Apocalypse Facts and Fantasies

Apocalypse Facts and Fantasies

Truths Tested and Errors Exposed by God's Gracious Guarantees to Israel

by

Donald C. B. Cameron B.Th., MA, Ph.D., Cert.Ed.

Dedicated to my family

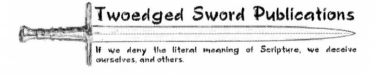

Twoedged Sword Publications

If we deny the literal meaning of Scripture, we deceive ourselves, and others.

First published 2006

ISBN-13 978-1-905447-07-7

ISBN-10 1-905447-07-8

Twoedged Sword Publications
PO Box 266, Waterlooville, PO7 5ZT
www.twoedgedswordpublications.co.uk

Foreword by Dr Alec R Passmore

When the writer of this significant book asked me to pen a foreword, I felt tremendously honoured to be associated with such a scholarly and intellectually satisfying work. The longer I plunged into its pages, the more I realised the deep significance both of what is written here and its timing. The whole world is moving towards a great crisis. Millions of earth's inhabitants live in fear, facing the future with universal apprehension. Devastating earthquakes, pandemic diseases, the demise of democracies, global terrorism (much of it increasingly seen as related to the intractable Middle East conflict) all prompt in the minds of millions, the question, "Where will it all end?" The Bible alone tells us the truth about man's destiny, and lays out God's plan and purposes for the end of time. And, puzzling for many, His plan is tied up with the destiny of the people of the Jewish nation, Israel, which is being restored before our very eyes!

From a lifetime study of Biblical theology, I regard Doctor Cameron's book to be a 'landmark publication', deserving the urgent study of every pastor and leader in the Church today. It is the result of some fifty-seven years of Biblical research undertaken by the analytical and concentrated mind of a man deeply committed to the Word of God and the God of the Word.

Donald Cameron says he left school with no qualifications and no confidence. Yet he advanced to a distinguished military career, rising to the rank of Major, RAEC, and being appointed British Liaison Officer to the Soviet Military Mission to the Commander-in-Chief, British Army of the Rhine. Later his linguistic skills and capable intellect were employed by Thorn EMI, Middlesex, as Senior Staff Trainer.

The writer's deep commitment to Jesus Christ guided him in his life's interests, and especially the study of God's inerrant Word. We are deeply grateful for his profound and, I believe, compelling study of Bible prophecy—the doctrine of the last things—in his many published articles and in this book. The writer has applied his considerable intellect to untangling the many differing and confusing views, which have sadly deterred many from an open and honest response to the divine *Eschatos* of Holy Scripture. This gifted writer clears much of the fog of confusion caused by conflicting and mistaken, though sometimes sincerely held views. His closely reasoned and detailed treatment of schools with differing claims is outstanding and most helpful. His assertion that Israel is the key to a correct understanding is ably set forth.

The Church has been robbed of the 'purifying hope', and seems to live as the secular world lives, without any awareness of the time on God's 'prophetic clock' and of the call to "Awake out of sleep!" (Romans 13:11). In the following pages you will discover a "Reason for the hope that is in you" (I Peter 3:15).

This book will unlock the prophetic Scriptures, which have so long been obscured, and even denied, through blind Anti-Semitic prejudice and use of inconsistent hermeneutic. I find many unique insights into God's amazing purposes for Israel and the world's future in these engrossing pages! My prayer is that this scholarly work will provide the urgent wake-up call the 21st century Church so badly needs.

Dr Passmore was formerly Director of Ministries with Prophetic Witness Movement International. He is currently Director of Omega Ministries and is a Fellow of the European Theological Seminary.

Acknowledgements

My first thanks are to God for a godly heritage from my mother's side—Canon Robert Baker Girdlestone, Rev Charles Girdlestone and my aunt, Ethel Girdlestone, who led my parents, and indirectly me, to Christ, and who fired me as a child with a keen interest in the predictive prophecy of the Bible and promises concerning the Lord's return.

Thank you to my tutor and mentor, Professor Gordon Beck of the European Theological Seminary, for his encouragement and constant monitoring. Thank you also to Dr Roy Miller, Dr Michael Phelan and Professor William Thomson, Seminary Staff or Adjunct Faculty members, who have been only a telephone call away for advice, information or discussion. Thank you also to Dr Theodore Danson Smith of Edinburgh—a ready source of much valuable information.

I would like to thank Rev Glyn Taylor, Editor of Prophetic Witness, and Rev Colin Le Noury, General Secretary of Prophetic Witness Movement International, for encouraging my writing over many years and also being available for discussion. They have their finger on the Nation's prophetic pulse, so to speak, and have been able to offer advice when required.

Rev Bob Higham, retired (but very active) Church of Scotland minister and former college lecturer, may have different views on some aspects of eschatology; but he has been immensely helpful over books at those times when my remoteness from the nearest theological library has been a handicap. Thank you Bob!

Having in Paul Rose of Twoedged Sword Publications, an Editor who not only loves the Lord, but also loves His appearing and is familiar with all the key Scriptures, has been an enormous asset in the later stages of preparation.

At times I would have been greatly hampered, but for the timely help of Michael Guile, friend, erstwhile neighbour, preacher and computer guru. Since my wife persuaded me to invest in a new computer, demands on his time have been considerably reduced, but I still have occasional battles of will with Microsoft and associated hard and software. Thanks, Michael.

I have appreciated the fellowship of Eric and Isobel Bellward of Eyemouth, fellow workers with my wife and me in Gospel services for the very elderly. They have a great love for God's people, the Jews, and have not only encouraged me in my writing, but have sometimes been the source of useful literature.

Thank you to my learned sons, Gordon and Colin, both authors in their own right, who, though probably faintly amused by Dad's recent ventures into theses, have been interested and supportive, and to my youngest son, Angus, who is an expert at keeping things in proportion and helping me to relax when I need to. Thanks to my mother, now 98 years of age, for faithfully sending me prophetic journals when I was a young soldier.

Finally, thank you to my wife, Greta, for her encouragement and forbearance, not necessarily at the same time (spouses have the most to contend with in times of academic hyperactivity), and for persuading me that this latest computer was a sound investment. She has been proved right, of course!

Contents

Part One—Testing Truths

Chapter One: Prophetic Principles And Definitions

Chapter Two: A Future For Israel—The Big Issue

Chapter Three: Some 'Untils' Concerning Israel

Contents

Part Two—Exposing Errors

Contents

Chapter Fourteen: Conclusions

Appendices

Glossary

The purpose of bold text in the column headed 'Definition' is to refer the reader to another entry in the Glossary under the heading of the text that is emboldened. More information on most of these terms can be found on pages 38–45.

Term	Definition
Amillennialist, Amillennial, Amillennialism	A teaching that denies the thousand year **Millennium** period altogether or assumes it to refer to the **Church Age**. Conservative Amillennialists see the earth as deteriorating; they believe that Jesus Christ will return in due course, in a single major event, to wind up earth's history and judge all classes—men and angels—before setting up the eternal heavenly state. They see the many widely varying accounts as applying, usually figuratively, to the same event. The resultant complexity of prophetic possibilities discourages all but a very few to study eschatology seriously. Virtually all Amillennialists embrace **Replacement Theology**. Those that do believe that God has a future for Israel tend not to attempt to reconcile this with their Amillennialism, their stance being by conviction, rather than on a coherent doctrinal basis. Amillennialism is generally associated with Augustine of Hippo, although there were earlier exponents.
Armageddon	See Rev 16:12–16; 19:11–21. The name 'Armageddon' comes from Revelation 16:16 and is generally accepted to be the mountain of Megiddo to the north of the plain of Jezreel. Armageddon has been the scene for many battles recorded in the Bible and is the place that the **Beast** and his armies will be drawn to at the end of the **Great Tribulation**. At the battle of Armageddon, Christ will defeat the Beast and his armies with His sword *"which... proceeded out of his mouth"* (Rev 19:21).
Beast	Other titles for the beast are 'Antichrist', 'man of sin', 'son of perdition', 'the prince that shall come'. The Beast is the second person of the latter day trinity of evil, along with the Dragon (Satan) and the Second Beast or False Prophet.
Church Age	The period from Pentecost to the **Rapture**.
Covenant Theologian	Conservative Bible scholars who reject Dispensationalism (see **Dispensation**) are generally Covenant Theologians. They believe that there are two contrasting Divine covenants, corresponding roughly with the Old and New Testaments. These are the Covenant of Works and the Covenant of Grace. Covenant Theologians are almost invariably also Replacement Theologians (see **Replacement Theology**).

Christ's Coming in Power	Will occur at the end of the **Great Tribulation**, when He will visibly return in judgement with an army of angels and His Bride or glorified Church. Christ's Coming in Power is the start of the **Millennium**.
Daniel's Seventy 'Weeks'	See Daniel chapter 9. The 'weeks' are heptads, weeks of years, or groups of seven years, each year being 360 days long. Daniel's Seventy 'Weeks' commenced shortly after Daniel's vision and ended, but for one group of seven years, with the rejection of the Messiah. One unfulfilled week or 'seven' therefore remains. We find both from Daniel and Revelation that the final year will be broken into two distinct halves, variously described as 'three and a half years', 'times, time and half a time', 1260 days and 42 months.
Dispensation, Dispensationalists	Any one of a number of periods (most commonly classified as seven) in earthly human history, starting with the Age of Innocence in Eden and culminating with the **Millennium**. Following the Fall, each dispensation either anticipates or looks back at Calvary as the sole means of salvation. God administered His call to mankind in different ways in dispensations past, but offered no alternative underpinning means of redemption except by faith in Him. All **Pre-Tribulationalist Pre-Millennialists** are Dispensationalists. They believe that during the current dispensation, namely the Church Age, the Nation Israel is being set aside or judgementally 'sidelined', while the Church, as it were, occupies the 'main line'. When the Church is removed at the **Rapture, Israel,** firstly in the form of evangelists and later as a restored nation, will return to the 'main line'.
Great Tribulation	The second half, or three and a half years, of the seven year **Tribulation** period.
Historicism	The teaching that the **Great Tribulation** prophecies are being fulfilled in the **Church Age**. It juggles with a multiplicity of historical dates and has periodically to be up-dated.
Israel	(1) The new name given by God to Jacob. (2) The descendents (hence Children) of Israel, forming a nation which God says will never cease to exist. (3) The Northern Kingdom, formed by the split following the death of Solomon, until deportation by Assyria. (4) The present Middle Eastern nation, still in unrepentant form, occupying only a small part of its title territory. (5) The future glorious Millennial Kingdom, following Christ's **Coming in Power** and national repentance, which will occupy all land between the River of Egypt and the Euphrates. (6) *Not* the Church, although there are **Jews** within the Church.

Jews	Originally those, mainly of the tribe of Judah, who returned from the Babylonian captivity. Often used in the New Testament to refer to all identified as being of **Israel** and now popularly assumed to refer to all Israelites.
Millennium	The literal future thousand-year period, free of Satanic influence, mentioned six times in Revelation chapter 20, which will follow Christ's **Coming in Power.**
Neo-Post-Millennialism	A modern form of **Post-Millennialism**, most likely to be encountered under the titles of 'Kingdom Now', 'Restorationism', 'Reconstructionism' or 'Dominion Theology'. Associated ideas include 'Theonomy', 'Manifest Sons of God', 'Latter Rain' and the 'Human Potential Movement'. Neo-Post-Millennialism is dealt with in **Chapter Twelve: Neo-Post-Millennialism And Israel's Future.**
Palestine, Palestinian	A title which never appears in the Bible, except in the Authorised Version (KJV), where Philistia or Philistines would be the correct translation. It was in the 2nd century BC applied by the Romans to the area between the Mediterranean and the Jordan and its inhabitants, and has illogically been applied to the same area and its people for the past century. There are no true Palestinian or Philistine people today.
Partial-Rapturism	The belief that only the most spiritual believers will be raptured and the others left to undergo seven years tribulation. It has aptly been described as Christ returning for His Bride and His being ruptured, rather than raptured.
Post-Millennialist, Post-Millennial, Post-Millennialism	The teaching that Jesus Christ will not return to earth until after the **Millennium.** Some Post-Millennialists believe that this has already started, but others see it as being entirely future. They believe that the world is to improve or be 'Christianised' before Christ's return, thus, through the Church's completion of the Great Commission, making the world fit for its Saviour. Many see this happening only through the efforts of a Church empowered by the Holy Spirit, but some see some sort of spiritual, moral or cultural evolution of mankind playing a role. Post-Millennialism was widespread during the great missionary era, but received a near death-blow with the outbreak of the First World War. Its revival in recent decades has been associated with the optimism of the Neo-Charismatic movement (see **Neo-Post-Millennialism**). The absence of subsequent much heralded world-wide moral improvement has dampened enthusiasm. It sees no special future role for **Israel**.

Post-Tribulationist, *Post-Tribulation,* *Post-Tribulationism*	The form of **Pre-Millennialism** which believes in a single event Second Coming **(Rapture and Coming in Power)** at the end of the **Great Tribulation**. They see the Church as going through the Great Tribulation. The term Covenant Pre-Millennialist is also applied to them. It is not currently widespread. Most Post-Tribulationists believe in a Millennial future for Israel, but generally do not perceive a key **Tribulation** role for Jews. Their most significant teaching is that the **Rapture** cannot be imminent, because of the outstanding preconditions of the **Tribulation.**
Pre-Millennialist, *Pre-Millennial,* *Pre-Millennialism*	The doctrine that Christ's Second Coming will occur before the **Millennium**. Pre-Millennialists believe that the world is currently deteriorating, and that only after Christ's personal judgemental intervention at **Armageddon** will an ideal state on earth be achieved.
Pre-Tribulationist, *Pre-Tribulation,* *Pre-Tribulationism*	Sometimes referred to in America as 'Dispensational Pre-Millennialism'. May occasionally be referred to in our pages as 'Dispensational Israelology' when there is a need to emphasise the Jewish element of the doctrine. It is the only form of **Pre-Millennialism** which adheres rigidly to the ever present possibility of the Lord's immediate return to take His Church home before the **Great Tribulation**, and to return later with it. The doctrine of God's central purposes for the **Jews** following the removal or **Rapture** of the Church is critical to Pre-Tribulationism.
Preterism	The teaching that most end-time prophecy was fulfilled in events surrounding the AD 70 sack of Jerusalem or in subsequent history. It relies heavily on the assumption that Jesus and the prophets exaggerated the awfulness of latter day events.
Rapture	The sudden catching up to Heaven of the resurrected bodies of all Church believers (the dead in Christ) and the translation to heaven of all living believers, both **Jew** and Gentile. The souls and spirits of the dead in Christ are already in Heaven. On earth at least seven years will elapse thereafter before Christ's **Coming in Power.**
Replacement Theology	The teaching that, following **Israel's** formal rejection of her Messiah, God has discarded the nation and transferred her blessings to the Christian Church. Most date this to the Crucifixion, but a few to AD 70.
Times of the Gentiles	The period from the reign of Nebuchadnezzar to the start of the **Millennium**.
Tribulation	The period of seven years **(Daniel's seventieth 'week')** following the **Rapture** of the Church. Sometimes it is seen to refer only to the first three-and-a-half years in contrast to the **Great Tribulation** of the remaining three-and-a-half.

Introduction

Naming a book is not as simple as it may seem. The thesis, which was the basis for this book, was prepared for the European Theological Seminary. Its full title was *God's Guaranteed Future for Israel— Establishing this as a Valid Benchmark and Applying it to Schools of Prophetic Interpretation*. This was an accurate description, but is rather unwieldy for a book. A more attention-grabbing title has therefore been chosen, one that relates more directly to perceived topical concerns and needs.

Apocalypse means unveiling. *The* Apocalypse refers to God's Unveiling, as contained in Revelation, the final book of the Bible. It foretells future happenings, some glorious, some horrendous and some 'either/or', depending whether one is a believer or not. Other books of the Bible contain important apocalyptic sections, such as Jesus' own lengthy Olivet Discourse. These add much to our knowledge; but Revelation supplements them and puts all into perspective. We must accept that these gracious disclosures are only partial. It would be foolish to expect all future events to be detailed. God knows that we do not need to know everything in advance.

'Everybody's opinion is equally valid' is the theory which underpins modern society, with its multi-cultural, multi-faith philosophy. Of course Christian living is not intended to be regimented. We are allowed considerable liberty and initiative in matters of conscience and conduct. But when it comes to God's laws and to serious doctrine, the 'anything goes' approach is utterly unacceptable. No Christian who takes the Bible seriously can countenance it. Whether it is 'politically correct' is irrelevant in the light of the unique and exclusive revelation of God in Christ Jesus. The Creator of the universe is omniscient. What He decrees *is*. When, for instance, His Son says that He is the only Way to the Father, we know beyond any shadow of doubt that this is the truth. We would not want it any other way.

Yet there is one area of theology, eschatology (the study of latter day predictive prophecy), where believers are so cautious, because of the presence of so many competing claims and interpretations, that they are afraid to take any particular stand. Some, who are strict elsewhere, adopt

19

the liberal theory that all believers' prophetic views are equally valid and should not be challenged. Individuals and congregations therefore remain confused, susceptible to every wind of change and at the mercy of the persuasive preacher, author or hymnologist. This ought not to be. Indeed, it need not be. Some conscientious and caring pastors and teachers are, on the one hand, eager to preach about the Lord's return and other key end-time matters, but are, on the other hand, hesitant to enter contentious territory. Consequently churches are perceived as sending out mixed messages. This inevitably undermines the authority of Scripture in the eyes of the world outside.

We believe that there is a unique, God-given key to help us unravel the conflicting prophetic programmes which abound. Moreover, there is benchmark or yardstick for validating the results of our investigations. We might define these as *Israel's guaranteed future as a nation and race, based upon God's faithful promises*. This does not disallow Jews from becoming Church members in the present age. In due course we shall be noting that God's promises to Israel include both conditional and unconditional, both short term and long term, both fulfilled and unfulfilled, both blessings and cursings. These classifications are of course significant, and we will have to differentiate between them. But what is paramount is God's faithfulness. That cannot be negotiated. Any scheme which does not allow God to fulfil His unconditional promises must surely be fatally flawed. Where God has promised ultimate forgiveness and restoration, let no man dare to know better!

In Part One we will examine what the Bible has to say about Israel and the future. Only in Part Two will we apply this benchmark to different teachings, demonstrating that those schools of prophecy which selectively deny God's promises to Israel effectively invalidate themselves. This sounds simple, but of course we will have to consider the defences offered. We should not patronise those who disagree with us.

As will become clear as we proceed, Bible prophecy concerns much more than the people Israel. However if we fail to recognise the significance of the vast number of prophetic passages in Scripture which refer to Israel, we are doomed to fail to perceive the overall programme of latter day events.

As we approach the time of which Jesus spoke, of *"men's hearts failing them for fear and the expectation of those things which are coming on the earth"* (Luke 21:26), I believe that there is a very real need for young people, many of whom are deeply troubled about our environment, to be aware of the fact that God has both ordained global events which match or surpass people's worst fears, and promised a period of glorious restoration—in His good time and in that sequence. Almost every week, it would seem, experts who leave God out of their reckoning produce some new doomsday scenario. Too often Christians produce their own solutions and expect God to go along with these!

Such terms as "The Four Horses of the Apocalypse", "The Mark of the Beast" and "The Battle of Armageddon" tend to be better known to film directors than to churchmen. There is a need to rectify this imbalance and to address two dangerous extremes. One is the teaching that such things are the province of pessimists, and that predicted calamities were deliberate exaggerations on the part of prophets to drive lessons home. The other is the scoffing attitude foretold by Peter, leading to apathy akin to that of Jesus' First Coming. None should willingly share the condemnation of the two disciples returning to Emmaus on the evening of the Resurrection day: *"O foolish ones, and slow of heart to believe in all that the prophets have spoken"* (Luke 24:25). Their folly had led to unnecessary heartbreak.

A further need is for enquiring Jews to receive assurances that there are evangelical Christians who do not believe that they *as a nation* have been for ever dismissed from God's future plans, as some teach, and that their displacement from the centre of God's purposes over the centuries by the largely Gentile Church has a strict time limit. They need to be re-assured that God has beautifully co-ordinated plans for all His people. In the meantime they may be individually welcomed into the Church on the same basis as everyone else.

There is a need too to emphasise that, from the earliest ages of human history until this planet passes away, there never has been, never will be and never can be any means of salvation for sinners than through the blood of the Lamb, Christ Jesus, shed on Calvary's Cross. Jesus is described as the Lamb more often in Revelation than in any other book of the Bible. God has worked in different ways in different times, but He has never saved by any other means. Whether one is Jew or Gentile, repentance and faith are required in order that this redeeming blood may be applied.

Let us take time to study what God has so graciously revealed to us. With many others, I am utterly convinced that one day the Lord Jesus Christ will come suddenly to take His redeemed home before the darkest chapter of earth's history. To us it is the *"Blessed Hope"*, though no believer can be sure of being alive at that wonderful moment. However those who have died will be the first to be caught up. This book should help readers to decide for themselves whether this is a Bible based hope or merely fanciful speculation.

Most literature on the Second Coming of Jesus Christ and other end-time events is studded with terms such as 'Post-Millennial' and 'Pre-Tribulational'. This may give the impression that any debate or conflict of opinion is to do solely with the sequence of future events. Certainly the sequence of events is important, and there is indeed a wide variety of views amongst different interpretive schools. But, at best, only one can be correct. That is simple logic.

Important criteria for validating prophecy relate to:

1. whether we interpret it consistently with our approach to other doctrines—in other words as literally as possible, bearing in mind that some visions are quite explicitly presented symbolically, and

2. whether we believe that much of Bible prophecy is yet to be fulfilled—as opposed to it having been fulfilled in the 1st century.

But the most important benchmark, yardstick or standard for assessing schools of prophetic interpretation must surely be the fact of the future literal, personal, visible return of the Lord Jesus Christ. The book of Revelation opens with: *"Behold, He is coming with clouds, and every eye will see Him"* (1:7), and closes with, *"He who testifies to these things says, 'Surely I am coming quickly.' Amen"* (22:20). To deny these facts totally undermines the authority and inspiration of Scripture, not to mention the trustworthiness of Jesus' own words and the angelic promise at His ascension. There are plenty of good books dealing with the certainty of His return; we will certainly touch on all these matters, but concentrate on Israel's involvement.

For over fifty years I have from time to time preached on the Second Coming of the Lord Jesus Christ. Reactions have varied from grateful thanks for preaching on a neglected subject to deep resentment. Prophecies concerning Israel's present position and future role have regularly featured; indeed, there are so many such promises, widely scattered in Scripture, that it is hard to avoid them. Latterly I have found more and more occasions when I have been led to champion, in a small way, the truths concerning Israel's future against those who assert that she has none, these include, incidentally, Roman Catholics, 'Jehovah's Witnesses' and Mormons. Among those calling themselves evangelicals, there are many more of these so-called Replacement Theologians than there were half a century ago.

I have recently become even more aware of how closely intertwined are the doctrines of a potentially ever imminent Pre-Tribulation Rapture and God's continued purposes for the nation Israel. This does not in any way mean that either *cannot* stand alone in its own right. Either can; but it is that much more difficult to prove. Why should we handicap ourselves by failing to use all Scriptural resources available?

Some believe in an ultimate restoration for Israel which is too remote for any practical present day consideration. Some believe that the nation-state of Israel and the Israel of the Bible have nothing to do with each other. Some believe that the Church has forever replaced Israel in God's plans and that 'Israel' is now an alternative name for the Church. Some, at the opposite extreme, believe that the nation-state can do no wrong and that a glorious future awaits her without her undergoing any further trials. All these I believe to be misapprehensions.

Some who call themselves Christians hate the Jews, some are indifferent, some are ambivalent, while yet others love them, but without perceiving their current spiritual state. I have become ever more aware of how a love among concerned Christians for the evangelisation and welfare of Jews is undermined, if they do not appreciate that Israel nationally is still subject to spiritual blindness, and that they will remain so until their final holocaust is over and their Messiah returns in Person. A nation occupying the Promised Land is only a first step in the prophetic programme. In the meantime only individual Jews can be saved; though winning them is indeed a blessed activity. These, while not losing their Jewish identity, immediately become members of the Church, and will therefore be taken to heaven at the Rapture.

So intricately interwoven are the supporting arguments for Israelology and the programme of a Pre-Tribulation Rapture, followed in turn by the Great Tribulation, Coming in Power, Millennium and Eternal State, that I have been convicted that it is time to examine the relationships and implications of all the main eschatological positions, looking chiefly from the perspective of the role of Israel. Some positions weaken, some undermine, whilst yet others actively deny Jewish roles which are massively confirmed in Scripture. We must be fully aware of the implications of our prophetic perspectives, for if any of our teaching implies God's unfaithfulness, it must be exposed. It is imperative that this should be done as objectively and fairly as possible, avoiding the more extreme versions of any position.

When I began my preliminary notes for this study, I had for some time been aware of a highly recommended book, *Israelology—the Missing Link in Systematic Theology* by Dr Arnold Fruchtenbaum[1]. When I eventually acquired a copy, I found that its reputation was well deserved; moreover it deals in great depth with some of what I had proposed to cover. However Dr Fruchtenbaum has approached the subject from a very different angle, examining each theory's views of Israel in turn and arguing his case for Israel's future as he proceeds. I propose to present my arguments for God's future purposes for Israel before using these to validate or discredit, as may be the case, alternative views.

Dr Fruchtenbaum naturally uses mainly American text-books. I intend to make considerable use of British sources, as we have much excellent material which is becoming forgotten and neglected; we are ignoring a fine heritage. However I will certainly use Trans-Atlantic sources as well, because most of the best modern material comes from there. America tends to be so associated with the leading cults and with certain recent extreme religious phenomena, that conservative British Christians have become suspicious. So good American books also need publicity in Britain. The Replacement Theology against which I propose to take a stand, is rife on both sides of the Atlantic. I will quote as far as possible directly from its proponents in Part Two of this book, rather than rely too much upon what those with whom I agree write.

I have unashamedly adopted Dr Fruchtenbaum's term, 'Israelology'. As, like him, I am a fervent believer in a future for Israel, I shall assume the term to imply a doctrine of Israel which encompasses its history from the Patriarchs at least to the end of the Millennium. The fact that at times Israel is far from being in favour with God does not alter His everlasting commitment. The term was suggested to me by Rev. Colin Le Noury of *Prophetic Witness* as I was searching around for a term which implies the antithesis of Replacement Theology. Dr Fruchtenbaum himself tells me that he feels that the term 'Dispensationalism' provides a more direct antithesis. I shall use both terms, and also 'Pre-Tribulationism' as appropriate. Each in its own way counters Replacement Theology.

Dr Fruchtenbaum has one huge advantage. He is a Jew. *"What advantage then has the Jew...? Much in every way! Chiefly because to them were committed the oracles of God."* (Rom 3:1–2). Nobody who does not understand Hebrew and Hebrew thought can fully appreciate all the nuances of the Old Testament original. However it is important that Gentile Christians should also be seen to believe in and to teach God's future purposes for Israel. It is a formidable and humbling task to tackle. Sadly there are also Messianic Jews who have been encouraged to believe that the great end-time Holocaust or Great Tribulation can be by-passed. This is a grave error. As we shall later see, God will have sealed witnessing Jews at that dreadful time, but it will be more blessed by far to be saved first and *"Be counted worthy to escape all these things, and to stand before the Son of Man"* (Lk 21:36).

Jesus said: *"Look at the fig tree and all the trees. When they are already budding, you see and know for yourselves that summer is now near. So likewise, when you see these things happening, know that the kingdom of God is near."* (Lk 21:29–31; see also Matt 24:32–33). The Olivet Discourse context refers to His future return. The vine and fig tree represent Israel in different ways (Joel 1:7). Jesus had just delivered His scathing condemnation of the Jewish leaders, the faithless keepers of God's vineyard, and had publicly and symbolically cursed a fruitless fig tree (Matt 21:19–21 and 21:33–41).

The fig tree was apparently dead, as many now would believe Israel to be. Yet within the last few decades it has budded and put on leaves—the very long awaited sign to which Jesus drew our attention. It is vital to note that Jesus did not say that bearing fruit was to be a prerequisite to His return. But, Oh dear! Recognising the sign and reading its significance is theologically and politically inconvenient. So many Christians studiously ignore it. Some fear to be ridiculed within their own congregations! We humbly wish to refer the reader's attention to this national fig tree which men say is dead, but which Jesus said would one day flourish. It is a matter of whom to believe. However we cannot build our theology on parables alone. We must take time to explore everything that Scripture has to say about this vital matter and its relationship to Christ's return.

Our stand, for which we make no apology, is one of constant vigilance, expecting our Lord to return for us and take us to the place He has gone to prepare for us. Any teaching which 'switches off' believers from talking about the return of the Bridegroom must be suspect. *"My beloved put his hand by the latch of the door, and my heart yearned for him"* (Cant 5:4). Samuel Francis picked up Solomon's theme in that lovely, but sadly neglected, hymn. 'I am waiting for the dawning':

> "I am waiting for the coming
> Of the Lord who died for me;
> Oh, His words have thrilled my spirit,
> 'I will come again for thee'.
> I can almost hear His footfall,
> On the threshold of the door,
> And my heart, my heart is longing
> To be with Him evermore."

The old jibe about being so heavenly minded that we are no earthly use is admittedly sometimes appropriate, though probably less frequently than it once was. But are we not in danger of neglecting something very precious? Do we not all too easily lapse into Laodicean lukewarmness and distance ourselves from the blessed hope of our Saviour's return?

There are some Christians who seem to be able to embrace Replacement Theology without their faith being diminished. But many see this as God having made a disastrous experiment with the Jews, and having wasted two thousand of the last four thousand years on a people for whom He has no further use. Their confidence in the infallibility and Divine foreknowledge of Almighty God thus comes under attack. Sceptics have a field day. We believe that the Dispensational Pre-Millennialism, which underpins this book, will help undecided or unconvinced readers to dispense with the constant allegorisation and explaining away of the obvious, which Replacement Theology demands, and to appreciate better the Infinite Wisdom behind a plan of salvation which spans earth's history from before the foundation of the world to the New Jerusalem. And this plan has always involved both Israel and the Church.

While we will from time to time pause to define certain key terms, we have, for the benefit of those less familiar with prophetic terminology, included a brief Glossary of Terms. There are also appendices: Appendix I contains a chronological table of events from the time of Daniel to the New Heaven and Earth; Appendix II contains Fifty Reasons For A Pre-Tribulation Rapture.

We do not intend to analyse the Middle East crisis and growing global confrontation. However we believe that it is imperative that Christians should have, as far as is reasonable, a Scripturally based perspective. This is particularly true in the United Kingdom and the United States of America, as we see our nations ever more bogged down in a perilous and intractable quagmire. So many Christians simply do not comprehend Israel's place in prophecy. Were they to do so, their faith would be boosted by an appreciation of the extraordinary reliability of predictive prophecy and would be motivated to know more.

Whatever our findings in these studies, as Christians, we must never forget that, whilst punishment and defence of the realm are legitimate government responsibilities, vengeance is exclusively God's prerogative (Deut 32:35, Rom 12:19). We dare not put ourselves in God's place. Ethnic cleansing and genocide are **never** human prerogatives. This is still the Year of Grace; the Day of Vengeance of our God is yet to come, as is the Year of the Lord's Redeemed. Our central responsibility is the Gospel—"For God so loved the world…".

Part One

Testing Truths

Chapter One

Prophetic Principles And Definitions

Some Christian Certainties And Uncertainties

Christianity is a religion of faith. Indeed, Christianity is a faith. Anything which claims to be Christianity, but which denies the necessity of faith, is a fraud. *"Without faith it is impossible to please... God"* (Heb 11:6). *"By grace you have been saved through faith..."* (Eph 2:8). During the Reformation between one and a half and two million people died for this faith. It is immensely precious.

To those who would challenge our confidence, we would reply that our faith is appropriate, inasmuch as it is based not upon our works but upon a faithful God, who made perfect provision for our redemption through the death of His Son. We recognise this in our creeds (Latin *credo*, I believe), whether it be one of the historic creeds drawn up by the early Church or our own personal adaptations, or statements of belief based upon the Scriptures. Faith can of course be misplaced; Christian faith is faith in God and what He has revealed about Himself and done for us. It is not faith in faith, which is a concept which can take one down dangerous psychological and pagan bye-ways.

These matters are fundamental to Christianity. They are certainties and cannot be negotiated or compromised. We have no authority to recognise anything else as truly Christian. Those who recite such creeds, and then go on to deny them, are apostate hypocrites; that is not an opinion, it is simple logic. Leaders who recite them aloud in front of congregations, but fail to preach them, abdicate responsibility.

However there are other great Bible truths which, for a variety of reasons, are not to be found in any of the great creeds of the 2nd to 4th centuries. This is partly because these creeds consist of brief unelaborated fundamental statements. One suspects that, had they been drawn up a few generations earlier, they might have included more. Nowadays even some of the fundamentals are widely neglected or conveniently ignored, suggesting at best apathy and at worst resistance. If the skeletal truths are neglected, how much more the flesh on them!

Two of the great truths—for that is what we believe them to be—excluded from the creeds, and thus subject to greater apathy and neglect, are:

1. God still has significant future plans for the nation Israel, despite their having formally rejected their Messiah at His First Coming.

2. The Second Coming of Christ is to be viewed by the Church as potentially ever imminent. While signs of the times should put us on a heightened state of alert, there are no absolute prerequisites such as the achievement of a golden age, or the undergoing of the Great Tribulation. These must happen, but not until the Church Age is over.

We believe that, whilst either of the above statements can stand on its own merits, these two truths are mutually supportive. If either can be demonstrated to be in accordance with Scripture, the case for the other will be much stronger. It is our intention to examine this mutually supportive relationship.

One contrast between these two is that with the first there are only two possible viewpoints. Either one does or one does not believe in God's future purposes for the Jews. The second is much more complex; one may believe devoutly in the Lord's future literal return, but consider it not to be potentially imminent, or one may assume the Lord's return to be purely symbolic, impersonal or non-literal. Furthermore one may believe, as we do, that the Lord will come first *for* His Church and then later *with* His Church, or one may believe in the Lord's return as a single event. All these viewpoints have names, which we will soon define.

The traditional approach for those sharing our persuasion is to start with the second question, namely the more complex issue of timing and imminence. However we propose to break with this tradition and to begin with the first and simpler statement, demonstrating the certainty of God's future purposes for Israel.

We will accordingly devote Part One, namely Chapters One to Six, to this cause. This will avoid the usual difficulties of keeping too many balls in the air, so to speak. The juggling of multiple positions can come later in Part Two (Chapters Seven to Thirteen), when we have firmly fixed the Jewish question as a prophetic benchmark or yardstick.

Thus in Part Two we will look a variety of alternative prophetic schools, concentrating on the major ones, and consider how these relate to God's future purposes for Israel. If these prove to be incompatible, we will enquire what is thus compromised or discredited. Nobody who believes the Bible to be the inspired word of God can reasonably expect there to be contradictions in such major issues. The discrepancies are in human minds.

Daniel in fact did not understand the full significance of one of Jeremiah's prophecies until the time of fulfilment was almost upon him; thus we have justification for intensified prayerful study and increased comprehension as we see signs of the times materialising.

Naturally some difference of opinions regarding details and sequences will inevitably arise in matters which Scripture singles out for special study and exploration; even *"angels desire to look into these things"* (I Pet 1:12). There are almost certainly questions which are not intended to be answered in full until the events are imminent or actually taking place. Then *"none of the wicked shall understand, but the wise shall understand"* (Dan 12:10). But the wise surely will understand more readily if they have hidden these words in their hearts and pondered over them. The fact that the early Church saints, despite their real commitment to study, understood end-time prophecies less comprehensively than latter day generations, should come as no surprise.

We are thus contending that, if God indeed has future purposes for the Nation of Israel, any prophetic scheme of interpretation must make sense in the light of this. Lest there be any misunderstanding at this stage, let us stress a few basic interpretative principles. Some of these have been covered by the writer in the seventy odd articles written by him in 'Your Tomorrow' and 'Prophetic Witness'[1] during the period 1993 to 2003, and will not be enlarged upon here. Others will be dealt with in greater depth later. In this chapter only we will minimise our Bible references and quotations from respected authorities. Thereafter we will make abundant use of both references and quotes.

Interpretive Principles For Prophecy

1. Prophecy is not intended to be history written in advance. Many details are yet to be revealed or clarified. We are expected to be familiar with the signs of the times, so that when events do overtake us, we will not be caught out, like the two disciples on the way to Emmaus on the evening of the Resurrection day. We should not be described as, *"Foolish ones, and slow of heart to believe in all that the prophets have spoken!"* (Lk 24:25). Despite certain gaps which Scripture leaves in our knowledge, we are provided with a great deal of precious material to give us a mix of absolute and tentative answers.

2. Prophetic study must never be divorced from general theology—from other central doctrines. After all, within Scripture it is closely integrated with the personality and attributes of God, with His plan and provision of redemption, with Christian conduct and relationships with the fallen world, with man's responsibility to his Creator, and much more.

3. Prophecy can and should be used as a powerful aid to evangelisation. We learn from Heb 11:7 that Noah used it in this way, and we find Peter and Paul, for instance, incorporating the certainty of coming judgement into their Pentecost and Athenian addresses. Noah was the least successful in terms of numerical results; but he was faithful, which is what God required him to be.

4. Prophetic study is not to satisfy our curiosity, but is a sacred duty (see Rev 1:3 etc.), though one to be kept in balance. If we truly love our Lord, surely we should be thrilled by the prospect of His return and wish to know more about His promises!

5. Apathy and wilful ignorance within churches towards matters concerning the Lord's return are themselves Signs of the Times (II Pet 2:3–5). In some respects this should comfort us; in other respects it should challenge or even rebuke us.

6. Many prophecies were written in such a way that they would be of relevance to those living in the intervening centuries before their final fulfilment. Some actually have double or even triple

34

fulfilments. But, however relevant the earlier fulfilments may have been, the language, which may initially have appeared dramatic and exaggerated, will prove eventually to be fully justified in the future horrendous time, when our planet will be literally at the brink of self-destruction (Dan 12:1 and Matt 24:21–22).

7.   While figurative language is plainly used, and events, especially in Heaven, have descriptions far beyond present human comprehension, everything should be understood in the plainest meaning possible. If we assume, without very good reason, that prophetic statements are simply parables, we leave ourselves open to every kind of nonsensical interpretation, and discourage others from studying God's word. Long ago Ezekiel complained bitterly to God that his hearers were dismissing his words as mere parables (20:49). This same form of escapism from prophetic truth is rampant among 21st century Christians. Having itching ears, they clamour to hear only what is convenient and palatable (II Tim 4:3).

8.   When we refer to the Second Coming without being specific, we are speaking of a complex series of events, which, we believe, will commence with the resurrection of the dead in Christ and the snatching to heaven of the living saints, and culminate with Christ's visible return to earth, accompanied by these same saints. If we try to see only one single event, portrayed in Scripture in a variety of different ways, we are likely to be confused by evident disparities in the accounts, and thus be discouraged from studying further. However we do recognise that, despite this, some Christians sincerely foresee only a single event. This we will discuss in due course. Logically both views cannot be correct. It is our duty to come to a conclusion which is in accordance with Scripture.

9.   It must be stressed that we believe that any Jew, who has been saved at any time from Pentecost until God winds up the present Church Age, became or becomes a member of the Church on exactly the same basis as any Gentile. We would also stress that, as Dispensationalists, who are often either unwittingly or deliberately misrepresented or misunderstood, we firmly believe

that from Genesis to Revelation, no one is ever saved from their sin except by the blood of Jesus Christ shed at Calvary. But we also recognise that God *"at various times and in different ways spoke in times past to the fathers..."* (Heb 1:1), and that revelation was progressive from Genesis to Revelation.

10. We recognise the very special place for Israel in God's plans. We believe that His promise to Abraham still stands: *"I will bless those who bless you, and I will curse him who curses you"* (Gen 12:2). We believe that it is still true that *"he who touches you touches the apple of His eye"* (Zech 2:8). But this does not give us licence to assume that the Jews are faultless, or that Israel's current policies vis-à-vis its Arab neighbours are *never* questionable. We are to love them 'warts and all'. After all, God Himself does not hold them guiltless; but on the other hand neither does He hold the Gentiles guiltless. We must maintain a sense of proportion here.

Other principles will emerge in due course. These are enough for the present. As we have indicated, we believe that it would be helpful first to spend some time looking at our first major issue, almost in isolation from the various prophetic interpretations which we shall enumerate. Then we will examine a number of Old Testament Scriptures which plainly predicted a future for Israel, and where the main bone of contention is whether these were or were not rendered void by national rejection of their Messiah two thousand years ago. It will also from time to time be necessary to look at the contentious issue of whether texts referring to a restoration of Israel refer to the return from Babylon, a future restoration, or perhaps even to both.

As Replacement Theologians assert that the Jewish nation has been rendered spiritually obsolete by the Church, it is inevitable that their views will be commented upon at all stages. However we will leave until our closing chapters the ways in which the main schools of prophetic interpretation differ from one another in how they relate to Israel. *We believe and intend to demonstrate that the views of each school stand or fall on this single issue.*

Some Definitions

Some readers will be familiar with the 'technical' terms which we will be using; others will not. We hope that this section will be helpful for those unfamiliar. The use of such terms will be essential if we are to avoid constant explanations. After all, the New Testament writers referred to Pharisees, Sadducees, Zealots, Herodians and so on; we need some understanding of the names in order to read the Gospels intelligently. Some resistance to modern labelling is understandable, because even within many evangelical churches serious study of the word of God is becoming the province of only a small minority. Far too many are too busy with other matters to spend time on Theology—the study of God. People who are quite prepared to learn vast vocabularies for topics like computers, sports and hobbies, seem to resist the acquisition of even a minimal number of theological terms. Where do our priorities lie?

Even Bible colleges seem to be spending much less time on doctrine and more on the peripherals, such as Christian sociology, philosophy and psychology. The result is that there is far greater scope for fads and fashions and a vulnerability to false teaching. Challenging or questioning the pulpit is depicted as a sin. Those with the strongest personalities or most appealing or entertaining programmes on offer are having a field day with the Lord's flock. These things ought not to be, but are themselves signs of the times. We have lost the Berean spirit—*"they received the word with all readiness, and searched the Scriptures daily to find out whether these things were so"* (Acts 17:11). We are reverting to the Dark Ages.

Thus, whilst we append labels to different prophetic views or schools of thought, we must be aware that, even at leadership level, there is often a frightening vagueness of all but the most basic concepts. Many hold a mix of views, which, if properly explored, are quite incompatible with one another. The result is that, if and when individuals do begin to dig deeper, they tend to be mystified; some give up, assuming their puzzles to be unanswerable.

We are particularly interested in definitions which bear some relationship to what people believe or do not believe about Israel. For those unfamiliar with eschatology (the doctrine of the last things), we will provide sufficient detail to save interrupting our flow of thought to offer explanations; authorities and further references will be given later. All these terms will be familiar to students of prophecy. We present them here in a logical rather than alphabetical sequence. An alphabetical list of short definitions may be found in the Glossary.

Replacement Theology has been mentioned already. It lies at the heart of what we wish to disprove, so we will re-emphasise that it is the teaching that, following Israel's formal rejection of her Messiah, God has discarded the nation and transferred her blessings to the Christian Church. It is incongruous that few ever claim for the Church the curses which were prescribed for Israel at the same time as the blessings! Thus it is a dogma which has not been thought through to its natural conclusions. Much more will be said about Replacement Theology in due course. It does not preclude the possibility of Jews being saved and joining the Church. We in no way dispute the fact that from Pentecost to the end of the Church Age, the Church rather than Israel has dominated God's witness to the world.

Dispensation, in the theological sense, applies to any one of a number of periods (most commonly classified as seven) in earthly human history, starting with the Age of Innocence in Eden and culminating with the Millennium (q.v.). Following the Fall, each dispensation either anticipates or looks back at Calvary as the sole means of salvation. God administered His call to mankind in different ways in dispensations past, but offered no alternative underpinning means of redemption by faith in Him. As we shall see later, the popular idea that Dispensationalism is a 19th century invention is anything but true.

All Pre-Tribulationalist Pre-Millennialists (q.v.) are Dispensationalists. They believe that during the current dispensation, namely the Church Age, the Nation Israel is being set aside or judgementally 'sidelined', while the Church, as it were, occupies the 'main line'. When the Church is removed, Israel, firstly in the form of evangelists and later as a restored nation, will return to the 'main line'. They demonstrate separate but God appointed roles for both Church and Nation. Sadly when Dispensationalism is taken to intellectually logical human conclusions, for which no scriptural evidence exists, Ultra- and Hyper-Dispensationalism occurs. The unscrupulous (or ignorant) have set up Aunt Sallies of these two minority extremes in order to attack and discredit ordinary Dispensationalists. Therefore the Dispensational title is sometimes dropped, even though the principles are still observed.

Conservative Bible scholars who reject Dispensationalism are generally **Covenant Theologians**. They believe that there are two contrasting Divine covenants, corresponding roughly with the Old and New Testaments. These are the Covenant of Works and the Covenant of Grace. Covenant Theologians are almost invariably also Replacement Theologians.

Preterism is a major disincentive to the study of the signs of the times. It is the teaching that most end-time prophecy was fulfilled in events surrounding the AD 70 sack of Jerusalem or in subsequent history. It relies heavily on the assumption that Jesus and the prophets exaggerated about the awfulness of latter day events.

Historicism is the teaching that the Great Tribulation prophecies are being fulfilled in the Church Age. It juggles with a multiplicity of historical dates and has periodically to be up-dated. We will encounter it in Chapter Thirteen.

The **Times of the Gentiles** commenced with Nebuchadnezzar, and were summarised to that king by God in the dream interpreted by Daniel, as recorded in the second chapter of his book. They will continue until the start of Christ's Messianic Kingdom, when the last earthly power is smashed.

Daniel's Seventy 'Weeks' (or heptads, weeks of years or groups of seven years) are described in Daniel 9:24–27, when they were about to begin. They amount to 490 years. 483 of these had elapsed when Jesus presented Himself as Messiah and was rejected and crucified. The remaining seven year period or 'week' will commence only after the Rapture, when the false prince, Beast or Antichrist will impose a seven year covenant upon Israel. We find both from Daniel and Revelation that it will be divided into two distinct halves, variously described as 'three-and-a-half years', 'times, time and half a time', 42 months and 1,260 days, thus disallowing the historisists' alternative interpretations.

The Promised Land. For convenience we sometimes use this self explanatory term to describe the territory promised by God in perpetuity in Gen 12;7, 17;8 etc., etc., and narrowed down firstly to Isaac's and then to Jacob's (Israel's) descendents. It stretches from the River of Egypt to the Euphrates. It was to be occupied little by little, and has to date been held in its entirety by Israel only latterly by David and by Solomon. Technically it is all Israel. Other nations may have occupied parts of it, but have never held the title. The original name of the central part was Canaan. The earth is the Lord's to give to whomsoever He will.

Palestine. This term, or Palestinia is incorrectly used four times in the AV (KJV) for the coastal area including the 'Gaza Strip'. Almost all modern translations have corrected this to 'Philistia' or 'Philistines', based on the non-Semitic people who once lived there. The term is first mention by Herodotus in the 5th century BC but was not used by the Romans until the 2nd century AD, when it applied to the area between the Mediterranean and the Jordan, as it was by the League of Nations during the last century. The self-styled Palestinians of today are mixed Semitic descendents of Esau, who were excluded from God's promise to Abraham. The current title has no basis in history or genealogy, but is used for political identity and manoeuvring.

The **Rapture,** a term which is derived from *raptare*, the Latin word for *to catch up*, in the Vulgate version of I Thess 4:17, means the sudden catching up to Heaven of the resurrected bodies of all Church believers (the dead in Christ) and the translation to heaven of all living believers, both Jew and Gentile. The souls and spirits of the dead in Christ are already in Heaven.

The **Church Age** started at Pentecost and will continue until the Rapture.

Daniel's Seventieth Week (or group of seven years) cannot start until after the Rapture. It is a detached week of Jewish history. It is often called, for convenience rather than accuracy, the Great Tribulation to distinguish these seven years from general tribulation, which is promised to Christians of all ages as a matter of course: *"In the world you shall have tribulation; but be of good cheer, I have overcome the world"* (Jn 16:33).

The term **Great Tribulation** applies in fact to only the second half or three and a half years of the seven. It is referred to by Jesus in Matt 24:21, *"Then there will be great tribulation, such as has not been since the beginning of the world"*. In Rev 7:14 it has a definite article (wrongly omitted in the AV): *"'Who are these arrayed in white robes, and where did they come from?' 'These are the ones who come out of the great tribulation, and washed their robes and made them white in the blood of the Lamb.'"*

The Beast will be the second person of the latter day trinity of evil. Along with the Dragon (Satan) and the Second Beast or False Prophet, he is described in Revelation 13 as the First Beast. He is often called the Antichrist, but, as there are other lesser antichrists, it is safer simply to refer to him as The Beast. *"The man of sin (will be) revealed, the son of perdition, who opposes and exalts himself above all that is called God or that is worshipped.* (II Thess 2:4).

Christ's **Coming in Power** will occur at the end of the Great Tribulation, when He will visibly return in judgement with an army of angels and His Bride or glorified Church.

By **Millennium** we mean the literal future thousand year period, free of Satanic influence, mentioned six times in Revelation 20. We contend that many will be alive then in their mortal bodies, but that resurrected saints of all ages will be present in their immortal bodies. We believe that Christ will reign on earth from his capital at Jerusalem and that long postponed promises to Israel will be fulfilled. Some question whether the period is present or future, actual or figurative and accurate or approximate. Some question whether the nation Israel exists or will exist during the Millennium, and whether the Church is undergoing or will undergo the Millennium. In fact one's views on the whether the Revelation 20 statements are to be taken literally or otherwise, will determine more than any other factor to which of the following prophetic schools one will subscribe.

Post-Millennialism teaches that Jesus Christ will not return to earth until after the Millennium. Some believe that this has already started, but others see it as being entirely future. Significantly they believe that the world is to improve or be "Christianised" before Christ's return, thus, through the Church's completion of the Great Commission, making the world fit for its Saviour. Many see this happening only through the efforts of a Church empowered by the Holy Spirit, but some see some sort of spiritual, moral or cultural evolution of mankind playing a role. To some Post-Millennialists, the Lord's return appears to be so far ahead as not to be worth studying except in the most superficial manner. Post-Millennialism was widespread during the great missionary era, but received a near death-blow with the outbreak of the First World War. Its revival in recent decades has been associated with the optimism of the Neo-Charismatic movement. The absence of subsequent much heralded world-wide moral improvement has dampened enthusiasm. It sees no special future role for Israel.

Amillennialism describes a wide ranging doctrine held both by conservatives and liberals. It either denies the thousand year period altogether or assumes it to refer to the Church Age. Conservative Amillennialists see the earth as deteriorating; they believe that Jesus Christ will return in due course, in a single major event, to wind up earth's history and judge all classes—men and angels—before setting up the eternal heavenly state. They see the many widely varying accounts as applying, usually figuratively, to the same event. The resultant complexity of prophetic possibilities discourages all but a very few to study eschatology seriously. Virtually all Amillennialists embrace Replacement Theology. Those that do believe that God has a future for Israel tend not to attempt to reconcile this with their Amillennialism, their stance being by conviction, rather than on a coherent doctrinal basis. Amillennialism is generally associated with Augustine of Hippo, although there were earlier exponents.

Pre-Millennialism is the doctrine that Christ's Second Coming will occur before the Millennium. All Pre-Millennialists are Bible-believing fundamentalists—fundamentalists in the better sense of the word. They believe that the world is currently deteriorating, and that only after Christ's personal judgemental intervention at Armageddon will an ideal state on earth be achieved. It was found in the early Church, but then almost, but not totally, disappeared until it was revived only slowly after the Reformation. The two main forms of Pre-Millennialism are summarised below. We will refer to Mid-Tribulation and Pre-Wrath Rapturists in Chapter Thirteen.

Post-Tribulationism (also Post-Tribulationalism) is that form of Pre-Millennialism which believes in a single event Second Coming (Rapture and Coming in Power) at the end of the Great Tribulation. They see the Church as going through the Great Tribulation. The term Covenant Pre-

Millennialist is also applied to them. It is not currently widespread. Most Post-Tribulationists believe in a Millennial future for Israel, but generally do not perceive a key Tribulation role for Jews.

Pre-Tribulationism (also Pre-Tribulationalism) is the form of Pre-Millennialism which we hold. It is also sometimes referred to in America as **Dispensational Pre-Millennialism,** and may occasionally be referred to in our pages as **Dispensational Israelology,** when there is a need to emphasis the Jewish element of the doctrine. It is the only form of Pre-Millennialism which adheres rigidly to the ever present possibility of the Lord's immediate return to take His Church home before the Great Tribulation, and to return later with it. The doctrine of God's central purposes for the Jews following the removal or Rapture of the Church is *critical* to Pre-Tribulationism. This is why it tends to be singled out for attack by Replacement Theologians. We would contend that this is also why it tends to be targetted by the Enemy.

'Jew' And 'Gentile'

It is most important at this stage to define what we mean be these terms, as there will otherwise be much scope for ambiguity. We could find more accurate terms, but these, we feel would fail to communicate so well to the average reader. Thus we shall use them as per modern parlance; in other words, to distinguish between those who are of Abraham's line through Jacob (Israel), and those who are not. This should serve our declared aims and objectives.

Thus we are going on the assumption that both refer to natural descent, and are a fact of life. A Jew will always be a Jew and a Gentile will always be a Gentile, even following Christian conversion. We recognise that, in both cases, being a Christian has the over-riding priority, giving the supreme spiritual status, with many ensuing benefits and privileges. But that it does not annul human lineage. We will leave until Chapter Eight consideration of the few scriptures which might suggest otherwise.

The word 'Israeli' is inappropriate for this study, as it is understood only in its political sense. It is taken to apply to Jews whose citizenship is in the state of Israel. Israelite and Israelitish may be more accurate words, but they are somewhat clumsy and unfamiliar to most people. Moreover they tend to be associated historically with the northern kingdom, following the disruption under Rehoboam and Jeroboam, rather than with the united nation. 'Hebrew' is a good word, and has been adopted by some Messianic Jews. It was occasionally used by Paul. However for most people nowadays it is associated with the language rather than the people.

We can and must use the term 'Israel' for the covenant nation, which has existed as a recognisable ethnic entity almost since the time of the Patriarchs, whether it was politically independent or not. In Part Two we will consider objections to and variations of the interpretation of this nationhood.

Originally 'Jew' indicated a member of the tribe of Judah, as opposed to one of the other tribes. However, as Unger says:

> "From the time of the Babylonian captivity, as the members of the tribe of Judah formed by far the larger proportion of the remnant of the covenant people, Jews became the appellation of the whole nation." [3]

'Gentiles' is the common Old Testament translation of *goyim* (*goi* in the singular). It simply indicates foreigners as opposed to Israel. In the New Testament the term 'Gentile' produces all sorts of translation problems. We must concede that our beloved Authorised Version (KJV) is full of inconsistencies in its renderings.

The Greek word most commonly translated Gentiles is *ethne*; the singular form, *ethnos*, means 'nation' and should not be a problem. Walvoord is very succinct in saying:

> "...Gentiles (Gr. *ethne*), which, although sometimes used for Jews (Lk 7:5; 23:2; Jn 11:48, 51, 52; 18:35; Acts 10:22), is more characteristically used of the Gentiles as distinguished from Jews, as for instance in Romans 11:13; 15:27; 16:4; Galatians 2:12; and is used in contrast to Jews in Romans 2:29 and 9:24." [4]

Richards says:

> "Ethnos occurs 164 times in the NT. Some occurrences designate all peoples. Several times the word specifies believers won from paganism. Typically, however, it is used

to designate pagan peoples who stand in contrast to the Jews or to Christians." [5]

He gives many references to illustrate these uses. The apparent confusion is not in the word of God, but in the fact that there were so many uses of this single word current when the New Testament books were being written. This is a common feature in linguistics.

While it can be demonstrated that *ethne* does sometimes refer to groups or members of the Jewish *Diaspora*, claims that this is the *only* legitimate translation lead to a dangerous extreme, where a sort of reverse Replacement Theology emerges, and Jews are encouraged to pre-empt the end of the Church Age. We will look briefly at this phenomenon in Chapter Thirteen. As it has been fairly well proved that the other word occasionally translated 'Gentile' in the AV, namely *Hellen,* implies either Greek *per se* or dispersion Jew, this exclusively Jewish claim for *ethne* would result in the Gentiles being mentioned only once in the New Testament, with the word *ethnikos* in Gal 2:14. This would of course be absurd!

We re-emphasise the fact that our use of 'Jew' and 'Gentile', will throughout this thesis refer to human ancestry and descent, unless otherwise indicated.

Interpreting Revelation

We shall be making frequent excursions into the book of Revelation. There are four main schools of interpretation for this book; we shall be adhering strictly to the Futuristic view. For a concise summary, we quote Dr Walvoord :

> "This approach is limited to conservative expositors who are usually premillennial... Under this system of interpretation, the events of chapters 4 through 19 relate to the period just preceding the coming of Christ. This is generally regarded as a period of seven years with the emphasis on the last three and one-half years, labelled the 'great tribulation'. Chapter 19, therefore, refers to the second coming of Christ to the earth, chapter 20 to the future millennial kingdom

which will follow, and chapters 21 and 22 to events either contemporary with or subsequent to the millennium". [2]

The Futurist interpretation in no way denies that Revelation has had legitimate applications for saints down through the ages, or that there are practical non-prophetic lessons and applications to be gleaned from its pages. But when one considers that Jesus Himself warned of a period of intense and unprecedented suffering immediately before His return in power, one finds it not at all unreasonable that much of the last book of the Bible should be devoted to this period. No other book in Scripture opens and closes with so many blessings, admonitions and warnings; no other book is personally 'signed off' by the risen Lord. This is the only school of interpretation which currently encourages widespread study of the book, rather than the plucking of short extracts as and when convenient.

Because our Pre-Millennial, Pre-Tribulational stand is so closely integrated with Israel's intermediate and long-term future, we will allow the following chapters, namely Chapters Two to Six, to testify to the appropriateness of this school of prophetic interpretation.

Broadly speaking, *whether* there is a distinct, identifiable future for Israel in God's revealed plans will determine whether Amillennialism, Post-Millennialism or Pre-Millennialism is correct. *When* such a future commences will determine which school of Pre-Millennialism is correct.

Chapter Two

A Future For Israel—The Big Issue

Ambivalence

> "Some people believe that God still has future purposes for Israel, while some do not, but rather that it has been replaced by the Church. Both sides have good arguments. I'm not sure where I stand. I'm easy."

These astonishing words were spoken recently by a pastor from the platform of one of those many churches which would still describe themselves as Bible-believing and evangelical, but where serious study is steadily being eroded by other activities which are supposedly good for 'church growth'. I wanted to shout out, "And is God easy too?" Church growth is a term which differs from 'evangelisation' in several subtle, and some less subtle, ways. Were this an isolated incident, one might almost let it pass. However as it probably reflects the positions of a few thousand other churches and leaders in Britain, it must be confronted, or at least examined.

Whether the Nation Israel was cast off forever by God after Calvary is one of those issues which potentially divide the Church into two camps. For this reason alone, many modern Christians shy away from tackling it. It is deeply unfashionable to deal with any matter which is seen as being divisive. *"Contending for the faith"* (Jude 1:3) has apparently become an activity in which one may participate, only if it can be guaranteed not to be offensive or cause disquiet to any individual or any other denomination. Causing offence to Jews is evidently the one exception to this rule. If the conscience is pricked, it is easy to quieten it by pointing out that there are many other 'more important matters' demanding our attention. This sort of attitude relegates the issue to a trivial status.

But is it trivial? Can it be right not to be sure whether or not God revoked His promises to Israel? Can it be right not to be able to take significant passages of the Old Testament at face value? For this is what Replacement Theology inevitably implies. Here are a number of reasons why we must not regard the question of whether Israel still has a place in God's plans as a trivial matter.

While we will regularly be challenging Replacement Theology, we must on no account misrepresent it. We will indeed encounter Replacement Theologians who insist that God has forever totally rejected the nation Israel since the Crucifixion, Pentecost or AD 70. But there are many others who, mainly on the basis of Romans 9 to 11, believe that God has guaranteed a time of repentance for the nation, and may even love the Jews. Our quarrel with this latter group is that their prophetic scheme does not allow for any distinctive role for Israel following this repentance. At best they seem to see some sort of integration with the Church; and this is no different from what has happened to repentant Jews since Pentecost!

No Trivial Pursuit

The space devoted in Scripture to Israel's future is considerable. Most is to be found of course in the prophets. But there is also much in the historical books and the Psalms. There are even clear indications in the Gospels and other New Testament references right through to Revelation. Even if one discounts those passages which one may argue have already been fulfilled in the restoration following the Babylonian Exile or in the earthly life of Jesus, much remains which, by no stretch of the imagination, has yet been fulfilled. No Replacement Theologian can reasonably deny this.

Some of the prophecies concerning Israel are conditional; but others are couched in unconditional terms and actually include texts which God gave on oath. Some of the most solemn promises in Scripture are included. If we maintain that God revoked or cancelled any of these promises, we are doing two very serious things. We are questioning God's integrity and trustworthiness, and we are giving people reasonable grounds for questioning God's other promises, including those upon which our very salvation is based. It is our duty as God's ambassadors (II Cor 5:20) to demonstrate the reliability of Scripture, not to give grounds for doubting it. Dr Walvoord says:

> "The question of the future of Israel is important because it determines the interpretation of so many passages of the Bible. To some the theological arguments may seem

technical, but the question simply put is whether the prophecies about Israel should be taken in their plain and natural meaning as revealing Israel's future." [1]

Despite the above facts, there is a growing number of theologians who would claim to be fundamental and evangelical but who espouse Replacement Theology, asserting that Israel forfeited her special rights and roles at or soon after Calvary. These, by and large, are not stupid people. Their case must be taken seriously, if only because of their widespread influence. It is either right or wrong, as indeed is our case. There can be no compromise position. There must surely be an authoritative answer in the Word of God; it is our duty to persevere until we find it.

Replacement Theology developed during the second and third centuries AD and was eventually codified and publicised in his book *De Civitate Dei* (The City of God) by Augustine of Hippo around AD 400, when it became an accepted doctrine of the Roman Catholic Church. It has remained such until this day. This alone should compel us to review it and to ask whether it is one of those secondary but important areas which the Reformers neglected as they concentrated upon salvation by works, the Mass, Mariolatry, corrupt monasticism and similar matters. When we consider the role Replacement Theology played in the Holocausts and Pogroms, perhaps it is not so secondary.

The revival of widespread recognition of Israel's future role began in Britain about 1820 and received a huge boost in November 1917 with the Balfour Declaration. Many nationally known evangelical theologians joined F B Meyer's Advent Testimony Movement. While the central theme was the Lord's near return, a future for Israel was implicit. The confirmatory evidence in the world scene was rapidly accumulating. Christians were noting the Signs of the Times in an exemplary way, which would shame today's churches.

Commitment remained high until well after the rebirth of the nation Israel in 1948. In recent years it has slumped. There can be but two reasons. Either it was wrong in the first place, or the change has come about as part of prophesied growing end-time apostasy and scoffing at the Lord's return. We must decide which. Whether the information is inconvenient or embarrassing is irrelevant. The predicted falling away and scoffing are definitely to come, whether we like it or not, according to the Bible (II Thess 2:3 & II Pet 3:3). As individuals and congregations we are responsible for resisting these trends. But we cannot stop them altogether; God said they would happen.

Doctrines should be held or rejected purely on the grounds of Scripture. However there is a secondary and increasingly common reason, namely convenience or expediency. Perhaps these terms are almost too polite. But it has become popular to consider first what will attract people to or repel people from Christianity—Christianity in its widest terms rather than the Gospel specifically. It is the wisdom of the world, but it is happening. Doctrines must never be watered down to make them more palatable. Any kind of support for Israel is seen as being politically incorrect; we will gain the world's approval if we attack Israel, even if only verbally. We must ensure that we hold doctrines for the right reasons; and political correctness is most certainly not one of them.

Israel has for decades now been the world's biggest political 'hot potato'. Crises may flare up, simmer for a while and then slowly die down. But questions regarding Israel's status, her occupation of the Land and her relations with 'Palestinian' Arabs continue to dominate the world scene. Initiatives come and go; treaties and agreements are short lived. It is clear that those Arab states which have had all the financial and other resources to alleviate the 'Palestinian plight'[*] have for a variety of reasons, which they may or may not feel are justified, chosen to keep the pot on the boil, as it were. Israel is rightly or wrongly portrayed as a client state of certain Western and Christian nations. Christians must have convictions based on Scripture, always assuming Scripture has anything to say on the issue. With more Bibles available to us than ever, we cannot stand back, nor can we sit on the fence. We must search the

---

[*] Much is heard in the popular international media about the 'Palestinian plight'. Even if we momentarily exclude the over-riding spiritual perspective and look at this from the viewpoint of international law, we find that the plight of individual 'Palestinians' is imposed by their own regime. The first duty of any government is the defence of the realm. As long as it remains the avowed intent of large sectors of the 'Palestinian' leaders to annihilate the state of Israel, Israel, who has never made such reciprocatory threats, is obliged to take such stern counter-measures as are necessary. She has learned by bitter experience that half measures do not work. Unlike many of her critics, she is fully aware that, based on a precedent set by the Prophet himself, fundamentalist Islamic states believe that it is morally justified to make and later break treaties in order to gain the upper hand over initially stronger opposition.

Scriptures. Were there to be no definitive answer, we would have to accept it; but we maintain that an answer can and must be found.

God said something most remarkable about Jerusalem which is currently pertinent:

> *"In that day I will make Jerusalem a very heavy stone for all peoples; all who would heave it away will surely be cut to pieces, though all the nations of the earth are gathered against it"* (Zech 12:3).

To date this has never been fulfilled in quite these terms. The setting of this text is a state of military siege, on a scale which has never hitherto occurred, but which today seems so very feasible.

Thus Scripture indicates that the Middle East crisis will get worse, much worse, before any improvement can be looked for. The uniqueness of this Zechariah statement and our claim to believe Scripture should compel us to enquire. No other city in the world has ever been a burdensome stone for all nations. But God said that this one would be. Why, oh why do Christians not use this as convincing evidence that the Bible is utterly reliable and totally up-to-date? Two and a half thousand years ago the Bible predicted that Jerusalem would become a huge international burden. It has happened. Why ever do Christians keep quiet about this? Nominally Christian nations are likely to have to take a firm stand sooner or later. Individuals and congregations may have to lobby Parliament. Have we compared our convictions with Scripture? Do we know where we *should* stand?

The unparalleled survival, against overwhelming odds, of the one nation which God chose as His own thousands of years ago should challenge us to ask why, if its special status was revoked over nineteen hundred years ago, did it not disappear, like other cities and nations which God judged, such as Sodom and Gomorrah, Tyre and Assyria. Why did Jerusalem not vanish without trace unless God has some special future purpose for it?

Because Israel, as mentioned above, occupies such a prominent place in the Bible's predictive prophecy, we cannot hope to have a correct perspective of God's future plans for our planet, unless we first determine beyond any shadow of doubt whether this special future still stands, or has been forfeited. We will be as misguided as those disciples who could not countenance the idea of the Cross for their Master, because they had mental blockages about His programme. Their loyalty was no more questioned than that of many hard working churches who are today striving to 'bring in the Kingdom', but whose priorities are distorted— quite unnecessarily. Mental blockages about this and other major aspects of God's revealed plans for mankind are rife. Pre-, Post- and Amillennialism are utterly incompatible with one another, yet they are being given equal status in a Church where the word 'tolerance' has been redefined to mean 'anything goes'. At best, only one of these three views can be correct. Two embrace Replacement Theology, one does not.

Replacement Theology is a major obstacle to the evangelisation of the Jews. It is desperately patronising and bewildering for them. We cannot lift from them their large share of the guilt of crucifying their Messiah; that is not our right or privilege. But we can and should remove the insistence that God has forever abandoned them, if it is not true.

They do not have the New Testament, where are to be found nearly all the verses from which Replacement Theologians make their case. Jesus said that He came to neither to destroy the Law nor the Prophets (the two halves of the Old Testament) but to fulfil them, as they should not pass away before the end of the world (Matt 5:17, 18). Unconditional promises in the Old Testament must stand. Devout Jews should be able to find in their Scriptures alone all the necessary corroborative evidence for Yeshua being their promised Messiah as well as unchangeable non-negotiable revelation as to their Nation's future. Jesus Himself after His resurrection used these Scriptures to prove to the two Emmaus disciples: *"Ought not the Christ (the Messiah) to have suffered these things and to enter into His glory?"* (Lk 24:26). He did not indicate that hereafter these prophecies were to become obsolete. Indeed, His entering into glory was still ahead; the prophesied future was as literal and valid as the fulfilled prophecy.

Some Points And Questions To Ponder

We have produced a fairly comprehensive list of reasons why the question of Israel's future cannot reasonably be ignored by Christians. Many of these reasons can be dealt with later as we look at the various schools of prophetic interpretation. But some general comments at this point would not be inappropriate.

Even were it not for the spiritual aspect, we would have to concede that the survival of a nation without a homeland for nearly nineteen hundred years (AD 70 to 1948) is quite astonishing. No other people has survived more than a generation or two without a country. Israel has survived around sixty, depending how one defines a generation. Algernon Pollock quotes Mark Twain:

> "The Egyptian, the Babylonian and the Persian rose, filled the planet with sound and splendour, then faded to dream stuff and passed away; the Greek and the Roman followed, and made a vast noise and they are gone; other peoples have sprung up and held their torch high for a time, but it burned out and they sit in twilight now or have vanished.

> "The Jew saw them all, beat them all, and is now what he always was, exhibiting no decadence, no infirmities of age, no weakening of his parts, no slowing of his energies, no dulling of his alert and aggressive mind." [2]

Even without reference to Holy Scripture, are we not baffled? Do we not with Mark Twain want to know the secret of the Jew's persistence? We have the Bible; we have the answer at our fingertips. And, bearing in mind that we have the answer available, can we honestly say that the nation which gave the world Marx and Einstein has shown any sign of intellectual decline or enterprise, either since Calvary or since the AD 70 sack of Jerusalem? If God's judgement was final, why were these distinctive talents not diminished?

Replacement Theology is based on the supposition that the Church permanently replaced the Nation Israel in every respect from Pentecost onwards, this being the penalty for rejecting their rightful King. We in no way deny the consequences for the Nation of that rejection; we simply dispute the permanence of the sentence. In another book, Pollock records:

> "Not for seventy years exile, as happened when Judah was removed to Babylon, but for nearly two thousand years, has the Jew been in exile. If sin brought about seventy years exile, what **terrible** sin has the nation committed to bring this about? Surely the rejection of God's Son. Reader, see that **you** do not reject Him." [3]

But let us note at this stage that the main judgement did not fall on Jerusalem and Israel either at the time of Jesus' committal for crucifixion, or at the moment of His death, or at Pentecost, as one might have expected, but around forty years later. Now we can provide good reasons for this; but those who claim that Israel was finished with forever in God's purposes might ponder why judgement was not instantaneous.

Moreover let us be very sure that recognition of Israel's sin is in no way whatsoever a form of licence to begin thinking or acting in an Anti-Semitic manner. Rather we should be like Paul, whose heart's desire was that they should all be saved (Rom 10:1–2). He recognised that they still have a zeal for God, even if in ignorance. Do we seriously think that Paul would have expressed such sentiments for a nation forever cast off? We will have more to say about Anti-Semitism later.

Note that rejection of Replacement Theology does not mean that Dispensationalists, and anyone else who recognises a future for Israel, reject the fact that there are spiritual applications for us too. Indeed, we would both recognise and apply the import of Paul's words:

> *"Brethren, I do not want you to be unaware that all our fathers were under the cloud, all passed through the sea... Now these things became our examples, to the intent that we should not lust after evil things as they lusted... All these things happened to them as examples, and they were written for our admonition, on whom the ends of the ages have come. Therefore let him who thinks he stands take heed lest he fall"* (I Cor 10:1, 6, 11, 12).

Thus Paul makes it clear that members of the Church are equally vulnerable. Provided we remember who the original target audience was and the fact that we are now living under a different covenant, there is no reason why we cannot draw numerous moral, spiritual and practical lessons. Indeed, it is a requirement. But we should be careful not to concentrate on the blessings, whilst ignoring the warnings.

Because of her sin and her treatment of the various prophets whom He had sent to her, God during Isaiah's time imposed upon Israel (Isa 6:9–10) a spiritual blindness that still remained at the end Paul's ministry (Acts 28:26–27) and has yet to be lifted. Later we will consider

Zechariah's account of how that blindness will eventually be removed. Christians are equally vulnerable. What God did to Israel can He not do to individuals, congregations and even denominations in the Church Age? How else do we account for the Dark Ages? Is it possible that a sort of selective blindness regarding God's future purposes for Israel has been acquired through failure to take the prophets seriously? We cannot give an answer yet, but let us bear this question in mind as we shortly go through some Old Testament passages.

After all, the official representatives of 'Christendom', both Orthodox and Catholic, had become blind to many major Bible truths long before the Reformation. Are we immune today? Under such regimes there have always been individuals who have insight and saving faith despite their denominational hierarchies and dogmas, just as at Jesus' first Coming and immediately afterwards there were significant numbers who recognised and welcomed Jesus of Nazareth, despite the official line.

Stephen berated an audience which included the High Priest:

> *"You stiff-necked and uncircumcised in heart and ears! You always resist the Holy Spirit; as your fathers did, so do you. Which of the prophets did your fathers not persecute? And they killed those who foretold of the Just One, of whom you have now become the betrayers and murderers"* (Acts 7:51–52).

Never was there a more serious consequence for ignoring the prophets than that. But we are living in a day of increasing disregard for Bible prophecy. Is not ignorance concerning the Saviour's Return and God's future purpose for Israel among the consequences of this neglect? Can Christians not be stiff-necked too?

We tend to think of the *Diaspora* or dispersal of the Jews throughout the world only as a consequence of their national rejection of their Messiah and the sack of Jerusalem in AD 70. But in fact Jewish exile began back in the 8th century BC with the defeat by Assyria of the ten tribe Northern Kingdom. It was extended in the following century to include the Babylonian exile of Judah (with Benjamin and the Levites who had not been deported by Assyria). In addition there were many 'economic refugees'—Jews who wished to acquire more comfortable lifestyles and prosperity, using their business acumen elsewhere. Only a minority, mainly but not exclusively from Judah, returned when Cyrus gave permission and encouragement to return to the Promised Land. By Esther's time Jews were apparently scattered throughout the 127 provinces of the Medo-Persian empire (Est 8:9). Consider the widespread home cities of the crowds in Jerusalem to whom the apostles preached at Pentecost. A fair number of Jews remained in the Land until the Bar Kochbar rebellion of AD 135, when eviction was virtually complete. If, as we have shown, dispersal as such was not exclusively for handing Jesus over for crucifixion, but was occasioned by other factors as well over a period of hundreds of years, how can Replacement Theologians maintain that that alone was the cause of Israel's everlasting rejection from God's purposes?

If there is to be no future for Israel, we lose the significance of some beautiful Old Testament typology. Take Joseph, *"him who was separate from his brothers"* (Gen 49:26) for instance. A J Pollock writes:

> "Joseph is a beautiful type of Christ, in that he was loved by his father, hated by his brethren, sold for twenty pieces of silver, passing in figure through death and resurrection in his prison life in Egypt, and finally exalted to the place of rule and authority, becoming in figure the Saviour of the world." [4]

The eventual reconciliation with his brethren, was carefully arranged by Joseph, so they were compelled to admit their appalling guilt and to fear for their very lives. This was an essential part of the collective repentance process, which eloquently extends this prophetic portrayal of Jesus the rightful King of Israel and His sinful but still beloved brethren. The Replacement Theologian makes no room for this collective repentance and restitution of Israel, believing them nationally to be beyond redemption.

False expectations can influence our views both of Israel's future and of the manner and timing of the Lord's Return. Dr Prasch observes:

> "There were three main reasons the Jews were not ready for Jesus to come the first time. They had a 'signs and wonders gospel' and they had a 'kingdom now gospel' and they had a 'prosperity gospel'. As it says in Daniel chapter 7:21,22, the saints take full possession of the kingdom **after** the return of

Christ—not **before**… They were taken up by a false spirit of dominionism and triumphalism, almost exactly what we see throughout much of the church today. The Jews had no desire to know about a suffering servant Messiah." [5]

The prosperity gospel has caught on less in Britain than in the USA, but the other two phenomena are rampant enough. Two thousand years ago these expectations did not allow the Jews to find room in God's plans, as they saw them, for the Church. Conversely similar false expectations, including a future without the Great Tribulation and Armageddon, do not allow many Christians to find room in God's plans, as *they* see them, for the Jews.

God's Witnesses

That great English expositor, F B Meyer, writes:

"In chapter xlii. 19 they are blamed for being blind and deaf; but for all that they are addressed as capable of giving evidence. Though they had misused their opportunities, and had made less progress than they might have done in their knowledge of God, yet they knew more of Him than any other nation beside upon the face of the earth, and could tell secrets which the profoundest thinkers had missed. "Ye are My witnesses, and My servant whom I have chosen." [6]

"'You are My witnesses' says the Lord, 'and My servant whom I have chosen'." (Isa 43:10). Who was God addressing? The answer is very simply found by reading the rest of the passage, starting with *"Thus says the Lord, who created you, O Jacob, and He who formed you, O Israel"*, (v1) and continuing with further specific references to Jacob and Israel, their history, their Land and their transgression. The passage continues into chapter 44. We read *"Thus says the Lord, the King of Israel... You are My witnesses"*. (vv. 6 & 8).

If, on the other hand, we look at the chapter or page headings of the AV (KJV) we find surprising statements such as, "The Lord comforteth the Church with promises" and "God calleth Cyrus for his church's sake". These headings are not inspired Holy Writ. They are 17th century additions, designed to be helpful to the reader, as indeed many of them are. Most modern translations have dispensed or amended them, but their legacy remains. We still cling to the mixed heritage of the 17th century.

If one reads the rhetoric of the 17th century Covenanting Scottish Presbyterians, one finds them constantly referring to themselves as Israel—to the exclusion of, for instance, Episcopalians, who might be classed as Amalekites or Canaanites! To be fair, many of them were devout believers, clinging to the Gospel of grace and prepared to be driven from their homes and even martyred for their faith. The local representatives of the English Bishops tried, by military means, to impose upon them their prayer-book-based liturgical worship, which smacked too much of the Catholicism which they had in the previous century cast off. But pride had taken its toll; they classed themselves as the only true Israel.

This is only one of the more extreme examples; there were others in Europe from the same period. Of course we Christians can apply the lessons of Isaiah to ourselves today, providing we never forget who the original addressees were, because they tell us how God deals with His own people and warn us of common pitfalls.

It is true, of course, that Israel has for the present collectively forfeited the blessings. She is obviously not the main source of witnessing for God today. The Church is currently doing that. However even now Israel is in an obscure way witnessing for God. She is witnessing by default, witnessing in spite of herself. She is still a powerful witness to God's faithfulness.

If we turn to Deuteronomy chapters 28 to 30, we find recorded on the one hand the list of blessings and privileges promised by God to Israel should they remain obedient, and on the other land the list of curses and penalties to be incurred should they prove disobedient. Many of these are to be found elsewhere as well, but this is the most comprehensive passage. As we know, after many warnings and lesser judgements, the great exiles to Assyria and Babylon and the even greater world wide *Diaspora* in AD 70 were sanctioned by God. These were the most bitter fruits of their disobedience.

The curses begin at 28:16. We need not go through them individually. But consider some of the following:

> *"The Lord will cause you to be defeated by your enemies; you shall go out one way against them and flee seven ways before them; and you shall become troublesome to all the kingdoms of the earth."* (v 25).

Has any nation ever been considered quite so troublesome to all nations? Has God not faithfully kept this promise—for a promise it is. Are the Jews not mutely witnessing to God's faithfulness.

> *"A nation whom you have not known shall eat the fruit of your land and the produce of your labour, and you shall be only oppressed and crushed continually. So shall you be driven mad because of the sight which your eyes see."* (vv. 33–34).

Have greedy eyes not looked upon the labour of the diligent Jew in many a country through the centuries and plundered or confiscated property, belongings and wealth? Have they not been driven to distraction by their suffering. Is not this precisely what God foreordained?

> *"And you shall become an astonishment, a proverb, and a byword among all nations where the Lord will drive you."* (v37).

What other nation has ever deserved this description? It is not the kind of promise which God wanted to keep for His ancient people, but it is the one which they chose. Had they chosen the way of obedience and received the remarkable blessings available, they would even now be witnesses to God's faithfulness in a very different way.

> *"Then the Lord will scatter you among all people, from one end of the earth to the other... and among those nations you shall find no rest, nor shall the sole of your foot have a resting place; but there the Lord will give you a trembling heart, failing eyes, and anguish of soul."* (vv. 64–65).

Was there ever a more eloquent summary of the history of the dispersed Jew? F B Meyer, in a chapter entitled "Ye are My Witnesses", says:

> "The very existence of the Jewish people scattered throughout the world, and yet preserved from absorption amid the populations that surround them—that they have no rest for the sole of their foot; that they have a trembling heart, and failing eyes, and pining of soul; that they fear night and day, and have none assurance of life; that they are evidently being kept for their land, as their land is being kept for them—all this is in exact conformity to the words of Moses in the Book of Deuteronomy." [7]

In our next chapter we shall consider from other Scriptures whether the promises for an ultimate golden future, when national repentance eventually comes, is to be taken equally literally. We must ask ourselves whether the standards of literal fulfilment, evidenced in the Scriptures which we have just quoted, should not also apply to as yet unfulfilled promises. Will there not be a faithful witnessing role for Israel in the final golden chapter of earth's history? Is the *"comfort ye My people"* not to be realised? We shall see.

There are dangers in dwelling incautiously upon these things—dangers not only for the Jews, who *need* to ponder them, because this can be a stepping stone to repentance, but dangers for the rest of us. The "serve them right" mentality is the first step to what is to God one of the most abhorrent evils in this world, Anti-Semitism. It should be the simplest matter of faith to accept that God can both love and judge.

> *"He who spares his rod hates his son, but he who loves him disciplines him promptly."* (Prov 13:24).

> *"And the vessel that he made of clay was marred in the hand of the potter; so he made it again into another vessel, as it seemed good to the potter to make... 'O house of Israel, cannot I do with you as this potter?' Says the Lord. 'Look, as the clay in the potter's hand, so are you in My hand, O house of Israel!'"* (Jer 18:4:6).

"No, He cannot!", says the Replacement Theologian, failing to notice that the potter did not take a fresh lump of clay, but remoulded the marred one. "Yes, He can!", we would challenge.

W E Vine, commenting on Isaiah 43, writes:

> "God's challenge to the nations is to 'bring' their witnesses that they may justify their acknowledgement of those who are no Gods (*verse 9*)... In contrast to this Jehovah makes the twofold declaration concerning His earthly people, 'Ye are My witnesses' (*vv. 10 and 12*). Connected with the first of these is their witness to the unoriginated and self-sustained nature of His Being. I am He... Before Me there was no God formed, neither shall there be after Me'... The second declaration that His earthly people are His witnesses, is put into connection with the facts, not only that He is the one and only God, the great Jehovah, but that He alone is the 'Saviour' (*verse 11*), and that, besides this, there is none that can deliver out of His hand (*verse 13*)... Since all this is so with regard to His national witnesses, let us take courage and renew our strength, as those whom He has called to be His witnesses through the Gospel." [8]

Later we may return to Vine's discourse, because commenting on God's declaration of Israel's witnessing function in Isaiah 44, he goes on to show how this is tied in with a future restoration

In the meantime, as we have noted, Israel is still unconsciously witnessing for God, if only through her sufferings and through her survival down through the centuries against enormous odds. But what about the Church? Is she not witnessing too, and witnessing in a much more positive manner? Yes she is, even if not always consistently. Are both therefore, as separate entities, expected to witness at the same time? This is one of the questions which the Replacement Theologian would pose. It is a very good question, an understandable one. Later we will face up to it and find out which response answers all the queries and is totally consistent with Scripture.

The very last words which Jesus spoke before He was caught back to Heaven, whence He came, were:

> *"You shall receive power when the Holy Spirit has come upon you; and you shall be witnesses to Me in Jerusalem, and in all Judaea and Samaria, and to the ends of the earth."* (Acts 1:8).

This was a prophecy—a very familiar one to all Christians. Is it not interesting and instructive to note how we tend to pay much more attention to those prophecies which appeal to us or give us a sense of importance, than those which have elements of warning or condemnation?

Certainly this one should give us a sense of importance. Some of the elements of Israel's witnessing must be continued by us. After all, Israel has been 'sidelined' and we occupy the 'main line'. Even though it may one day become illegal, we too must be witnesses to the fact that there is no other God, and that all other gods and faiths are false. Preaching this makes us feel a bit uncomfortable, doesn't it? But then any form of Christianity with which the unsaved can be totally comfortable must be false. Proclaiming the Gospel must have an element of making people feel uncomfortable. We, like the Jews of old, must bear witness to the fact that there is no other Saviour. This is central to our Gospel.

But we, the Church, have one glorious additional responsibility. We are witnesses to Jesus Christ's death and resurrection. In fact we are more than witnesses; we are ambassadors, accredited representatives of our heavenly homeland and our Lord and King.

> *"Therefore we are ambassadors for Christ, as though God were pleading through us; we implore you on Christ's behalf, be reconciled to God. For He made Him who knew no sin to be sin for us, that we might become the righteousness of God in Him."* (II Cor 5:20–21).

However privileged Israel's ancient role was, ours is greater. Denial of Replacement Theology robs us of nothing we should have.

Words Of Caution

We believe we have given ample evidence that the question of whether God still has purposes for Israel is a major issue, one which cannot be ignored, but which must be tested against Scripture. We have also seen some evidence, although we have yet to gather much more, that Israel's future and the timing of the Lord's return are inextricably linked. Despite having a different perspective on many of these matters, Bruce Milne admits:

> "Another 'sign' which lies right at the heart of discussion about the Lord's return is the nation of Israel".

He then asks:

> "Do we conclude then that the Jews have no place in God's purpose since their rejection of the Messiah? Certainly the case for claiming that the Israeli state as it presently exists has a place is unproven." [9]

From this the unwary reader might assume that all those who believe in a future for the Jews see the present nationhood of Israel as having virtually fulfilled the conditions for the return of the Messiah. Now this may be true of a few, whose preoccupation is almost exclusively with getting as many Jews back into the Land as possible. These are, by and large, neither Dispensationalists nor Pre-Tribulationists. They simply love Israel; and for this they must be commended, because they have a zeal for winning Jews for Christ. But they tend to underestimate the significance of the as yet unrelieved national blindness. We must re-emphasise the fact that the budding fig tree is still fruitless, and no more than a pointer or sign of the times. We believe that Israel still has to undergo its final and most bitter holocaust before salvation comes for the survivors.

The other cautionary point concerns the risk of being seen to be taking any kind of stand for Israel. If we take a stand on the matter of the imminence of Christ's return, at worst we are in danger of being seen as cranks or eccentrics by the 'scoffing brigade' within our churches. That is a small price to pay for recognising this great spur to evangelisation and this witness to the reliability of the Bible. But soon if we take a stand for Israel, we could well become the target of that arch-Anti-Semitist himself, Satan.

As Islam increases its political muscle within our land, we could conceivably be portrayed as Zionist agitators. Islam simply cannot differentiate between Judaism and Zionism. Supporting Israel in any form could be seen as being politically unacceptable and racist, such is the growing hypocrisy of international politics. Weaker churches are likely to distance themselves from anything Jewish. Only the United States consistently vetoes United Nations Security Council anti-Israel resolutions. Britain's national stand rarely goes beyond abstention. As the European Community's political stranglehold over our foreign policy is tightened, that option may soon no longer be available to us.

However we can safely ally ourselves with David, who was told: *"When you hear the sound of marching in the tops of the mulberry trees, then you shall go out to battle, for God has gone out before you to strike the camp of the Philistines"*. (I Chron 14:15). Neither need we fear to be identified with Israel's prophet, who, when the Syrian army invaded, prayed that his young servant might be able to see that *"the mountain was full of horses and chariots of fire all around Elisha"* (II Kings 6:17). God has allotted Israel an angelic champion—*"Michael, the great prince who stands watch over the sons of your people."* (Dan 12:1). We will see more of him in this special role when we look at Revelation 12. If we are on Israel's side, we are on the Lord's side.

Chapter Three

Some 'Untils' Concerning Israel

'How Everlasting?'

We are now going to spend some considerable time looking at passages of Scripture which, we believe, demonstrate either individually or collectively God's future plans for Israel. These plans are consistent with a nation set aside, whilst the Church occupies centre stage throughout the most populous part of the world's history hitherto.

Dispensationalists are generally content to demonstrate that Israel has a future extending to the end of the Millennium, or perhaps a little beyond to the end of this world and this creation. If we can prove this future, we will have achieved our task as far as our defence against A- and Post-Millennialism is concerned. But perhaps we can go a little further into the future with Israel.

We read in Revelation 21 that, in the eternal state, the New Jerusalem will have gates bearing the names of the twelve tribes of the children of Israel (v12), and foundations with the names of the twelve apostles of the Lamb (v14). Both Israel and the Church are clearly identified, whether we fully understand the significance or not. Is this alone not overwhelming evidence that God still has a future for Israel? At least a memorial of both Israel and the Church are recorded eternally in heaven. Surely had Israel been 'written off' this would not be the case. The Church in Scripture is never divided into twelve Israelite tribes.

The common defence against inconvenient information supplied in these last two chapters of the Bible is that they are so far beyond our comprehension, that we cannot build reliable doctrines upon them. This of course is pure escapism and should not be tolerated. It is within this wonderful vision that the Lord Jesus Christ imparts His final universal message to the Church before His return; is that too difficult to comprehend? Do we thus lightly dismiss His message for the ages? If the tribes of Israel are specifically mentioned, it is for a very good reason indeed; we have no grounds for quibbling. Surely were Israel a discarded part of God's evaluation of human history, its tribes would on no account be included in this ultimate future! Whether we fully understand the life and architecture of the New Jerusalem is irrelevant; it does not permit us to ignore the passage.

Charles Ryrie simply comments:

> "The wall has 'twelve foundation stones,' and on them are the names of the 'twelve apostles'. Notice that even in eternity Israel and the church are distinguished, though both are included in God's redeemed people." [1]

William Newell helpfully notes:

> "We know positively that at least *one* nation and *one* seed, ISRAEL, will belong upon the new earth. In Isaiah 66:22 we read, 'As the new heavens and the new earth, which I will make, shall remain before Me, saith Jehovah, so shall your seed and name remain'. This is eternity for national Israel, and no escaping it! Because Isaiah 65:17, 18, which belongs to the new creation, has been confused with the millennial verses (20–25) men have rushed to the conclusion that all that Isaiah says concerning the new creation is millennial. But God says Israel's 'seed and name' shall *remain* in the new heavens and earth, that is, in that new order beginning in Revelation 21:1." [2]

Ethel Girdlestone, my great aunt, who led my parents, and indirectly me, to the Lord, and perhaps thanks to whose prayers this book has been written, writes in her inimitable way:

> "It is a fact worthy of note that not only do the precious jewelled foundations bear the names of the twelve Apostles of the Lamb, but we also find the names of the twelve tribes of Israel written upon the twelve entrances to this most hospitable City. Does not this fact tend to confirm my notes on Chapter xii, where I suggested going back to the call of Abraham for the origin of the Sunclad Woman: for 'he looked for a City which hath foundations, whose Builder and Maker is God'? In Heb. xi:40 we are told concerning Old Testament saints that 'they without us shall not be

made perfect.' Is it not evident from this verse that those dear old saints, *Israelites indeed,* to whose lives and writing we owe so much, are some day to receive blessing even through us? Also is it not possible that the finally restored wife of Jehovah, and the Bride of the Lamb may in some wonderful way be united in God, 'that God may be all in all'?" [3]

She has been with her Lord since 1955, but she used to speak just like that! We have lost the generations who so loved the graciously revealed promises of God. Now this little diversion into eternity took some time, but surely it was worthwhile. For if it is proved, as surely it has been, that Israel has a future in the New Jerusalem, all further Scriptures which we can add, to support our case for a future within our planet's history, can be no more than supplementary.

Unconditional Promises

We have already acknowledged the fact that Replacement Theologians have a number of verses or passages which they use to support their position. Some of their arguments are presented very convincingly, although they do tend to be oblique attacks; they offer passages which do not actually say that Israel has no future, but rather try to demonstrate that this is true. We will look at these in Chapter Eight. What they seem to be reluctant to admit is the overwhelmingly greater number of passages which the Israelologist can quote to prove Israel's distinct future.

Thus whatever else Replacement Theologians may argue, their case depends ultimately on proving that the numerous Old Testament passages, which at face value prove Israel's future, are conditional. If they fail to do that, they are tacitly accusing God of breaking His promises, whether they intend to or not. This largely explains why churches which are not Pre-Millennial devote so little time to predictive prophecy, in relationship to the space which Scripture accords it. The implications of such study are downright awkward for them; they are inconsistent with other truths which they hold dear. Their easiest course is to divert attention from the problem by accusing Pre-Millennialists of being pre-occupied with prophecy.

Of course there are many conditional promises, which we must consider. However the majority of promises appear to have no conditions attached. Therefore the initiative lies with the Dispensational Israelologist, rather than with the Replacement Theologian. Before the birth of modern Zionism, T B Baines, having referred to the promise of the Land, perceptively wrote concerning *tenure* of, as opposed to *title* to the territory:

> "The Israelites never had more than a conditional tenure of the land, and it is needless to say that a conditional gift is no fulfilment of an unconditional promise. This is not left to our own judgement, however, for we are plainly told in the language of Paul, 'that the covenant, that was confirmed before of God in Christ, the law, which was four hundred and thirty years after, cannot disannul, that it should make the promise of none effect. For if the inheritance be of the law, it is no more of promise, but God gave it to Abraham by promise' (Gal iii: 17,18)." [4]

Let us repeat Baines' statement: "a conditional gift is no fulfilment of an unconditional promise". We will have more to say about the Land in the next chapter.

There is a particular type of unconditional prophecy regarding or affecting Israel, which has an important conditional clause regarding the timing. As children we quickly learned the difference between 'unless' and 'not until', always assuming we had reasonably consistent and reliable parents. "No pocket money this week unless you tidy your bedroom" has different connotations from "you don't go out to play until you have eaten your vegetables". That particular week's pocket money *could* be forever forfeit; but sooner or later we *would* get out to play. Sometimes the message was put in a positive form—"You stay at the table until you have eaten your vegetables." The effect was similar, even although the emphasis was changed. In the positive approach emphasis may be put on the activity or condition which is to prevail before the 'until' can take effect.

As adult Christians, are we equally alert to the fact that God distinguishes between 'unless' and 'until' or 'not until' situations? He means what He says, for He is more consistent and reliable than any earthly parent. We find other reliable people in the Bible using them appropriately too.

Thus we find Jacob wrestling with God and saying, *"I will not let You go unless You bless me"*. (Gen 32:26). God recognised and honoured that albeit human 'unless'. Joseph, as unrecognised governor of Egypt, warned his brethren, *"You shall not see me unless your brother is with you"* (Gen 43:3). They understood the import and hastened to comply. Jesus said, *"Unless you are converted and become as little children, you will by no means enter the kingdom of heaven"* (Matt 18:3). Would we challenge that? Paul said to the master of the ship, *"Unless these men stay in the ship, they cannot be saved"* (Acts 27:31). The wise captain heeded this man of God, whom he had learned to respect. Not a single life was lost. Now where in Scripture do we find comparable 'unlesses' tied to Israel's actual survival? We don't! But there are many 'untils' regarding postponed blessings.

Yet the Replacement Theologian takes a line which implies that God said to Israel something along the following lines: "Unless you accept My Son as Messiah the first time I send Him to you, you will have no further place in My plans". But of course God never said any such thing, though He did say many severe things about Israel. The Jews are indeed still receiving *"from the Lord's hand double for all her sins"* (Isa 40:2). But from Isaiah we learn that it is ultimate comfort, not annihilation, which is to follow the double punishment.

The Dispensational Israelologist does not in any way underestimate the seriousness or consequences of the national rejection of the Messiah, but believes that God has set a number of milestones, time conditions, 'untils' or 'not untils' for an eventual restoration of this beloved but wayward nation. These are very strict prerequisites, but they offer promised certainties when they are ultimately met.

We will take a look now at some of these 'untils' and 'not untils'. Deciding upon a sequence of presentation was difficult, inasmuch as there is a good deal of overlap both of themes and timing. They are not intended at this stage to be seen as a setting forth of a particular view of the prophetic timetable. In the next chapter we shall look at some more 'untils' which concentrate on Israel and the future return of her Messiah.

We must not be tempted in these passages to stray into comprehensive expositions. We need give only sufficient background and comment to illustrate how they confirm some aspect of God's future purposes for Israel.

Until The Cities Are Laid Waste

Our first 'until' comes in the positive form. It is extremely significant, as is proved by the number of times it is quoted in part in the New Testament. We need therefore to spend some time on it. Extra time is also required here, as some principles will be laid down for application to subsequent passages.

> *"And He said, 'Go, and tell this people: "Keep on hearing, but do not understand; keep on seeing, but do not perceive". Make the heart of this people dull, and their ears heavy, and shut their eyes; lest they see with their eyes, and hear with their ears, and understand with their heart, and return and be healed.' Then I said, 'Lord, how long?' and He answered:* **'Until the cities are laid waste and without inhabitant,** *the houses are without a man, the land is utterly desolate, and the Lord has removed men far away, and the forsaken places are many in the midst of the land. But yet a tenth will be in it, and will return and be for consuming, as a terebinth tree or as an oak, whose stump remains when it is cut down. So the holy seed shall be its stump.'"* (Isa 6:9–13).

This of course is the surprise commission given to Isaiah when He replies, *"Here am I! Send me"* (v8). However useful these words may be out of context, we must be aware of their original setting. Jesus thought it was important; so should we. One cannot but wonder whether those who deliberately ignore this inconvenient sequel to these words, when they have chosen them for commissioning believers for some entirely unrelated task, may sometimes be inviting for themselves a sort of selective blindness and perhaps even prejudice or hardness regarding Israel's future. Where such hardness spills over to unbelievers, it can promote Anti-Semitism. The fact that the heavenly scene preceding Isaiah's commission speaks of judgement, should make us stop and think. *"Here am I, send me!"* may take us into unexpected areas in the Lord's service.

We find part quotations from these words in Matt 13:14, 15; Mk 8:17, 18; Jn 12:38–41; Acts 28:26, 27 and Rom 11:8. There are other less direct references elsewhere. Those who claim that the prophecy foretold Israel's change of heart at the return from the Babylonian captivity, rather than anything later, must note well these New Testament quotations, which carry the message on into the Church Age and beyond—a much more distant 'until' than 536 BC.

It is of course quite wrong to assume that there was no reference here to the Babylonian return. There most certainly was a limited fulfilment then; after all, Jerusalem had been desolated by Babylon. Jeremiah says,

> *"After seventy years are completed at Babylon, I will visit you and perform My good word toward you, and cause you to return to this place. For I know the thoughts that I think towards you, says the Lord, thoughts of peace and not of evil, to give you a future and a hope. Then you will call upon Me, and I will listen to you. And you will seek Me and find Me, when you search for Me with all your heart."* (Jer 29:10–13).

This was one of those offers for much greater blessing than was actually claimed when the time came. God's offer was genuine enough; but He knew what was going to happen and the extent and duration of the limited, half claimed blessing. His plans took this into account—plans for instance for the birth, life, rejection, crucifixion and resurrection of His Son.

Now of course there was no comparable return from the Assyrian captivity of the Northern tribes; and, even of Judah, more chose to remain in their new homes in the Babylonian empire than actually returned to avail themselves of this blessing. However there was a considerable revival under the leadership of Ezra for Judah-with-Benjamin and their attached Levites, plus a tiny representation of spiritual refugees from other tribes. Idolatry was firmly dealt with, and the zealous Pharisees arose to become faithful custodians and interpreters of the Scriptures—for a while (their classical image dates back to Maccabæan times). In fact the conditions of Isaiah's 'until' were potentially met, and theoretically might have endured, had hardness not crept in through religious pride.

When Jesus began His ministry, this deafness, blindness and hardness were widespread, but by no means fully in place. Some of the recovered Post-exilic spiritual hearing and sight was still available. So Jesus at first preached openly and straightforwardly, because He knew that His hearers had the ability to hear, see and understand had they wanted to. It was only after the religious leaders, as recorded in Matthew chapter 12, having followed Jesus around and weighed up His teaching, declared His message to be Satanic.

This was the juncture, in certain respects as critical for the next twenty centuries as Jesus' later trial and crucifixion, at which He re-imposed the judicial sentence which in His pre-incarnate glory, He had passed more than seven centuries before. Hardness of hearts was the factor over which they had the greatest personal control, and for which therefore they bore the greatest responsibility. These conditions prevail within the Jewish nation to this day. Isaiah's original 'until' applies to this day, being confirmed in many parallel passages.

Only after this rejection of His teaching did He resort to parables. Dr Walvoord writes regarding Mt 13:10–17:

> "After the first parable the disciples came to Jesus asking, 'Why do You speak to the people in parables?' (v10). The secret of why parables are used is that those who have rejected Jesus Christ as presented without parables now are not entitled to understand the secrets that belong to those of the faith. Accordingly Jesus said, 'Whoever has will be given more, and he will have an abundance. Whoever does not have, even that which he has will be taken from him' (v12)." [5]

Any Preterist ideas we may have that the desolation of the cities associated with this 'until' could refer to the sack of Jerusalem in AD 70 by the Romans is quickly dismissed, when we consider that that was a time of *diaspora* and deepening spiritual crisis, and not one of remnants and spiritual enlightenment. We will review this in Chapters Eleven and Twelve.

Going back to Isaiah chapter 6, we find W E Vine writing:

> "The people had so persistently perverted their ways that they had gone beyond the possibility of conversion and healing... The prophet, while willing and obedient, was so weighed down by the nature of his message, that he cried, 'Lord, how long?' For Isaiah knew that He would not cast off His people for ever (cp. Exod 32:9–14). The Lord responded by foretelling the wasted, depopulated condition of the cities, the uninhabited state of the house... Even so this remnant will come through a time of trouble. It will be 'eaten' or 'burnt' by a purifying fire (see Mal 3:3). This was the case with those who returned from captivity by the decree of Cyrus... So in the coming "Time of Jacob's Trouble" under Antichrist (Jer 30:7)... All this describes, in a twofold application, the circumstances of the remnant both after the return from captivity and hereafter in the Great Tribulation. The nation, consisting of the remnant, will, under the hand of their Messiah-Deliverer, revive and be glorified (Is 11:1)." [6]

We will later note the conditions of the repentance, which will eventually lift the hardness, blindness and deafness, when we look at texts from Zechariah. That will be a more comprehensive and long lasting remedy than that of Ezra's day. It will include all Israel (all the tribes, cf. Rom 11:26) rather than merely Judah and a few others. We observe that both Malachi, just referred to by Vine, and Zechariah prophesied after the return from the Babylonian exile. Their fulfilment can *only* be a latter day one. As we shall see from other 'untils', the return from world-wide exile which started in the 20th century is not the only prerequisite.

Until The Fullness Of The Gentiles

This spiritual state of Israel, with its three symptoms, is picked up by Paul. His reference is to Isa 29:10, written after the chapter 6 vision; the effect of the sentence had been immediate. In Romans 11 he says,

> *"God has given them a spirit of stupor, eyes that they should not see and ears that they should not hear, to this very day"* (v8),

and

> *"hardening of heart has happened to Israel **until the**
> **fullness of the Gentiles has come in"** (v25).*

Dr Walvoord writes:

> "In God's programme the project of calling out His Church
> of both Jews and Gentiles must be completed first
> (I Cor 12:12–13; Eph 1:22–23; 4:11–13)... Prior to Israel's
> deliverance, during the present age they are experiencing a
> 'hardening of heart', that is, many turn away from the
> Gospel. This will continue until God's purpose in His
> Church is complete." [7]

There may be minor variations of opinion about the exact moment of the
fullness of the Gentiles ending; but it is most certainly future.
Walvoord's statement about the Church being complete rather suggests
that the Rapture will be the moment for the lifting of the recalcitrance,
deafness and blindness. Certainly it cannot be before this. But
completion of the spiritual recovery will have to wait an extra seven
years or so, until after the Great Tribulation. After all, it is during this
brief interim period between the Rapture and His Coming in Power in
which Jesus' words will be fulfilled:

> *"I have come in My Father's name, and you do not receive*
> *Me; **if another comes in his own name, him you will***
> ***receive."** (Jn 5:43).*

Those who will be duped by the False Prophet into worshipping the
Beast will certainly not have regained their spiritual faculties and are
excluded. This is the clearest reference to the coming Beast or Man of
Sin, who will deceive many.

> *"And then the lawless one will be revealed, whom the Lord*
> *will consume with the breath of His mouth and destroy with*
> *the brightness of His coming. The coming of the lawless one*
> *is according to the working of Satan, with all power, signs*
> *and lying wonders, and with all unrighteous deception,*
> *because they did not receive the love of the truth, that they*
> *might be saved."* (II Thess 2:10).

Vine helpfully comments on Rom 11:25, clarifying any lingering doubts about the 'fullness of the Gentiles':

> "There are thus two limitations to the 'hardening', (a) extent; (b) duration... The time limit is the coming in of 'the fullness of the Gentiles'. This phrase cannot mean the blessing of the Gentiles as a whole, for that is to be consequent upon Israel's restoration, and not preliminary to it. Nor, again, does it denote the consummation of the times of the Gentiles, the period during which dominion is granted to the Gentile powers. Nor can it mean the consummation of Gentile iniquity. The reference seems to be to the whole number of Gentiles who partake of the blessings of salvation in the present age. The phrase does not stand for quite the same thing as the Church. For Jews who have accepted Christ have become part of the Church and are distinct here from Gentiles. Paul is speaking of God's dispensational dealings with Jew and Gentile."[8]

Probably the spiritual restrictions which afflict the 144,000 Jewish witnesses (Rev 7:2–8), which will prevent them being saved earlier and being counted part of the Church and thus raptured, will be lifted as they see their Messianic kinsmen suddenly disappear. They will have their minds, eyes and ears opened by the Holy Spirit, as they 'see the light', and are sealed by Him to preach the Gospel of the Kingdom. Like Saul of Tarsus, their zeal for God and knowledge of Scripture will suddenly be liberated from past obtuseness; they will be ready immediately to preach. One suspects that their hearts will become right before their ears and eyes, allowing God to use them. But just as the rest of the Jewish nation did not join Paul in the recovery of spiritual sight nearly two thousand years ago, no more will many of those Tribulation period Jews who close their hearts to the Gospel. There is a reference in Zech 13:8 to two thirds of living Jews remaining hardened; we will note the consequence later.

Was there ever more conclusive evidence, taking into account both Isaiah 6 and Romans 11, that the spiritual deafness, blindness and hardness of Israel will one day be removed and that her long exile from centre-stage will be over? We will return in due course to these verses from Romans. But we have a further 'until' to look at regarding the end of Gentile domination.

Until The Times Of The Gentiles Are Fulfilled

*"For there will be great distress in the land and wrath upon this people. And they will fall by the edge of the sword, and be led away captive into all nations. **And Jerusalem will be trampled by Gentiles until the times of the Gentiles are fulfilled.**"* (Lk 21:23, 24).

We have already stated that the 'fullness of the Gentiles and ending of the 'Times of the Gentiles' do not appear to coincide exactly.

Just when one is considering the arguments of those who assert that much of predictive prophecy concerning Israel is no longer relevant, because it was 'spent' at the return from Babylon or in AD 70, one finds a further text which unambiguously proves the opposite. So it is here with the times of the Gentiles. As far as Jesus was concerned, the ending of the 'times of the Gentiles' was still very much in the future, along with other events which by no stretch of the imagination have been fulfilled. John, well after AD 70, wrote:

"The court which is outside the temple... has been given to the Gentiles. And they shall tread the holy city for forty-two months" (Rev 11:2).

The 'times of the Gentiles' are still current, and the vast majority of the nations would like things to stay that way.

Writing about the Babylonian captivity, John Savage writes:

"We now come to a memorable, but very sad, epoch in the history of God's people,—the captivity and complete break-up of the nation that had for many centuries enjoyed the protection and favour of Jehovah... The first dismemberment of the nation took place when Shalmaneser carried the ten tribes of Israel captives to Assyria over a hundred years before the captivity of Judah (II Kings xvii). With the captivity by Nebuchadnezzar of the two remaining tribes of Judah and Benjamin the dissolution of the whole nation was complete. For though Judah had returned after the seventy years of captivity (see Ezra and Nehemiah), they were subject always more or less to other nations until their final dispersion at the destruction of Jerusalem by Titus, the Roman general, in the year AD 70. Israel thus having forfeited and lost its position of power as a nation before God, the sceptre of earthly government was transferred to the Gentiles, in the person of Nebuchadnezzar, and is to continue in their hands 'until the times of the Gentiles be fulfilled'." (Luke xxi.24). [9]

He then goes on to follow through the Times of the Gentiles as outlined in the great prophetic chapters of Daniel, starting with the overall scheme in chapter 2. In that chapter the five successive world empires, which were to control the part of the world which included the Promised Land, were revealed through the awesome image, which Nebuchadnezzar saw in his dream, starting with his own Babylon, the golden head, and ending with the Revived Roman Empire, the feet of incompatible iron and clay, with toes representing ten constituent kingdoms, which, after a long interval, shall follow on from the legs of iron, ancient Rome. The Church Age is not covered, except inasmuch as the old Roman Empire continued long into the Church's early history. The entire Church Age in fact lies within the Times of the Gentiles. This fifth future empire is the real focal point of the vision and is elaborated upon later in Daniel.

"There is a God who reveals secrets, and He has made known to King Nebuchadnezzar what will be in the latter days." (2:28).

Dr Rice writes in his commentary on Luke 21:24:

"Note the worldwide dispersion foretold in verse 24. Jews will go all over the world. And note the specific prophecy in verse 24 'and Jerusalem will be trodden down of the Gentiles, until the times of the Gentiles be fulfilled.' As this is being written (1971), Jews have control of the old city of Jerusalem, but it is inhabited primarily by Arabs and we would think from this Scripture that the Jewish control is only temporary and limited. Yet according to this verse it seems that an independent Jewish nation cannot have undisputed claim to and possession of the city of Jerusalem proper *'until the times of the Gentiles be fulfilled'*, that is, when the last Gentile rulers will be put down with the destruction of the Antichrist in the tribulation time and when Christ Himself shall return and *'the God of heaven set up a kingdom'*, the Jewish kingdom of Christ in Palestine, although it will be a kingdom of the whole world (Dan 2:44, 45). If we understand verse 24 correctly, then the ownership and control of Jerusalem is likely to be put into international hands and not left permanently under the control of Israel." [10]

Yet there are still Christians who believe that God has no future purposes for Israel! The Church simply does not fit in to Daniel's vision, as some would claim. It did not overthrow Rome; neither will it overthrow the Beast's kingdom—*"whom the Lord will destroy with the brightness of His coming"* (II Thess 2:8). Whether the switch to international control occurs before or after the Rapture is one of the questions we cannot answer. Certainly, according to Daniel 9:27, the Temple area will be under Jewish control for three and a half years, but, as we have seen from Revelation 12, the outer court will not.

Until The Spirit Is Poured Forth

Jerusalem is still the topic as Isaiah writes:

> *"On the land of My people will come up thorns and briers... because the palaces will be forsaken, the bustling city will be deserted... **until the Spirit is poured upon us from on high**, and the wilderness becomes a fruitful field... Then justice will dwell in the wilderness, and righteousness remain in the fruitful field. The work of righteousness will be peace, and the effect of righteousness, quietness and peace forever"* (Isa 32:13–17).

We saw something of this desolation as a precursor to the removal of deafness and blindness in our Isaiah 6 passage. Here we read of something else, which, if we think about it, is intimately linked, which will follow the ending of this spiritual incapacity. Kelly writes of these chapter 32 verses:

> "The allusion is to what precedes Jehovah taking His place and reigning in the land. And all the sorrow is to be **until**

the Spirit is poured down upon them. Then comes the great change in Israel. There is not of course the same dwelling of the Holy Ghost in any sense in the believer as now, for that He has a special dwelling in the church is now manifest. But there will be a suited and large outpouring of the Spirit in that day, as we have seen already. It is a mistake to suppose that Jehovah's reigning is incompatible with the Spirit's being thus poured out." [11]

It was for spiritual reasons that the earth came under a curse in Genesis 3; it should not surprise us that God will, in response to spiritual revival, one day lift that curse. The land long lay desolate following the AD 70 sacking of Jerusalem by the Romans. Its new inhabitants did little for the recovery of the countryside. It is only within the last century that parts of the desert have blossomed as a rose, as is often proclaimed. But to date this has been largely as a result of Jewish industry and enterprise—the *"sweat of your face"* (Gen 3:19). There are still tracts of unreclaimed desert. This is only a dim foreshadowing of the full promise of Isaiah 35, when the desert will spontaneously blossom as a rose. But that will not and cannot happen until the Spirit is poured out. Indeed, the worst desolation is still to come first, during the awful Trumpet and Vial or Bowl judgements of Revelation.

Some might be surprised at the first of Kelly's sentences quoted above. But this is consistent with Zech 12:10,11.

> *"And I will pour on the house of David and on the inhabitants of Jerusalem the Spirit of grace and supplication; then they will look on Me whom they pierced; they will mourn for Him as one mourns for his only son... In that day there shall be a great mourning in Jerusalem."*

True repentance is a ministry of the Holy Spirit. Those Jews who have worshipped the Beast and accepted his mark will not and cannot be included (Jn 5:43; Rev 14:9,10). Zech 13:8,9 indicates, as previously mentioned, that only a third will achieve this repentance:

> *"Two thirds in it shall be cut off and die, but one third shall be left in it; and I will bring that one third through the fire... they will call on My name, and I will answer them.*

I will say, 'This is My people'; and each one will say, 'The Lord is My God'."

There is no ambiguity in the passage. These are Jews; and one day God will bless them.

Bearing in mind this final holocaust, referred to in those verses, those who evangelise Jews must realise how blessed is their work if they do it now, because Jews born again in the Church Age will not have to undergo these horrors; they will partake in the Rapture.

Writing about this Isaiah passage, F B Meyer, founder of the Bible and Advent Testimony Movement in Britain, makes the simple but profound statement which the world would do well to heed:

"Let us remember that righteousness must precede peace." [12]

He draws our attention to Matt 5:24 and Heb 7:2. When we pray for the peace of Jerusalem (Ps 122:6), we are addressing One who keeps His promises; and we should have our eye on that future day. The prior seven year bogus peace treaty, which will be agreed or imposed after the Rapture will be brokered by the Beast, but be most outrageously broken when the 'abomination of desolation' is set up in the Jerusalem temple three and a half years later. Jesus warned His listeners on Olivet that that would be a time of untold suffering and strife—not one of peace or security. His predictions should help us to set our priorities and values.

Until Her Righteousness Goes Forth

Here we have two related 'untils' within a few verses of each other. We can deal with them together. They are very significant, but, because their message concerning Israel's future in God's plans shouts out so loudly and clearly, we can afford to be quite brief.

> *"For Zion's sake I will not hold My peace, and for Jerusalem's sake **I will not rest, until her righteousness goes forth as brightness, and her salvation as a lamp that burns**. The Gentiles shall see your righteousness, and all kings your glory... You shall also be a crown of glory in the hand of the Lord, and a royal diadem. You shall no longer be termed Forsaken, nor shall your land any more be termed Desolate... I have set watchmen on your walls, O*

Jerusalem, who shall never hold their peace day and night.
You who make mention of the Lord, do not keep silent, and
give Him no rest till He establishes and till He makes
Jerusalem a praise in the earth" (Isa 62:1–4, 6, 7).

The ultimate righteousness of chapter 32 is here also. But now we learn that, even during the foretold desolation, God is neither unconcerned nor inactive. Desolation was deserved; it had to happen. But God is fully aware of those guilty of the abhorrent crime of Anti-Semitism; the perpetrators will not escape judgement. God has His angelic watchers. Christians must be careful to disassociate themselves completely. Replacement Theology can bring a sense of comfort to those who persecute Jews.

Replacement Theologians would do well to ask three questions of this short passage:

1. Are the promises conditional or unconditional? They are clearly unconditional except inasmuch as certain things must happen before they can be fulfilled.

2. Is this Israel? Or is it the Church which is supposed to have annexed all Israel's blessings? Consider v4: *"You shall no longer be termed Forsaken, nor shall your land any more be termed Desolate".* Has that ever applied to the Church? This is about something which has been forsaken and desolate but which will be restored. The apostate church of Revelation 17 is doomed for destruction. This is about Israel.

3. Have they been fulfilled already? At no time since Isaiah prophesied has this international acclaim and renown occurred. As yet they are *"an astonishment, a proverb and a byword"* (Deut 28:24). Can Christians not trust that He who kept His promises as to Israel's curses will equally keep them as to her blessings?

Once again that old diversion that all was fulfilled at the return from Babylon is seen to be contemptible. Nehemiah prayed (4:4) *"Hear O our God, for we are despised; turn their reproach on their own heads".* Amid the rejoicing of the younger generation at that restoration, there was weeping among the priests and oldest of the people, who could recall the greater glory of Solomon's temple (Ezra 3:12,13). However Isaiah speaks of a future magnificence even greater than Solomon's or Herod's temples. Dr Fruchtenbaum writes regarding Isa 54:1–8:

> "This remarriage is further described in Isaiah 62:4–5. Israel's land that she lost because of her adultery is to be totally restored (v4). Like a new husband rejoices over his virgin bride, in this same way God will rejoice over His restored wife (v5). Hosea, who had much to say about the adulteries of Israel, also spoke of her reunion with her husband in 2:14–23. Hosea began by describing the courtship and wooing in the wilderness (vv.14–15). Israel will again be allured into the wilderness where God will speak to her heart in courtship. When she responds, all her vineyards will be restored." [13]

It is strangely sad how many are prepared to accord to Israel the passages identifying her spiritual adultery, but not those promising her future restoration when God welcomes her back.

Until The Time Of The End

This 'until' is rather different in nature, but is nevertheless significant because it is closely identified with Daniel's people, Israel (Dan 12:1).

> *"But you, Daniel, shut up the words, and **seal the book until the time of the end**; many shall run to and fro, and knowledge shall increase... And he (the angel) said, 'Go your way, Daniel, for the words are closed up and sealed till the time of the end.'"* (Dan 12:4,9).

Arguments are sometimes presented to suggest that the 'time of the end' refers in the Old Testament to anything in the New Testament. This provides a useful escape clause for those who wish to regard any implications for the future. However this final chapter of Daniel is emphatically about the *"time of trouble such as never was since there was a nation"* (v2). This has not happened yet. It has still to happen and it features an Israel easily identified with the Israel of the Old Testament and not at all with the Church. It is the Great Tribulation foretold by Jesus (Matt 24:21,22,29), to which we have referred previously; this is Daniel's seventieth 'week' with its mid-point desolation. Both Daniel and Matthew confirm that this will be disaster on an unprecedented scale. The fact that there was a 2nd century BC first version of the Abomination of Desolation (Dan 9:27; 12:11) does not invalidate the even more important future occurrence, though the prophecy was important enough at that time too. The main version is still ahead. Jesus said so.

We are by no means suggesting that parts of the book of Daniel did not have prior relevance; they certainly did, especially in the times of both the profaning of the temple by Antiochus Epiphanes in 168 BC and of the sack of Jerusalem in AD 70 and AD 135. We are simply asserting that the book also has highly significant latter day messages, which Jesus makes it quite clear should be read and understood. *"Know therefore and understand"* said the angel to Daniel (9:25). *"Whoever reads, let him understand"*, adds the Gospel writer (Matt 24:15).

If we are not meant to understand, why is the book of Daniel to be sealed or protected until the end time? Were Justin Martyr (*c.* AD 100–165) and Irenaeus (*c.* AD 130–200) wrong to study Daniel's prophecies in such detail and to come to Pre-Millennial conclusions? Dr Skevington Wood recounts in some detail the interest of some of the early Church Fathers: they came to Pre-Millennial conclusions too.[14] Should indeed we be ignoring Daniel for the present and leaving it for the Tribulation saints? Or is this simply a misinterpretation of the injunction to seal this wonderful old book?

Geoffrey King seems to have it right:

> "I am sure that it is not sealed in the sense of being hidden away, but, as we shall see in a moment, for the opposite reason. Why else do you shut up a book and seal it? I quote from Seiss, who again is helpful. I think this is the right understanding. 'Just as valuable official documents intended to direct and inform successive generations are carefully secured and held inviolable against all tampering, that they may be preserved entire... In this sense was Daniel to shut up and seal the words of this book.' Look carefully at the Hebrew, the explanation is much simpler and in keeping with the opening of this verse. The variorum: '**Many shall peruse the book**'. Tregelles: 'Many shall scrutinise the book from end to end'. Pember: 'Many shall search it

through and through': Darby: 'Many shall diligently investigate'. Seiss: 'Many shall examine it'. But Fausset is best: 'Many shall scrutinise it, running through every page'. I would accept that as the best and right meaning. You see what the angel is saying to Daniel: 'Shut up the book: seal it to the time of the end. It is to be taken great care of, because at the time of the end many shall run through it eagerly and knowledge shall be increased.'" [15]

God the Holy Spirit is omniscient. He knew how Daniel would come under attack from the scoffers and sceptics more than most other books of Scripture, because the amazing accuracy of the prophecies challenge those who find its predictions uncomfortable or inconvenient. So he had it safeguarded—preserved for future generations. Through Daniel He foretold that the tribulation saints will prize it highly. How privileged we are to have a preview. Israel is to undergo her greatest trial ever. But the faithful remnant will have available this divinely prepared and preserved guide. There are still 'difficult' passages in some chapters of Daniel. They will no longer be difficult when the final predicted events take place; nations will become easily identifiable and personages will become unmistakable. As Geoffrey King said, they will be running through every page. It could be top of the reading list for the sealed 144,000! Not only has God got a future plan for Israel; He has revealed it.

Chapter Four

'Untils' Concerning Israel And Her Messiah

Great David's Greater Son

In the previous chapter we looked at a number of situations which must continue until something else significant happens, and events which cannot happen until certain preconditions have been met. All concerned Israel, and pointed to its carefully outlined future in God's plans. Those who believe Israel has no future tend to skip lightly over these points and concentrate on a limited number of 'proof passages', which we will examine later.

But we would respectfully draw these 'untils' to the attention, not only of those who believe that Israel has no future, but also of those Christians who are well disposed to Israel, but believe that its ultimate future has begun already. We have already stated that we believe that the fig tree has been budding during the last century or so, with Zionism, the Balfour Declaration, the birth of the new state and much more. But sadly we cannot agree with those who would see a Millennium-like age emerge from the present situation without the prior rise of the Beast, the Great Tribulation and Armageddon.

In fact, unless one is to distort or artificially divide what, to all appearances, is the continuous narrative and single vision of Revelation chapters 19 and 20, the Millennium cannot start until after the return of Jesus Christ. In 19:11 we see heaven opened to reveal a white horse *"And He who sat on him was called Faithful and True, and in righteousness He judges and makes war."* At that future point He is not static in heaven; He is revealed as coming, for in v14 the armies in heaven are seen *following*. One does not follow a person who is not moving. Here there are many other significant things to which we will refer later, but now we note in particular that, as the result of Christ's return in power, the Beast and False Prophet are cast into the lake of fire (v20), that the opposing earthly armies are destroyed (v21) and that Satan is bound for a thousand years (20:2).

So it is time to turn to some more of the 'untils' which God has ordained and which concern the personal role vis-à-vis Israel of the returning Jesus Christ, her once rejected Messiah. Let us introduce this crucial personal role with some succinct quotes from the Victorian writer, T B Baines. These help to remind us that Israel is no afterthought of God, conceived some centuries after the Flood and Tower of Babel, but has from earth's earliest ages been central to His plan for the whole of human history. This plan has always required His personal involvement in Redemption through His Son, born of a select line.

> "All Scripture is the history of two men, who are thus described—'The first man is of the earth, earthy; the Second Man is the Lord from heaven' (1 Cor XV. 47). [1] There is no promise of the removal or mitigation of the curse, no hint of moral or spiritual improvement, given to the first Adam. A promise is given, but it centres in another, the woman's seed... From these two fountain-heads—the fallen Adam and the woman's seed—flow two streams... The history of ruined man, the first stream, rolls on in the gathering gloom, till it issues in the rejection of the Christ and the reception of the Anti-Christ. The unfolding of God's promises in His Son, the second stream, also moves on without interruption... Man left to himself goes from bad to worse." [2]

> "But the increasing wickedness of man only serves to show forth more conspicuously the boundless resources of God. He calls Abraham from the midst of this idolatry, leads him forth into a distant land, and there makes to him and to his seed two closely connected but distinct promises. One of these, often repeated and variously expressed, is thus first announced—'In thee shall all the families of the earth be blessed' (Gen xii. 3)'". [3]

The other promise to which he refers is, of course, the Land. He further writes:

> "The conditional and temporary possession enjoyed by Israel is not the fulfilment of the covenant with the fathers... A partial fulfilment doubtless took place, and this we shall find to be God's general mode of acting. When a

promise is given the first man is tried to see whether he can inherit it. This is partial fulfilment and the result invariably is to prove the inability of man after the flesh to receive any blessing from God's hands. This, however, does not cause God to change His purpose, or the promise to remain unfulfilled. He has in reserve, as the focus in which all the promises centre, the Second Man, the Man of His own right hand, whom He will bring forth in His own time to receive all that the first man has failed to obtain, and to do all that the first man has failed to accomplish. The Scripture evidence that Israel's national blessing and glory are fulfilled in the reign of Christ, as well as the character of that reign, will occupy us hereafter." [4]

He then goes on to deal with the great promises made to David in 2 Sam 7:8–16, and its double application to David's immediate successors and his ultimate Successor. He does not, but very easily could, quote complementary verses from Ps 89:19–37.

"It is manifest that the terms of the prophecy correspond only in very small measure with the history of the Jewish sovereigns, and that nothing has yet taken place at all resembling the permanent dominion here described. There can be no doubt, then, that the prophecy has yet to receive its fulfilment, and that this fulfilment is to be found in 'the Second Man'. Indeed, the language of Hebrews makes this plain, for there is a portion of this prophecy, 'I will be to Him a father and he shall be to me a son,' expressly quoted as referring to Christ. And that David himself so understood it, is clear from Peter's language on the day of Pentecost, when he speaks of David as 'knowing that God had sworn with an oath to him, that of the fruit of his loins according to the flesh He would raise up THE CHRIST to sit on his throne' (Acts ii. 30)... Though this prophecy (to David) was uttered at the moment of Israel's greatest glory, God speaks of their establishment in peace and security as still future— 'I *will* appoint a place for My people Israel, and *will* plant them, that they may dwell in a place of their own, and move no more;' and He further connects this stable possession with the reign of the Son of David of whom He said, 'I will stablish the throne of His kingdom for ever.'...

"Committed to the first man, they have utterly failed. Entrusted to the Second Man, they will be triumphantly accomplished. He it is who will crush the head of the deceiver of the world; He it is in whom all the nations of the earth shall be blessed; He it is that shall deliver Israel out of the hand of her enemies to serve Him without fear; He it is who shall have dominion from sea to sea...". [5]

May we pause for a moment to contemplate these things? Have these promises been fulfilled already? No, they have not! Do they clearly point to an earthly or to a heavenly fulfilment? To an earthly! Has there or has there not to be a vindication and glorification of this Second Man, the Man Christ Jesus, upon this planet before it passes away and the kingdom is transferred to a new heaven and earth? Yes, there has to be!

The Second Man is wholly man. But He is also wholly God.

> *"When the fullness of time had come, God sent forth His Son, born of a woman, born under the law, that we might receive the adoption of sons"* (Gal 4:4, 5).

Indeed, He is a Man. But the writer to the Hebrews quotes Ps 2:7, saying:

> *"You are My Son, this day I have begotten You"* (Heb 1:5).

He quotes God the Father as saying:

> *"Let all the angels of God worship Him"* (v6)

and adds,

> *"To the Son He says, 'Your throne, O God, is forever and ever'"* (v8).

Indeed, He is fully God.

Is it not strange that Christians are more than willing to acknowledge His right to the heavenly throne, where He is seated with His Father, but are so reluctant to accord Him His right to His earthly one, the future Jerusalem throne? Why do many Christians so resist the right of the Second Adam to redeem on earth all that the first Adam lost? What has happened to the truth of the Restoration of all things? This is why we must challenge Post-Millennialism.

The Hebrews writer quotes a Psalm of David—David, to whom or through whom so many of the Messianic promises were made, David the national hero prophet-king. David is mentioned no less than fifty-four times in the New Testament. Jesus was acknowledged as the Son of David by angels, needy individuals, multitudes who thronged to hear Him and by Gospel writers themselves. Peter in his Pentecost address mentions David three times, noting (Acts 2:34) that, unlike the ascended Christ, David was yet in his grave.

Until The Times Of Restoration

Ten days earlier, as He was about to be taken up to heaven, Jesus was asked by the disciples, *"Lord, will You at this time restore the kingdom to Israel?"* (Acts 1:6). This, one would think, would have been the appropriate juncture for Jesus to have made it clear that there would be no future restoration of Israel, had this been the case. Dr Walvoord writes:

> "If they were incorrect in their expectation of a kingdom on earth, this would have been a proper time to correct the disciples. The answer that Jesus gave... indicated the event was still ahead... From the perspective of almost 2,000 years, it is obvious that God is fulfilling in this present age His purposes unannounced in the Old Testament, of calling out a people of both Jews and Gentiles to form the church of Christ." [6]

In both Acts 2 and 3 Peter develops the truth that, through their rejection and crucifixion of the Christ, God's plan of salvation has been furthered.

> *"Yet now, Brethren, I know that you did it in ignorance, as did also your rulers"* (3:17).

He then confirmed what they should have known, namely that Christ's suffering had been prophesied (3:18). But he was very quick to ensure that they understood that their ignorance did not exonerate them, by immediately demanding their repentance. While there are Old Testament verses which, seen in retrospect, indicate that the Messiah would be rejected by the Jewish leaders (e.g. Ps 22:7), it must on no account be assumed that God manipulated these leaders to have Jesus crucified. They may have done it in their ignorance, which, as we saw in our previous chapter, was brought upon themselves by their hardness of heart; but they did it of their own free will, within God's foreknowledge. Some would like to portray Dispensationalism as God's manipulation of events. That is a travesty of the truth.

In his first address after Pentecost, Peter covers Jesus' ascension, sojourn in heaven and future return, as he addresses his own people:

> *"Repent then and be converted, that your sins may be blotted out, that times of refreshing may come from the presence of the Lord, and that He may send Jesus, who was preached to you before,* **whom heaven must receive until the times of restoration of all things,** *which God has spoken by the mouth of all His holy prophets since the world began* (Acts 3:19–21).

That takes us of course back to Eden. The Church is not specifically prophesied by the prophets; the restoration is—in great detail.

The meanings of the Greek words for *restore* of Acts 1:6 and *restitution* in the AV (KJV) of Acts 3:21 have no significant difference. They refer to the same event. Jesus Christ is thus said to be remaining in heaven *until* such a future time of restoration of all things on earth. By then it will be even more desperately needed than at present. We are given no information that He is currently restoring anything in heaven. The sin-blighted heaven which will one day be destroyed (Rev 21:1) refers to the visible and atmospheric heaven or firmament. There Satan has his seat as Prince of the Power of the Air (Eph 2:2).

It is clear from the continuous narrative of Revelation chapters 19 and 20, where no change of vision occurs, that the Restoration of all things does not precede, but rather follows the Great Tribulation and the vanquishing of the leaders of the rebellion which will culminate with the open challenge to God at Armageddon. The restoration is to be both physical and spiritual, to reflect the two aspects lost in the Fall. The need for both is evident if we consider the catastrophic future global events which Jesus foretold through angels (it is *His* Revelation, as the opening verse of the Apocalypse confirms). There He elaborates His general predictions of Matt 24:21, with the Seals (6:1–8:3), Trumpets (8:2–9:19) and Bowls or Vials of Wrath (16:1–21).

On the physical side there will be global warfare, slaughter, famine. There will be lethal pollution of land, rivers and oceans, destruction of most plants and crops, and annihilation of marine life. There will be fearful atmospheric pollution, colossal earthquakes and terrifying cosmic and climatic phenomena—apparently asteroid strikes and meteorite showers.

On the spiritual side, a vast demonic army will be released from the bottomless pit. Satan will be aided by the first Beast or final Antichrist and the second Beast or False Prophet. They will receive the adulation of massed millions, and inspire the most blasphemous idolatry. Men will harden their hearts and curse and challenge their Creator. The final religious abomination of Mystery Babylon will hold sway.

Of course, as Pre-Tribulationists, we believe that the Church will no longer be on earth at this time, and that an innumerable martyred multitude from all the nations, who have responded to the preaching of the Gospel of the Kingdom during the Tribulation, will be soul and spirit with their Lord in heaven (Rev 9:9). Their resurrection will occur after Christ returns (Rev 20:4). The unsaved, however, will be in the resurrection of the damned 1000 years later (20:5, 12). Nothing could be clearer.

The restoration is something He is coming to do on earth. The restoration cannot apply to the heaven and earth of Revelation 21 and 22; those are to be new, so will not require to be restored then or ever. It can therefore apply only to the atmospheric and cosmic heaven and to the present earth; moreover Peter says that it has been widely prophesied in the Old Testament. Replacement Theologians will be hard pressed to find many such prophecies regarding restoration which do not specifically mention Jewish people, tribes of Israel, Zion, Jerusalem or the geography of the Promised Land.

By allegorising prophecies concerning Christ's paramount role in the Restoration, we are in our own minds—and, worse, in the minds of congregations to whom we may preach—denying to the Lord Jesus

Christ, the Second Adam, the glory and vindication which must rightly be His; we are even implicitly denying the fact that He *will* accomplish such a restoration. Let us be clear; no such restoration is happening now, despite the wild claims of recent decades. There is a decisive future 'until'. The clouds received Him from the sight of His disciples. He remains in heaven until one day He comes again with clouds *"in like manner as you saw Him go into heaven"* (Acts 1:11), and to the same spot just outside Jerusalem, the Mount of Olives (Zech 14:4). Do we seriously imagine that He has no further purposes with Israel when we consider that fact? He is to return to Jerusalem, not to Rome, Babylon, Mecca, Amritsar, Brooklyn or Salt Lake City. This is overwhelmingly significant.

Jesus himself asked the Pharisees the very searching questions,

> *"'What do you think about Christ, whose Son is He?' They said to Him, 'The Son of David.' He said to them, 'How then does David in the Spirit call Him "Lord", saying "The Lord said to my Lord, 'Sit at My right hand, **till I make Your enemies Your footstool'**"? 'If David then calls Him "Lord", how is He his Son?'"*

We will be returning to these verses soon.

Until You Say "Blessed Is He"

We now come to what is probably the 'until' most quoted by Pre-Millennial writers and preachers. That is hardly surprising, because the text speaks volumes and is not easily distorted.

> *"'O Jerusalem, Jerusalem, the one who kills the prophets and stones those who are sent to her! How often I wanted to gather your children together, as a hen gathers her chicks under her wings, but you were not willing! See! Your house is left to you desolate; for I say to you, **you shall see Me no more till you say, "Blessed is He who comes in the name of the Lord!"**'"* (Matt 23:37–39).

The first 'Palm Sunday', with Jesus' ride into Jerusalem, was now past. He had just delivered His final, most scathing, attack on the scribes and Pharisees. He was very shortly going to deliver one of His greatest sermons, the Olivet Address (Matt 24 & 25). It was to concern events and conditions leading up to and during His coming in power.

It would be useful to remind ourselves briefly about Olivet (or Mount of Olives), that hill crest, no more than two miles or a Sabbath day's journey from the city centre.

- It was from the Mount of Olives that the Shekinah Glory of the Lord left Jerusalem at the time of the Babylonian captivity (Ezek 11:23).

- It was from the Mount of Olives (Matt 23:1) that Jesus set off on His ride into Jerusalem on a donkey, presenting Himself in fulfilment of the 'just and lowly' King foretold by Zechariah (9:9).

- It was from the Mount of Olives that the personified Glory of God, Jesus Christ (Jn 1:14), departed into heaven (Acts 1:9, 12).

- It is to the Mount of Olives that He will return at the moment of Jerusalem's greatest need ever (Zech 14:1, 4).

- The Mount of Olives will at that moment split into two, its usefulness being completed, its striking fault, long known to modern geologists, having been preserved until that stupendous moment (Zech 14:4).

Is this not yet another proof that God still has a future for Israel? Might He not otherwise have chosen some other conspicuous point to which to return, thus dispelling any further doubts about Israel? As it is, it is there, just outside the old city boundaries, that Jerusalem will first see Him when He returns. How dramatic! How convincing! How pathetic is the diversionary excuse sometimes given, that references to Jerusalem after Acts refer to *'Jerusalem above'*. All the details given confirm that it is *'Jerusalem which is now, and is in bondage with her children'.* (Gal 4:25, 26).

As He formally presented Himself to the city the previous Sunday, He was escorted by a crowd of devout Passover pilgrims from all over the known world, who had made what, for most of them, was a once-in-a-lifetime journey to the home of their fathers and the sanctuary of their God. The crowd probably included many who would be saved on the day of Pentecost. Acts 2:9, 10 relates the distant places from which they had travelled, mostly on foot. They sung the *Hallal Rabbah* or great Praise (Psalms 113–118) customary for Passover pilgrims. In their midst was the One of whom the Psalmist prophetically spoke those culminating verses: *"The stone which the builders rejected has become the chief cornerstone; this was the Lord's doing; it is marvellous in our eyes... Blessed is He who comes in the name of the Lord!"* (Ps 118:22, 23, 26).

But as He arrived at Jerusalem, the citizens saw Him as He presented His credentials and heard the crowd cry *"Hosanna to the Son of David!"* (Matt 21:22). Their reaction was, *"Who is this?"* There was no spark of recognition. Jesus was to indicate a few days later the long delay before there would be another opportunity to see Him presenting His kingly credentials.

This will be at the time when God makes Jerusalem an intoxicating *"cup of drunkenness to all the surrounding (Arab) peoples"* and *"Jerusalem a very heavy stone for all peoples; all who would heave it away will surely be cut to pieces, though all the nations of the world are gathered against it"* (Zech 12:2, 3). Zechariah then goes on to describe how God will personally intervene, and how He will empower certain of His people. All the world's armies will be gathered against Israel (Rev 16:14–16). Lest any question such military madness, they should observe that those verses tell us that they will be demonically driven—and God will summon them. Military strategy and common-sense will play little or no part.

David Baron writes:

> "When the enemy lifts his hand for the final blow in order utterly to destroy them, 'that the name of Israel may be no more in remembrance'—the visible appearance of Jehovah in the person of their Messiah Jesus takes place... Not only shall Jehovah Himself 'go forth and fight against those nations,' but when once the weak and broken remnant of the people recognise their Divine Saviour, and hear the shout of the King in their midst, they are suddenly girt with superhuman strength." [7]

"I will pour on the House of David and on the inhabitants of Jerusalem the Spirit of grace and supplication; then they will look on Me whom they pierced; they shall mourn for

Him as one mourns for his only son, and grieve for Him as one grieves for a firstborn." (Zech 12:10).

The prophet goes on to describe vividly that mourning—national penitence for two thousand years of rejection, brought down to family and even individual level. How Jewish scholars have wriggled and struggled down through the years to avoid the implications of these words, even turning the 'Me' of the oldest manuscripts to 'him' in order to avoid the fact that the pierced speaker is Jehovah Himself. Some modern translations have adopted the marginal reference 'him' too. 'Jehovah Witnesses' likewise squirm.

This time there will be no *"Who is this?"*. True, there will be the two thirds, apparently, who will have recognised the False Messiah and accepted the mark of the Beast, thus putting themselves beyond salvation. Jewishness will not exempt them.

> *"The smoke of their torment ascends forever and ever; and they have no rest day or night, who worship the beast and his image, and whoever receives the mark of his name"* (Rev 14:11).

Probably some of these will be slain or taken captive during the siege, (Zech 14:2).

Others repent—repent as opposed to bemoan or regret. To quote Baron again,

> "But suddenly the noise of war and the shout of triumph is turned into wailing and lamentation as the spirit of grace and supplication takes possession of the heart of the remnant of Israel, and the eyes of the blind are opened, and they behold in the King of Glory, at whose presence the earth trembles and the mountains are cleft... none other than the one whom they have pierced, and whom for so many centuries they have despised." [8]

> *"And it will be said in that day: 'Behold, this is our God; we have waited for Him and He will save us. This is the Lord. We have waited for Him; we will be glad and rejoice in Him; we will be glad and rejoice in His salvation'"* (Isa 25:9).

This surely is the prime fulfilment of Paul's prophecy,

> *"And so all Israel will be saved, as it is written: 'The Deliverer will come out of Zion, and He will turn away ungodliness from Jacob; for this is My covenant with them, when I take away their sins'"* (Rom 11:26, 27).

Those destined for destruction will have already met their doom. Where, Replacement Theologian, is the Church in all these prophecies? Do you seriously think that this can be allegorised?

F B Meyer puts it graphically and with a Dispensationalist perspective:

> "It was when his brethren were in their greatest straits that Joseph made himself known unto them; and when the Jews are in their dire extremity, they will cry aloud for help and deliverance from Him whom they rejected This memorable scene in the ancient land of the pyramids will be reproduced in all its pathos, when the long-rejected Brother shall say to His own brethren after the flesh, 'I am Jesus, your Brother, whom ye sold unto Pilate: and now be not grieved, nor angry with yourself, that ye delivered Me up to be crucified; for God did send Me before you to preserve a remnant in the earth, and to save you alive by a great deliverance' (see Gen xlv 1–15)." [9]

The Church, Gentile and Jew alike, do not have to wait for that 'until'. We have first repented and recognised Jesus of Nazareth as Christ, Lord and Saviour. We are waiting for Him to take us home. And that will be before He returns to earth. It will be from a resurrected or raptured perspective that we will witness all these 'untils' come to maturity.

Until He Comes Whose Right It Is

Our next 'until' was uttered by the prophet Ezekiel in the seventh year of his personal exile to Babylonia, along with ten thousand of his countrymen. The profane puppet king still ruled in Jerusalem and, as we know from Ezek 8:3–18, heathen abominations were being performed in the temple. This was the countdown to the final sack of Jerusalem by Nebuchadnezzar's army and the start of the Times of the Gentiles. At the most, four years of Zedekiah's reign remained. He is thus addressed:

"Now, to you, O profane, wicked prince of Israel, whose day has come, whose iniquity shall end, thus says the Lord God: 'Remove the turban, and take off the crown; nothing shall remain the same. Exalt the lowly, and abase the exalted. Overthrown, overthrown, and I will make it overthrown! **It shall be no longer, until He comes whose right it is, and I will give it to Him.'"** (Ezek 21:26, 27).

We are really more interested here in what will happen after the 'until' conditions are met than in what is about to cease. However we must look briefly at the vain attempts to fill the long interim gap which God indicated was to occur.

It would also be useful to introduce a second relevant 'until' from Jacob's prophetic last words to his sons, as we will wish to refer to them:

"The sceptre shall not depart from Judah, nor a lawgiver from between his feet, until Shiloh comes; and to Him shall be the obedience of the people" (Gen 49:10).

The Jamieson Fausset & Brown's Commentary describe the AV *diadem* and NKJV *turban* as the high priest's mitre (referring to Ex 28:4 and Zech 3:5), or priestly emblem.

"Both this and the 'crown', the emblem of the kingdom, were to be removed, until they should be restored and united in the Mediator, Messiah (Ps 110:2, 4; Zech 6:13). As, however, King Zedekiah alone, and not the High priest also, is referred to in the context, English version is supported by Genesius... This shall not be the same—The diadem shall not be as it was, nothing shall be the same."

Fairbairn and Rosenmuller are quoted as authorities.[10] Gardiner writes:

"There shall be an utter change and overturning of the existing state of things... After the emphatic repetition of the 'overthrow', it is now added that the condition which follows the overthrow shall not be permanent... 'until He comes whose right it is'. This is generally acknowledged as a reference to Gen xlix.10 Shiloh)... The promise here made refers plainly both to the priestly and to the royal

> prerogative, and a still more distant foretelling of the union
> of both in the Messiah may be found in Zech vi:12–13." [11]

There was to be no rightful king of Israel thereafter, until the One whose right it is—the King who was coming (Zech 9:9), but who would be rejected and crucified, before He was to rise and be taken to heaven, there to remain until the *time of restoration of all things.* *"Then"* says God (Ezek 21:27) *"I will give it*—the kingly crown—*to Him".* Here is another nail in the coffin of Replacement Theology. The crown of Israel, the Davidic crown, is not obsolete, but merely suspended until it is one day claimed by *'Him, whose right it is'*, namely Jesus Christ.

In 153 BC Jonathan, youngest son of the godly Mattathias and brother of Judas Maccabeus, received from Demetrius a golden crown and purple robe, which he wore at the Feast of Tabernacles, thus inaugurating the Hasmonean prince-priests. But he and his successors, one of whom was to be the Edomite Herod, were always more or less subject, first to the Seleucid Empire, that quarter of Alexander the Great's 'bronze' kingdom (see Dan 2:32; 8:8; 11:4) and later to Rome. The later Maccabees, from the tribe of Levi, vainly tried to claim legitimacy for their non-Judaean rule by claiming that the curse of king Coniah (Jer 22:24–30) disinherited David's line. But of course Jesus' fleshly descent (Lk 3) is through the line of David's son Nathan, which was not thus disqualified. Jonathan's appointment to the High Priesthood was by the Roman curator, of all people. He was not even of Aaron's branch of Levi. Now of course neither is Jesus. But He does not need to be. He is a Kingly High Priest after the order of Melchizedek. The Aaronic priesthood became obsolete after the Cross.

Jeremiah makes the point that Coniah ruled only over the house of Judah, not over Israel (Jer 22:30). From Ezek 37:15–22 we are reminded that Christ will rule over the united house of all the tribes of Israel. We may not understand *how* this amazing promise involving the 'lost tribes' will be fulfilled. We simply take God at His word.

> *"'Behold the days are coming,' says the Lord, 'that I will raise to David a Branch of righteousness; a King shall reign and prosper, and execute judgement and righteousness in the earth. In His days Judah will be saved, and Israel will dwell safely'"* (Jer 23:5, 6).

As the perceptive Nathaniel, the Israelite in whom was no guile, declared, *"Rabbi, You are the Son of God! You are the King of Israel."* (Jn 1:47,49). Unless one is going to preposterously claim that the two sticks of Ezekiel 37 are the Catholic and Orthodox churches, or Catholic and Protestant churches, or some other product of a vivid imagination which cannot face facts, this is all about Israel.

But more than that; He is to be acclaimed at last *"King over all the earth"* (Zech 14:9), with His capital at Jerusalem, to which the nations will come to worship (Mic 4:1–3; Zech 14:16). He will rule the nations with a rod of iron (Rev 12:5 & 19:15). We will have more to say about this rule later.

Between writing the previous and the following paragraphs, I was appalled to find in Montreal, a cathedral dedicated to "Mary, Queen of the World". One cannot but ponder how that lovely but humble woman will react in her future resurrection body to the blasphemies which, down through the centuries, have been perpetrated in her name. But the One who is both her human Son and God's divine Son will most certainly be King over all. Mary never was and never will be the Mother of God; that false title is derived from the earliest paganism of Nimrod's time.

Until That Day In My Father's Kingdom

> *"But I say to you, I will not drink of the fruit of the vine from now on **until that day when I drink it new with you in My Father's kingdom"** (Matt 26:29).*

Jesus was celebrating with His disciples that Passover feast for which He had longed *"with fervent desire"* (Lk 22:15) to eat before His suffering. He made this simple unambiguous statement about the next occasion on which He would share wine with them. It certainly did not concern events between His resurrection and ascension, for there is no record, as there surely would be, of His drinking wine then. Whereas His eating fish and a piece of honeycomb is singled out for a mention, providing evidence for the ability of those in their resurrection bodies to eat (Lk 24:42).

We know practically nothing of the anatomy of our future glorious resurrection bodies or how they will function on earth, other than the very basic conclusions which we can deduce from the accounts of Jesus' brief appearances to the eleven during those final forty days, and from the fact that our bodies will be transformed into conformity with His glorious body (Phil 3:21). Jesus was talking of a yet future occasion. This is another 'until' which has not yet been fulfilled, but most certainly will be. At that time He had not been acknowledged King of the world. Nor will He be until He comes again in power.

Jesus was not talking of a future occasion in heaven. He has never drunk wine there with His disciples, for no single believer is as yet in his or her resurrection body. Neither Peter, nor Mary, nor any other saint is with the Lord except in soul and spirit. They are blessedly conscious, but are still classed as 'asleep' (II Thess 4:13, 14), and will remain so until their human trinity of body, soul and spirit are at last reunited (I Thess 5:23). They have no power to answer the vain pagan based prayers of those on earth. That should not trouble any believer, as we have the infinitely greater privilege of praying with confidence to the Father in the name of the Son.

No. Jesus was talking about a future time on earth—of the Millennium.

> *"And I bestow upon you a kingdom, just as My Father bestowed one on Me, that you may eat and drink at My table in My kingdom, and sit on thrones judging the twelve tribes of Israel"* (Lk 22:30).

All the tribes are to be there, as promised in Ezek 37:16–22.

> *"And I will make them one nation in the land, on the mountains of Israel; and one king shall be king over them all; they shall no longer be two nations, nor shall they ever be divided into two kingdoms again"* (v22).

If we read on further in this great chapter of Ezekiel, it becomes ever clearer that this healing, of a rift that dates back to around 980 BC, has not as yet taken place. It is a significant promised feature of God's future for Israel.

Does *"this fruit of the vine"* sound like heaven? Indeed, it does not. The vine, which will be devastated during the Great Tribulation (Rev 8:7), will once again flourish in Israel.

> *"And it will come to pass in that day that the mountains will drip with new wine... and all the brooks of Judah will be flooded with water* (Joel 3:18).

"'I will bring back the captives of My people Israel; they shall build the waste places and inhabit them; they shall plant vineyards and drink wine from them... no longer shall they be pulled up from the land I have given them', says the Lord your God" (Amos 9:14, 15).

This is (a) not already fulfilled, (b) not about the Church, (c) not about heaven, but (d) emphatically about the future and about Israel. We may admire what the kibbutzim and the Israeli government have done by way of irrigation; but that is nothing compared with the changes which God will bring about in the future.

Dr Walvoord in his Matthew commentary simply notes:

"Here he was referring to the millennial kingdom, when Christ will return to the earth with His resurrected disciples and participate once again in the earthly scene. There is no indication anywhere that wine will be drunk in heaven." [12]

In Lk 13:28, 29 Jesus told His adversaries (see v17):

"There will be weeping and gnashing of teeth, when you see Abraham and Isaac and Jacob and all the prophets in the kingdom of God and you yourselves thrust out. They will come from the east and west, north and south, and sit down in the kingdom of God."

This cannot be heaven. North, south, east and west are the directions from which the Lord will summon, with angelic help, the outcasts of Israel (Isa 11:12) and the sheep and goats of the Gentiles (Matt 25:32); they are not celestial compass points. And most certainly Jesus' adversaries are not going to be admitted to heaven and subsequently cast out! The resurrection of the Old Testament saints will take place following the Great Tribulation when Christ returns (Dan 12:13).

The judging by the disciples is further confirmation of the earthly scenario of this fulfilment. Only God, in the Person of the Son, judges in heavenly realms (Jn 5:22, II Cor 5:10, Rev 20:11). On the other hand we read in I Cor 6:2,

"Do you not know that the saints will judge the world?"

The Greek *krino* is used for the verb 'judge' both here and in Lk 22:30. Richards says:

> "*Krino*, the verb, means one or more of the following in a given usage: to judge, evaluate, decide, assess, distinguish between, pronounce judgement, select or prefer. The whole process of evaluation is thus expressed by this one word." [13]

Thus we are given a clear picture of a future in which Jesus Christ will reign supreme over the whole world, in a theocracy greater than the failed one of Israel before Saul in the Old Testament. Israel will be back in the Promised Land, with twelve tribes reconstituted, each having as judge one of the twelve apostles. Until that glorious day comes, Jesus, by His own confession, will not partake of the fruit of the vine. We have noted earlier how the remnant of Israel will repent, be saved and enter the Millennial Kingdom.

However it will be Jesus Christ personally who will conduct the Judgement of the Nations (the Gentiles), which will determine to whom the welcome summons will be given:

> "*Come, you blessed of My Father, inherit the kingdom prepared for you from the foundation of the world*";

or upon whom the sentence will be pronounced:

> "*Depart from Me you cursed, into the everlasting fire prepared for the devil and his angels*" (Matt 25:34,41).

The determining factor will be the treatment of "*these, My brethren*" (v40), and of the Gospel of the Kingdom, which they will have been preaching between the Rapture and Coming in Power. Any other interpretation implies salvation by works. Note that Paul in the above quoted I Cor 6 passage does not specify rule over *Israel,* as Jesus did to the twelve. The whole world is to be judged by resurrected saints. But Israel will at last be "*the head and not the tail*" (Deut 28:13). Jerusalem will be the centre or focal point of the entire planet (Is 2:2–4; 11:10; 35:10; Micah 4:1,2).

We will deal further with the identity of this earthly kingdom and some of the denials of the reality of these prophecies in other chapters.

Until I Make Your Enemies Your Footstool

*"The Lord said to My Lord, 'Sit at My right hand **till I make Your enemies Your footstool.'** The Lord shall send the rod of Your strength out of Zion. Rule in the midst of Your enemies."* (Ps 110:1, 2).

Here we are privileged to eavesdrop on a conversation within the Godhead; the Father is addressing the Son. Jesus later in fact challenged the Pharisees with this verse, and included the third Person of the Trinity in His question—*"How then does David in the Spirit call Him 'Lord', saying: 'The Lord said to My Lord'...?"* etc. It is noteworthy that the most recent English version of the Tanakh or Jewish Bible uses a lower case 'L' for the second 'lord'.[14] The translators have yet to learn the lesson with which Jesus confronted the Pharisees.

Dr Walvoord writes:

"The crushing judgement on those who oppose Christ is described in verses 5 and 6. The contrast is between Christ's present position in heaven, where He is waiting for the time when judgement will fall on His enemies, and the judgement that will take place at His second coming. In Peter's Pentecostal sermon he called attention to the fact that the resurrection of Christ was necessary for Christ to fulfil these prophecies (Acts 2:34–36). Christ in His resurrection is pictured as ascending into heaven and sitting on the throne of God, waiting until His enemies be made His footstool. The implication of this passage is that the Davidic kingdom has not yet begun, but awaits the time of Christ's second coming when judgement will fall upon His enemies and He will assume actual rule over the children of Israel."[15]

So we are left in no doubt as to where Jesus Christ is at present.

"I also overcame and sat down with My Father on His throne" (Rev 3:22).

This is not David's earthly throne which was promised (Lk 1:32), where places will be given on His right and left to the two as yet unidentified disciples chosen by His Father (Matt 20:23). We also know that He will remain in heaven until He goes forth to wage war against His enemies, and to rule with a rod of iron (Rev 19:15).

However even in heaven He is identified as *"The Lion of the tribe of Judah, the Root of David"* (Rev 5:5). That revelation was given five or six decades after the start of the Church Age and long after the sack of Jerusalem. Yet He had not relinquished His specifically Jewish titles, nor renounced His claim to the Jerusalem throne. He still has masses of unfinished business with Israel.

God is faithful, though some would dare deny Him the right to keep His promises.

> *"'As soon as Zion travailed, she gave birth to her children. Shall I bring to the time of birth, and not cause delivery?' says the Lord. 'Shall I who cause delivery shut up the womb?' says your God. 'Rejoice with Jerusalem and be glad over her, all you who love her; rejoice for joy with her, all you who mourn for her'... For thus says the Lord: 'Behold, I will extend peace to her like a river, and the glory of the Gentiles like a flowing stream'"* (Isa 66:8, 9, 10, 12).

Answer if you will, Replacement Theologian, has this ever happened to date?

No less certain is the fate of the opposing armies of the nations.

> *"The indignation of the Lord is against all nations, and His fury against all their armies... For the Lord has a great sacrifice in Bozrah, and a great slaughter in the land of Edom... For it is the day of the Lord's vengeance, the year of recompense for Zion"* (Isa 34:2, 6, 8).

See also Isa 63:1–7, where we read of His treading the winepress alone and tramping them in His fury. Truly His enemies will be under His feet. While righteousness will prevail, the Adamic curse upon the earth will be removed and suffering will be eliminated in an Eden restored. From Zion Christ will rule with a rod of iron (Ps 2:6, 9; Rev 19:15).

However there is one further step to be taken, as notified in what some find the surprising prophecy of Rev 20:7–9, where are told that, at the end of the Millennium, Satan will be loosed for sufficient time to deceive the nations again. He will lead a huge army of the deceived against the saints and the Holy City. Fire will come down from heaven and destroy them, and Satan will at last be cast into that place from which there can be no return or relief, the eternal lake of fire.

We must recall that, whereas the Beast or counterfeit Messiah and the False Prophet will have been thrown into the lake of fire at the time of Armageddon (Rev 19:20), Israel's most bitter foe, *"the dragon, that serpent of old, who is the devil and Satan"* will only have been bound and cast into the Abyss for the duration of the Millennium. There is a strong indication in Isa 24:21,22 that this will be the fate of the other fallen angels. The Abyss can be unsealed at God's behest, as it will indeed be during the fifth trumpet of the Great Tribulation, when Satan's hosts will be massively reinforced by a multitude of demons, incarcerated there since the Flood. Their release will however be brief.

Only the living saved will be permitted to enter the Millennium. There will be the *"ransomed of the Lord"*, Jews who will *"come to Zion with singing, with everlasting joy on their heads"* (Isa 35:10, 51:11). From the Gentiles there will be the aforementioned *"blessed of My Father"* (Matt 25:34). Their salvation is eternal. But children will be born to them. *"The streets of the city (Jerusalem) shall be full of boys and girls playing"* (Zech 8:4,5 etc.). As noted in an earlier chapter, the resurrected saints of previous ages, who will be present, will not and indeed cannot marry or become parents.

But these children, as they grow up, will never have been subjected to the wiles of the devil. They must be tested and make conscious decisions if they are to be qualified to enter the new creation when this old earth passes away. Some evidently will devise serious sin independently; the penalty will be death (see Isa 65:20). However this will be the exception rather than the rule. The reigning saints will be there to monitor events, but may not be given the ability to see into hearts and minds. So Satan must briefly be released.

Dr Tatford writes:

> "During the Millennium there will be universal submission to Christ and He will be outwardly acknowledged as supreme Lord. Since the human heart is ever sinful, in many

cases the subjection will be but a feigned obedience, and lip-service will hide inward opposition and enmity. At the close of this glorious dispensation, the true character of man will be manifested." [16]

So much for the psychologist's assertion that bad behaviour is dictated by adverse environment! Writing at about the same time on the other side of the Atlantic, Newell says:

"Here we see the Devil loosed after the thousand years of imprisonment, and immediately rushing back to his old task of deluding earth's inhabitants to that 'war' against God, to which the 'enmity against God' of the 'mind of the flesh' was ever prone, but for which, during the thousand years, leadership was lacking." [17]

The primary target of the rebellion must inevitably be Jesus Christ Himself. A thousand years of peace will lead to extraordinary naivety. But the hatred will be poured out in an attack on Jerusalem and on 'the camp of the saints', which we may assume to be the dwelling of the resurrected believers, who have been reigning and perhaps resented, for ten centuries. It appears from Zech 14:16–19 that, during the Millennium, there will be some resistance (Egypt is cited) to the mandatory annual international pilgrimage to worship the Lord in Jerusalem.

Satan, it would seem, will use that age-old phenomenon, Anti-Semitism, to inflame the passions of those destined for destruction. Whatever the Replacement Theologian thinks about God's future purposes for Israel, Satan knows better. No doubt Replacement Theology suits him very well indeed, for without it there could never have been Anti-Semitism within Christendom. God's reaction will be the swiftest and most decisive ever.

Then follows the end of this old earth (II Pet 3:10), and, for the redeemed of all ages, a new heaven and earth. But for the remainder of mankind there remains only the fearsome Great White Throne, upon which will be seated the now utterly beyond appeal Lamb of Calvary, from whose face heaven and earth will flee away (Rev 20:11–15). Newell adds:

"Let us distinguish therefore the Great White Throne judgement from all those dealings with His enemies which God has heretofore had; as for instance, at Armageddon.

> Hereto God's enemies, though vanquished, have been permitted the opportunity to oppose Him, even after such an iron-rod rule as the Millennium. Eternal, final action has not been taken against those who remained unregenerate upon earth." [18]

This takes us to the 'until' which needs no further comment from us. It marks the utter and eternal vindication and victory of the One who is the Lamb of God, the Lord of the Church and the King of Israel.

> *"For He must reign till He has put all enemies under His feet"* (I Cor 15:25).

Conclusion To The 'Untils'

We have looked in some depth at eleven 'untils', and referred briefly to a few others. All had three common features:

- There was a condition that was to continue until some specific event yet in the future. A change could not take place until something first happened.

- There was the event itself, not necessarily enlarged upon in the key text, but nevertheless essential to the fulfilment.

- There was the guaranteed new condition or happening.

While various other factors were involved, all of the eleven 'untils' bore some significant relationship to a future for Israel. The critical juncture of each 'until' is at or following the return to earth in power of the Lord Jesus Christ. The correlation of Replacement Theology, which denies to Israel these future roles, conditions and blessings, to Peter's predicted scoffing must be plain to all.

> *"Scoffers will come in the last days, walking according to their own lusts, and saying, 'where is the promise of His coming? For since the fathers fell asleep, all thing continue as they were from the beginning of creation'"* (II Pet 3:3,4).

It is a sobering thought that Peter is talking of at least nominal Christians—those who are aware of the promises and who believe in creation.

Finally, as a further challenge for Replacement Theologians, two of these 'untils' which have a relevance to Israel, were recorded after the national rejection of the Messiah, namely in the Acts and Epistles, in other words after those events which are claimed to have disqualified that people from any further place in God's plans.

Chapter Five

Israel's Nearer Future

Israel In The Church Age

This chapter is devoted largely to Israel's future immediately following the Rapture of the Church. We will take time to justify our assertions, with frequent quotes from Scripture and other sources. In Chapters Nine to Twelve and particularly in Thirteen, we will be looking at the different interpretations of this intermediate future by various prophetic schools.

But first let us very briefly make some comments about Israel's status in the Church Age, or present dispensation, which began at Pentecost. Jesus Himself was a Jew. The Church started with Jews. It had to. All the Apostles were Jews; they were to be *"witnesses to Me in Jerusalem, in all Judaea and Samaria, and to the ends of the earth"* (Acts 1:8). This was of course the sequence in which the Gospel spread, and can be traced through the Acts. All of the Day of Pentecost converts were Jews, mainly pilgrims of the Diaspora (2:8–11). The Samaritans were being targeted by the time of Stephen's death (8:25). Gentile worshippers of Jehovah, like Cornelius, were soon evangelised (Acts 10:35), and so on until, by the end of the book, Paul berated the Jews (28:25–28), thereafter concentrating on the Gentiles; *"Therefore let it be known to you that the salvation of God has been sent to the Gentiles, and they will hear it!"*

Paul did not say that only now would the Gentiles be evangelised. They had already been for some time. However Paul, Barnabas, Silas and the other missionaries had invariably started their mission to each new town at the synagogue, or wherever Jews met. It was the appropriate place, because there the Old Testament Scriptures were known (the New Testament was not of course in existence). These were the people with inestimable privileges;

> *"What advantage then has the Jew, or what is the profit of circumcision? Much in every way! Chiefly because to them were committed the oracles of God."* (Rom 3:1, 2).

But for centuries they had failed as God's witnesses to the nations, being pre-occupied with their own religious observations.

But it must be clearly understood that, whilst God was giving individual Jews the privilege of hearing the Gospel first, and of repenting and being converted, <u>in no way was the national penalty for rejection of the Messiah open to cancellation</u>. The AD 70 sack of Jerusalem was ordained. The penalty for rebellion first imposed at the Assyrian and Babylonian captivities was about to be re-invoked;

> *"The Lord will scatter you among all peoples, from one end of the earth to the other... and among those nations you shall find no rest, nor shall the sole of your foot have a resting place; but there the Lord will give you a trembling heart, failing eyes, and anguish of soul"* (Deut 28:64–65).

The partial return over the past century has not reversed this. We have already considered the preconditions.

Jews have certain advantages within the Church; God has never forgotten the lineal descent of any Jew. But their spiritual status is the same as that of Gentile converts, and will remain so until the end of the Church Age.

> *"...the mystery of Christ, which in other ages was not made known to the sons of men, as it has now been revealed by the Spirit to His holy apostles and prophets: that the Gentiles should be fellow heirs, of the same body of His promise in Christ through the gospel."* (Eph 3:4–6).

We Gentiles believers are in fact indebted to the Jews and should never forget this (Rom 11:20); we are also capable of provoking them to jealousy (Rom 11:11).

Most of the epistles were written to churches in which there were significant numbers of Jews, and where an understanding of the Old Testament Scriptures could be assumed. Even the new Gentile converts were being grounded in those Scriptures, which underpin the Christian gospel. Some books, such as Hebrews, James and I Peter were specifically addressed to Jews. Now two great dangerous extremes of Bible interpretation are (a) failing to note to whom a passage of Scripture is addressed, and (b) assuming that, because a passage is addressed to a specific person or group, everybody else may ignore it.

Thus Peter in his first epistle addressed *"the pilgrims of the Dispersion* (1:1), in other words Jews, we must on no account assume that that well known passage (2:9–12) excludes Gentile Christians from the priesthood of all believers—that most precious truth which was one of the central tenets of the Reformation:

> *"But you are a chosen generation, a royal priesthood, a holy nation, His own special people, that you may proclaim Him who called you out of darkness into His marvellous light."*

Most certainly there were special applications for Peter's direct addressees; but that was partly because the Jewish converts had still failed to grasp all that their new status implied. There is no special Jewish reference in Rev 1:5; it applies to all believers:

> *"To Him who loved us and washed us from our sins in His own blood, and has made us kings and priests to His God and Father..."*

We can share Peter's pronouncement, but those of us who are not Jews do not require the lesson to be hammered home quite as firmly as the original recipients of that lovely epistle.

Tribulation Jews

Our 'until' studies in the previous two chapters ranged through Scripture from Genesis 3 to Revelation 22. We encountered conditions, some of which started as far back as the Babylonian Captivity, which are to apply until some intervention yet future. In other words, some 'untils' imposed conditions which were to prevail for over two and a half millennia before an awaited change could materialise. The *"until Shiloh comes"* condition has in fact a life-span of over three and a half thousand years. But in each case ultimate fulfilment is guaranteed. Sooner or later beyond each 'until' lies a golden age for Israel and the world.

By demonstrating that Israel has this golden future, we have in one sense met our terms of reference, proving that any school of interpretation, which does not recognise God's future purposes for that nation, must be fatally flawed.

We considered the general state of things before each 'until' and the changed situation which is to follow it. Like Replacement Theologians, we have agreed that Israel's rejection of her Messiah led to dreadful national consequences. Unlike them, we have maintained that this did not cause God to break His everlasting covenants with them. We have in fact dealt with the past, the present and the long-term future of Israel, and have found all to be in accordance with the most obvious and literal, as opposed to parabolic and obscure, interpretation of the prophetic Scriptures.

What we require to do now, before summarising our case for Israel's future, is to take more time to consider the events of that intermediate future, which immediately precedes many of these 'untils'. We cannot of course quote Scripture for events preceding the Rapture, except very generally in the signs of the times and continuing applications of the ancient curses for disobedience. We have already noted a number of significant matters about this period, but some need further exploration. Closely associated with the critical points of many of the 'untils' are tribulation, judgement, suffering and death on both local-to-Israel and global scales. Here are events which the Bible describes in great detail, but where Replacement Theologians try hard, as they are bound to, to prove that Israel is not in fact Israel.

So wonderful is the promised restoration—the good news—that one may be inclined to ignore the more immediate future—the bad news, or at least not-so-good news. Only the most ardent and optimistic Post-Millennialist perceives a currently improving world. So desperate is our current world situation that many Christians see the Utopian conditions described by the prophets as so remote and unrealistic that they can, for all practical purposes, be forgotten. We must therefore devote a little more time to those events which bridge the gap between the present and Christ's return in power. We must also look in greater depth at the evidence for any Jewish participation in God's revealed plans for this interim period.

However the prophetic time clock, or future revealed through the prophets, will not begin to tick again until the end of this present Church Age. Israel's future starts with Christ's coming for His Church, not at His coming in power. We believe that this present age, in which Israel is set aside, is rapidly drawing to a close. God's eye is still upon her and none can touch her with impunity, but her main role is a waiting one until the

Church is taken from centre stage. The stage for the next act in God's programme is being set, if we may use this analogy. Already we see Jewish and other end-time actors gathering in the wings.

For the Jews who have recognised and accepted Jesus Christ as their Saviour, their next change in status is a heavenly one. Like ours, their hope is the sureness of Christ's coming to take them to the place He has gone to prepare (Jn 14:2). In the meantime, although part of the Church, they may be said to constitute God's faithful Jewish remnant, maintaining continuity as the recipients of the great covenants. For those other Jews, elect in God's foreknowledge but as yet unenlightened, who are to survive the Great Tribulation, their great hope is initially, as we have seen, an earthly one.

Just as in the Church Age, Jews do not cease to be Jews just because they have become Christians on the same basis as Gentiles, and have become free from the bondage of the Law, so, following the Rapture, God will not cease to recognise the status of Jews left on earth. Indeed, Jewishness will never be more important. It would be strange indeed should Jews have a distant past and distant future, but no future immediately after the departure of the Church. To use our two familiar analogies, they will move back from the siding to the main line; they will return to centre stage. There will be a faithful minority, different from the one just received into heaven, with a key role in presenting the Gospel to the world. But there will also be a faithless majority, for whom this short period will prove disastrous. They will have a potential glorious future but will reject it. We have in Chapter Three looked at their fate and the reasons for it.

The fact that we are dealing with a mere seven year period may tempt us to dismiss it as not worth the effort or time to study. But this approach would be a grave error. Not for nothing did the OT prophets devote so much space to it. Not for nothing did Jesus address His Olivet Discourse to it. Not for nothing is the central part of Revelation (chapters 6 to 19) dedicated to it. We know from Scripture how God has in the past used short periods of human history to achieve enormous changes. Consider the Flood, which lasted only a year, or the momentous events of the first year after the flight from Egypt, or Jesus' three year ministry, or those three hours of light and three of darkness as our Saviour hung on the

Cross. Gabriel, who was sent by God to announce this seven year period, is not noted for being used to impart trivial messages!

Tim Lahaye writes:

> "The Tribulation is one of the most significant periods of God's dealings with humankind and certainly occupies a most prominent place in His prophetic plan. More space is dedicated to that little seven-year period than any other comparable time frame in the Bible. It is mentioned over fifty times in the Old Testament by such expressions as 'the day of calamity', 'day of wrath', 'the day of the Lord's wrath', 'the day of Jacob's trouble', 'the day of vengeance of our God', 'time of trouble', and 'the day of the Lord'. In every case it is talking about the nation of Israel. There are over a dozen references to that period in the New Testament." [1]

I believe that it would be safer to say that these various names all refer to times *within* the seven years, rather than necessarily implying the whole period. He adds, and here he probably echoes the thoughts of every Pre-Millennialist:

> "The main purpose of the Tribulation is to compress into seven years of trauma, conditions that will be conducive to bringing every person to a decision about Jesus Christ and the Antichrist. [2]

In the same book Lahaye goes on to demonstrate, using a brief statistical analysis, that, on the basis of available population data and projections:

> "There are probably more people living in the world today than have lived from the time of Christ to the generation before this present generation" [3]

Here he makes no claim to be more than approximate in his figures. He illustrates how, immediately following the Rapture of the Church, and before the major judgements of Revelation commence, there will be a very much larger world population than at any time in postdiluvian human history until recently. God's mighty dealings with mankind may be mercifully confined to a very short period, but it will be with a significant proportion of the population of the ages—say no less than

30% and no more than 50%. Exact figures are quite impossible to calculate and would not alter our case.

All these will face God's final challenge to repent or be damned, to chose Christ or Antichrist. It will also be the time of Satan's most desperate and bitter onslaught. God will apparently bring in angelic forces to help (Rev 14:6); there will be an unprecedented outpouring of the Holy Spirit, of which Pentecost was but a foretaste (Joel 2:28, 29); and there will be Jewish missionaries, doing at last what that nation should have done many centuries ago. We will explain soon. Of course the Holy Spirit's unique indwelling of the Church will not re-occur.

Israel has yet to undergo a final holocaust. Whether we feel comfortable with the idea or not is irrelevant, if God deems it necessary and has decreed it. Even here we shall find ensuing blessings, though they may not be apparent at the time. Heaven's love and justice will yet again be seen to meet.

We would not dare to claim to be able to answer all the questions posed by Revelation; and certainly we would not claim that all Pre-Tribulationists are agreed in every detail. It would be unreasonable to expect this, given the nature of prophecy. But we 'Pre-Tribs' achieve almost a complete consensus in our Israelology of the Tribulation. Dr Stanton sums up Israel's role very neatly:

> "The Tribulation does not deal with the Church at all, but with the purification of Israel. It is not the 'time of the Church's trouble', but the 'time of Jacob's trouble'. The emphasis of the Tribulation is primarily Jewish. The fact is borne out by Old Testament Scripture (Deut 4:30; Jer 30:7; Ezek 20:37, Dan 12:1, Zech 13:8, 9), by the Olivet Discourse of Christ (Matt 24:9–26), and by the book of Revelation itself (Rev 7:4–8; 12:1, 2, 17, etc.). It concerns 'Daniel's people', the coming of 'false Messiahs', the preaching of the 'gospel of the kingdom', flight on the 'sabbath', the temple and the 'holy place', the land of Judaea, the city of Jerusalem, the twelve 'tribes of the children of Israel', the 'song of Moses', the 'covenant' with the Beast, the 'sanctuary', the 'sacrifice and oblation' of the temple ritual. These all speak of Israel and clearly demonstrate that the Tribulation is largely a time

of God's dealing with His ancient people prior to their entrance into the promised kingdom... Moreover, it is evident that the Tribulation also concerns God's judgement upon Christ-rejecting Gentile nations..." [4]

The following classes or groups of tribulation period Jews can be traced. The list is not exhaustive. Obviously there must be a certain amount of overlap. Some will be martyred and others slain in judgement. Some will survive to the end. The evidence for their Jewishness is much stronger than that against, if our hermeneutics are consistent.

1. The two thirds who will go through the fire or holocaust and remain unrepentant (Zech 13:8).

2. Those who will accept the Man of Sin as their anti-messiah.

3. Those who will acquiesce to the seven year false covenant.

4. The 144,000 of Revelation 7:2–9.

5. The 144,000 of Revelation 14:1–5.

6. Those who are given 'great wings of an eagle' to flee to the prepared refuge in the wilderness (Rev 12:6).

7. Those who heed Jesus' warning of Matt 24:16–18, Mk 13:14–16 and Lk 21:21 and who flee to the mountains.

8. The one third who will go through the refining fire and come forth as pure gold (Zech 13:9).

9. The two mighty, miracle working witnesses of Rev 11:3–13.

It is not essential to identify beyond any shadow of doubt exactly who each group consists of. If most can be proved to be Jews, our case is complete. However the nearer we can come to positive identification, the stronger our case becomes.

Groups 1, 2 and 3 apply to the same people. We have already referred to them. They were potentially part of God's future for Israel, but they have eternally excluded themselves, Sadly we need say no more about them.

We know, from Rev 12:4, 13, 17 and from other passages, that Satan's ancient hatred of the Jews will reach its highest level ever at this time, that persecution against those whom he does not succeed in duping will be intense. We also know that God's special intervention on their behalf will be more spectacular than at any time since the plagues upon Egypt.

However we must not be so taken up with the roles and experiences of the Jews in the Tribulation, that we fail to realise that God's dealings with mankind are to be global and multi-national, with special judgements devoted to the Beast's kingdom and to Babylon.

Whether groups 5 and 6 of the above list are identical depends upon timing. We shall look briefly at them later. We have already considered group 8, for these are survivors of the coming holocaust. This leaves us with groups 4 and 5; we will leave until later in this chapter the question of whether the Revelation 14 group is the same as the Revelation 7 group.

The 144,000

How paradoxical it is that film makers, novelists and cult leaders seem to know more about certain great features of the book of Revelation than the average evangelical Christian. These are:

- The Four Horsemen of the Apocalypse (6:2–8).

- The 144,000 (7:2–9; 14:1–5).

- The Mark of the Beast (13:16–18; 14:11; 15:2, 16:2).

- The Battle of Armageddon (16:12–16, 19:19).

When one considers the special blessings, warnings and admonitions of the opening and closing verses of Revelation, one is astounded at the lack of interest in churches, and at the ability to find, if pressed, bland explanations which inspire no further study. We have in the two previous chapters referred to all four of these phenomena, however we believe that this Revelation 7 group of 144,000, is of prime importance.

As we mentioned in our first chapter, we are viewing Revelation from a Futurist standpoint. We believe that the Church will be translated or raptured to heaven between Revelation 3 and 4, and before the opening of the seven Seals, else there would be no rewarded saints to cast their crowns before the throne (4:10). We are about to devote much more time and space to the 144,000 than to any other group, because we believe that they are to play a central end-time role and have not been described in detail without good reason. We do concede that fully understanding their role requires a certain amount of exploration of and comparison with other scriptures. However we would also point out that, if *they* are not going to perform the evangelistic function, for which we believe they are to be sealed, there is going to be an enormous vacuum of witnesses. This we cannot accept.

Are they Jews or are they not? Do those who would dispute this seriously pause to consider how the reliability of Scripture is undermined when they dare to question statements so explicit? We would contend:

1. They are sealed.

2. They are Christ's.

3. They are Jews.

In Chapters Nine to Twelve and Thirteen in particular we will see what other prophetic schools of interpretation have to say about them. The other crucial related question is, whether they are indeed missionaries. They have been variously claimed by 'Jehovah's Witnesses' as themselves (or did until their numbers inconveniently rose beyond this figure, when they became their 'overcomers'!); by Seventh Day Adventists as those who will observe the Saturday Sabbath at the time of the Lord's return; by Christadelphians as themselves and by Mormons as their elders and so on. Denial of Jewishness comes from all quarters; sadly not only from cults.

Girdlestone's comments here are not only consistent with the broadest Pre-Tribulation teaching, but help to clear up certain apparent difficulties:

> "'Now if the fall of them be the riches of the world, and the diminishing of them the riches of the Gentiles, what shall the receiving of them be but life from the dead?' (Rom xi. 12–15). In this seventh chapter of Revelation we have an account of the *beginning* of that nation's spiritual restoration to favour; and the mighty result it has in the troubled world—for we soon read of an innumerable multitude out of *all* the nations who evidently owe their salvation to the Spirit-inspired ministry of the sealed 144,000." [5]

"Then I saw another angel ascending from the east, having the seal of the living God... saying, 'Do not harm the earth, the sea, or the trees till we have sealed the servants of our God on their foreheads' And I heard the number of those who were sealed. One hundred and forty-four thousand of all the tribes of the children of Israel were sealed." (Rev 7:2–4).

The following four verses tell us how there will be twelve thousand of each named tribe. Opinion is divided over whether the number is actual, approximate or symbolic. We are inclined to agree with Newell:

"The 12,000 of each tribe means, of course, 12,000. In Elijah's day God had left for Himself seven thousand (I Kings 19 and Romans 11). We believe that these were exactly seven thousand persons... We shall and must receive God's words concerning the future as literally as we do concerning the past." [6]

A number being symbolic does not necessarily affect its accuracy. Take, for instance, the seven deacons, seven churches of Asia, ten plagues, Ten Commandments, twelve tribes, twelve apostles and so forth. Whatever their precise numbers, these tribal companies are without exception Jewish.

We must take time to look at the Gentile group, as well as the Jewish group, as they are closely related in space and time. Both fit into the same parenthesis. While there is a steady progression of events in the prophetic part of Revelation, that is from chapter 4 onwards, there are breaks or parentheses to describe various personalities and groups, whose time span of activity may extend beyond the intervals at which they are inserted.

John saw:

"a great multitude which no one could number of all nations, tribes, peoples, and tongues, standing before the throne and before the Lamb, clothed with white robes and with palm branches in their hands... 'These are the ones who come out of the great tribulation, and washed their robes and made them white in the blood of the Lamb. Therefore they are

before the throne of God and serve Him day and night in His temple... They shall neither hunger any more; the sun shall not strike them, nor any heat... And God shall wipe away every tear from their eyes'." (Rev 7:9, 14–17).

Comparing the earlier Jewish group and latter Gentile group, Baines writes:

"Everything here agrees with God's ways of dealing with the world after the Church is taken... While the Church consisted of a remnant of Israel, together with saved Gentiles, they were, when once converted, 'baptised by one Spirit into one body', and formed in Christ 'one new man'; whereas nothing is more marked in this scene than the prominence given to Israel, and the difference between God's ways towards these tribes and towards the Gentiles... yet sharing the same salvation." [7]

The parenthetical nature of these two passages has been understood at least since Darby's time. Back in 1842 he said:

"Chapter vii forms a parenthesis between the sixth and seven seals, for God is going to intervene in a more special and positive manner at the centre of everything, in Canaan; but He will not do anything before He has separated His Jewish people and set His seal upon them." [8]

We do not necessarily agree with all that Darby said about these two visions. Others have had time to develop or modify his views. Scott, one of Darby's successors, writes:

"There are two separate visions contained in this (7th) chapter. The first concerns Israel (vv.1–8); the second refers to the Gentiles (vv.9–17). There can be no question as to the parenthetic character of both. The contents of our chapter form no part of events under the Seals... Thus between the sixth and seventh seal, yet forming no part of either, a deeply interesting episode of blessing to the Israel and to the Gentiles is introduced. The course of judgement is suspended and the veil drawn aside that we might witness the heart of God... The vision of the saved Gentile multitude after coming out of the great tribulation regards them in full and millennial blessing on earth, for it is an earthly scene (vv.16, 17)." [9]

Dr Ironside makes similar comments on the parenthetical nature of Revelation 7:

"Now we find that before the Lord gave John the vision of the opening of the seventh seal, He gave him this parenthetic seventh chapter in which are recorded two important visions." [10]

He then goes on to describe these in similar terms to what we have already noted. He contributes more to our understanding of the location and timescales of the great multitude:

"It seems very strange that some have taught that in this great multitude we have the raptured church. They have supposed that the Lord would not come for his church until the middle of the tribulation period. But a careful study of the passage makes it very evident that we are gazing here on an earthly, not a heavenly company. This great multitude embraces the Gentile nations who will enter into millennial blessing. It is the great ingathering of the coming dispensation... During the dark days of the great tribulation they will heed the testimony which will be gathered to the end of the earth by Jewish missionaries. The wise among the people will instruct many in righteousness (See Daniel 12). They are identical to the 'sheep' of Matthew 25... But nowhere does it say they are taken away to heaven—quite the contrary. They are in a scene where it is necessary for the Lamb to feed them, lead them, and spread His tabernacle over them... It is probably because people have not realised the blessedness of the millennial day that these verses are made to refer to Heaven." [11]

Dr Tatford points out that there are similar parentheses between the 6th and 7th trumpets and 6th and 7th Vials as there are here between the 6th and 7th Seals. [12]

This understanding helps us in many ways. It saves explaining, when and how the multitude had been raptured, had the description been of Tribulation martyrs in Heaven. It is consistent with earth, inasmuch as there is no night in Heaven, no sun and no tears to wipe away (see vv.16 and 17). Assuming that the 144,000 are the same as those in Revelation 14, and there is admittedly some dispute about this, it would explain why these are described as the 'firstfruits to God and the Lamb'. They seem to be in fact the firstfruits of the Tribulation, whose conversion could go back to the time of the opening of the first Seal; Girdlestone's comments on the 144,000 being the beginning of the prophesied revival fit perfectly. This again is consistent with their mission, which we have as yet only briefly alluded to, but which must start very soon after the Rapture. This passage presents huge problems for those with a simplistic eschatology, which believes that when believers die, they go to heaven and stay there.

Acknowledging the parenthetical nature of Revelation 7, we have seen that the 144,000 do not have to wait for the completion of the judgement under the Seals to make their appearance, even if we do encounter them in Revelation 7 following the opening by the Lamb of six Seals. We must emphasise that what is heralded or instituted by these Seals does not have to be completed before the next activity can commence. Indeed, whilst the *opening* of the Seals precedes the *sounding* of the Trumpets, and the Trumpets in turn precede the *pouring out* of the Bowls or Vials of God's wrath, these three series are not consecutive. Borrowing a term from Dr E J Miller, we might say that they are *coterminous.*[13] We will comment on this later. Each series *starts* well before the next, but each finishes with the Lord's coming in power. The intensity of the Trumpets, compared with the Seals, is greater and the time span shorter, and so it is with the Vials vis-à-vis the Trumpets.

So in fact the sealing of the 144,000 takes place very early in the seven years. If they are missionaries or evangelists, they need time for their mission. Immediately following their listing, we are introduced to their apparent converts, the afore-mentioned great multitude.

Ryrie, writing about the 144,000, observes:

> "These 'bond-servants of our God'… are Jews from each of
> the twelve tribes, and they do a particular service for God…

> A seal is principally a guarantee of ownership and security, and both these ideas are evident in the sealing of these 144,000... They are kept secure by God, which means they have physical safety from their enemies on earth while they are accomplishing their service for the Lord. It is commonly assumed that their service includes evangelism, though this is not specifically stated." [14]

So are they evangelist and missionaries? Where does this teaching come from? Why do we encounter the great multitude here? Surely it is because they are placed next to the only people who are qualified to preach the Gospel to them, namely the 144,000. The Church will no longer be there. Were the Church still to be around, wherefore the sealing of these Jews? If the 144,000 are somehow representative of Christians, as some have taught, having a merely symbolic number, why list them by Jewish tribal names? There is no precedent whatsoever for that in the New Testament. God rarely clarifies prophetic revelation to the point where everyone, irrespective of spiritual status, may understand, but He certainly does not deliberately confuse believers.

Many fundamental Christian doctrines, such as the nature of the Holy Trinity, are understood not from a single definitive statement, but from reflection on several passages. An understanding of the 144,000 and their ministry is similar, except that we would not be quite so outspoken in pinning our colours to the mast, as we would be with our belief, for instance, in a Triune God. We suggest that the following passages, when viewed together, indicate their missionary purpose.

- The sealing and description of the 144,000, as found in Rev 7:1–8, partly quoted above.

- The description of the great multitude. As found in Rev 7:9–17, likewise partly quoted.

- The Judgement of the Nations, or 'sheep and goats', as prophesied by Jesus in Matt 25:31–46.

- The Olivet Discourse context of Jesus' words, *"This gospel of the kingdom will be preached in all the world as a witness to all the nations, and then the end will come"* (Matt 24:14). Once again it will be, *"Repent, for the kingdom of God is at hand"*.

- Jesus' sending forth of the seventy (Lk 10:1–16), inasmuch as it gives us precedents for the preaching of the gospel of the kingdom, the emphasised call for repentance and the penalties for rejecting the call of Christ's evangelists.

The Sheep And Goats Link

Not all the early Pre-Tribulationist writers made the connection between the 144,000 and great multitude of Revelation 7 and the persecuted 'brethren' and 'sheep' of the Judgement of the Nations, described by Jesus at the end of His Olivet Discourse (Matt 25:31–46). However the resultant picture seems to fit together perfectly and explains fully the familiar words of God through Isaiah:

> *"You are My servant, O Israel, in whom I will be glorified…*
> *I will give you as a light to the Gentiles, that you should be*
> *My salvation to the ends of the earth".* (Isa 49:3,6).

While we do not deny a Millennial application, surely the primary one— the preaching of salvation—will start earlier, when some Jews again begin to fulfil their suspended destiny.

Kelly is one of those earlier writers who is humble enough to admit that he had previously had problems with a passage:

> "But the moment I learned that it was all a parenthesis, and that the actual time when the sealed remnant of Israel and the saved Gentiles come into public action and take their place upon the stage is another thing altogether, that difficulty was at an end… Still more striking is the resemblance of the sheep of Matt xxv, because these are not merely the blessed Gentiles of the millennial day, but had stood the test during the interval of grievous trial which preceded it. And observe that the sheep in that passage are distinguished from the King's brethren who have a position yet nearer to Himself— Jewish saints who, after the church is taken to heaven, will be entrusted with the gospel of the kingdom, which is to be preached in all the world for a witness to all nations before the end comes. Thus in Matt xxv 31–46, Israelitish brethren of the King, just before the close, test the Gentiles, who at

His appearing are summoned before His throne, and discriminated as blessed or cursed, their faith or unbelief being proved by the way they had carried themselves towards the messengers of the coming kingdom, in the time of their sorrowful testimony." [15]

Hal Lindsay's scholarship tends to be underestimated because of his racy 'seventies style' of writing, which was so effective for his time. He writes:

"A seal also guarantees the protection of the person bearing it. Since these are marked men, they will be under constant attack by the followers of Antichrist as well as demonic forces. But God will supernaturally protect them against all attacks. They will apparently suffer from hunger, exposure, ridicule, torture, and imprisonment at times, but all these special servants will be preserved to continue their witness through the whole Tribulation period... I personally believe that the ones whom Jesus describes as 'these brothers of mine', in Matthew 25:31–46 are the 144,000 described here. The way a person treats these evangelists during the Tribulation will reflect whether he is a believer in their message or not, because it will be extremely perilous to help these men who will no doubt be on Antichrist's most-wanted list. The great lesson I learn from this forecast is that God's man or woman is indestructible until God has finished with him here on earth!" [16]

We could go on almost indefinitely adding quotes which help to link the 144,000 with the 'My brothers' and the great multitude with the 'sheep' of Matthew 25. Each adds a little to our understanding. Let us finish our case for this connection with some words from Dr Walvoord, whose start point on this occasion is the Matthew rather than the Revelation text. We will wish to return to his commentary on this chapter much later. He says, and here we must take brief extracts from quite a long passage:

"At this judgement. 'all nations' better translated as 'all Gentiles' are gathered before Him and are described as sheep and goats intermingled... The sheep are invited to inherit His kingdom, and Christ will address them... *'For I was an hungered, and ye gave Me meat: I was thirsty, and ye gave*

*Me drink; I was a stranger, and ye took Me in: naked, and ye
clothed Me: I was sick, and ye visited Me: I was in prison,
and ye came unto Me... Verily I say unto you, inasmuch as ye
have done it unto one of the least of My brethren, ye have
done it unto Me...'* In mentioning 'My brethren', He is
referring to a third class, neither sheep nor goats, which can
only be identified as Israel, the only remaining people who
are in contrast with all the Gentiles." [17]

Walvoord then goes on to discuss lucidly the problem, often perceived in
this Matthew 25 passage, of souls apparently being saved through good
works, rather than by grace. He concludes with:

"The answer to this question is found in the context of this
passage. Those described here are the people who have
lived through the great tribulation, a time of unparalleled
anti-Semitism, when the majority of Jews in the land will be
killed. Under these circumstances, if a Gentile befriends a
Jew to the extent of feeding and clothing him, it could only
mean that he is a believer in Jesus Christ and recognises the
Jews as the chosen people. Accordingly, in this context,
such works become a distinctive evidence that the Gentiles
described as the sheep are those who are children of God by
faith in Jesus Christ." [18]

Those who are still unhappy with some of the correlations which we
have made might consider the mission of the seventy sent out in pairs by
Jesus (Matt 10:1–6). He gave them certain specific instructions. Then He
added words of the strongest commendation and condemnation for those
who would accept or reject these disciples.

*"He who hears you hears Me, and He who rejects Me
rejects Him who sent Me"* (v16).

We find Jesus making the statement about those who would reject the
ministry of the Twelve (Matt 10:5 et seq.), where the instructions given
nearly two thousand years ago are going to apply again, except in the
matter of geographical limitation.

Jesus indicated that evidence of reception of the disciples would be
repentance (v13). It was a central theme in John the Baptist's message

(Matt 3:2 etc.), of Jesus' own teaching (Matt 4:17 etc.) and a primary sign of Jewish rejection of Jesus (Matt 11:20). Peter preached repentance (Acts 2:38 etc.); Paul preached repentance (Acts 17:30). Even today, repentance is all too often the missing element of Gospel preaching. In the Great Tribulation failure to repent will be synonymous with damnation (Rev 9:20, 21; 16:9, 11). The great contrast between the mission of the seventy and the 144,000, apart obviously for timing, is the scope. During His earthly ministry, the mission of the disciples was to the *'lost sheep of the house of Israel'* (Matt 10:6). In the Tribulation it will be world-wide.

The angel who imparted to Daniel his closing vision about *"your people"* in the *"time of trouble such as never was since there was a nation, even to that time"* (Dan 12:1) declared, *"Those who are wise shall shine like the brightness of the firmament, and those who turn many to righteousness like the stars forever and ever"* (v3). This clearly refers to the Great Tribulation. We would expect such special people to be mentioned in the New Testament elaborations of the Great Tribulation. And we do surely find them mentioned—in the "My brethren" of Matthew 25 and the 144,000 of Revelation 7—and every single one a Jew!

We mentioned earlier that there was some debate over the 144,000 of Revelation 7 and the similar number of Revelation 14. We feel it inappropriate to take time to delve into this admittedly fascinating debate. Whether they are the same or not; and who in Revelation 14 is seen in heaven and who on earth, does not affect our case. We believe, beyond any shadow of doubt, that there will be 144,000 sealed Jews, and that everything points to their being the missionaries or evangelists who will be bitterly persecuted, but who will win the great multitude for Christ. Dr Barnhouse's comment on Revelation 14, where he notes that there are singers in heaven, the church, singing the same song as the 144,000 on earth, seem to get over the problem of identifying the two groups as being identical. [19]

Lest we wonder how so much can be achieved by so few in so short a space of time, let us not forget that the testimony of these sealed evangelists will be hugely supported by the unprecedented portents in the heavens and the earth—people's hearts will indeed fail them for fear.

Nevertheless the innumerable multitude will be in the minority compared with the unrepentant (Rev 16:11 etc.).

The Two Witnesses Of Revelation 11

We find another parenthesis, this time between the 6th and 7th trumpets, in which we are told of two special witnesses with almost unprecedented power and authority. There are certain imponderables here, which may have to wait for full clarification until the events described actually transpire. However we do know sufficient to be able to confirm both the Jerusalem and Jewish identities, which is what is currently required of us.

- Their mission is future, lying within the final seven year Tribulation period (v3).

- It is described as lasting both 1,260 days and three and a half years, thus removing any ambiguity (vv.2, 3).

- The location will be Jerusalem, however uncomplimentary the description (vv.1, 2, 8).

- Jerusalem will still be unregenerate; *"the great city which spiritually is called Sodom and Egypt, where also our Lord was crucified"* (v8). Well-meaning Messianic Jews cannot pre-empt the end of the present dispensation. Compare that with the more distant Millennial description: *"The name of the city from that day shall be THE LORD IS THERE (Jehovah Shammah)"*. (Ezek 48:35).

- Following the principle that 'if the plain sense makes sense, seek no other sense', the witnesses will be individuals—*'My two witnesses'* (v3) with all the characteristics of mortal people, however influential they may be,

- Their powers will be miraculous, spectacular and global (vv.5, 6).

- Their characteristics are those of Old, rather than New, Testament prophets. Baines writes:

"The attitude of these two witnesses towards their opponents is not that of Christians, but that of Elijah, who prayed for drought, and called down fire from heaven, and Moses, who turned water into blood, and smote the earth with plagues. This is God's way in government, but it is quite foreign to His present long-suffering grace… The testimony therefore, is not that of Christians proclaiming the gospel of God's grace, but of the Jewish remnant, proclaiming again the gospel of the kingdom, the glorious and triumphant advent of the Messiah." [20]

We could speculate endlessly about whether these will in fact be Enoch and Elijah, neither of whom has yet tasted death, or Moses and Elijah, the more commonly held view. Moses' body and grave have been miraculously preserved for some specific purpose (Deut 34:6 and Jude 1:9). Either way there will be at least one Jew, divinely appointed and preaching from Jerusalem, who will have a world wide audience and whose deaths at the hand of the Beast will be celebrated by many races. God will, three and a half days later (v10), vindicate and glorify them, summoning them bodily and visibly up to heaven, to the discomfort of their enemies (v12).

Sanctuary During The Great Tribulation

We have persisted in using Revelation as our main source of data for the Great Tribulation, as it avoids the problem of the claims that the Olivet Discourse warnings of Jesus relate solely to the Roman sack of Jerusalem forty years after He spoke. We have already conceded that this was a legitimate secondary application, for indeed, history tells us that both in AD 70 and AD 135, Christians fled the city as they saw Roman armies approaching. However so much more which Jesus prophesied has not yet taken place, and His words harmonise perfectly with other end-time prophecies. This is true of the refuge promised by Jesus in Matt 24:15–20; Mark 13:14–18; Lk 21:20,23 compared with, for instance, Rev 12:6,14–16. This pre-occupation with AD 70 is called Preterism and is dealt with in some detail in Chapters Eleven and Twelve.

The text of the Olivet Discourse includes many spectacular future happenings, including the Lord's return in power to the earth, which bear no relationship to the first century. One reason why some, especially Replacement Theologians, do not like to see the Olivet Discourse applying beyond the first century is the fact that Jesus made provision only for Jerusalem, the surrounding area and Jews, rather than for the whole Church. Our answer to that is simply that the Church will not be here. But Jesus knew that Satan's fury would be poured out on these Jews during the Great Tribulation, and He planned to make gracious special provision for as many as would or could heed the warning He was giving.

The actual moment for fleeing will the setting up of the Abomination of Desolation (Dan 9:23, Matt 24:15, Mk 13:14) and will be just as the Great Tribulation is starting—in other words at the three and a half year point. From Revelation 12 we find that this is the juncture where Satan, having been cast out from the heavens (v10), will pursue the Jews. Why will he pursue the Jews? For the very good reason that the Church will be safe in heaven, and beyond his reach. It all fits together!

Revelation 12 fits into the same parenthesis as chapter 11, where the two witnesses are foretold. But this time we have licence to interpret signs, rather than accepting the plain unvarnished text, for 12:1 talks of a 'great sign' or 'symbol' in the form of *"a woman clothed with the sun, with the moon under her feet, and on her head a garland of twelve stars"*. This is neither the Church nor Mary—neither fits the picture—it is about Israel and conforms perfectly to Joseph's dream in Genesis 37 and the description of Israel in Isa 66:7–9. The vision spans human history, before focussing on that future point in time with which we are here concerned, namely at the mid-point of the Tribulation. Lahaye writes:

> "The entire picture of the sun-clad woman is best understood when one keeps in mind that the Christian dispensation of almost two thousand years is entirely omitted here. This parallels the seventy weeks of Daniel, which predicts 483 years until Messiah the Prince shall be cut off and then, making no reference to the Gentile Church Age, goes on to the seven-year Tribulation period, completing the seventy weeks of years. Between Revelation 12:5 and 12:6 have occurred thus far nearly two thousand years of Church history... Verse 6 refers to the Tribulation period, when it says 'the woman fled into the desert' where God had prepared a place for her. As He provided for the nation Israel

> for forty years in the desert, so He will feed Israel during the Tribulation's 1,260 days." [21]

Israel has already long since given birth to the Man-child, who is to rule the nations with a rod of iron (v2 with Ps 2:9 and Rev 19:15). The Man-child or Son of Man has long since been caught up to heaven (Acts 1:9), utterly beyond the power and reach of the Serpent or Dragon (vv.3, 9) who would, had he been able, have destroyed Him whilst on earth (e.g. Lk 4:29). Now we come to the point where Satan, hitherto the Prince of the Power of the Air (Eph 2:2), is forcibly ejected from the heavens, where he has had access to accuse the brethren day and night (v10). His wrath is immense; Hal Lindsay writes:

> "The last half of the Great Tribulation will be a time of unparalleled persecution of the Jews. Satan will not only incite men on earth to hound them, but he and his angels will give special attention to their destruction. He'll be particularly angry over Jews who have finally placed their faith in Jesus as their Messiah. When this great outpouring of Satanic fury began, the believing Jews will be reminded of the words of Jesus in Matthew 24:16, 17, where He forewarned those who would be alive at the time of the 'abomination of desolation' to flee to the mountains, not even stopping to go back into the house for their coats." [22]

From verses which we have noted in the Olivet Discourse, not all will avail, or apparently be able to avail, themselves of this refuge. The Revelation vision closes with the words:

> *"The dragon was enraged with the woman, and he went to make war with the rest of her offspring, who keep the commandments of God, and have the testimony of Jesus Christ." (v17)*.

Whether these will be the ones who, because they were pregnant, for instance, will be unable to flee, we cannot say. Perhaps they will be latecomers to Jerusalem. Perhaps they will be later converts, impressed with the testimony of those believers whose heeding of the New Testament based warnings will be seen to have been vindicated. We know for certain from Zechariah passages encountered earlier that there will be believing Jews in Jerusalem right up to the time of the Lord's return.

Whatever the answer, it is abundantly clear that Jews in various roles will be mightily used, and in many cases mightily shielded, by God during that future dark time, when the Church will be safe with her Lord, awaiting to accompany Him when He returns in power in *"the Day of Vengeance of our God"* (Is 61:2; 64:4). We will be reminded briefly of that Day of Vengeance towards the end of our next chapter.

Chapter Six

Completing Our Case For Israel's Future

Nothing More Certain

In completing our case for God's future purposes and a promised restoration for Israel, we will in this chapter take time to consider the following in a little more depth:

- What, if anything, is negotiable and what is not negotiable with God concerning the future—especially the future of Israel.

- What Anti-Semitism has to tell us about Israel's future.

- The nature of God's covenants with Israel and how these relate to any other covenants.

In our 'until' studies we have found much concrete evidence for God's future purposes, all subject to certain time prerequisites. Before looking at what the 'opposition' in the form of Replacement Theology, has to say, we will devote one more chapter to presenting our case for this future for Israel constituting a benchmark against which any eschatological school may be evaluated.

In his excellent and remarkably comprehensive little volume of 1879, Edward Dennett opens his chapter on "The Restoration of the Jews" as follows:

> "There is nothing more certain from the word of God than that the Jews, who are now dispersed throughout the world, will be restored to their own land; 'for He that scattered Israel will gather him.' (Jer xxi.10)."

We would wholeheartedly agree, pausing again to commend the faith of people like Dennett, Darby, Kelly, Baines and Anderson who, long before the Balfour Declaration, took God at His word. He continues:

> "The time of their restoration is not revealed; but inasmuch as they are found in the land soon after the rapture of the

saints, it is evident that it will take place about that time, whether before or after it would be impossible to say, but probably afterward, because otherwise there would be a visible sign of the Lord's being at hand." [1]

Now here is the mark of the faithful student of prophecy. He has declared what Scripture unambiguously affirms, but is unashamed to admit what he cannot be sure of, and is prepared to go no further than 'probably' when there appears to be insufficient evidence. In the light of 20th century history we are able to amend that 'probably'. We know, for instance that the independent nation-state of Israel has been founded and that millions of Jews are in fact back in the Land before the Rapture. We know that as yet most of these have returned in an unrepentant and therefore unregenerate condition.

Nevertheless we must concede that his reasoning is sound in the light of what he knew. What he and other Victorian Dispensationalist writers were *certain* of is still true; only some of the things they were *uncertain* of have turned out rather differently, especially regarding timing. There are still more Jews scattered around the globe than there are resident in Israel; that is significant. The progress in the last century towards the end-time scenario has been so startling, and the signs of the times regarding Israel have been so convincing, that one feels that men like Dennett would be astonished at the unbelief within today's evangelical circles.

However what Peter had to say about scoffers (II Pet 3:3) has also materialised; so the rebirth of Israel, growth of Anti-Semitism and other features, which Dennett and his contemporaries might have assumed would alert the vast majority of Christians to the Lord's return, have not actually done so. We have to admit to our shame that we are living in a generation of Christians, which has more reason than any previous one to believe that the Lord is at hand, but whose apathy is becoming proverbial.

We are compelled to agree totally with Dennett when he writes about the basic fact, that nothing is more certain from the Bible than Israel's restoration. There are other *equally* certain doctrines. In fact there are other doctrines which conservative Bible scholars would regard as being fundamental to their faith, yet which are supported by many fewer passages than Israel's eventual restoration. Any person denying these other fundamental truths would be classed as being liberal or worse. It is a strange and sad anomaly indeed that there is not an evangelical consensus regarding Israel. It can be explained only in terms of the various predictions, mentioned in early chapters, of a latter day falling away, lack of faith and scoffing attitude to matters relating to the Lord's return, plus the activity of the common Enemy.

This blindness to the most prominent signs of the times seems to be as rife as that of the Pharisees and Sadducees of nearly two thousand years ago to the signs of their times (Matt 16:2,3). The fig tree, Israel, is at last in leaf, but it is as fruitless as it was when Jesus cursed it. The sky is, as it were, ablaze with a glorious red sunset, and those who should be interpreting it do not perceive the coming even more glorious day. The Jewish leaders whom Jesus condemned were simply not sufficiently interested to be perceptive. What does that say about Christians today?

Now we are not claiming that all those who deny Israel's coming restoration do not look forward to the Lord's return. But there is a considerable coincidence or overlap between the apathy toward prophecy, Replacement Theology and passive (rather than active) Anti-Semitism. Many would be horrified were they only to stop and consider the implications. We will have more to say about this soon.

It would be a fair summary at this stage to say that, while there is overwhelming evidence in Scripture to indicate a number of hugely important roles for the Jews in the future, there will always be resistance to this truth, not only from pagans, sceptics and atheists, but also from those who would consider themselves to be Christians; not only from nominal Christians, but also from some who would in all other respects consider themselves to be Bible believing Christians. Is that last comment too harsh? We will consider later.

One might well ask whether, under these circumstances, there is any point in pressing on with our case for Israel's future, if in fact many Christians are going to remain unconvinced, or are unwilling to be convinced. Two answers immediately leap out at us.

- We would be giving in to Satan, whose hatred for the Jews, particularly Jewish believers, is, as we have seen, at least as strong as his hatred of Gentile believers. We would be bringing comfort to our Enemy and tacitly turning a blind eye to growing

Anti-Semitism. Every member of the Church has the inestimable benefit of the gift of the Holy Spirit, a mighty shield against the attacks of the Enemy, which, as we will remind ourselves later in the chapter, has not yet been given to Jews outside the Church.

- There is a principle, particularly well illustrated in Ezekiel chapter 34, which says that it is the believer's responsibility to *proclaim*, irrespective of whether that proclamation is heeded. The responsibility for heeding or not heeding the proclamation is between the individual and his or her Creator. The faithful preacher is absolved; the negligent one assumes the guilt. Admittedly Ezekiel's topic for proclamation is different; however so much Scripture is devoted both to Israel's future and to the Lord's return, that one feels that it is not wrong to apply these principles to both.

Negotiable And Non-Negotiable

Commenting on Lk 21:5–26, Algernon Pollock writes:

"How deeply interesting is this scripture when we reflect that it contains a prophecy that fell from the lips of the Lord Himself. For our purposes we would draw attention to the different part of this prophecy:

1. The Temple should be razed to the ground.

2. Jerusalem should stand a siege and fall into the hands of the enemy.

3. That it should be accompanied by terrible bloodshed.

4. That the Jews should be dispersed among the nations.

5. That Jerusalem should be trodden down of the Gentiles 'until the times of the Gentiles be fulfilled'." [2]

Now we have already looked at this Luke passage in a previous chapter, but wish to make the point here, which is emphasised by the clarity of the above agenda, that this prophecy, which deeply concerns the Jews and Jerusalem, is simply not negotiable. It is an agenda rather than a proposal. Sometimes God is prepared to negotiate. He allowed Abraham to do so over Sodom's fate (Gen 18:22–33), and Gideon regarding his commission (Jud 6:39). We saw other instances in our third chapter, when we compared the conditional and unconditional.

Following Jesus' ascension, God graciously allowed almost forty years for individual Jews to repent and to recognise their Messiah; but He emphatically did not indicate that the national penalty for the crucifixion of their King could be rescinded. A new dispensation, the Church Age, had already replaced the previous one. There could be no reversion to the previous state of affairs. The national remedy would now have to wait two thousand years or so.

Tens of thousands were deported by Titus in AD 70. Thirty thousand of these Jews worked as slaves building the Colosseum. But some were allowed to remain until the AD 135 Bar Kochbar uprising, when Hadrian deported the remainder. So the full impact of Jesus' prediction of the dispersal was not felt for at least a century.

Jews began to trickle back into the Land in the late 19th century. By the mid 20th century the trickle became a flood. But to this day many more Jews remain outside the Land than are to be found within it. We are still in the Church Age. Neither can the next dispensation begin, nor can complete Jewish sovereignty occur, until, as Jesus said, the Times of the Gentiles be complete. And we have already seen what cataclysmic events must precede that.

Too much attention paid to the writings of Post-Millennialists is leading to premature hopes and ambitions of some Messianic Jews. Instead of clearly defined dispensations (whether one uses the term or not), there is a vague ambition to drift from one age to another, avoiding the clear mileposts of Scripture. Neither the short not the long term prerequisites can be skipped. God's plans are infinitely wiser and more thorough than those of even the best intentioned Jew or most avid Gentile supporter of Israel. Man's pre-emptive solutions would be short-term and would never solve the problems of this earth. The refiner's fire cannot be by-passed (Isa 48:10; Zech 13:9). This refining must not be confused with any sort of purgatory for the dead, a concept, which, as Hislop confirms, dates back to Plato of ancient Greece, Virgil of Rome and even earlier to

Egypt, and is still found in many pagan religions, as well as in Roman Catholicism.[3] This refiner's fire is about living Jews, not dead people. It is worth remembering that *holocaust* is derived from the Greek for burnt offering.

There is a kind of negotiation which we should never dare indulge in with God. That is manipulation, which betrays a lack of humility and suggests an arrogance towards our Creator. It implies that we think we know better than Him. It seems to be particularly common with people's views concerning what God should and should not do about Israel. When faced with promises of Israel's future restoration and glory, some, like Peter of old, would offer that contradictory challenge, *"Not so, Lord!"* We cannot say and mean 'Not so' and 'Lord' in the same breath and expect God's approval. Jesus' reply was *"Get behind Me, Satan"*—the toughest words ever spoken of an apostle, but appropriate, because Jesus knew the source of the thought process. Since the time of Constantine, Christian bodies have effectively been demanding that God should never forgive the Jewish nation. If God cannot forgive the Jews, many of whom were not even in the Land at the time of Jesus rejection and crucifixion, what chance has the Gentile Church for its frequent failures and apostasy?

Blackstone challenges:

> "Divest yourself of prejudice and preconceived notions, and let the Holy Spirit show you, from His Word, the glorious future of God's chosen people, 'who are beloved' (Rom 11:28), and dear unto Him as 'the apple of His eye' (Zech 2:8)."[4]

Yes, there is room for punishment:

> *"And first I will repay double for their iniquity and their sin, because they have defiled My land; they have filled My inheritance with the carcasses of their detestable and abominable idols"* (Jer 16:16).

Note that 'and first' in this passage which ties in with the famous *"Comfort ye"* opening of Isaiah 40, where the comfort *follows* the doubly paid recompense.

But there is also room for mercy:

> *"Who is a God like You, pardoning iniquity and passing over the transgression of the remnant of His heritage? He does not retain His anger for ever, because He delights in mercy. He will again have compassion on us, and will subdue our iniquities. You will cast all our sins into the depth of the sea. You will give truth to Jacob and mercy to Abraham, which You have sworn to our fathers from days of old"* (Mic 7:18–20).

We Gentile believers should beware, *"If God did not spare the natural branches, He may not spare you either"* (Rom 11:21). Beware the heart-hardening effect of Replacement Theology, which dares to know better than God.

Anti-Semitism

Here is a vast subject which we have already touched on several times. We cannot give it comprehensive cover, but must explore it sufficiently to understand its relationship to Replacement Theology. It is by no means the same thing. We have referred to Anti-Semitism a number of times, but have not considered whether this remarkable phenomenon is a reason for denying God's future for Israel or confirming it. Certainly some would say that it is evidence for God's everlasting rejection of Israel. Some would say that it is fully justified, going as far as to claim that its very antiquity without apparent interference by God is itself justification. Ignorance of God's control and restraint in the affairs of men abounds. For those for whom it is not inconvenient to trace God's dealings, both in love and in discipline, with Israel, there are almost four thousand years of evidence readily available.

Dave Hunt devotes to the topic a chapter, which he entitles 'The Mystery of Anti-Semitism'. It is a good title, inasmuch as, while to the serious student of the Bible it is no mystery, it remains a profound one to the world. In it he asks:

> "Why should the Jews, in contradistinction to all other people, be pursued with such relentless hatred wherever they go in search of a home? There is something truly mysterious about this heinous phenomenon! Yet it cannot

be without explanation. Are the Jewish people after all the most obnoxious, wicked, hateful people on the face of the earth? Have the Jews, in every generation and in every place, brought anti-Semitism upon themselves? Do they, to the last member of that race, really deserve such treatment? Some Jew-haters might say so, but that is surely not the consensus of rational people world wide." [5]

One thinks of passages such as Lamentations 4:15:

"They cried out to them, 'Go away, unclean! Go away, go away, Do not touch us!' When they fled and wandered, those among the nations said, 'They shall no longer dwell here.'"

The context does not find Jeremiah claiming that His people were innocent; anything but. But Jeremiah knew what Anti-Semitists fail to recognise, that ultimate forgiveness is promised.

"The children of Israel shall come, they and the children of Judah together; with continual weeping they shall come, and seek the Lord their God." (Jer 50:4)

That has never happened to date. Only Judah returned from Babylon, and only the volunteers of that tribe. Jeremiah spoke of the entire nation.

While the misery reflected in Lamentations was widespread, the contrition recorded in Jeremiah's lament was far from being general. No doubt Jeremiah was not totally alone in being penitent, but here he is confessing and interceding for his wayward people at the start of the seventy year captivity, in the same way as Daniel did at the close (Dan 9:3–19). Typically, the few take on the prayer burden of the many. We have already noted from Zechariah 12 when and how repentance will occur, and how widespread it will be. The Acts 2:38 call to repentance was heeded by only a few thousand; they entered the new-born Church.

In Jeremiah's day repentance was demanded by God for a variety of sins, chiefest of which was spiritual adultery or idolatry.

"And the Lord God of their fathers sent warnings to them by His messengers, rising up early and sending them, because He had compassion on His people and on His dwelling place. But they mocked the messengers of God,

despised His words, and scoffed at His prophets, until the wrath of the Lord arose against His people, till there was no remedy" (II Chron 36:15, 16).

Six hundred and forty years later their chiefest sin was the rejection and crucifixion of their long-awaited Messiah.

"Which of the prophets did your fathers not persecute? And they killed those who foretold the coming of the Just One, of whom you now have become the betrayers and murderers" (Acts 7:52).

Stephen's appropriate words cut them to the core. The account of this incident is followed with:

"At that time a great persecution arose against the church which was at Jerusalem" (Acts 8:1).

At Iconium:

"the unbelieving Jews stirred up the Gentiles and poisoned their minds against the brethren" (Acts 14:2).

The Jews were not slow themselves to persecute, as well as to incite Roman persecution of the early Christians. The God who has kept records of atrocities against Jews by Gentiles has not forgotten those by Jews against Christians.

Nobody can reasonably deny that the Jews, both in their history and in their present circumstances, are unique. That very uniqueness is a testimony to God's faithfulness to His promise; people should take note. Replacement Theologians would do well to consider how the ushering in of the Church Age has never altered God's declaration (Ezek 20:32–34):

"What you have in mind shall never be, when you say, 'We will be like the Gentiles, like the families in other countries, serving wood and stone'. 'As I live,' says the Lord God, 'surely with a mighty hand, with an outstretched arm, and with fury poured out, I will rule over you. I will bring you out from the peoples and gather you from the countries where you are scattered...'."

That does not describe the return from Babylon or even the hitherto partial return and birth of the modern Israeli state. This three and a half thousand year old uniqueness remains undiminished. How remarkable! Nobody on the international scene and few in the world of religion can avoid having an opinion about Israel.

Before looking again at the Scriptures, let us briefly list those who whether actively or passively, whether out of rancour, out of apathy or out of genuine Christian conviction, or for purely political reasons, oppose the possibility of *any* future, let alone a Divinely planned one, for Israel. Then we can see who, if anyone, is undecided or uncommitted over this issue. Finally we can see who are Israel's true friends. The sequence will be fairly arbitrary. Some groups we have already encountered; others we have yet to meet. On this occasion we are not going to differentiate between the state and the people.

Opponents of Israel's future

- Self-styled 'Palestinians'—Arabs living in enclaves and elsewhere between the Mediterranean and the Jordan, by no means all of whose ancestors lived there—who see the Jews as Zionists who have stolen their homeland. Zionism is actually a modern term, little over a hundred years old. They see this as an affront to Islam and believe it to be a religious duty to regain their former territories. The former desert state of much of the land, the fact that a lot of land was legally bought by Jews from absentee Arab landlords, and other embarrassing details are conveniently forgotten. They live in an explosive atmosphere of truth, myth and propaganda and are easily manipulated. Their god is Allah, the moon god whom Mohammed adopted, and who is specifically proclaimed in some mosques as having no son. They naturally do not believe that our God, who sent His Only Begotten Son into the world, has any right to promise a future for Israel, particularly in 'their' land. 'Once Islamic territory, always Islamic territory or House of Islam' they claim, although God has often proved them wrong. They obviously deny Jews and Christians similar rights.

- Muslims in general. Because Islam is a cultural, legal and political as well as a religious system, they assume that Judaism and indeed Christianity also embrace those four features. Their faith tells them that Islam must ultimately be victorious, and so have found Israel's military superiority inexplicable. They cannot countenance defeat, yet have had to, even when overwhelming odds have been on their side. One can understand their point of view when we leave God out of the reckoning.

- Other 'Third World' nations, who, rightly or wrongly see Israel as a client state of Western imperialism or an extension of colonialism. Whether their assessment is valid has nothing to do with the situation.

- Many nominally Christian states, particularly Roman Catholic countries, whose faith embraces Replacement Theology. Also countries who, for the sake of moral weakness, or political or economic expediency, find it more popular to be seen to side with Israel's enemies.

- Pacifists, who would compromise anything or everything for peace—peace at any price. Where these are Jews, who would cheerfully bargain away what God has promised, they are greatly mistaken if they believe that such deals are justified. The episode of Naboth's vineyard (I Kings 21) is salutary.

- Atheist Jews who crave a national future, but do not recognise the God who has miraculously preserved their race through so many centuries in the face of such adversities. Incongruously there are proportionately more atheists among Jews than in almost any other community.

- Satan and his angels, as we noted in our last chapter, from Revelation 12 etc.

'Fence Sitters' Regarding Israel's Future

- Some countries, like Great Britain, waver between the two positions. The personal stance of our prime minister or foreign secretary, at any given time, may tip the balance in either direction. Britain can take credit under God for the 1917 Balfour Recognition, and at other times there has been more tacit support for Zionism and Israel than is generally realised. Nevertheless we have much more of which not to be proud, especially during the immediate post-War years.

- Some Christians, who simply cannot or will not make up their minds.

Supporters of Israel's Future

- Orthodox Jews. For centuries Jews around the world celebrated the Passover saying hopefully, "Next Year in Jerusalem!". At last some of them are back in Jerusalem, though under enormous pressure to quit. They devoutly believe that God still has a purpose for them. Atheist or agnostic Jews simply rely on moral, historical, traditional and cultural arguments for a homeland. They rely upon the arm of flesh.

- Christians without any strongly held eschatological views. They may have been brought up in homes where the Bible was read and revered, or may simply have read their Bibles thoroughly since becoming Christians. They cannot but take at face value the numerous promises made to Israel, even though they do not necessarily see how these promises fit together.

- Pre-Millennialists, particularly those with Bible-based Dispensational or Pre-Rapture Return convictions. They can reasonably be termed Israelologists.

- On the international scene, there are nations and statesmen, who either openly or secretly support Israel, but do not necessarily bring God into the equation. The reasons may be pragmatic. Some see Israel as the champion against what they believe to be the growing threat of militant Islamic fundamentalism. Others admire her tenacity, industriousness and so on. Hitherto the United States of America has been the leading champion of Israel. But the USA has her share of Anti-Semitic pressure groups, and is now being blackmailed by terrorists to discard her conscience.

- Lastly we would remind ourselves that there is God Himself— Jehovah the Covenant God. *"If God is for us, who can be against us?"* (Rom 8:31). His time-table is not ours; but it is available for those who seek to know at least the main sequence of events.

Wrong perceptions may be held in all sincerity, although we should be aware that God does not necessarily excuse ignorance (see Acts 17:30, Rom 1:19 etc.). Of course, as history bears witness, Christians are liable to suffer exactly the same kind of treatment as Jews, particularly in Islamic and Communist countries. Jesus warned His disciples of impending hatred and persecution (Jn 15:18–25) and said, *"The time is coming that whoever kills you will think that he offers God a service"* (Jn 16:2). The Palestinian suicide bomber has been brainwashed to believe this fervently. However the blood of God's martyrs is precious in His sight in both Old and New Testament times (Ps 116:15; Heb 11:32–40; Rev 6:10, 11).

Dave Hunt records:

> "From earliest childhood Jews are taught the role of Christians in their persecution and pogroms. Yet the vast majority of Jews don't really know what being a Christian means. That confusion has caused the Jews to blame Christ and Christianity for anti-Semitism... Out of ignorance, Jews equate Christianity with Roman Catholicism, unaware that the Roman Catholic Church, though it claims to be Christian, has killed far more Christians than it has Jews." [6]

> "Most Jews are not aware of the fact that the Inquisition consumed probably 100 times as many Christians as it did Jews. For 15 centuries (for 1200 years *before* the Reformation) the Roman Catholic Church, at the same time it was killing Jews by the thousands, was torturing and killing Christians by the millions." [7]

However if one considers the numbers of Jews killed with active encouragement of the Vatican, such as in the Crusades, or tacit support of Rome through many centuries, or adds to this those massacred by regimes in predominantly Catholic countries, when Popes could have used their influence but have not done so not, then the Jewish statistics do surpass those of Christian non-conformists martyred for their faith. The Russian Orthodox Church might have stopped or at least moderated the pogroms. They too are seen by Jews as typical Christians.

God has the most severe things to say about the perpetrators of Anti-Semitism. Speaking of Pharaoh's persecution, God said:

> *"The nation whom they serve I will judge; afterward they shall come out with great possessions"* (Gen 15:14).

Jeremiah says:

> *"'Israel was holiness to the Lord, the firstfruits of His increase. All that devour him will offend; disaster will come upon them' says the Lord"* (Jer 2:3).

The Psalmist writes:

> *"They have said 'Come, and let us cut them off from being a nation, that the name of Israel may be remembered no more'. For they have consulted together with one consent... Deal with them as with Midian, and as with Sisera, as with Jabin at the Brook of Kishon, who perished at En Dor, who became as refuse on the earth"* (Ps 83:4, 5, 8, 12).

He could have been writing in the 20th century, but for the names. History tells us how God did in fact deal decisively with all the nations against whom the Psalmist lodged this complaint.

The antiquity of these passages reminds us that the plight of the Jews down through the centuries has not been exclusively for rejecting the Messiah, monumental though this offence was. In fact in the case of the Egyptian slavery, national sin is not even associated with their suffering. Pharaoh's attack is seen to be directly against God.

> *"You shall say to Pharaoh, 'Thus says the Lord: Israel is My son, My firstborn'"* (Ex 4:22).

We know the rest of the history and consequences of Pharaoh's continued defiance. Isaiah gave good King Hezekiah a reply to give to the Assyrian king, Sennacherib:

> *"Whom have you reproached and blasphemed? Against whom have you raised your voice, and lifted your eyes on high? Against the Holy One of Israel"* (II Kings 19:22).

Neither then, nor now, nor in the future will any indulge in Anti-Semitism with impunity. The total unanimity of hatred of Israel, described in ancient times by the Psalmist in Ps 83, has yet to be achieved in our time within the United Nations; but it will surely come soon within the international community (Zech 14:2). Woe to those weak 'Christian' nations who despise the God of Israel, and hide behind political correctness! It is bad enough to be counted among the abstainers, though worse to be a perpetrator.

Basilea Schlink writes:

> "It is not without reason that the apostle Paul exhorts us who believe in Christ not to adopt a superior attitude towards the Jews but to remain humbly aware that the Jews are the root of the tree. They bear us, not we them, for we are only grafted in (Romans 11). But the evil one succeeded in luring the Christian Church away from this humble, brotherly attitude when, in self-glory, she appropriated all the graces and promises meant for Israel, thereby expunging Israel from God's redemptive history. Such arrogance made it possible for those assertions promoting hatred of the Jews to thrive even within Christendom. It was argued, 'Did not God Himself say in His Word that the Jews are a stubborn, disobedient people, full of sins, lies and unfaithfulness?' Admittedly the Holy Scriptures speak thus of the people of Israel; there is no denying that…" [8]

Basilea Schlink has much of importance to say regarding Israel. However she is somewhat over-optimistic about Israel's present spiritual state. We shall refer to this and its significance in Part Two.

There is one kind of Anti-Semitism perpetrated by some Christians today which is actually welcomed by many religious Jews and by some Israeli government bodies. It is the denial of the Christian Gospel to the country, through anti-missionary or anti-proselytising laws. Writing about one Christian organisation, J J Prasch, a Messianic Jew, writes:

> "X has published a mission statement with a covering letter explaining its position on non-evangelisation of Jews. It claims to fulfil Isaiah chapter 40 by comforting Israel, telling Israel that her iniquity is removed—without telling Israel the gospel message which is the only biblical way her iniquity

can be removed. To say that the sin of Israel can be removed without the Blood of Jesus—the Jewish Messiah—is a blasphemous heresy known as 'dual covenant theology'." [9]

He devotes some considerable space to the topic, including a section aptly titled, "Israel, We Love You—But Go To Hell!". He also gives details of recent cases of persecution of Messianic Jews by Orthodox Jews. In Britain we tend to be smug over Anti-Semitism; but we have little cause. England has been more guilty in this respect than Scotland. King Canute, Richard the Lion Heart and Edward I banished Jews; William the Conqueror and later Oliver Cromwell allowed them to return. Shakespeare's portrayal of characters like Shylock reflects contemporary attitudes. Persecutions in London, Norwich and York Castle are shameful episodes in English history.

The Final Holocaust

Most people without any particular religious leanings would blame Zionism for any Anti-Semitic feelings. But Zionism is a movement of the last hundred and twenty or so years. Anti-Semitism has been around for thousands of years. It will not last much longer, but as we have noted, it has yet to assume its final and most terrible form. There is only one sure way for Jews to escape at present. That is by accepting Jesus Christ as Messiah now and being included in the *"gathering together to Him"* (II Thess 2:1). The option of fleeing from Jerusalem during the Tribulation is not open to anyone currently aware of but resisting the full truth of the Christian Gospel. It will be only for those Jews who come to a saving knowledge of their Messiah after the Rapture.

Phillips and Vines summarise this future final holocaust within the general context of Anti-Semitism:

> "When one thinks of the terrible sufferings of the Jewish people in all ages, especially of their sufferings during the Nazi holocaust, it seems impossible that anything could be worse. The Holy Spirit assures us, however, that the great tribulation will be worse than anything ever to take place on this planet.
>
> Think of the sufferings of the Jewish people. Egyptian pharaohs have tried to exterminate them. Assyrian kings,

148

Babylonian emperors, and Persian potentates have turned their hands against them. Xerxes ordered their total extermination from all his realms. Greek tyrants and Roman Caesars, neighbouring princelings and church officials, Spanish inquisitors and Roman popes, medieval kings and swashbuckling tsars and commissars—one and all have persecuted this people. The dungeon and the sword; the thumbscrew and the rack; gigot, flame and fire; concentration camps and gas chambers; starvation and tortures; sadistic experiments in the name of science—all that fallen men or raging demons could devise—all have been used against this people. But the great tribulation will be worse than them all." [10]

Inevitably we are drawn back time and time again to the blessings and curses which God imposed before Israel entered the Promised Land with instructions to drive out the wicked inhabitants (Deut 28:1–31:21 with Num 33:52–55 etc.). If God considered those inhabitants worthy of eviction, who is going to gainsay Him? Is it not strange how many approve of God's scattering of Israel in the past, but would dare to criticise His eviction of others, even denying His right to supplant inhabitants if He wishes to? It is God the Holy Spirit, not some misguided Christian or some Zionist, who inspired Zechariah to close his great prophecy with the words,

> *"In that day there shall no longer be a Canaanite in the house of the Lord of Hosts"* (Zech 14:21).

This of course does not give us licence to take the law into our own hands.

In view of the fact that the curses have not failed when they were deserved, why ever do some Christians suppose that God is going to allow His promises of blessings, issued at the same time, to fail? The curses have yet to run their full course. The storm clouds have long been gathering for the final onslaught.

> *"For behold the day is coming, burning like an oven... but to you that fear My name the Sun of Righteousness shall arise with healing in His wings"* (Mal 4:1–2).

The context is exclusively Jewish.

For the perpetrators of Anti-Semitism, the demon-driven nations which will converge on Jerusalem, the message from the Son of God will be:

> *"For the day of vengeance is in My heart, and the year of My redeemed has come"* (Isa 63:4).

Isaiah cried:

> *"Oh, that You would rend the heavens! That You would come down! That the mountains would shake at Your presence."* (Isa 64:1).

Later prophecies confirmed that Isaiah's yearnings will at last be satisfied.

Confusion Over Covenants

From time to time in Part Two we will be referring to covenants concerning Israel, so it would be appropriate to devote a little space at this stage to clearing up some misunderstandings. Problems arise partly through Christians ignoring the Old Testament, except as a sort of series of historical novels, to be treated less seriously than the New Testament. It is ironic that Replacement Theologians should sometimes style themselves 'Covenant Theologians', when in fact they base their theology on fewer covenants than Dispensational Israelologists.

People read in the Epistle to the Hebrews that the New Testament or New Covenant has replaced the Old worn out temporary one, and assume that any covenant made in Old Testament times is therefore no longer valid or relevant. The teachings of Dispensationalists are thus undermined through ignorance rather than prejudice.

In no way whatsoever are we discounting the Covenant teaching of the Epistle to the Hebrews. It was written to Jewish Christians who had yet to come to terms with the very important fact that their Mosaic or Levitical Covenant was obsolete. Let us quote a few verses to confirm this:

> *"On the one hand there is an annulling of the former commandment because of its weakness and unprofitableness, for the law made nothing perfect... by so much more Jesus has become a surety of a better covenant"* (7:18, 19, 22).

"But now He has obtained a more excellent ministry, inasmuch as He is also Mediator of a better covenant, which was established on better promises. For if that first covenant had been faultless, then no place would have been sought for a second" (8:6, 7).

Now this passage is very important, for it gives the timing of the establishment of this covenant, which was to replace the previous one:

"'Behold, the days are coming says the Lord that I will make a new covenant with the house of Israel and with the house of Judah—not according to the covenant that I made with their fathers in the day that I took them by the hand to lead them out of the land of Egypt...'" (8:8, 9).

The superseded covenant was established in the Sinai desert in the first year of their forty year sojourn. It refers to this and no other Old Testament covenant. The writer to the Hebrews is actually quoting Jeremiah 31 regarding the replacement covenant; so this is something planned and promised beforehand by God. It is not an attack on the Old Testament. Kelly, regarding the Jeremiah prophecy, writes:

"It will be no dishonour to the law of Moses that God will establish a new covenant under the Messiah; in fact Moses himself predicted it. He foretold that the Lord God was to raise up a prophet like unto himself, but although like unto himself, superior to him (Deut xviii. 15, 18). There would be no superiority in this prophet if he did not introduce a better state of things, that is the new covenant. Moses brought in the old covenant. Christ will bring in the new covenant." [11]

The late Dr John F Walvoord, a leading Israelologist and Pre-Tribulationist theologian, sees no conflict with his dispensational stand when he writes:

"One of the most obvious facts about the Bible is that it is divided into the Old and New Testaments, or the old and new covenants. Though the entire Bible bears witness to a gracious, loving God, there is a sharp contrast between the basic revelation of the Old Testament as compared to the New. This is captured in the simple statement of John 1:17,

> 'For the law was given through Moses; grace and truth came through Jesus Christ'." [12]

Having made it absolutely clear that we have no dispute with what is the generally accepted stand of all evangelicals on the contrast between the Mosaic or Levitical covenant on the one hand, and the New on the other, let us now emphasis that our case for Israel's future is based on very different ancient covenants between God and Israel, plus of course the New one.

The Mosaic covenant, unlike the other old covenants with Israel, foreshadowed Calvary and was about the means of salvation. Thus it involved the shedding of the blood of the lamb, which was absent from the other, as outlined in Hebrews chapter 10. The other old covenants were different kinds of contracts between God and Israel. The fact that circumcision was required by God in two cases does not make them the same covenant.

We read in the Bible of covenants between individual and individual, or people and people, such as that between Abraham and Abimilech (Gen 21:27), or between Jacob and Laban (Gen 31:44). We also know of the covenant between God and Noah and his descendents, not to drown the world again for as long is it should last (Gen 9:11–17). That is an unconditional, unilateral covenant, an example of God's faithfulness, which some would wish to deny to His covenant dealings with the Jews. But we are concerned now with covenants other than the aforementioned Mosaic or Levitical one, between God and Israel.

We first read of covenants between God and Abraham and his descendants in Genesis 12:1–3:

> *"Now the Lord had said to Abram: 'Get out of your country, from your kindred and from your father's house, to a land which I shall show you. I will make you a great nation; I will bless you and make your name great; and you shall be a blessing. I will bless those who bless you, and I will curse him who curses you; and in you shall all the families of the earth be blessed'."*

This is the background to the Abrahamic covenant, of which we read more in Genesis 15:18 and 17:2–21 (where the word 'covenant' occurs ten times).

One wonders how so many can play fast and loose with such a straightforward and solemn declaration. Walvoord comments:

> "In attempting to understand the revelation God gave Abraham, the interpreter of the Abrahamic promise is faced with the decision as to whether this should be taken in its literal meaning, that is physical descendants, as Premillenarians believe, or whether it should be spiritualised to represent the spiritual company of the elect of Israel and even Gentiles, as Amillenarians believe. As the exposition of the covenant throughout the book of Genesis will demonstrate, the promise was literal, that is, Abraham understood the promise of a great nation to refer to his spiritual descendants, and this was also God's intent... That Abraham would also have spiritual children (Gal 3:6–9) does not change the literal promise." [13]

Pollock imposes a cautionary perspective on these covenants. He starts by quoting Romans 9:4, 5:

> "*'Israelites, to whom pertaineth the adoption, and the glory, and the covenants, and the giving of the law, and the service of God, and the promises; whose are the fathers, and of whom, as concerning the flesh Christ came, who is over all, God blessed for ever. Amen.'*... God made *'covenants'* with Israel, but what had they in view? One verse tells us. God had a long look-out down through the centuries. It is not a question of Abraham and his individual blessing, though that is, perforce, secure, but the blessing of mankind. We read: *'And the Scripture, foreseeing that God would justify the heathen (the Gentiles) through faith, preached before the gospel unto Abraham, saying In thee shall all the nations be blessed'* (Galatians iii. 8)." [14]

So ultimately God's covenants with Israel were for the blessing of all mankind, but, apart from the Levitical one which, as we have seen, was to be superseded, they are for the duration of this planet. The Levitical covenant was conditional, and those conditions could not be met. So how many *unconditional* covenants between God and Israel are there? We have already referred to these covenants in our 'until' studies in our second and third chapters, sufficiently to prove that these were not declared void after Calvary. So we can afford to be brief here.

Dr Fruchtenbaum[15] quotes Dr Dwight Pentecost[16] as listing "four unconditional and eternal covenants God made with Israel". We could use other sources, but this is a particularly succinct summary.

- "The Abrahamic Covenant promised 'a land, a seed and a blessing which would be universal and eternal'."

- "The Palestinian Covenant 'gives the basis on which Israel will occupy the land'."

- "The Davidic Covenant promised 'a king, a kingdom and a throne to the seed of Abraham' and 'an everlasting earthly kingdom over which David's son should reign'."

- "The New Covenant promised a national salvation and restoration of Israel".

It will be noted that the Levitical covenant (the 'Old Covenant' spoken of in the New Testament) is not included among these. By 'unconditional' we are referring to their final outcome as guaranteed by God Himself.

Fruchtenbaum writes:

"An unconditional covenant can be defined as a sovereign act of God whereby God unconditionally obligates Himself to bring to pass definite promises, blessings and conditions for the covenanted people. It is a unilateral covenant. This type of covenant is characterised by the formula *I will* which declares God's determination to do exactly as He promised. The blessings are secured by the grace of God. Covenant Theologians have misinterpreted what Dispensationalists mean by 'unconditional' Their claim is that Dispensationalism teaches that these covenants contain no conditions whatsoever... God's fulfilment of His promises are unconditional and He will accomplish all promises stated in the covenants. In other words, the conditions stated in those same covenants are not the basis by which the covenants will be fulfilled." [17]

Fruchtenbaum writes regarding the Mosaic Covenant and the Law of Moses:

"While the previous four covenants were unconditional, this one is conditional. A conditional covenant is a bilateral covenant and may be defined as a proposal of God to man conditioned by the formula, *if you will*, whereby He promises to grant special blessings to man providing man fulfils certain conditions contained in the covenant. Man's failure to do so often results in punishment... The Mosaic Covenant was the basis for the Dispensation of Law. It was the one Jewish covenant that was conditional." [18]

So we have seen ample evidence from the New Testament, notably from Hebrews, that this one conditional covenant was declared obsolete nearly two thousand years ago, whilst the others still stand firm, with reassurances which in no way clash with the impermanent nature of the Mosaic/Levitical covenant:

- Abrahamic   *Unconditional*
- Palestinian   *Unconditional*
- Davidic   *Unconditional*
- New   *Unconditional*

As opposed to:

- Mosaic or Levitical   *Conditional*

Some might argue that the Palestinian and Davidic covenants were merely an extension of the Abrahamic one, in which the Land was first promised. Whether it is or is not makes no difference whatsoever to our cases for God's future purposes for Israel. Baines, for instance, does not see it as separate; however his general comments are useful in re-enforcing what we have already noted elsewhere and in providing food for thought:

"Thus there are three covenants; the first an unconditional one, with Abraham, not yet fulfilled; the second, a conditional one, with Israel, which prevented the accomplishment of the first, by making it contingent on the people's obedience; the third, an unconditional one, also with Israel, which sets aside the second, and so renders possible the fulfilment of the first. But though the condition of the Sinai covenant is to be removed, national restoration and the fulfilment of the unconditional covenant with Abraham is not to take place until the time of national repentance." [19]

Baines, who is not unique in this, is in effect listing three covenants thus:

- Abrahamic (including Palestinian and Davidic)   *Unconditional*

- Mosaic or Levitical   *Conditional*

- New   *Unconditional*

Zacharias' prophecy (Lk 1:68–79) refers apparently to a single covenant— *"To perform mercy promised to our fathers and to remember His holy covenant"*. He had been talking about the promises to David and was about to refer to those to Abraham. However, as the Palestinian covenant (Deut 29:1,9,12) and the Davidic covenant (II Sam 7:12–16) seem to qualify for independent status, it would appear that Fruchtenbaum, Pentecost and Lightner, who uses the same four headings,[20] are right, rather than Baines.

It is interesting that the term 'covenant' is not used in God's promise to David as recorded in II Samuel 7, but it is confirmed to be such in no uncertain manner in Ps 89:28,34:

"My mercy I will keep for him forever, and My covenant shall stand firm with him... Nevertheless My lovingkindness I will not utterly take from him, nor allow My faithfulness to fail. My covenant I will not break, nor alter the word that has gone out of My lips. Once I have sworn by My holiness; I will not lie to David; his seed shall endure for ever, and his throne as the sun before Me; it shall be established forever like the moon, even like the faithful witness in the sky."

For Israel the unconditional covenants can be fully promulgated only when the Messiah returns in power. This must of course include the New Covenant. We have already in this chapter referred to the Hebrews 8 quote from Jeremiah 31. That passage continues:

> *"'But this is the covenant that I will make with the house of Israel after those days, says the Lord; I will put my law in their minds, and write it on their hearts; and I will be their God, and they shall be My people... If those ordinances depart from Me, says the Lord, then the seed of Israel shall also cease from being a nation before Me forever.' Thus says the Lord: 'If heaven above can be measured, and the foundations of the earth beneath, I will also cast off all the seed of Israel for all they have done says the Lord.'"*
> (Jer 31:33, 36, 37).

Does that sound like the Church? Surely the final few words alone deny any possibility. What an awesome responsibility the Replacement Theologian takes upon himself in non-literal interpretations, when literal ones make profound sense.

It goes without saying that currently Jews and Gentiles alike participate in the New Covenant at the moment of their salvation. The addressees of the Epistle to the Hebrews were already recipients. But here we are discussing future national participation.

The following quotation from Pollock is particularly useful in that it shows the interrelationship between the Church and Israel in the terms, timing and possession of the New Covenant:

> "The New Covenant to be made with Israel, following on her deep repentance at the end of the great tribulation, and synchronising with the personal reign of Christ in the Millennium, is one of pure sovereign grace, consisting of new birth, the forgiveness of sins, and the gift of the Holy Spirit. What a day that will be for Israel! The righteous foundation for this New Covenant is already laid in the death of Christ, and though not ratified with Israel as a whole, it has been antedated in God's dealing in blessing with His saints from the earliest times. Apart from new birth

there can be no link with God in blessing. The forgiveness of sins and the gift of the Holy Spirit were alike promised in Old Testament times. As to Christians, though not formally under it, they have the blessings of it already. The cup at the Lord's Supper signifies 'the blood of the New Testament [Covenant]'... The Christian has, indeed, larger and fuller blessings than those of the New Covenant, but, as the greater includes the lesser, so do Christian blessings include the New Covenant blessings. Meanwhile these blessings are found in connection with the Church, but when the Lord comes for His people, and Israel is set up under Christ, as Priest and King upon His throne, the New Covenant will be made with Israel in a public way." [21]

If we find Pollock's words difficult to accept, we should read again those Jeremiah 31 verses where the New Covenant is first promised in detail, and ask ourselves whether it has ever been fulfilled to date in the terms there described. We will find that it has not been. Even if we argue, as we may do, that the Church inherited every aspect of the New Covenant immediately after Calvary or at Pentecost, it in no way negates God's promise through Jeremiah of Israel one day receiving it too.

Concluding Comments On The Case For Israel's Future

We have by no means used all the material available in Scripture for proving God's future purposes for Israel; but we must draw a line somewhere. In our second part we shall be referring again to some of the texts which we have already used, and introducing others as appropriate.

As we have stated before, we believe that the number of passages supporting the truth of God's future plans and purposes for Israel is overwhelmingly greater than those suggesting the contrary. This is not prejudgement. In a series of articles published in *Your Tomorrow* in 1998,[22] I examined, in defence of the Pre-tribulation position, rather than the Israelology one, a number of texts which I now find to be common to both.

We are likely also to note as we study those schools of prophetic interpretation which largely or wholly support Replacement Theology, that their proof passages do not so much *deny*, but rather, in their view, *imply* that there is no future for Israel. Indeed, if they cannot prove that

God permanently discontinued His special relationship with Israel and annulled all His covenants, then we may safely conclude that Replacement Theology is a heretical relic of the Dark Ages.

Those are tough words; are they justified? Well, consider this. Isaiah cries:

> *"But now, O Lord, you are our Father; we are the clay and You our potter; and all we are the work of Your hands. Do not be furious, O Lord, nor remember iniquity forever... Will you restrain Yourself because of these things, O Lord? Will you hold Your peace, and afflict us very severely?"* (Isa 64:12).

Would *we* deny forgiveness to the penitent nation to be? Would we limit Jesus' Calvary prayer?

> *"And when they had come to the place called Calvary, there they crucified Him... Then Jesus said 'Father, forgive them, for they do not know what they do'"* (Lk 23:33,34).

Was that plea really confined to the Roman soldiers? We know that many would not accept that forgiveness. But who are we to deny it to the nation who, as we have seen from Zechariah 12, will one day repent not only individually, but also collectively and nationally?

My friend and fellow ETS research student, Dr Michael Phelan writes:

> "We must take note of the fact, that this prayer from the dying Christ was for forgiveness of those who earlier had cried, 'His blood be upon us, and on our children' (Matt 27:25), a verse so abused by the established churches over the centuries in order to justify the most dreadful, yet official and systematic, persecution of the Jews. To believe that the awful act of condemning Christ to crucifixion excluded Israel from their promises involves believing that this prayer of Christ, the High Priest after the order of Melchizedec (Heb 5:6ff), uttered at the most sacred moment in the world's history, went unheard! It also, of course, involves believing that Peter was not led of the Holy Spirit to preach in the way he did in Acts chapter two." [23]

Many centuries before, as recorded in Exodus 32:1–14, God had declared the Children of Israel to be worthy of annihilation for making and worshipping the golden calf. Moses took upon himself the role of intercessor. He did not excuse his brethren; rather he reminded God of His covenant promises to the patriarchs and of the potential cynicism of the Egyptians to His abandoning His people. Would we, as Christians, dare to take the opposite line from that of Moses? Do we make full use of the powerful witness to the unbeliever of the way in which God has been faithful to both His declared blessings and curses regarding Israel? Why should the world scoff?

It is to that 'greatest of the Minor prophets', and to the commentary of my pastor of more than fifty years ago, Dr James Sidlow Baxter, that I would turn in closing. He is commenting here on Zechariah chapters 12 to 14:

> "In this third part of Zechariah's great Messianic prophecy, we need only to translate snatches here and there by way of guidance. The language makes it clear that this passage passes over the present 'Church' interval, when, after all the tragic delay caused through the rejection of the true Shepherd-King, Jehovah shall again take up and complete His grand purpose for Israel." [24]

He concludes with:

> "Such then is the Book of Zechariah… Yet both in the earlier movements (i–viii) and in the later (ix–xiv) we hear the same recurrent key-note all the way through—Jehovah is 'jealous for Zion'. The Pulpit Commentary remarks on chapter ix 13, 'Nothing but inspiration could have enabled Zechariah and Daniel to foresee the rise of the Macedonian dynasty, and the struggles between the Syro-Grecian power in Maccabæan times, which is here announced.' What then shall we say about those passages in Zechariah which look right on to the Messiah's first and second comings—to His public entry into Jerusalem in lowly dignity, riding on an ass; to His being 'wounded' in the house of His own kinsmen; to the 'smiting of the Shepherd and the scattering of the flock'; to the preservation of the 'remnant' even as at this very day; to the 'mourning' for Him, which is yet to be,

when the Jews 'look on Him whom they pierced'; to the last super-conflict and the final kingdom-glories? Yes, what shall we say to all this? Is it not a marvel of inspiration? Oh for that final triumph which Zechariah has predicted! 'Even so, come Lord Jesus!'"[25]

How can anyone who knows and loves the word of God, believing it to be infallible, deny that God yet has purposes for Israel? However, being theologically correct does not guarantee our personal spirituality. We must walk humbly, as we study these awesome matters.

No Escape Clause

We have made much of unconditional promises as a basis for belief in God's guaranteed future for Israel. But we must be careful to maintain a balance, by reminding ourselves that there were important conditions and warnings too, the observance or neglect of which have determined Israel's prosperity and usefulness at any given point in history. For almost 2,000 years the Church has fulfilled what was potentially Israel's role, albeit within the foreknowledge and plans of God.

Their initial role was accorded in response to an offer made to God immediately before He gave them the Law through Moses at Sinai:

> *"If you will indeed obey My voice and keep My covenant,*
> *then you shall be a special treasure to Me above all people;*
> *for the earth is Mine. And you shall be to Me a kingdom of*
> *priests and a holy nation"* (Ex 19:5,6).

Jewishness has never exempted any child of Israel, who is as prone to breaking God's law as any Gentile, from the same need for repentance, faith and redemption through the shed blood of the Lamb provided by God. That Lamb was formerly foreshadowed in the Tabernacle and Temple sacrifices; but He was slain once for all at Calvary. Jews whom Jesus encountered in the incident recorded at Jn 8:31–59 had forgotten this. Being a Jew brought incalculable privileges and awesome responsibilities in Old Testament times. One day, God's word assures us, those privileges and responsibilities will be borne and exercised in a truly worthy manner.

I would respectfully and earnestly challenge any Replacement Theologian who claims to be Bible-believing to read carefully Ezek 39 verses 21 to 29 and to reconsider their position. The passage is too long to quote in full, but note in particular vv. 22, 23, 27 and 28:

> *"So the house of Israel shall know that I am the Lord their God from that day forward. The Gentiles shall know that the house of Israel went into captivity for their iniquity; because they were unfaithful to Me, therefore I hid My face from them. I gave them into the hand of their enemies, and they all fell by the sword... When I have brought them back from the peoples and gathered them out of their enemies' lands, and I am hallowed in them in the sight of many nations, then shall they know that I am the Lord their God who sent them into captivity among the nations, but also have brought them back to their land."*

The precise timing of the fulfilment of this passage is not the issue; but the bare facts are. By no stretch of the imagination can the passage be applied to the Church. By no stretch of the imagination can the promises be described as conditional. And by no stretch of the imagination can it be said to have been fulfilled at the return from Babylon or at any other time in history. Therefore it *must* be future, if God's word is to be believed. God must still have purposes for the nation Israel. The very demise of Replacement Theology is foretold in this passage: *"The Gentiles shall know..."*. Hallelujah!

Part Two

Exposing Errors

Chapter Seven

Taking Stock

Adhering To Terms Of Reference

We are taking stock—not closed for stocktaking. One involves moving forward and the other standing still. We cannot afford to stand still. As we move forward we must ever be aware of our terms of reference, which are to demonstrate how God's future for Israel is a vital benchmark for validating schools of prophetic interpretation. But we have also indicated that we intend to use this process in defence of or to promote Dispensational Pre-Millennialism, with its strong Israelologist implications. So, whilst we will concentrate on our chosen benchmark, we will by no means disregard other aspects.

We are not claiming that any school which guarantees a future for Israel must needs be correct. Were that true, we would have to recognise Orthodox Judaism as being a valid alternative to Christianity! Moreover we would have to accept all the widely differing forms of current Messianic Jewish teaching on eschatology, rather than only some.

For the purposes of this book, God's future for Israel is an invaluable benchmark for verification of prophecy. But it is much, much more. In other words, it is not true merely so that after the Lord returns to the Mount of Olives, and all the Messianic promises are being fulfilled, we can turn round, albeit in the courteous manner that would be expected of saints in their resurrection bodies, and say to old Replacement friends the suitable equivalent 'Yah boo! We told you; didn't we?' Far too many humbling things will have taken place to allow any pride in our own theological accuracy or achievements. Even when words of commendation have passed from the lips of our Saviour, or crowns of recognition have been awarded by His hands, pride will be banished. A grand old hymn helps to put it all into perspective.

"The Bride eyes not her garments
But her dear bridegroom's face.
I will not look on glory,
But on my King of grace,
Not at the crown He giveth,
But on His pierced hand;
The Lamb is all the glory
Of Immanuel's land."

Anne Ross Cousin

And of course if we believe in God's future purposes for Israel, we will find it very much easier to monitor and recognise the signs of the times, and to avoid coming into the same condemnation as the Emmaus pair; *"O foolish ones, and slow of heart to believe in all that the prophets have spoken!"* (Lk 24:25). Jesus did not say that they had not believed *anything* of what the prophets had foretold, but that they had not believed *all* that they had spoken. Is this not what happens with Replacement Theology? Belief in Bible promises becomes strangely selective, conforming to human aspirations rather than to God's purposes.

Some prophecies, which are credible and comprehensible in their most straightforward form, are interpreted 'spiritually'—almost as if use of the word 'spiritually' adds some praiseworthy element, when all it actually conveys in this context is 'not literally'. We would expect the word 'spiritual' to have positive overtones. Instead, it is all too often used in a manipulative, diversionary or even patronising way, to suggest the superiority of the insight of those who cannot or do not wish to face plain language when plain language makes sense. This is the technique of the cult members who call at our doors. It should not be the practice of fellow believers.

Bone Of Contention

Our bone of contention, then, is almost entirely with Replacement Theology, the teaching that the Church has replaced Israel in all God's plans for the future, and that the blessings once promised to Israel have now been passed on to the Church. So, having demonstrated that God most certainly has future purposes for Israel, including a complete restoration, need we proceed any further?

One problem is that Replacement Theology occurs in different levels of intensity and leads to more conclusions than the most obvious one, which we have defined in the above paragraph. Generally speaking it underpins both Amillennialism and Post-Millennialism; but we may find exceptions here and there. It would be unrealistic to expect to study every minor variation within either of those schools, or indeed all the variations within Pre-Millennialism which are not Pre-Tribulationist. But we should take note of attitudes to, as well as belief or disbelief in, God's purposes for Israel. Attitudes can be very telling—and sometimes very damaging.

Pre-Millennialists may very well get the impression that only they are interested in predictive Bible Prophecy. This is probably truer in Britain and other countries which have access to very many fewer religious television and radio channels than the United States and Canada. Such access has disadvantages as well as advantages, unless one is very thorough in testing teaching against Holy Scripture. The *"prince of the power of the air"* is an expert in manipulating our air waves.

Certainly the Dispensationalist, the Pre-Tribulationist and the Israelologist (and we have noted a huge overlap between the three) are usually either admired, ignored or ostracised for their interest in matters concerning the Lord's return. The 'Left Behind' books[1] of LaHaye and Jenkins are so popular across the Atlantic that they are to be found at supermarket checkouts and even some larger newspaper stalls. I noticed in two recent visits that they are also much cheaper! Certainly there is much greater awareness of prophetic matters there, even although this tends sadly to be balanced by more chasing after other spiritual extremes, deviations and cults.

Among serious theologians of all the major prophetic persuasions who face up to these matters, the debate is directed less exclusively against Pre-Millennialists by the others than one might suppose. Thus we find Post-Millennialists and Amillennialists attacking fiercely each other's eschatology. This is hardly surprising as they are utterly incompatible, even though in many British churches they do seem to co-exist happily. We shall see examples of all these things in due course. Usually this is done in a much more civilised way than one would expect from politicians with their divergent views, because, by and large, these are people who love and serve Jesus Christ and who recognise brothers and sisters in the Lord. However there is a place for the fervent holding and defending of what we believe to be precious Bible truths. Sometimes feelings run high, just as apparently they occasionally did among the early Church leaders over matters like the reintroduction of works into the Gospel of grace (Gal 1 & 2). A *laissez faire* approach on the Apostles' part would have been utterly irresponsible.

David Pawson, writing about the Millennium, says:

> "I am no stranger to controversy... I find that honest debate sharpens my own mind and, I believe, that of those with whom I disagree. I do not think that divisions from fellow believers are justified by differences in this particular area... Mind you, I cannot agree that God's promises for the future are a secondary matter." [2]

As we shall find later, there are some areas in which I cannot agree with David Pawson, but I believe that these words are eminently sensible, both in the sense that bitterness should be avoided and that fear of controversy is no excuse for failing to address the more 'difficult' passages of Scripture. The blessing promised by the Lord for keeping the words of prophecy of Revelation (1:3 and 22:7) are not to be gained by sticking to a milk diet any more than they are to be by cramming with head knowledge.

Those writers whom we will be able to treat with the greatest respect and to whom our hearts are most likely to warm are those who, whether we agree with them in every detail or not:

- Love the Lord

- Love His coming again

- Love His ancient people, Israel

At one time the schools divided more or less along denominational lines; but these have long since become blurred. Nowadays we may find a love of the Lord's return and a recognition of Israel in the most unlikely places, and a complete absence of them where would most expect to encounter them.

The question of whether Israel has a future in God's plans is a straightforward 'either/or' one, as is, for instance, the question of whether the Rapture is a separate event from the Lord's return in power. Admittedly there are complex issues closely related, but this does not stop us from safely concluding that logically only one of either pair of options can be correct; the other must be wrong. Thus we believe that we have been reasonable in contending that, by demonstrating that God has future purposes for Israel, Replacement Theology, as it is generally understood, must inevitably be false. However, as we said earlier, it is not sufficient to prove one's own case merely by disproving somebody else's.

So we will look at both 'hard-line' and 'soft-line' books of the major schools, doing our best to get a fair representation of their teaching, particularly regarding Israel. Again we will try to ensure that both sides of the Atlantic are represented. Some authors seem to go out of their way to avoid giving themselves labels, although they may be liberal enough in their labelling of others. The result is that they tend to be ignored by those critical reviewers who prefer the easy option of dealing with extreme cases. We will try to compensate for this.

Replacement Theology Sources

There are certain elements which are common to virtually all Replacement Theologians. This is reflected by a number of what we might call shared 'proof texts', which they believe support their cases. It would be grossly unfair to deny that there are texts which, taken in isolation or along with a few others, do give some sort of case for Replacement Theology, especially the denial of Millennial kingdom aspects. These must be considered carefully.

Rather than repeating ourselves too often, we will select a few of the most significant of these and tackle them in our next chapter. Thereafter we will need simply to refer back to them. However, more often one actually finds that the proof texts are in fact used more to *dis*prove what others believe than to prove anything. They are used as ammunition rather than building bricks.

Some proof texts really deserve chapters to themselves; we cannot afford this, but will try to allocate space according to the amount of usage they receive from the different schools, and how critical their correct understanding is to our cause. What we should be prepared to take note of is the overlapping use, among different schools of interpretation, of the very few texts which are employed to disprove Israel's future. It is strange that some of these are mutually exclusive schools. This is curious and should be investigated. Some seem to be clutched like drowning men holding on to straws.

I am not pre-empting my findings, but simply commenting on something which has struck me in my initial research into the apparent Israelite implications of these proof texts. I have encountered most of them before whilst arguing for the Pre-Tribulationist stand. Indeed, some I dealt with a number of years ago whilst writing for *Your Tomorrow*. I will be quoting from these articles later and will give references as appropriate.

One of our biggest difficulties in validating prophetic schools vis-à-vis Israelology is that some writers are open and vigorous in their assertion that Israel has had no future in God's plans since New Testament times, and go to some lengths to support their views by logical argument. These are easy to come to terms with. But others simply assume this to be the case and make comparatively few comments, apparently taking the permanent rejection of Israel as an uncontroversial foregone conclusion. Perhaps denominational backgrounds have something to do with this. Some Christians just do not seem to realise that there is a debate, and regard the evangelisation of Jews in the same way as they would regard any other missionary enterprise.

Understanding 'King' And 'Kingdom'

Included among the texts which we will be looking at in Chapter Eight will be three in which the term 'kingdom' occurs—three texts which are frequently used to deny any future Millennial kingdom for Israel. Consequently they are employed to deny the literal fulfilment of numerous precious prophecies. We will deal briefly now in strategic terms with the concepts of king and kingdom, and in subsequent chapters look at the inappropriate applications and interpretations of these texts made by certain schools of prophecy.

Woolly thinking about the Scriptural use of the words abounds. Expressions such as 'extending the kingdom' are generally regarded as being positive, but do not necessarily convey the same meaning to every believer. Hymn writers use the terms ad lib. The more modern the hymns, the less likely we are to find them being used appropriately. However antiquity is no guarantee of accuracy, nor modernity a denial of accuracy. Some modern compilers are casual or even ignorant; but a few still take care.

If we search the Scriptures for passages containing either word, we find a wide variety of applications; some contrast with one another, but never clash. All will be equally valid in context. We will find, for instance, that the term 'king' is applied both to the Triune God, as the eternal Creator, Ruler and Sustainer, and to the Lord Jesus Christ personally; but it is a different kind of kingship. He has set strict time limits, and graciously shared the main features of His restoration programme with those who care to examine it.

Although the earth is still in rebellion against its Creator, His rule is absolute. His permissive will can and does impose sanctions upon man's activities, *"In order that the living may know that the Most High reigns in the kingdom of men…"* (Dan 4:18).

Jesus Christ has kingly roles because He is *"the Word who became flesh and dwelt among us"* (Jn 1:14), and because He was *"born of a woman, born under the law, to redeem those who were under the law"* (Gal 4:4–5). Thus, for instance, the promise which we have already noted (II Sam 7:12–16; Ps 89:27–29 and Lk 1:32–33), that Christ should sit on David's throne is to be fulfilled in the Man Christ Jesus, not in God the Father. Moreover it will be upon earth, not in heaven.

This helps us to understand the parable which Jesus told concerning Himself, as the nobleman who went into a far country to receive a kingdom (Lk 19:12 et seq.). He was clearly to receive this kingship from His Father; but His Father did not have to abdicate His own kingship in order to do this. The realms and roles contrast sharply with one another. In Dan 7:13 we read of the Father, as the enthroned Ancient of Days.

> *"And behold, One like the Son of Man, coming with the clouds of heaven! He came to the Ancient of Days, and they brought Him near before Him. Then to Him was given dominion and glory and a kingdom, that all peoples, nations and languages should serve Him. His dominion is*

> *an everlasting kingdom, which shall not pass away, and His kingdom the one which shall not be destroyed" (Dan 7:13–15).*

By no stretch of the imagination can we say that this vision has been completely fulfilled.

There is no conflict between the everlasting kingdom and the limited duration of the Millennium; for it is at the *end* of the Millennium that the very last enemies will be destroyed (Rev 20:9–10). Then He will hand over to the Father that kingdom which has flourished upon the earth—an earth which is now reserved, and will then be ready, for destruction by fire (I Cor 15:25–28 and II Pet 3:7). Christ's kingdom will outlast all. We find much of this in Isaiah 65, but have to wait until Revelation 20 to learn of the break between the temporal and eternal states; this is progressive revelation.

Before He ascended into that 'far country', He, who had come to Jerusalem with the rightful title of King of Israel (Jn 12:13; also Jn 1:49, Mk 15:32), was crucified under the man-given superscription of King of the Jews. When He returns, inscribed upon Him will be the title, *"King of Kings and Lord of Lords"* (Rev 19:16) *"and the Lord shall be King over all the earth"* (Zech 14:9). His earthly capital will be Jerusalem, where He once triumphed over sin; now He will triumph over His enemies (Ps 1:6). This will be a new situation, as prophesied by Daniel:

> *"And in the days of those kings the God of heaven will set up a kingdom which shall never be destroyed; and the kingdom shall not be left to other people; it shall break in pieces and consume all these kingdoms, and it shall stand for ever"* (Dan 2:44).

As one reads in subsequent chapters of Daniel of further details of those earthly kingdoms, it becomes ever clearer that this verse cannot possibly refer, as some would claim, to the Church. It is yet future, when Christ will be both King of Israel and King of the Earth.

In Matthew 10 we read of Jesus sending out His apostles exclusively to *"the lost sheep of the house of Israel"* (v 6) with the Gospel of the Kingdom. They were to seek out 'the worthy'(v 13); contrast this with the later Gospel of Grace, which is for the unworthy. As Kelly writes:

172

"They were to declare the kingdom of heaven. 'As ye go' said our Lord, 'preach saying, The kingdom of heaven is at hand' (v 7). But the great characteristic feature of the mission was the conferring upon them power against demons and diseases. The appropriateness of this, in connection with Israel, is manifest. It was bright evidence that the true King, Jehovah, was there, who was able Himself not only to cast out demons, but to confer that power upon His servants." [5]

Jesus went on to give them a preliminary warning that, as the rightful King's representatives, they might anticipate rejection (v14). Later, after His own initial rejection was evident, He was much more specific about His impending crucifixion (Matt 17:22). Jesus was beginning to fulfil Ezekiel's detailed prophecy (chapter 34) about the needy sheep of the house of Israel, neglected by their spiritual leaders. There are in that chapter unconditional divine promises of ultimate salvation following the travail, which Replacement Theologians would dare to repudiate.

> *"'And they shall no longer be a prey for the nations... nor bear the shame of the Gentiles any more... They shall know that I the Lord their God am with them, and that they, the house of Israel, are My people,' says the Lord God"* (Ezek 34:28–30).

When we consider Jesus' strict injunction about the Gospel of the Kingdom and the house of Israel, it is outrageous to claim that the predominantly Gentile Church is Israel.

Many misconceptions stem from a lack of overview of the kingdom teaching, and of viewing the kingdom parables simplistically and out of context. We will be hopelessly at sea if we fail to recognise the Bible's own succinct summary, that *"He came to His own and His own did not receive Him"* (Jn 1:11). In other words, during His earthly ministry He presented Himself to His own people as the coming King, and was rejected by them. Failure to note the differences in Jesus' ministry, after the accusation by the representative Jewish leaders, the Pharisees, of His power being Satanic (Matt 12), leads us to embrace an anachronistic kingdom programme.

To quote Dr Ryrie:

> "The story of the King is a story of loneliness. First He was received and acclaimed; He proved Himself in every way; His teaching was recognised; but now the repudiation climaxes in the rejection. This clearly is the Christology of the theology of the synoptics." [6]

Dr Walvoord puts very succinctly into perspective the relationship of the kingdom to Jesus' rejection:

> "With this background of rejection, Jesus recognised that the kingdom He was offering would not be fulfilled soon, but would come about at His second coming. This is the theme of Matthew 13. There has been much resistance to the idea that the kingdom was postponed. It must be understood that what is postponed from a human standpoint is not postponed from the divine standpoint. With God, all contingencies and seeming changes of direction are known from eternity past, and there is no change in God's central purpose... On the divine side this was no change of plan, but on the human side it was a change of direction regarding fulfilment of the kingdom promise... The Israelites' widespread unbelief at this point in the life of Christ changed His message from one of offering the kingdom to one of contemplating what would result in view of Israel's rejection of Him. In keeping with this, Matthew 13 reveals the general character of the present age between the first and second comings of Christ. This is done by revealing aspects of the mystery of the kingdom." [7]

Note particularly that, in the first line of the above quote, Walvoord said, "Jesus recognised"; he did *not* say, "Jesus realised". Those who attempt to discredit Dispensationalism seem to be unable to grasp the difference between these two concepts. This is no trivial matter of semantics; it is a fundamental difference in understanding God's divine plan. The first allows for the fact that Christ knowingly and willingly came to die for our sins (Gal 4:4,5). The second implies that His rejection came as a complete surprise or even shock to Him. We want to be associated with no part of that latter idea, which, if one follows its logic, is heretical, denying the omniscience and very divinity of the Second Person of the Godhead.

The kingdom in the Church Age is in mystery. This is basic but very important teaching. The kingdom parables, such as the Sower, the Wheat and Tares and the Pearl Merchant, will be familiar to all Christians. Dispensationalists fully recognise their significance; but we simply do not believe them to be the full sum and substance of kingdom teaching; they concern only the present interim state. Their temporary nature, culminating in the end of this age, becomes apparent as we read the parables. Vine in his Dictionary writes:

> "The 'kingdom' is said to be in 'mystery now, Mark 4:11, that is, it does not come within the range of the natural powers of observation, Luke 17:20, but is spiritually discerned, John 3:3 (cf. I Cor 2:14). When, hereafter, God asserts His rule universally, then the 'kingdom' will be in glory, that is it will be manifest to all; cf. Matt 25:31–34; Phil 2:9–11, II Tim 4:1, 18."[8]

In the epistles the term 'king', except when it applies to secular monarchs, occurs only twice (I Tim 1:17 and 6:15). The term 'kingdom' occurs eighteen times, but is sometimes used in negative terms of exclusion, sometimes in futuristic and sometimes in eternal terms. On eight of these occasions it occurs within the expression, 'the kingdom of God'. Rather than being used of the Church, the term 'kingdom of God' is used, to quote Unger's Dictionary, "as embracing all created intelligences both in heaven and on earth who are willingly subject to God and thus in fellowship with Him."[9] This, of course, includes the Church. But Christ's relationship to the Church is principally that of 'Lord'. In due course it will be that of Bridegroom; at present we are at the espousal stage. This does not mean that we recognise His kingship any less than Esther did her husband's kingship after Ahasuerus had held out his sceptre to her (Est 5:2). But it does mean that the relationship is just that much closer and more precious than that of King and subjects. Far too many churches seem unaware of this.

Before leaving this topic, we must stress that, ever since His ascension, Jesus has been and still is our Kingly High Priest after the order of

Melchizedek, as declared in Ps 110:4 and enlarged upon in Hebrews 6 and 7. But that is a heavenly role, and is therefore not in dispute.

> *"This hope we have as an anchor of the soul, both sure and steadfast, and which enters the Presence behind the veil, where the forerunner has entered for us, even Jesus, having become High Priest forever according to the order of Melchizedek"* (Heb 6:19, 20).

We will summarise this short interlude into kingdom doctrine with Dr Pentecost's words:

> "First we have seen that in order to understand the biblical concept of *kingdom,* we must recognise that it involves several ideas, including the *right* to rule, a *realm* in which ruling authority is exercised, and the *reality* of that authority actually being exercised. In laying the foundation for clearing up misconceptions concerning God's kingdom, we have understood that the Bible presents truth concerning two aspects of the kingdom of God; the *eternal* aspect as well as the *temporal* aspect. And finally, the kingdom is characterised by four essential truths:
>
> 1. It is timeless,
> 2. It is universal,
> 3. It is providential,
> 4. It is miraculous." [10]

There are both simple and complex aspects of these matters. Any further comment on kingship can wait until we encounter the so-called 'proof texts'.

We have taken time in this chapter to give a brief overview of the various aspects of the King and Kingdom, as a precursor to our further studies, as herein lies one of the major sources of contention. The other major source is, of course, the issue of whether Israel has been replaced by the Church. As this question dominates our study from start to finish, no further comment is required at this point. We are now in a position to launch straight into our proof texts.

Chapter Eight

Some Proof Texts Of Replacement Theology

"My Kingdom Is Not Of This World"

These are the opening words of Jn 18:36. They were spoken by Jesus at His trial before Pilate. They are frequently used and, out of context, seem to make a good case for some of the main tenets of Post- and Amillennialism; particularly the latter. Actually Pre-Millennialists have no problems at all with this statement of Jesus, but some seem to assume they have!

We will have to investigate a few matters, such as:

- What were the circumstances in which these words were uttered?
- What is the immediate context?
- What do they really mean?
- Is the verb tense significant?

The situation is well known. Jesus was on trial before Pontius Pilate for His life, having been referred by the High Priest, who had no power of capital punishment. Pilate was completely out of his depth, with very little understanding of the underlying circumstances or their accusations. Caiaphas, the High Priest thought he had, but as a Sadducee, a 'liberal' compared with the Pharisees, his spiritual insight was shallow. His power base depended upon intrigue. To Pilate this was an awkward and embarrassing trial which he could well have avoided, but, for reasons of political expediency, was forced to conduct.

We read:

> *"Then Pilate entered the Praetorium again, called Jesus and said to Him, 'Are you the King of the Jews?' Jesus answered him, 'Are you speaking for yourself on this, or did others tell you this about Me?' Pilate answered, 'Am I a Jew? Your own nation and the chief priests have delivered You to me.*

177

> *What have You done?' Jesus answered, **'My kingdom is not of this world.** If My kingdom were of this world, My servants would fight, so that I should not be delivered to the Jews; but now My kingdom is not from here.' Pilate therefore said to Him, 'Are You a king then?' Jesus answered, 'You say rightly that I am a king. For this cause I was born, and for this cause I have come into the world, that I should bear witness of the truth. Everyone who is of the truth hears My voice.' Pilate said to Him, 'What is truth?'"* (Jn 18:33–38).

Now we do not propose to look at this passage in its entirety, but several things are relevant to the interpretation of that short statement, *"My kingdom is not of this world"*. Jesus did not in fact answer Pilate's question as to whether He was King of the Jews. We have earlier noted that this was not one of His titles, or certainly not a full title. Moreover we should observe that this is not His full answer to the next question, *"What have You done?"* It was the first part of a three part answer to the question which Pilate *ought* to have asked; all three parts are equally relevant. However let us focus briefly on the first statement.

Well, the words are simple enough; there is no great linguistic conundrum to be tackled. The translation, "My Kingdom is not of this world" is the most common one, occurring in the AV, Darby, NIV, NKJV etc. The RSV renders it, "My kingship is not of this world" and the NEB, "My kingdom does not belong to this world". All are reasonable enough if one wishes to avoid clumsiness. But that "of" is not, as one might suspect, from a genitive case with "this world", but actually translates the exceedingly flexible preposition *'ek'*. Young's Concordance lists it as being translated in the AV, 400 times as 'of', 182 times as 'from' and '131' times as 'out of'; all other uses pale into insignificance.[1] The sense of origin or belonging is indisputably there in normal usage; so in this case it includes a sense of not belonging to this world. A word-for-word translation of the Greek would be, "The mine the kingdom is not out of the this world".[2]

What the statement does *not* say is "My kingdom is not *in* this world". What some people apparently want it to say is: "My kingdom is not of this world and never will be in this world". But Jesus did not say that either. What we particularly object to is the common implication that this statement proves that Jesus Christ can never have a kingdom on this earth. We will have more to say about the nature of such a kingdom on earth when dealing with another 'proof text'. In the previous chapter we looked at the various different kingly titles which God and Jesus Christ hold. Too few Christians recognise the multiplicity of these.

Walter Chantry, who fiercely asserts his Amillennialism and Replacement Theology, and whom we are due to meet again later, writes:

> "Our Lord completely disavowed any identification with the world's methods. 'My kingdom is *not of this world*: if my kingdom were of this world, then would my servants fight...' (John 18:38). His servants do not launch clever political manoeuvres against earthly institutions, nor set up their own counterparts. His kingdom is no threat to the legitimate claims of even earthly rulers. Its members 'render unto Caesar the things that are Caesar's and unto God the things that are God's' (Matt 22:21). They work peacefully within the existing system." [3]

Now this is what one might expect of somebody who makes very little reference indeed to the Old Testament prophets and to God's promises through them. He is utterly absorbed in the truths concerning the 'kingdom in mystery' and is blinkered regarding anything else. Of course his remarks in the paragraph we have quoted are relevant to the 'kingdom in mystery' during the Church Age, but he is so scathing about Dispensationalism in his book quoted here, that He cannot perceive that there have been and will be times in which Christ has exercised and will exercise His Kingship in a very different manner.

Consider the following texts, some of which we have already referred to:

> *"The Lord has said to Me, 'You are My Son, today I have begotten You.'"*

The reference here is to what was then the future Incarnation.

> *"Ask of Me, and I will give You the nations for Your inheritance, and the ends of the earth for Your possession. You shall break them with a rod of iron; You shall dash them in pieces like a potter's vessel.'"* (Ps 2:7–9).

"It shall break in pieces and consume all these kingdom, and shall stand forever." (Dan 2:44).

Such divine interventions in the rule of men hardly match Chantry's term 'political manoeuvring'; yet they foretell direct action by the Judge of the world, whose actions are always righteous.

Lest any are still naïve enough to believe that this conquest will be achieved through missionary endeavour, however fine and appropriate that is in its place, consider:

"Behold, the Lord comes with ten thousands of His saints, to execute judgement on all...' (Jude 1:14–15),

or:

"The armies in heaven... followed Him on white horses. Now out of His mouth goes a sharp sword, that with it He should strike the nations. And He Himself will rule them with a rod of iron. He Himself treads out the winepress of the fierceness and wrath of Almighty God." (Rev 19:15).

The Revelation passage continues in the same vein. People cannot even hide behind the Old Testament excuse; these are all in the New. These clear unconditional prophecies make Chantry's statement about what God's servants can or cannot do quite ridiculous; what is worse is that he makes it appear that God's foreknowledge is faulty. Has Chantry, who would describe himself as a fundamentalist, considered that?

Let us bear in mind that the One who will rule with the rod of iron is the same One, who, as He stood awaiting the sentence of crucifixion, told Pilate that His kingdom was not of this world. Is it really all that difficult to reconcile these different forms and timings of Christ's kingship? So preoccupied is Walter Chantry with the single mystery aspect of Christ's kingdom, that we find Him writing:

"Third among the spiritual goods of the kingdom of God is *truth*. In his fateful interview with Pilate (John 18:33–38) our Lord plainly declared himself to be a king. Yet he avowed that his kingdom is not of this world. What our Saviour contrasted with this world was truth." [4]

He links this with v 37. Is this as much as we can expect of the hitherto unfulfilled glorious Messianic prophecies for Israel and the world? We do not in any way deny the truth aspect, but believe fervently that all the old kingdom promises are still to be honoured in the terms in which they were made; and most of these terms are physical as well as spiritual. Truth can be associated with Jesus Christ in any of His many roles.

William Cox, a well-known Amillennialist whom we will be meeting again in the next two chapters, is unable to grasp the appropriateness of different types of kingship in different times and circumstances. He writes:

"The non-believing Jews expected their Messiah to appear and set up a kingdom. And this belief was based on the Scriptures. Their hyperliteral interpretation of the Old Testament blinded their eyes to the genuine kingdom and kept them from recognising the real king. The Messiah did come into the world, and he did establish his kingdom; or, rather he manifested a new phase of the on-going eternal kingdom of God. The Jews expected a warrior-type Messiah who would inflict vengeance on their enemies and place Jews in chosen places of leadership. To their dismay Jesus did not come into Jerusalem on a white charger, but rather he entered the city on a lowly donkey... And while his kingdom was a disappointment to hyperliteral interpreters of the Old Testament, it was indeed the fulfilment of the kingdom predicted therein."[5]

What a travesty of a mixture of truth and error! Cox persistently uses the term *hyperliteral,* usually patronisingly. He applies it to everything in the Bible which has a perfectly simple meaning, but which inconveniently does not fit his own eschatological scheme of things. His frequency of use of this term reflects the vast number of Old Testament passages and Revelation which he stubbornly refuses to accept at face value. The implications for the veracity of Christ's own revelation of His coming in power (Rev 19) are appalling. These Jewish expectations summarised by Cox are not, in fact, far off the mark—they are wrong only in timing and in their own personal ambitions. Incongruously Cox is prepared to recognise the Zech 9:9 prophecy of Christ coming in humility on a donkey, but not the Rev 19:11 one of Him returning on a white war-horse. What bankrupt standards of interpretation!

Jn 18:36 is in the present tense and is primarily concerned with what was happening then and there. It is crucial to understand this. A number of years ago in a Pre-Millennial journal I wrote:

> "Those who use this verse in Jn 18 to discount the Lord's millennial reign should ponder hard and long over two other verses, *viz*, Jn 12:47 and Acts 17:31. In the one Jesus said, 'I did not come to judge the world but to save it;' in the other Paul states that 'God hath appointed a day in which He will judge the world in righteousness by that Man...', going on to demonstrate that this Man is the risen Saviour. Is there conflict here, one correct and one false? God forbid! It is simply a matter of timing and occasion. One refers to the time when Jesus came expressly to suffer and die; the other refers to His coming to judge and to reign. So it is here. Just as He did not come to judge the world then, but will do in the future, so He did not come to reign then, but He most certainly will do some day." [6]

There are many other contrasts between the Lord's actions at His first and at His second coming. Surely it is not difficult to see that the differences do not add up to inconsistency, but to the appropriateness of the different occasions. The closing statement of Jn 18:36 is, *"But now is My kingdom not from here"*. 'Now' is translated by *nun,* the standard Greek adverb for 'at this point in time' or 'at this present time'. Pilate probably got the message that Jesus was talking about that present time. So should we. But we should also have no difficulty in understanding, or in accepting, that one day He will impose His rule upon the long rebellious earth.

> *"He shall have dominion also from sea to sea, and from the River to the ends of the earth"* (Ps 72:8).

Neither the new heaven nor the new earth will have any sea (Rev 21:1). The Psalmist can only be talking about this earth, which does have.

We have used only a tiny proportion of the texts and arguments we could muster. However we must move on; let us close this section with a quote from William Blackstone:

> "It is objected that Jesus said: 'My kingdom is not of this world' (John 18:36). True! Not of the spirit of the world (I John 2:15–17), just as believers are not of the world (John 15:19)... Both Christ and His kingdom are from above. But it will be set up on this earth, in accordance with the prayer He taught us: 'Thy kingdom come. Thy will be done, as in heaven, so in earth' (Luke 11:12)... Earthly kingdoms are corrupted by the deception of Satan. But in the millennial kingdom he will not deceive them, for he will be bound." [7]

"The Kingdom Of God Is Within You"

This is the rather unfortunate AV and NKJV rendering of Jesus' words recorded in Lk 17:21. The NKJV translators were reluctant to change more than necessary the AV (KJV), and the translation itself is technically acceptable. One can understand an exclusively non-literal understanding of the kingdom being taken from this rendering. However, if we point out at the outset that Jesus was talking in the present tense, as He was in Jn 18:36, we need not elaborate on the fact that Jesus was not talking about a permanent situation, but rather about the situation which prevailed during His earthly ministry.

The context reads:

> *"Now when He was asked by the Pharisees when the kingdom of God would come, He answered them and said, 'The kingdom of God does not come with observation; nor will they say, "See here!" or "See there!" For indeed the kingdom of God is within you.'"*

The main problem is with the variety of legitimate uses of the preposition, *'entos'*, translated as 'within' (AV, RV and NKJV), 'among' (NEB), 'in the midst of' (Darby and RSV) and 'in your midst' (Moffat and NASV). Marginal references in the AV and RV give 'in the midst' as alternatives. 'Within' is not in itself an incorrect rendering; but it is inappropriate to the context. We are not quibbling over irrelevancies.

This problem with the translation of prepositions must not be thought to be peculiar to Greek-to-English; it occurs between modern languages too, as I well know, having in my day been a teacher of Russian. The whole sense, as lawyers know only too well, often depends upon the correct rendering of the humble preposition.

All are legitimate renderings of the preposition in general. Before determining which is best here, we might consider Jesus' audience and ask ourselves which could reasonably apply in this particular situation. Are there any common renderings which are linguistically admissible but spiritually unacceptable? To whom was Jesus speaking? Well, there is no question of doubt; He was addressing the Pharisees. Was the kingdom within *them*? It was to one of the best of the Pharisees, a secret enquirer, that Jesus said: *"Except a man be born again, he cannot see the kingdom of God"* (Jn 3:3). Were the majority of the Pharisees born again? Surely not, for it was to Pharisees that Jesus said, *"You are of your father the devil"* (Jn 8:44)—severe words indeed. So the AV translation *"within"* can hardly apply here, especially as there are better alternatives.

Dr Scofield comments on this verse,

> "It could not be said of a self-righteous, Christ-rejecting Pharisee, that the kingdom of God, as to its spiritual content was within him. Our Lord's whole answer, designedly enigmatic to the Pharisees (cf. Matt 13:10–13), has a dispensational meaning. The kingdom in its outward form, as covenanted to David (II Sam 7:8–17) and described by the prophets had been rejected by the Jews; so that, during this present age, it would 'not come with observation' (literally outward show) but in the hearts of men (Lk 19:11–12; Acts 1:6–8; Rom 14:17). Meantime the kingdom was actually 'in the midst' of the Pharisees in the persons of the King and His disciples. Ultimately the kingdom of heaven *will* come with outward show. (See v 24).[8]

Dr Rice adds in his comment on this Luke passage:

> "Eventually Christ will come openly, publicly at His return to reign with all the saints and angels, but at present, and

until then, the kingdom grows as people are converted, and the kingdom is not with outward observation." [9]

There is no hint of lack of outward observation in the kingdom promised to the Jews at some future date. As usual, we are spoiled for choice by the number of scriptures available. We will take snippets from just a few to demonstrate a highly observable future kingdom specifically for Israel, but also for the world as a whole. Should any doubts linger, the passages should be read in full:

"Why do the nations rage...? The kings of the earth set themselves, and the rulers take counsel together against the Lord and against His Anointed... I will give You the nations for Your inheritance, and the ends of the earth for Your possession. You shall break them with a rod of iron" (Ps 2:1, 2, 8–10).

We have quoted before from this remarkable psalm, where we have all the authority of God the Father addressing God the Son (see v7).

"Out of you (Bethlehem) shall come a Ruler who will shepherd My people Israel" (Matt 2:6 quoting Mic 5:2).

This fulfils some of the great Shepherd of Israel prophecies of Ezekiel 34:

"Indeed, I Myself will search for My sheep and seek them out" (v11).

At His first coming He practised only His Shepherd role (Matt 9:36; 10:6),

"the Good Shepherd who gives His life for the sheep" (Jn 10:11).

When He comes again He will also exercise His Ruler role.

Blackstone, writing about this passage, says:

The sense then is as follows: The kingdom of God does not come with 'careful watching'; that is, not in such a way as to be concerned only by sagacious critics. Neither is it to be seen only by those who are scrupulously watching for it. They will not say 'Look here or there' for the kingdom of God is among you; that is, it was then visibly present among them in the person of Jesus the King. And so it will be visibly present when He comes again." [10]

Those who so misunderstand or misrepresent Lk 17:21 should skip a couple of verses and read v24:

"For as the lightning that flashes out of one part under heaven shines to the other part under heaven, so the Son of Man will be in His day. But first He must suffer many things and be rejected by this generation" (vv. 24–24).

Is it *really* so difficult to comprehend these two contrasting, but equally valid, conditions of the kingdom?

We also find promises of the returning Lord in *the midst* in a Messianic kingdom unmistakably set upon earth.

"At that time Jerusalem shall be called The Throne of the Lord, and all nations shall be gathered to it" (Jer 3:17).

"The name of the city from that day shall be: THE LORD IS THERE", or Jehovah Shammah (Ezek 48:35).

"O daughter of Jerusalem! The Lord has taken away your judgements, He has cast out your enemy. The King of Israel, the Lord, is in your midst; you shall see disaster no more" (Zeph 3:14–15).

The whole passage is about a future restoration following God's indignation upon the nations.

"Thus says the Lord: 'I will return to Zion, and dwell in the midst of Jerusalem'" (Zech 8:3).

The passage goes on to describe in detail mortal family life in Jerusalem.

By no stretch of the imagination are these pictures of heaven. Denying the fulfilment of these promises would not only be a punishment for Israel; it would be a denial by God the Father of promises made to God the Son—denial of His future recognition and acclamation in the city, land and world which once rejected Him. Would Replacement Theologians really be party to *this*? Apparently most would. We are not, of course, suggesting that the unsaved dead will return to earth to acknowledge Him. That is clear from Rev 20:5; their turn to bow to Him will be later—disastrously later. But all the living will worship Him.

It should be observed that most of the above quoted passages refer to or at least include on-going situations—life in the Millennial Kingdom. Certainly some, such as Psalm 2, start with summary, retributive judgement, equating with the Judgement of the Nations or Sheep and Goats. However we have already noted that that judgement will result in the 'goats' being consigned to Hades for a thousand years to await the Great White Throne and awful Second Death (Rev 20:5, 11). But the 'sheep' who are invited to inherit the kingdom, and especially their yet-to-be-born descendents, will require to be judged in the same way as Israel was judged before Saul's time, by God-appointed judges, such as Gideon, Samson and Samuel. Unlike in those days, it will be totally beneficent; but it will also be strictly righteous and inflexible—not because of autocracy but because of theocracy. Christ will delegate to the resurrected David and the apostles special responsibility for Israel, whilst the faithful of the Church will have responsibility over the nations, *"If we endure we shall also reign with Him"* (II Tim 2:12).

The Hebrew verb for to judge is *sapat*. But it also means to deliver or to rule as well as to sentence or adjudicate. *Vine's Expository Dictionary* says,

> "Sapat can be used not only of an act of deliverance, but of a process whereby order and law are maintained within a group." [11]

One well known theologian who seems unable to grasp this range of meanings is Professor Berkhof, who makes the extraordinary statement:

> "The Bible speaks of 'the day of judgement' but this does not mean that it will be a day of twenty-four hours, Neither is there any ground to assert with Pre-millenarians that it will be a day of a thousand years." [12]

This is a flagrant distortion of Pre-Millennialism. Berkhof must surely have been aware that when we believe that Christ will reign as King, judging the nations with equity for a thousand years, we are referring to the duration of His ruling, rather than to the duration of His sentencing. We do *not* claim that the Judgement of the Nations (Matt 25:25–46) will last a thousand years, which is the natural conclusion of Berkhof's statement. On the contrary, we would assert, because of His invitation to the 'sheep' to possess the kingdom (v34), that this will be concluded at the start of the Millennium. We will return to Dr Berkhof's views on the Millennium in Chapter 10.

Pre-Millennialists are frequently misrepresented as asserting that the Millennial kingdom will be righteous throughout, with no sin present during the thousand years. Perhaps some of us have been careless at times in implying this, because many of us do, with some justification, refer to it as earth's Golden Age. Jay Adams, another well-known Amillennialist, but one who is much less prone to distorting what others believe than is Cox, whom we quoted above, writes:

> "The hope of a perfect, post-judgement 'new earth wherein dwelleth righteousness' is quite different from the expectation of an imperfect semi-golden age in which sin remains. A time of hypocritical (or at best, unwilling) conformity, where sin is barely restrained by an iron-fisted rule of force... The New Testament knows absolutely nothing of *imperfect* golden-age preaching."[13]

Well, firstly let us point out that the absence of any such teaching in the New Testament is no impediment. We would scarcely expect to find it taught there with the frequency it enjoys in the Old Testament, as it hardly concerns the present Church Age. However Adams is right in saying that Pre-Millennialists, or certainly most of them, do not claim that absolute perfection and righteousness will be willingly achieved upon earth during the Millennium; such a state must wait for the new heavens and earth. The resurrected saints will be holy and will not beget children (Matt 22:30). The 'sheep' who will enter the Millennium will be redeemed. But those who will be born to them will be in a world where Satan is bound safely out of harm's way (Rev 20:2, 7). Sin will be the exception, rather than the rule. However individuals will still have the personal ability to rebel, in the way that Satan himself once rebelled without any external tempting agency (Isa 14:13; Ezek 28:15). At the end of the Millennium, in an event about which we will have more to say later, Satan will be released briefly (Rev 20:7–10), in order to provide an opportunity for testing and decision making.

We share with Adams the expectation of "*a new earth wherein dwelleth righteousness*". Unlike Adams we also have expectations of a prior restored earth where Christ will rule with a rod of iron. And this *is* foretold in the New Testament (Rev 19:5). In Chapter Eleven we will see such an expectation of a golden age with Post-Millennialists, but then it will be upon earth and before Christ's return.

The compulsion to worship after the Lord's return is graphically described in Zech 14:16–19. How can anybody possibly claim that this has already been fulfilled or, alternatively, that it is figurative? Either approach breaks the rules of interpreting Scripture. God has declared it, and it must happen some day.

As we have previously observed, Isaiah 65 does not show the break between the end of this old earth and the creation of the new one. That was not revealed until the close of Revelation when God gave His final written programme for the Church to treasure. However we read the statement,

> "*No more shall an infant from there live but a few days, nor an old man who has not fulfilled his days; for the child shall die one hundred years old, but the sinner being one hundred years old shall be accursed... For as the days of a tree, so shall be the days of My people...*" (Isa 65:20, 22)

The passage should be read in full. God says it is to happen. It certainly did not happen in post-exilic Judah, nor has it happened within the Church Age. It *must* therefore be future. Only Pre-Millennialism makes allowance for it and explains how sin can be found on earth after the Judgement of the Nations, which some would naively call the last judgement. Finally, we must mention the prediction, referred to in an earlier chapter, of the Gog and Magog rebellion at the end of 1000 years, described in the plainest of plain language (Rev 20:7–9). And that also most certainly is in the New Testament, Dr Adams!

Were absolute perfection to be achieved upon earth, where would be the need for the apostles and saints to reign with Christ? David Pawson, who, incidentally, is a Pre-Millennialist but not a Dispensationalist, writes perceptively:

"Certainly there is no unequivocal statement about the millennium elsewhere in the New Testament. But there are a number of indirect references, perhaps all the more impressive because they are incidental. There are, of course, some clear promises in the rest of the book of Revelation. 'Overcomers' will rule the nations' (2:26–27). The redeemed will 'reign on the earth' (5:10). The 'kingdom of the world' will become the 'kingdom of Christ' (11:15). Chapter 20 is clearly the fulfilment of these predictions. When we turn to Paul's letters we find a number of hints. Perhaps the clearest is in his first letter to Corinth. Upbraiding the Corinthian believers for suing each other in pagan courts, he says: 'Do you not know that the saints will judge the world, are you not competent to judge trivial cases?' (I Cor 6:3). This cannot refer to the final judgement, which is in the hands of the Lord alone. It points to a day when Christians will be responsible for the administration of justice."[14]

If some Christians have difficulty in fitting all these God-revealed details into their own prophetic timetables, without resorting to endless explaining away of all that is difficult, should they not reconsider the programmes of those believers who have no need for such ploys?

"Flesh And Blood Cannot Inherit The Kingdom Of God"

We read in I Cor 15:50,

"Now this I say, brethren, that flesh and blood cannot inherit the kingdom of God; nor does corruption inherit corruption".

This is an understandably popular verse with those who would deny any future Messianic kingdom on earth, with or without Israel. Clearly we must consider this apparent problem. While doing so, we will also look briefly at that oft quoted verse,

"The kingdom of God is not food and drink, but righteousness and peace and joy in the Holy Spirit" (Rom 14:17).

190

Before proceeding further, we would invite those who quote these texts to disprove the Dispensationalist Pre-Millennialist position to ask two questions. We ask them because it may be that the answer to one or the other may make their own position untenable. People sometimes fail to follow through the implications of opposing the views of others.

- Do they or do they not believe that, from the moment of their conversion, they have entered Christ's kingdom, at least in its present form, despite still being flesh and blood and requiring normal sustenance?

- Do they believe that Jesus meant to be taken literally, or merely figuratively, what He told His disciples on His betrayal night? *"I will not drink from the fruit of the vine from now on until I drink it new with you in My Father's kingdom"* (Matt 26:29). We considered this passage at some length in Chapter Four.

Paul told the Colossians:

> *"Giving thanks to the Father who has qualified us to be partakers of the inheritance of the saints in the light. He hath delivered us from the power of darkness, and translated us into the kingdom of the Son of His love, in whom we have redemption through His blood, the forgiveness of sins"* (Col 1:12–14).

We are already in His kingdom, by virtue of the redemption which we have received as believers, despite being in our mortal bodies. So why is there a problem about people in their mortal bodies living on earth during the Millennium? Any problem is in people's own minds.

The context of the 1 Cor 15 passage is the key. Kelly writes:

> "It will be observed that God's kingdom is here viewed exclusively on the other side of death, in accordance with the great theme in hand. 'Earthly things' have their place very definitely elsewhere; here, for the reason given, they are not found. Flesh and blood, man, as he is here below, cannot inherit God's kingdom. It is not merely corruption that does not inherit incorruption, being incompatible, but man in his best estate is altogether vanity. Short of

resurrection, which is the intervention of another Man, who is also God, He cannot inherit where God reigns."[15]

However even back on earth, as we have seen whilst examining our previous 'proof text', the redeemed 'sheep' do inherit the earthly kingdom after the 'goats' or 'tares' have been weeded out, in the same way as long ago Adam and Eve inherited God's newly created earth. The unrepentant Jews will at that time be removed:

"I will make you pass under the rod, and I will bring you into the bond of covenant; I will purge out the rebels from among you, and those who transgress against Me, but they shall not enter the land of Israel" (Ezek 20:37,38).

That does not describe the return from the Babylonian captivity, as the wider context confirms.

Consider that lovely 35th chapter of Isaiah.

"Then the eyes of the blind shall be opened, and the ears of the deaf shall be unstopped. Then the lame shall leap like a deer, and the tongue of the dumb sing. For waters shall break out in the wilderness, and streams in the desert..." (vv. 5, 6).

Do we believe that? It cannot be talking about heaven; this is about miraculous healing. Our incorruptible celestial bodies, which we will receive when He meets us in the air to take us to the place He has gone to prepare, will be brand new and will require no healing. There will be no former wilderness in heaven requiring transformation. The chapter closes with,

"And the ransomed of the Lord shall return, and come to Zion with singing, with everlasting joy on their heads. They shall obtain joy and gladness, and sorrow and sighing shall flee away" (v10).

This is about people, who have evidently recently been afflicted, returning—yes, returning. And one cannot return to somewhere one has never been before. These are exiles. But their physical healing and everlasting joy does not describe the return from Babylon. They cannot be returning to heaven; so they must still be on earth. They will include those who will have heeded Jesus' Olivet Discourse warning to flee when the Abomination of Desolation is set up (Matt 24:15–16), and those, if they are not one and the same, who are to be given a prepared place of refuge in the wilderness (Rev 12:6). The only people who will *return* to heaven, apart from the Lord Himself, will be the raptured saints at the end of the Millennium; and they will already be in resurrection bodies and therefore not described here. That last verse is repeated in Isa 51:11; it must be important.

We could make similar, equally convincing, comments on the 41st chapter of Isaiah, so quaintly but misleadingly headed in most AV editions, but not Scofield's, "God expostulateth with his people, about his mercies to the church". We may claim a share of these mercies as Church Age believers, but must never forget that they were emphatically, repeatedly and strikingly applied to Israel by the *"Holy One of Israel"* (v14), *"God of Israel"* (v17) and *"King of Jacob"* (v21). The scene from v14 is unprecedented, but unmistakably about earth—where men and women are creatures of flesh and blood. There are many other passages with significant elements of these and similar promises.

I quote again from one of my own articles in *Your Tomorrow*:

> "It is not seen as a problem that flesh and blood (ourselves) should currently inhabit the Kingdom in mystery, so why should it be difficult to accept that flesh and blood should populate the Millennial earth? Once the kingdom has been handed over to the Father following the final rebellion, those born and saved during the Millennium will receive their immortal bodies. The subsequent verses of 1 Cor 15 describe the marvellous change from corruption to incorruption. 'Then shall be brought to pass the saying that is written, death is swallowed up in victory'. The eternal destiny of the redeemed of all ages is incorruption. Yet we here and now have corruptible flesh and blood. We have yet to receive our inheritance. The Millennial saints will be no different *except in timescale*." [16]

The common application of the Rom 14:17 'proof text' can be largely corrected by the above comments. However it is worthwhile returning again to Blackstone to round up our case:

"Indeed it is not simply 'meat and drink', or eating and drinking, or simply outward observances. Neither was the kingdom of Israel meat and drink. Nor the Roman Empire. But the subjects of each did eat and drink, and Paul simply taught that they should do so circumspectly and with charity. So will the subjects of the kingdom of God eat and drink. 'Blessed is he that shall eat bread in the kingdom of God (Luke 14:15). 'Blessed are they which are called unto the marriage supper of the Lamb' (Rev 19:9)... Jesus himself said... 'I appoint unto you a kingdom, as my Father hath appointed unto me; that ye may eat and drink at my table in my kingdom' (Lk 22:29–30). This is the strongest proof that the kingdom will be literal and material...".[17]

We cannot begin to explain how, in the Millennium, saints will be able to eat and drink in their resurrection bodies. It is a mystery which is not revealed to us; some questions will have to await the Millennium for answers! But we have an irrefutable precedent in the Lord Jesus Christ Himself. The Holy Spirit has gone out of His way, we might say, to record that Jesus, whist in His resurrection body, ate fish, and a piece of honeycomb (Lk 24:42), but significantly did not drink wine with the eleven, as He had already imposed upon Himself a time limitation which has yet to mature, as we noted earlier. His body was not ghostly, but tangible, as His invitation in Lk 24:39 and Jn 20:27 confirms. Yet He could and did pass through walls (Jn 20:26). No doubt He could have done this had He wanted to before His death; but we learn from his reply to the devil during his wilderness temptation that spectacular stunts were inappropriate (Lk 4:11). Following His resurrection it was no stunt, but doing what came naturally.

After His resurrection and before His ascension it was different; the Gospel writers are careful to give a few further details of how a resurrection body can function on earth. Even as the multitude of the holy angels who did not follow Satan's rebellion remain sinless; so during the Millennium we will be sinless in our resurrection bodies; this is a wonderful truth, but one that really challenges our faith. In the meantime, like Paul when he wrote to the Romans, we are still subject to this *"body of death"* (7:24).

We have by no means exhausted all the evidence available to counter the negative interpretations of these texts. We will keep some in reserve pending encountering the texts again as we examine the various prophetic schools. The 'proof texts' examined so far have long been used to attack Pre-Millennialism. We have seen that in fact they in no way undermine either Israel's future or a thousand year time of Restoration. The remaining texts are commonly used in more direct attacks on Israel's future.

The Antiquity Of These Interpretations

Lest any question the antiquity of our literal stand, let us go back to one of the Church Fathers who predates Augustine, the father of Amillennialism. Dr Glasson, who is not a Pre-Millennialist, but is scholarly enough to present cases fairly, writes:

> "Iraeneus, who wrote towards the end of the second century, set forth a profound interpretation of the Christian faith in his great work *Against Heresies*. In one section of this (Book v. 32–5) he deals at length with the material kingdom on the earth which the saints are to enjoy after the first resurrection. Christ's promises about drinking new wine is to be literally fulfilled during this period; creation is to be restored to its original perfection during this period and animals will be at peace as foretold in Isaiah 11. He protests against the spiritualising of such passages as Isaiah 65 and other descriptions of material prosperity... In addition to the risen saints there will be on the earth survivors from the present age, 'those whom the Lord shall find in the flesh, awaiting Him from heaven, and who have suffered tribulation and escaped the hands of Antichrist... And Jeremiah the prophet has pointed out, that as many believers as God has prepared for this purpose, to multiply those left on the earth, should both be under the rule of the saints to minister to this Jerusalem and that His kingdom shall be in it.'" [18]

Augustine himself provides further evidence for the antiquity of the literal interpretation of prophecy, which he took upon himself to deny for his own and coming generations. He wrote the following about Chiliasm or Millennialism:

"This opinion might be allowed if it is proposed only spiritual delights unto saints during this space; but seeing the avouchers hereof affirm that the saints after this resurrection shall do nothing but revel in fleshly banquets, where the cheer shall exceed both modesty and measure, this is gross and fit for none but carnal men to believe. But they that are really and truly spiritual do call these opinionists Chiliasts; the word is Greek, and may be interpreted Millenaries or Thousand-year-ists." [19]

What striking evidence! Clearly there was abuse or deviation among some Chiliasts; but the ancient belief still existed. One should not discredit any doctrine by singling out its most immoral or worldly exponents, as Augustine has selectively done here. We say selectively, because there were many other contemporary departures from the early faith and practices which Augustine actually espoused and encouraged, as Hislop enumerates. [20]

We are not in any way claiming universal acceptance of Millennialism in the post-Apostolic Church—we would hardly expect this when we consider the deviations listed in five of the seven churches in Asia in Revelation 2 and 3—and that was at the close of the first century. J N D Kelly, a church historian who makes no claims to be a Pre-Tribulationist, writes:

"Papias looked forward with wide-eyed wonderment to the literal fulfilment in that (future) epoch of the Old Testament prophecies of unprecedented fertility of field and vineyard. Justin writes in a kindred strain of the idyllic millennium, when Jerusalem will be rebuilt and enlarged and Christians, along with the patriarchs and prophets, will dwell there with Christ in perfect felicity. He confesses that he knows pious, pure-minded Christians who do not share this belief, but like others he considers it plainly authorised by the predictions of Isaiah, Zechariah and the prophets, not to mention Revelation, and it clearly counts in his eyes as an unquestioned article of orthodoxy." [21]

"Neither Jew Nor Greek"

We can afford to be brief with the remaining 'proof texts' of Replacement Theology, inasmuch as our entire study concerns Israel's future in relation to other prophetic matters; moreover we have picked up and dealt with many of the following points elsewhere. All the following texts are from Paul's epistles to young churches where, at the time of writing, there were significant numbers and often majorities of Jewish converts, particularly at leadership level. Some of these to varying degrees were attempting to re-impose Jewish laws, rituals and traditions. The most extreme case was, of course, the group of Galatian churches, who were reverting to another gospel, one of works, which was 'anathema' (1:7–10). Paul addresses them as *"O foolish Galatians"* (3:1). If we bear this in mind, the references to Jews and Israel will be seen in perspective.

The following verses are frequently quoted by Replacement Theologians:

> *"For there is no distinction between Jew and Greek, for the same Lord over all is rich to all who call upon Him"* (Rom 10:11).

> *"There is neither Jew nor Greek, there is neither slave nor free, there is neither male nor female; for you are all one in Christ Jesus"* (Gal 3:28).

> *"According to the image of Him who created him, where there is neither Greek nor Jew, circumcised nor uncircumcised, barbarian, Scythian, slave nor free, but Christ is all in all"* (Col 3:10–11).

We have dealt with this matter several chapters back, but touch on it again among the 'proof texts'. As far as our eternal standing before God and our means and method of salvation are concerned, there is no difference whatsoever. But God most certainly recognises on earth the difference between men and women, and laid down the strictest laws, which we flout at our peril. Provision is made for relationships between slaves and masters. The spiritual significance *within* the Church of the difference between Jews and Gentiles is almost eliminated; yet Jews are stated still to have certain advantages, and therefore are still recognised as being unique (Rom 3:1–2).

The first of the above texts is from Romans 10. Reading too much into any statement in Romans chapter 9, 10 or 11, without noting its point in a definite progression is dangerous. Some Pre-Millennialists have been criticised for calling these chapters a parenthesis. They are a parenthesis only inasmuch as together they are a case study on the theme which Paul has been developing, namely the oft misunderstood doctrines of election (see Campbell Morgan below) and sovereignty of God (see Vine). Most believers are familiar with the declaration and development of these truths in that great eighth chapter of Romans.

Campbell Morgan writes in his opening remarks on Romans 10:

> "On the basis of the principle of election, Israel as a nation is rejected. The apostle now proceeded to deal with that fact in order to show its real reason. In doing so, he first of all declared the fact of their failure in terms of his own sympathy and compassion; and then proceeded to show that their way of return must be through Christ; thus coming to the definite declaration of the reason of their rejection."[22]

The obtuseness of the Replacement Theologian lies in the inability to accept the scriptural truth of Israel's return and restoration along with that other scriptural truth of their rejection. Rejection goes down well with them, but they apparently resent and deny restoration and forgiveness, rather like the prodigal son's elder brother. This rejection of the wayward but penitent Israel surely grieves our Father in heaven. Vine, concentrating on the closely related sovereignty aspect in these three chapters of Romans says:

> "The Apostle is still continuing his subject of vindication of God's character and ways. He has shown in the first eight chapters that God is righteous in the exercise both of His wrath and of His grace. He now proceeds to establish the righteousness of God in His dealings with Jews and Gentiles."[23]

Distortion or misunderstanding is likely to stem from failing to follow through these chapters about God's dealing with Israel, past, present and future. Indeed partial reading might give some initial grounds for Replacement Theology, whereas by the end of chapter 11 the case for

Israel's future receives a resounding accolade. An extract from Sidlow Baxter's analytical table of the epistle is helpful:

"National: how the gospel relates to Israel (Roman ix–xi)

Does not annul the purpose with Israel (ix)

Because not all Israel true Israel (vv. 7–13)

And an elect remnant being saved (vv. 27–29)

Rather, it fulfils the promise to Israel (x)

But Israel bent on salvation by works (vv. 1–4)

And stumbles (ix v 32) *through unbelief* (vv. 18–21)

And confirms the prospect before Israel (xi)

Israel's fall made to bless Gentiles (vv. 1–24)

And all Israel shall yet be saved (vv. 25–29)"[24]

The distinction between Israel and the Church and between the Jew and Gentile in the forward looking chapter 11 is inescapable. We looked in some detail in our 'until' studies in our third chapter at the temporary nature of Israel's national hardening, and the guaranteed end of her ungodliness. In v28 we read,

"Concerning the gospel they are enemies for your sake, but concerning the election they are beloved for the sake of the fathers."

In v31 we read,

"Even so these also have now been disobedient, that through the mercy shown you they also may obtain mercy."

The Jew appears here in stark contradistinction to the Church and Gentile, and yet is to be shown mercy. Denial of this promised mercy is tantamount to denying mercy to ourselves. How absolutely preposterous it is for Replacement Theologians to claim for the Church promises like those in Hosea 14:

"O Israel, return to the Lord your God, for you have stumbled because of your iniquity... I will heal their

backsliding, I will love them freely, For My anger is turned away from him. I will be like dew to Israel" (vv. 1, 4, 5).

"They Are Not All Israel Who Are Of Israel"

This quote is taken from Rom 9:16. It is one of several verses which are used to assert that the Church has replaced Israel. Other texts sometimes used to this end are:

> *"He is not a Jew who is one outwardly, nor is circumcision that which is outward in the flesh; but he is a Jew who is one inwardly"* (Rom 2:28–29).

> *"And as many as walk according to this rule, peace and mercy be upon them, and upon the Israel of God"* (Gal 6:16).

> *"At that time you were without Christ, being aliens from the commonwealth of Israel and strangers from the covenants of promise, having no hope and without God in the world"* (Eph 2:12).

It is widely assumed among Replacement Theologians that, because all Jews are not true Jews, their number must be taken up by Gentile Christians who are now the Israel of God. This cannot be claimed to be a doctrine, because there is no single statement anywhere in Holy Scripture which states that the Church is Israel. David Pawson comments:

> "Then there is the application of the name 'Israel' to the church (based on one ambiguous phrase in Gal 6:6; over seventy other references in the New Testament all refer to the Jewish people). It would seem that prejudice may be operating when it comes to the millennium! ... Quite simply, if no other scriptures point in the same direction or if many other scriptures point in a different direction, a passage must be re-examined in this light." [25]

Some might criticise Pawson's use of 'obscure' here. But it is obscure in that the expression, *'the Israel of God'* is used nowhere else in Scripture, and is not actually defined by Paul. We may make deductions or assumptions from it, but not doctrines.

Well, we have seen a great many passages which point in another direction, namely to Israel's future as the direct descendents of the patriarchs. We can demonstrate from the Bible that not all members of Israel-after-the-flesh are Israelites in every sense. Dr Phelan writes:

> "Christ in Jn 1:47 referred to Nathaniel as 'an Israelite indeed, in whom is no guile' By referring to him as *an Israelite indeed* Christ seems to be saying that Nathaniel is a True, or Genuine-Israelite. This is in sharp contrast to those we encounter later on in the same Gospel who, although able to boast of having Abraham as their father, were referred to by Christ as children of the devil!... they could perhaps be referred to as *False-Israelites*, inasmuch as they were *untrue* to their forefather Abraham (Jn 8:39–44)... Thus with the ministry of Christ we see a narrowing of the definition of Israel. On the one hand Christ acknowledged that the Jews of John chapter 8 were the Seed of Abraham (v37), but because His word was not in them, they could not be considered to be the Children of Abraham, with God as their Father." [26]

None of this gives us licence to say that the Gentile Church is Israel. Again, we must remind ourselves that in Romans chapters 2 to 4 Paul was dealing with misguided Jewish Christians; this comes over very clearly. Paul, dealing in chapter 4 with righteousness being imputed to Abraham because of his faith, rather than works such as circumcision, shows how we share in Abraham's blessing. Vine quotes from v11:

> "'To all the seed; not to that only which is of the law, but to that which is of the faith of Abraham, who is the father of us all.' The seed here stands for all the children of Abraham who accept God's condition of faith, whether Jews or Gentiles. The promise given to Abraham will be secured to the nation of the Jews, but not on the grounds of law-keeping, and meanwhile all believing Jews are, alike with believing Gentiles, the spiritual children of Abraham." [27]

That is about as near as one ever gets to Gentile Christians being called Jews or Israel. But try substituting 'Church' for Israel in anything Paul wrote after this, and you find total nonsense, such as 'My heart's desire and prayer to God for the Church is that they may be saved'!!! This is, of course a deliberate distortion of Rom 10:1, but one which might be acceptable in modern Rome; but it is foolishness to those who believe that only the saved are in the Church, and that no saved are outside it.

John the Baptist said to the unrepentant Pharisees and Sadducees, who were relying upon their descent from Abraham, *"God is able to raise up children to Abraham from these stones"* (Matt 3:9). Note that he said 'is able to' and not 'will', and that he added 'from these stones' and not 'from the Gentiles'. Note also that the patriarch referred to in these passages is Abraham, and not Jacob (Israel), the only patriarch exclusive to Israel. Surely were we to consider ourselves as Gentile Christians to be some sort of new Israel, we would be termed spiritual children of *Jacob*. As Dispensational Israelologists we have no difficulty with verses such Rom 9:6, *"They are not all Israel who are of Israel"*. But neither do we see any evidence therein that anybody other than a Jew is Israel.

The reference in Eph 2:12 to the 'commonwealth of Israel' (AV and NKJV) brings no comfort to Replacement Theologians. The term is unique in Scripture, the Greek noun *politeia* occurring only here, and in Acts 22:28 as the *citizenship* which Paul received by birth but which the Roman commander had to buy. Writing of the Ephesian Gentiles, Kelly points out:

> "They had no hope. They were not expecting any divine intervention to deliver them on the earth... They had no connection with God in the world; whereas the Jews had Him to direct all their movements—how they were to live... everything was entirely under the distinct ordinance of God. If they had God thus in the world, the Gentiles knew nothing of the sort." [28]

We are reminded of Jesus' words to the Samaritan woman,

> *"You worship what you do not know; we know what we worship, for salvation is of the Jews"* (Jn 4:22).

Jesus went on to say that this would change. It had just changed for the Ephesian Gentiles:

> *"But now in Christ Jesus you who once were far off have been made near by the blood of Christ"* (Eph 2:13).

Fruchtenbaum deals at great length and very convincingly with Replacement Theological applications of Rom 2:28–29 and with the limitations of circumcision. We can quote only briefly:

> "What Paul was dealing with in this passage was the Pharisaic concept that all who were circumcised would definitely make it into God's kingdom… The mere act of circumcision does not exempt the Jew from judgement if he fails to keep the law. Circumcision avails only if the law is kept; but mere ritual will not bring justification… Jeremiah taught that circumcision without reality is uncircumcision. Paul taught the other side of the coin… Verse 27 states that, in fact, the righteous uncircumcision will judge the unrighteous circumcision. The morality of the uncircumcised Gentile can judge the immorality of the circumcised Jew."[29]

So again we see no suggestion whatsoever of any Gentile being converted into a Jew. Without that happening there can be no case for the Church being converted into or being synonymous with Israel. We will close this section and this chapter with a further quote from Dr Fruchtenbaum, which both re-enforces these points and explains how, following God's sifting of them, *"all Israel will be saved"* (Rom 11:26):

> "The purpose of this lengthy treatment of Romans 2:17–3:19 was to put 2:28–29 in its proper context. The context shows that Paul is not teaching that Gentile Christians become spiritual Jews, but that not all Jews are true Jews. The distinction is not between Jews and Gentiles, or between Israel and the Church, but between the remnant and non-remnant, between Jews who believe and Jews who do not."[30]

Glasson raises questions over the canonicity of Revelation, not surprising from somebody who seeks to find human sources for Jesus' ideas and teaching.[31] But he is perceptive and honest enough to observe what so many try to wriggle out of:

> "Revelation 20 teaches quite plainly that after Christ's return to the earth and the slaughter of his enemies He will reign over the earth for a thousand years. After this Millennium comes the Final Judgement and the eternal state

associated with the new heaven and earth. It is still the orthodox Jewish view that the reign of Messiah will be a literal reign of limited time on the present earth... This temporary Messianic kingdom is taught in the Talmud." [32]

What a paradox it is that most orthodox Jews are yet blind to the Person of their Messiah, whilst many Christians are blind to the scope of the faithfulness of God's promises to the Jews! We are now in a position to see whether various schools of prophetic interpretation are or are not validated by a scriptural certainty—*that God has faithfully declared and guaranteed a significant and glorious future for those people of Israel who have not become members of the Church of Jesus Christ*. We make no claim whatsoever for this being the only criterion for validation; only that it is a mandatory and uncompromising one. *Failure to meet this criterion must invalidate any school of interpretation, irrespective of other considerations.*

Chapter Nine

Amillennialism And Israel's Future—Background

Amillennial Authorities

Because of the current widespread nature, both doctrinally and geographically of Amillennialism, and because of its ambivalent, and in extreme cases hostile, attitude to Israelology, we are going to devote two chapters to it.

For reasons which will become clearer as we proceed through this chapter, even if we omit outright liberals, selecting a number of what we might term typical Amillennial authorities is problematical. Some writers give the impression that they write for all; then one immediately encounters others who say something entirely different. This is probably truer of Amillennialism than of any other school. We want to avoid the manipulative ploy of some apologists, who choose the most extreme spokespeople of their adversaries in order to discredit the more typical ones. On the other hand we need to know something of the extremists, because they can be very vocal and therefore influential.

Every school of prophetic interpretation has its internal divisions and differences, which, as we said earlier, are almost inevitable, given the nature of Bible prophecy. Some, like Adams, Cox, Hoekema and Milne devote whole books either to defending Amillennialism or to attacking other schools; but equally influential are those writers who devote only a chapter or so to eschatology within general theological treatises; such are Stott and Chantry.

In his book *Amillennialism Today*, William Cox, a comparatively fundamentalist writer whom we quoted in the previous chapter, starts sentences with "Amillennialists believe that...". This is totally misleading and gives the impression of a united front; yet few Amillennialists believe exactly the same as he does.

Some do not even attempt to defend their Replacement Theology, but seem to assume that it is generally accepted. And, after all, it is teaching about Israel's future with which we are most concerned. That in itself is immensely significant—a sign of the times, inasmuch as it reflects a failure to *"Look at the fig tree and all the trees"* (Lk 21:29). Another problem with which we have to contend is that many, though not all, tend to misunderstand Pre-Millennialism. Some pick on atypical rather than typical statements.

Some defend Amillennialism against Post- as well as Pre-Millennialism, while others see only Pre-Millennialism as a threat. The final problem, as we have already seen, is that, whilst some Amillennialists hotly deny any future for Israel in God's purposes, others, while accepting such a future in principle, simply leave no room for it in their scheme of things. This latter is a subtler deviation, one which at first sight seems almost harmless.

To two authorities, namely Berkhof and Hoekema, we will devote whole sections. They are scholarly, and the type of people with whom one feels one could do business, even though disagreeing with them. The others we will refer to when appropriate. Adams we choose because he is representative of the mass of Christians who are badly informed about Pre-Millennialism and base their own position largely on the imagined faults of others; however some of his points are well made. Space does not permit us to do full justice to each. Milne is another moderate; Metcalfe is an extremist, whilst Chantry, Stott and Cox fall somewhere between. These are imperfect classifications, because individuals may be extreme, for instance, on Millennialism, but moderate on Replacement Theology, or vice versa.

We have carefully chosen representatives from both sides of the Atlantic. One of the best known and most often quoted British Amillennialists we have omitted, because we have it on very good authority that in his old age he confided to a friend that he had been mistaken throughout his life. However we can provide no written evidence. We have already, we believe, presented in earlier chapters cast-iron evidence from Scripture for God's future purposes on earth for Israel, so can keep most of our responses fairly brief.

Amillennialism—Seeking A Definition

The internal differences to which we have referred make a fair definition difficult to find. But we must do our best, so should build up to it carefully. John Walvoord writes:

> "The history of modern liberalism has demonstrated that its adherents are drawn almost entirely from Amillennial ranks."[1]

This comment will not be popular with Amillennialists; but it is true. His point does not actually discredit Amillennialism, but it should certainly make us pause for thought. He does not suggest that *all* Amillennialists are liberals—far from it; there are some with whom we would agree on all other major areas of theology. However many are liberals, and hence justify the above quote. In fact we believe that Amillennialism through its subjective approach to prophecy actually encourages liberalism. Apart from that brand of Post-Millennialism (more in Chapter Eleven) which sees a coming golden age as a sort of humanist moral evolution, one finds virtually no liberals outside Amillennialism.

Ultimately in these two chapters we will have to determine whether or not Amillennialism is validated by its recognition, *within a consistent and credible eschatological framework*, of God's future purposes for the Jews. Initially the prospects do not look good inasmuch as most Amillennialists openly embrace Replacement Theology. But there are exceptions on a variety of grounds. So we must investigate further. Cox writes:

> (1) "Amillennialism is not liberalism. (2) Amillenarians stand for a scriptural approach to eschatology. (3) Their teachings are based squarely on the Bible as the inspired and infallible word of God. (4) It goes without saying that some liberal theologians hold the Amillennial view of eschatology. (5) But so do many liberals hold the other millennial views."[2]

The numbers in brackets we have added. The fourth sentence of this quote stands in sharp contrast to the first three! However it happens to be truer than the first three sweeping statements. I personally have known and heard several Amillennialist ministers who simply are not sure how literal the Lord's return is to be, but preach on it during 'Advent' because it is in their denominational calendar! They may be well-meaning but are generally very confused. Cox's final sentence is misleading. No liberals hold other Millennial views except the aforementioned moral evolutionists.

We will find some who, without being actively Anti-Semitic, are totally convinced that God has completely abandoned Israel as a people having a special relationship with Him. This was the official attitude of the Dark Ages and still lingers on among some Protestants, who, in most other theological respects, completely and vocally disassociate themselves with Rome. We will find others who are convinced—and here we will be looking later at Hoekema's exposition of Romans 9 to 11—that God has very definite plans for the *spiritual* restoration of Israel. Our complaint against them will be largely that they recognise no special future Jewish role in a restored earthly Kingdom, and no provision for Christ's future rule on earth with a rod of iron. Others, we will discover, fall between these two extremes. As we look at the history of the movement, we may decide that it is not unreasonable to describe Amillennialism as a Pre-Reformation hangover.

Right attitudes to God's wayward people, Israel, are highly commendable; but attitudes alone are not enough; we will be looking for *provisions*. It will certainly not be enough to prove that Jews can enter the Church on the same basis as Gentile believers. Surely all conservatives believe that, irrespective of eschatological stance! Crazily, some Amillennialists think they have the exclusive rights to this teaching; but Pre- and Post-Millennialists share it. It will not even be sufficient to recognise that God has plans to restore the *nation* Israel, which a few Amillennialists believe is due to happen in a modified form within the Church Age. It will be necessary to provide an opportunity within an eschatological plan—to demonstrate that there will be a time for the fulfilment of major Old Testament prophecies such as:

- A recognisable but restored earth, such as will commence with Christ's feet touching the Mount of Olives (Zech 14:4 et seq.), and having other specifically identified geological alterations such as are found in Isa 11:15 et seq., features which cannot by any stretch of the imagination be allegorised.

- A comprehensively healed and rejuvenated earth, as described in Isaiah 35, in contrast with the later brand new one of Revelation 21, with its absence of days, nights and seas.

- A glorious earthly Jerusalem such as we find described in Isaiah 2 and Micah 4, in contrast with the New Jerusalem as described in Revelation 21 and 22; in other words a Jerusalem that *"shall arise"* rather than the later one that *"shall descend"*.

We could add to the list almost ad infinitum: but this will suffice. Our earlier chapters laid down many requirements. Only if we can find Amillennialism matching these criteria can we give it a clean bill of health. It must be compatible with all God's unconditional promises.

We gave a brief definition of Amillennialism in Chapter One; but it was a general and therefore not a particularly satisfactory one. Indeed, one wonders whether there is a definition which would satisfy every adherent. Perhaps the most helpful course would be to refer again to Cox. Quoting Dr Walvoord, he writes:

> "A good definition of Amillennialism comes from the pen of one of its severest critics. 'Its most general character is that of a denial of a *literal* reign of Christ upon the earth. Satan is conceived as bound at the first coming of Christ. The present age between the first and second comings is the fulfilment of the millennium. Its adherents are divided on whether the millennium is being fulfilled now on the earth (Augustine) or whether it is being fulfilled by the saints in heaven (Kliefoth). It may be summed up in the idea that there will be no more millennium than there is now, and that the eternal state immediately follows the second coming of Christ.'"[3]

Kliefoth's 19th Century minority position is better known in Britain as Warfield's Amillennialism, as expounded more fully early in the 20th century. Warfield is a bit of an eschatological hybrid; some Post-Millennialists claim him too! However, as it shares with Augustinian Amillennialism the same view of a general resurrection and judgement; and as it interprets in an allegorical fashion all the promised blessing for Israel as being in heaven, we see no point in dealing with this splinter group separately. We will be referring to the more common Augustinian variety, or at least the modernised version. Many early Amillennialists actually anticipated the Millennium ending in AD 1000 and had to adjust their thinking—date fixers have to do this a lot!

Perhaps it is unfortunate for conservative Amillennialists that they have to live with a negative definition, rather like 'foreign' or 'Protestant', words which describe what a person is not or does not believe, rather than what they are or do believe. Cox writes:

> "Some have suggested the name 'realized millennialism'. This writer prefers the term 'biblical millenialism'".[4]

The first of these we would allow as a description of the belief; we will quote Adams to explain. However the second description, that of 'Biblical Millennialism', we would hotly dispute. Amillennialism has, from its earliest days, had at its heart the non-literal or symbolic interpretation of unfulfilled predictive prophecy. We contend that this far exceeds what is worthy of the title 'biblical'.

Welshman, C H Dodds, a comparative liberal, coined the term 'realized eschatology' back in 1935. Apparently it was Adams who first adapted it to 'Realized Millennialism'. He writes:

> "By definition, realized millennialism is the belief that the millennium is a present reality. All unrealized millennialists (whether of the pre- or postmillennial sort) deny this and look for a future millennium."[5]

That is a very reasonable definition. But our natural reaction to this could well be to ask why, if the Millennium is currently being realised, is Satan not bound. Sceptics and liberals poke fun at this Amillennial idea of a currently bound Satan, when they look at the world around them, and no wonder! We believe that the Amillennial case is pathetically weak and actually brings people's perception of Bible prophecy into disrepute.

Amillennialism In The Early Church

We turn again to Cox and read the following statements, full of half truths, which illustrate the backs-to-the-wall approach of many Amillennialist apologists. We add a few comments:

"Amillennialism is as old as the Christian church itself.
Contrary to its critics, Amillennialism is not an innovation
among modern theologians. Church fathers such as Origen
and Augustine struck out against chiliastic teachings in their
days. In fact chiliasm (millennialism) lay dormant from
Augustine's time until its revival in the nineteenth century."[6]

- Amillennialism is ancient, but *not* as old as the Church. It was not
  until the 3rd century that it made any serious impact and not until
  the 4th that it was widely accepted.

- No serious critic of Amillennialism would suggest that it is a
  modern innovation, but would trace it back at the very least to
  Augustine. Cox is being defensive against an imagined accusation.

- Rome might refer to Origen (*c.* 185–254) and Augustine (354–430)
  as Church fathers, but must we? They belong to the age where
  heresies were multiplying, rather than to the Apostolic or
  immediate Post-Apostolic age.

- Yes; Origen and Augustine did strike out at the chiliastic
  teachings, which were older than theirs. Sadly corruption had crept
  in there too; but that was no reason to discard them. They should
  have been taken back to basics, rather than replaced.

- While it is true that chiliasm lay dormant throughout the Dark
  Ages (does that in itself not strike Cox as significant?), important
  minority groups held it from the 15th or 16th centuries. Certainly it
  had a popular revival in the 19th century, spreading far beyond
  Brethren circles.

In the early Church, which was predominantly Chiliastic or Millennial, the
distinctions between Post- and Pre-Tribulationism had not crystallised; we
can discuss these contrasts in Chapter Thirteen. As Glasson records:

"It appears that Nepos, Bishop of Arsinoe, had written a
work entitled 'Refutation of the Allegorists' in which he
had insisted on a literal interpretation of Revelation 20."[7]

Nepos saw this new threat from Alexandria and elsewhere. Bishop
Dionysius led the attack on the established Millennial teaching,
confirming that even in the 2nd century the Church was still largely, but

much less exclusively Millennialist. Both Papias and Justin Martyr, notable Millennialists, admitted knowing fine Christians who did not agree with their eschatology, but the implication was that these were a minority. Clement of Alexandria, with what some might deem the worthy purpose of making Christianity more palatable to the Greek mind, introduced the thoughts of Philo, the philosopher, incorporating the non-literal philosophical approach to Scripture, hence the extensive allegorising. Whenever believers have sought to accommodate the wisdom of the world, spiritual disaster has followed. It happens today. Origen, the real developer of Amillennialism, is described in Hutchinson's Encyclopaedia as "chiefly remembered for his fanciful method of allegorical exegesis of the Bible"[8].

But it was not until Augustine's time that allegorical Amillennialism began to dominate and be given respectability. Glasson writes:

> "The final collapse of chiliasm, as far as the main Christian tradition was concerned, was due to St Augustine, the famous Bishop of Hippo in North Africa, who lived from 354 to 430. He was responsible more than anyone else for popularising the view that we are now living in the millennium... He writes: 'He that looks for great good in this world, is far wrong. The place therefore where this promised peace will dwell and abide is the heavenly Jerusalem.' For centuries all orthodox writers followed him in referring to the present Church-age, and the idea of a literal reign of Christ in the chiliastic sense was finally dismissed from the main trend of Christian thought. Jerome, Augustine's contemporary, took the same line and wrote: 'Let us have done with this fable of a thousand years'. Elsewhere he describes Millenarians as 'our half-Jews who look for a Jerusalem of gold and precious stones from heaven and a future kingdom of a thousand years'."[9]

It must be conceded that by Augustine's time there were excesses in Millennialism. Any sound doctrine is subject to deviations. Jesus identified false teaching within several congregations of the province of Asia at the end of the 1st century (Revelation 2 and 3), so later deviations from sound eschatology are hardly surprising. But He told them to repent, not to have a rethink! In Chapter Eight we found Augustine writing of these Millennialist excesses—we do not quote in full this time:

> "The avouchers hereof affirm that the saints after this resurrection shall do nothing but revel in fleshly banquets, where the cheer shall exceed both modesty and measure, this is gross and fit for none but carnal men to believe." [10]

One should not promote any new doctrine as a reaction to the worst excesses of what was formerly a sound one. Jerome is the guiltier of the two, displaying either ignorance or having picked upon the most extreme exponents of Millennialism. Here we see the 4th century Christian Church denying the main opportunity or 'window' in future history for the fulfilment of God's promises to Israel. This teaching concerning Israel had become obscured, as Christian leadership had increasingly become centralised in Rome and Byzantium. Those conservatives who follow Augustine's eschatology should consider his statement: "He that looks for great good in this world is far wrong", and then read Isaiah chapter 11, 35 and 65, where God foretells great good in this world on a scale yet to be realised. They should then consider whether they still want to be associated with such degradation of Scriptural truth.

In Jerome's words we detect a definite prejudice against Jews, in what is clearly intended to be a derisory term for those who recognise such a future. Here already are rearing their ugly heads the attitudes which were to lead to the Anti-Semitism of the Dark Ages and beyond. In fifty-odd years as a Pre-Millennialist I have never come across anyone who visualises the Millennium in the ways that Augustine's 'avouchers' are supposed to have done.

Amillennialism From The Reformation

It is interesting that among Protestants Augustine is currently being rehabilitated. Writing in what has become a predominantly Amillennialist journal, Nick Needham devotes a lengthy article to "Augustine: Vessel and Champion of Grace". While admitting that he does not agree with everything that Augustine wrote, he says:

> "Read Luther and Calvin, and you will find them quoting Augustine on almost every other page" [11]

Contrast that with Professor Renwick, who writes:

> "Augustine was the greatest Christian of his age; but he
> sanctioned certain beliefs and customs which were afterwards
> productive of much evil in the Church. Thus he taught that
> there was no salvation outside the visible Catholic Church
> (with its traditionalism and sacramentarianism). He also
> favoured ascetic monasticism, fostered the use of relics and
> encouraged belief in purgatory." [12]

Apparently such facts are no longer important to the *Evangelical Times*,
which once took an uncompromising Protestant stand. While we
certainly owe a huge debt to the great Reformers, we have to note that,
indeed, they did not separate themselves from all of the false doctrines
which had infiltrated Christianity down through the centuries; and of
course eschatology was not their prime concern. Catholic Amillennialism
was one doctrine which remained comparatively unchallenged by the
best known Reformers, except with regards to the Rome-Babylon
correlation, which naturally received maximum attention. Thus
Replacement Theology remained largely in place, and Anti-Semitism
found some sort of footing within Protestantism. It lingers on in some
quarters to this very day, and seems set to increase as quasi-moral
pressures are brought to bear over the 'Palestinian' issue. We would not
normally quote *Watchtower* as an authority, because 'Jehovah's
Witnesses' are a cult, as well as being Replacement Theologians in their
own way. They can be relied upon to make capital out of any Christian
failings. However a recent comment is interesting:

> "Furthermore Luther's later essays on those Jews who
> refused to convert to Christianity, particularly *On the Jews
> and Their Lies*, have caused many to brand the author anti-
> Semitic." [13]

Regarding Israel's future, Luther tended towards Replacement Theology;
but regarding the Lord's return, he was generally Pre-Millennial; this today
would be an unusual conjunction. Calvin in Geneva did his best to set up
what was intended to be at least a semi-theocratic kingdom, which was to
include various features of the Old Testament Millennial prophecies.
However neither the place, nor the time nor the people were right! The
17th century Westminster Confession, the nearest Presbyterians have to a

statement of faith, reflects the single judgement eschatology which is so central to Amillennialism; we will look at this in our next chapter. Dr Sinclair Ferguson writes:

> "The Confession affirms the reality of Christ's return, of the last judgement and of Heaven and Hell. The last day, when all men and angels shall be judged has already been appointed, but remains unrevealed." [14]

We will in due course discuss the problems raised by such a confession, which gives no further elaboration to Christ's return, thus leaving the way open for endless speculation.

By the 18th century, as the great revivals came and as the missionary age dawned, Post-Millennialism rapidly overtook Amillennialism. This is usually traced to 1700 and Daniel Whitby, though, as we shall see in Chapter Eleven, it actually goes further back than that. One need only look at the optimistic hymns of the period. However in due course Pre-Millennialism emerged in its modern form to challenge it. By the time Blackshaw wrote his influential book, *Jesus is Coming* [15] in 1908, Amillennialism had become so disconsidered that he defended his Pre-Millennial stand only against Post-Millennialism. He quotes Philip Melanchton, Joseph Mede, John Milton, Burnett, Sir Isaac Newton, Isaac Watts, Charles Wesley and Augustus Toplady as pre-19th century Pre-Millennialists [16]. We cannot take time over the precise stand of each one of these; they were anything but uniform in their eschatology.

It was only after the horrors of the Great War had shattered and discredited the Post-Millennial dream, that Amillennialism reappeared as a major force. It had to contend with the two great boosts to Pre-Millennialism of the 1917 Balfour Declaration of a Jewish homeland and the 1948 birth of the Israeli state. Balfour was accorded by the Jewish community far greater honour at his death than any previous Gentile. In more recent years it had to compete with the Neo-Post-Millennialism of those who were making well-intentioned but extravagant claims of great national revivals and 'Christianisation' of society. Cities and even nations were being 'claimed' for Christ and dozens of Old Testament prophecies for Israel were being firstly assumed and secondly annexed by the Church. The world was supposedly agog in the 'seventies and 'eighties to see *'manifestation of the sons of God'*. But the necessary national revivals never took place, because repentance was largely absent. Scepticism and apathy ensued.

Instead the world plummeted downhill, as the Bible, Pre-Millennialists and Amillennialists all said it would. Amillennialists did not make a fuss about it. They simply carried on as usual with their old brand of eschatology—one which leaves much less room for the optimism of the Post-Millennialist or the miraculous expectations of the Pre-Millennialist. Amillennialism is very much less demanding of credulity, much less challenging and therefore less disruptive to the 'anything-for-a-quiet-life brigade'.

In the meantime A- and Post-Millennialism seem to co-exist quite happily in many congregations, with people blissfully unaware of their mutual incompatibility. How? Why? Perhaps because few adherents of either group take time to investigate the implications and scriptural authority of what they believe. Perhaps it is because both are rather vague in their understanding of the Millennium, and fail to attach any importance to it. It is sufficient for many that there are verses dotted here and there around the Bible to which to cling. Whether these fit together coherently is of little concern, particularly if Israel is taken out of the equation.

Probably it is also true to say that a small admixture of Post-Millennialism gives a sense of optimism, purpose and progress. This is a poor basis for fellowship; it provides at best peaceful co-existence, which is not the same. The Bible's *"as it was in the days of Noah"* teaching (Matt 24:37*)* is seen as defeatist and is not at all popular, despite the fact that it was Jesus Himself who uttered these words. This accounts for recent Post-Millennial inroads into Amillennialism. Spectacular Divine intervention is seen as chiefly for Pre-Millennialists—and they of course are thought of as extremists and potential troublemakers!

The Old Allegorisation Excuse

Cox, as we mentioned in our last chapter, frequently uses the expression *hyper-literal* for any statement in Scripture which stretches *his* personal faith but is perfectly acceptable to Pre-Millennialists. This Latin-Greek hybrid term is not found in Chambers' Dictionary; perhaps he invented it himself. Chambers defines the prefix *hyper* as 'over, excessive, more

216

than normal', and *literal* as 'not figurative or metaphorical; inclined to use or understand words in a matter-of-fact sense...' Need we comment further? Other Amillennialists use different terms, but their eschatology and Israelology (if they have any) are entirely dependent on their preparedness to interpret prophecy in figurative or metaphorical ways. Such interpretation is inevitably subjective and gives rise to a host of conflicting options. Perhaps the greatest danger is the fact that, while the Bible contains concentrated areas of predictive prophecy, these are never totally divorced from other doctrines. Thus by being non-literal in one or two areas, we can open up the flood-gates of liberalism in other areas. It can be the start of a disastrously slippery slope. Cox writes:

> "Amillenarians accept the entire Bible as the Spirit-breathed, infallible Word of God." [17]

He does not actually specify *all* Amillenarians, but that is the most obvious meaning. Many Amillennialists simply do not believe in the infallibility of the inspired Holy Scripture. However many, like Cox, do, *provided*, as we noted above, they are allowed arbitrarily to interpret figuratively prophetic passages in a way which Millenarians have no difficulty in interpreting at face value. It is Cox who, more than once, uses the adjective 'materialistic'—what we might call a weasel word—to describe a literal Millennium. Were he to think the matter through, he would, on the same basis, have to describe the Garden of Eden, which God created, as materialistic. Manipulative words are dangerous.

Consider another statement from Cox:

> "Amillenarians... believe that the book of Revelation says, symbolically, what the rest of the New Testament says in clear language. And the twentieth chapter of this symbolic book can be no exception. The one thousand year period is mentioned only in that chapter." [18]

He omits to mention that, inconveniently for him, it is stated six times there. Of course there are many visions of scenes in heaven which we cannot fully comprehend with our present limited understanding. But try following through Cox's above quoted statement. We are left with the idea that Christ's return *"in like manner as ye saw Him taken into heaven"* is to be taken literally because it is in Acts, but His return as described in Revelation is purely symbolic because it is in Revelation! We could cite other examples, but one will suffice to make our point.

Like other Amillennialists, Cox cannot face up to the exactitude of the thousand years. Yet when Jesus gave John seven letters for the seven churches of Asia, there *were* seven. They are named. Likewise the seven Seals, Trumpets and Bowls are carefully enumerated; there are various other instances in this book of numbers being precise. The oft quoted thousand-year simile used in II Pet 3:8 does not justify evading the actual number when it is so heavily emphasised in Revelation 20.

Many numbers of Revelation and other books almost certainly do have special spiritual significances; but this does not stop them also meaning what they actually say, for instance, twelve named tribes, ten specified commandments, twelve named disciples etc. So why do Cox and virtually all other Amillennialists have such problems with the constantly repeated one thousand year declaration of chapter 20? We would suggest that it is because of the uncomfortable (for them) fact that the Church Age has now almost doubled that figure, proving, that, if taken literally, the Millennium is *not* the Church Age, and therefore something future. Without allegorisation they are without a case. They are compelled to defend the indefensible.

Milne, who, like Hoekema and Berkhof, is usually much more balanced and reasonable than Cox, writes:

> "Underlying the pre-millennial interpretation of Revelation 20 and the Old Testament accounts of the coming messianic kingdom there commonly lies a particular approach. This is the view that biblical prophecies should be interpreted literally rather than symbolically. Thus pre-millennialists regularly accuse those who dismiss the millennial idea as being guilty of two errors.
>
> 1. The first error is inconsistency, in that they treat some prophecies literally (e.g. the fact that Jesus is coming again) but others only symbolically (e.g. that there will be a millennial kingdom). The right to decide which is literal and which is symbolic lies apparently with the Amillennialist interpreter...

2. The other is lack of faith, since (it is alleged) underlying the attempt to interpret these prophecies symbolically is an element of unbelief..."[19]

Dealing with the second accusation first, we must be hesitant about condemning any other Christian of lack of faith unless it is demonstrated in other ways, which it is with some, but by no means with all, Amillennialists. However one is tempted at times to believe that the miraculous details of predictive prophecy are almost too much for some sincere believers to accept; and this is sad.

As regards the first of these accusations against Amillennialists, we believe that it is a fair one. Such Old Testament prophecies as Jesus' virgin birth, His birth in Bethlehem, His coming on a donkey and so forth are seen to be literal, whilst those promising a future restored earth akin to Eden and a glorified Jerusalem, are taken to be symbolical or allegorical. If this is not inconsistency, whatever is? So varied and subjective are the allegorical interpretations of Amillennialism, that it is not altogether surprising that it has been dubbed 'Mythical Millennialism'! The source for this is not available.

Allegory And Anti-Semitism

John Metcalfe takes his allegorisation beyond the normal bounds of those Amillennialists who claim to be Bible-believing. Allegorisation with him is 'spiritual'; face value interpretation is 'superficial'. Even God's promise to Abraham of the Land must not be trusted, according to him:

> "The truth is that Abraham, far from for ever, *never* inherited the land of Canaan. And yet certainly it was promised to him and his seed. Then of course it follows, as in the case of the first promise to Abraham, that a deeper, more profound and spiritual meaning was intended in the promise of God than appears on face value. And without this true interpretation everything becomes both contradictory and chaotic, as for example in the fantastic dispensational and premillennial notions."[20]

Our definition of 'promise' and his differ widely. He cites Hebrews 11 to support his case; but one can almost hear the pages of Deuteronomy and

Joshua crying out in protest. Such false logic from his own 'contradictory and chaotic' mind leads to further statements, such as:

> "There is no proof whatsoever that the people calling themselves Jews today—practising a hopelessly compromised and deviant departure from the pure law required under the Old Covenant—no proof whatsoever that they are the twelve tribes. There is only claim. Not proof. There can be no proof. There are no records... All that exists today is a people calling themselves Jews, practising a corrupted form of that Judaism which already had submerged the scriptures beneath a flood of puerile interpretations from the Rabbis and their traditions of the elders, over two thousand years ago."[21]

This kind of rhetoric would have gone down well in the Third Reich. That is not an overstatement. Such teaching was widely propagated in Germany in the 1930s. Yes, it is extreme, but we must include it here. It is an example of what can happen to a fundamentalist who allegorises what does not suit his preconceptions. The fact that there is a heavenly Zion blinds him to God's faithful promises for the earthly one. Quoting and commenting on Psalm 110, he writes:

> "'The Lord shall send the rod of thy strength out of Zion'... Obviously David cannot be regarding the earthly location of Zion at Jerusalem. In prophecy he is regarding Zion in terms of the spiritual, divine and heavenly concepts associated with that city. That was what made Zion, and Jerusalem, important. And nothing but that. Therefore David seeing this in the Spirit, disassociates all that God had wrought in and spoken about Zion from the mere heap of bricks, stones, earth and rocks of that name. He sees that all that matters about Zion is what came down from God out of heaven in connection with that place."[22]

This is extreme Amillennialism, which in turn leads to extreme Replacement Theology, which in turn brings comfort to, if it does not actually promote, Anti-Semitism. Worse, it effectively accuses God of being a liar when one considers a cross-section of unfulfilled promises. Dozens of scriptures are no doubt buzzing through our heads. Who is the enemy of Israel, we wonder, who has provoked such dismissal of the people who are the apple of God's eye? And we have quoted here only some of the worst examples of John Metcalfe. Needless to say he subscribes to many other familiar Amillennial doctrines, such as a single judgment; [147] however we have seen enough.

Other Amillennial writers dismiss Israel's national future less dramatically and more sympathetically. We will later see John Stott's comments. Stott is not the kind of theologian one wishes to criticise, but we believe that his Israelology is quite wrong. There are those who are quite enthusiastic about a future for Israel, but see it only as a spiritual one. Walter Chantry seems to be making a promising start, with statements away beyond what some fellow Amillennialists would admit. Writing about the "profound unity" between Old and New Testaments, he says:

> "It will also counter-act present-day teachers who without warrant teach that when God makes new covenants with men, He utterly cancels the terms of the former agreements… Those who recklessly imagine that a new covenant from the hand of God invalidates a former, have not carefully read Galatians 3:15–17." [23]

Disappointingly, we find that these promises, which Chantry claims to recognise, have to be fulfilled only 'spiritually'. According to him, Jesus' teaching should have changed our view of the prophets. Are we really to believe that the Old Testament prophets were prophesying about His First and Second Comings, using entirely different standards? What, we wonder, are we supposed to do with Daniel's Old Testament prophecy of the Abomination of Desolation (Dan 9:27), which was actually fulfilled in the 2nd century BC, but which Jesus, in the New Testament, confirmed was also future (Matt 24:15)?

> "Their expectations were national. They were looking forward to an external purification of a literal Israel, for renovation of rulers, temple and customs. But our Lord left all these corrupt institutions visibly intact. He did not materially dismantle the old. Nor did he set up a new nation discernible to human senses" [24]

Actually our Lord arranged, as we know from the Olivet Discourse and subsequent history, that these flawed institutions *should* be dismantled. That happened in AD 70. Chantry continues at some length on this theme, then later writes:

> "Eschatology sometimes does strange things to men's minds. One of these has been to produce in children of the kingdom a delighted expectation that in the future the structure of the Jewish state will return. How could any lover of Christ and his Spirit wish to erect again the theocratic system abolished at the high cost of the precious blood of Christ. If the Jews as an ethnic body are yet to see future blessing from God, it will be by their entering Christ's spiritual kingdom, not by a revival of a Mosaic state. A return to the theocratic order would be a rebellion against Christ, not blessing." [25]

So, having stated that God does not break promises, he proceeds to explain that these were to be only spiritually conceived. We are left staggered by the number of prophecies which seemed clear enough as we went through the many 'untils' in our earlier chapters, but are now told by Chantry to take as only figurative. His correlation between the abolishment of the theocracy and Christ's blood is both emotive and tortuously illogical.

We make no claim for the Millennial Israel to be Mosaic; that is not Pre-Millennial teaching. Chantry is misrepresenting us. Currently a small minority of Messianic Jews may do. There will be vast differences between the Mosaic and the Millennial, which we cannot now look into. Rebellion against Christ will be failing to worship Him in His theocratic Millennial Kingdom.

> *"And it shall be that whichever of the families of the earth do not come up to Jerusalem to worship the King, the Lord of Hosts, on them..."* (Zech 14:17); and there follows a list of punishments.

Try 'spiritualising' that, Walter Chantry! We patronise God when we ridicule promises which make perfectly good sense, if we are only prepared to investigate.

We have seen that, no matter how plausible it may seem in its allegorising, Amillennialism is a hangover from the Dark Ages, with roots going back to Greek philosophy. In our next chapter we will look further into Amillennial doctrine and how it impinges on Israel's promised future. So far we are not impressed.

Chapter Ten

Amillennialism And Israel's Future—Doctrinal

Louis Berkof

Dr Louis Berkhof is the first Amillennialist to whom we will turn in connection with Israel. He is one of those who foretells a partial future conversion of the nation Israel, and for this he must be given credit. But, like virtually all Amillennialists, he denies the most obvious opportunity for restoration *following* the Lord's return, as per Zechariah 12–14. This, of course, is one of the greatest objections of Israelologists to Amillennialism. He writes:

> "Great events precede the Second Coming. According to Scripture several important events must precede the return of Christ.
>
> a. The calling of the Gentiles...
>
> b. The conversion of the full number of Israel. II Cor 3:15 and Rom 11:25–29 refer to a conversion of Israel, and the passage in Romans seems to connect this with the end time. Some take these passages to teach that Israel as a whole, Israel as a nation, will finally return to the Lord. It is more likely however, that the expression 'all Israel' in Rom 11:26 simply refers to the full number of the elect out of the ancient covenant people." [1]

Unlike some Amillennialists he recognised that these 'great events' must indeed happen. But He is forced into stating that these events will precede the Second Coming, by assuming that Second Coming to be the end of the world. His 'Millennium' has already passed—just look at the problems that this concept causes! We have already looked at and dismissed what he deems 'more likely'. Hoekema also gives a convincing reason for dismissing the usual Replacement use of 'all Israel'; we will quote him in our next section.

We will stick with Dr Berkhof for a while. The following quote encapsulates more Replacement Theological material in a single paragraph than some writers achieve in a book. It illustrates how amazingly selective and subjective the so-called Bible-believing stance of some Christians can be. We accept that he gives Bible references for each point which he makes; we are omitting most of these from this quote because we have dealt them already or will deal with them elsewhere. We are adding numbers for reference.

> (1) "According to Pre-Millennialism Christ at His return will re-establish the kingdom of David on earth, and will reign at Jerusalem for a thousand years. (2) This theory is based on a literalistic interpretation of the prophets and of Rev 20:1–6. (3) It makes the kingdom of God an earthly and national kingdom, while the New Testament represents it as spiritual and universal, a kingdom that is even now in existence. (4) The New Testament knows nothing of such an earthly and temporal kingdom of Christ, but does speak of His heavenly and eternal kingdom. (5) Moreover, this theory seeks its main support in a passage (Rev 20:1–6), which represents a scene in heaven, and makes no mention of the Jews, of an earthly and national kingdom, nor of the land of Palestine, as the place where Jesus will rule." [2]

Let us repeat the above, sentence by sentence, and make brief comments on each point:

> (1) "According to Pre-Millennialism Christ will re-establish the kingdom of David on earth, and will reign at Jerusalem for a thousand years."

Yes; we acknowledge that that is a very fair summary of a key Pre-Millennial Israelologist teaching.

> (2) "This theory is based on literalistic interpretation of the prophets and of Rev 20:1–6."

The word 'theory' is patronising, when he claims to teach 'doctrine'; however we will overlook that. We have made it very clear that we believe that it is dishonouring to the word of God to interpret it in any way other than literally, unless there is good cause. And we perceive no such cause, especially in the simple and straightforward narrative of Revelation 19 and 20. The problem that people like Berkhof have with Revelation 20 is that it so devastatingly destroys their theories. Few passages compel Christians so to scrape the bottom of the barrel to avoid the obvious implications. It is he, not we, who should be on the defensive. It is he, who, having to re-interpret plain speech, holds a 'theory', while we hold fast to the simple doctrine.

> (3) "It makes the kingdom of God an earthly and national
> kingdom, while the New Testament represents it as spiritual
> and universal, a kingdom that is even now in existence."

The 'whereas' implies that we believe in the first kind of kingdom and he in the second kind. But we firmly believe in *both* and see no conflict whatsoever. We see no 'either/or' situation here; but he does. Were he ignorant of this fact, he could be excused; however as the author of a major work on Systematic Theology[3], he must surely have been aware of the normal Pre-Millennial stance, which recognises several forms of the Kingdom, which, as we noted in Chapter Eight, are not mutually exclusive. Thus we conclude his statement to be manipulative.

> (4) "The New Testament knows nothing of such an earthly
> and temporal kingdom of Christ, but does speak of His
> heavenly and eternal kingdom."

Most Amillennialist writers make claims of this sort. Of course there is much more about the Millennial earthly kingdom in the Old Testament than in the New, because it is particularly appropriate there. In the New we find, the Messiah and His kingdom being rejected, and, thereafter the kingdom in mystery for the duration of the Church Age. But there *are* clear references to a future earthly rule in the New Testament, such as:

> *"In the regeneration, when the Son of Man sits on the throne
> of His glory, you who have followed Me will also sit on twelve
> thrones, judging the twelve tribes of Israel"* (Matt 19:28).

> *"After this I will return and will rebuild the tabernacle of
> David which has fallen down. I will rebuild its ruins, and I will
> set it up, so that the rest of mankind may seek the Lord, even
> the Gentiles who are called by My name"* (Acts 15:16, 17).

This is something Christ will do when He *returns*. How can this possibly describe heaven? Yet it is clear New Testament teaching.

> (5) "Moreover, this theory seeks its main support in a passage (Rev 20:1–6), which represents a scene in heaven, and makes no mention of the Jews, of an earthly kingdom, nor of the land of Palestine, as the place where Jesus will rule."

This 'theory' does *not* seek its main support in Revelation 20; that chapter simply enables us to place the promised earthly kingdom accurately as to time. It finds, rather than seeks, its main support in a whole host of as yet unfulfilled Old Testament prophecies. These prophets are no more anachronistic now than they were when Jesus expounded from them on the way to Emmaus (Lk 24:27), when Peter quoted them at length in Acts 2 and 3, or when James answered, *"with this the words of the prophets agree"* (Acts 15:15).

As for the astonishing statement that Rev 20:1–6 'represents' a scene in heaven, just read those verses and those which immediately follow them! Are saints, as nations in heaven, going to require protection from the deception of Satan? Are Gog and Magog going out into the four corners of the earth *in heaven*? The earth and surrounding atmosphere and cosmos will not disappear until after the Millennium (v11). Had Berkhof any concept of God's avowed promises, he would talk about the land of Israel, and not Palestine, which is mentioned only four times in Scripture and *never* as the land of promise.

No, these facts we concede are not enumerated in Revelation 20; they do not need to be. But where else would one fit them relative to the Lord's return in power? So important is this point and the fact that the thousand year interval is not stated except in Revelation 20, that we will devote a whole section to it, following a brief look at the stance of Hoekema.

Anthony A. Hoekema

Here is one of the more thoughtful and courteous Amillennial writers. We will be quoting from two of his books. Like Berkhof he acknowledges a future of sorts for Israel. Some of the harder line Amillennialists would do well to note the following of his statements; he is referring to Romans chapters 9 to 11:

"One verse in chapter 10 deserves special attention, verse 12: 'For there is no distinction between Jew and Greek; the same Lord is Lord of all and bestows his riches on all who call upon him.' Paul's point here is that as far as obtaining salvation is concerned, there is no distinction between Jew and Greek. If this is so, a future period of time in which Jews will be saved, or in which Jews will be saved in a way different from the way in which Greeks or Gentiles are saved, would seem to be ruled out."[4]

Now we would agree with this. However what is implied in the last sentence is that Pre-Millennialists teach that Jews are not saved in the same manner as Gentiles. That is emphatically *not* normal Dispensational teaching, though some believe it is, whilst apparently others would have it thought to be so in order to discredit us or to 'score points'. While we agree that God has made different demands upon different ages and revealed Himself in different ways at various times (Heb 1:1), *in no dispensation has there ever been any means of salvation other than through the shed blood of Christ at Calvary*, whether for Old Testament, New Testament or Millennial individuals, or whether for Jew or Gentile. The doctrine of the Lamb extends from Genesis 3 to Revelation 22.

Then he writes regarding the Romans 11 passage about the fullness of the Gentiles and all Israel being saved: he makes an important point about Calvin's view. This is the point which we promised to quote whilst looking at Berkhof.

"Calvin, as we saw, thought these words referred to the salvation of the total number of the elect throughout history, not only from the Jews, but also from the Gentiles. The difficulty with this interpretation, however, is this: in Roman 9–11 the term *Israel* occurs eleven times; in each of the ten instances other than 11:26 where the term is used, it points unmistakably to the Jews in distinction from the Gentiles. What reason is there for accepting a different meaning of the term here? Why should Paul suddenly shift from the natural meaning of the term *Israel* to a wider, figurative meaning?"[5]

Many Amillennialists would side with Calvin here, but we wholeheartedly agree with Hoekema. A few paragraphs later he adds:

> "I interpret this passage, then, as meaning that God fulfils his promises to Israel in the following way. Though Israel has been hardened in its unbelief, this hardening has always been and will continue to be only partial hardening, never total hardening. In other words Israel will continue to turn to the Lord until the Parousia, while at the same time the fullness of the Gentiles is being gathered in."[6]

This sound plausible enough, and is about the best one can expect from Amillennialism; but there are major problems. This does not conform to our earlier 'until' texts in Chapters 3 and 4, where the repentance and conversion of Israel is clearly sudden and dramatic and is portrayed as being in sharp contrast to the intervening period, for instance: *"Ye shall not see Me henceforth until..."* (Matt 23:39). Spiritual conditions for the nation before and after the critical 'until' are entirely different. But it is probably the best that Hoekema can suggest if he will not accept that the Millennium follows the Parousia or Second Coming. Once this is denied, people have to find solutions which appear to fit in. Paul, writing of course within the Church Age, confirmed that the national hardening and blindness was still present. although this 'veil' could be removed from individual Jews who turned to the Lord (II Cor 3:15, 16).

We saw without any shadow of doubt in an earlier chapter, that Zechariah teaches that the Jewish *national* repentance will occur not in a trickle throughout Church history but in a single great event. It will happen thus:

> *"I will pour on the house of David and on the inhabitants of Jerusalem the Spirit of grace and supplication; then they will look on Me whom they have pierced..."* (Zech 12:10).

Even if that chapter is allegorised, the suddenness ought to be evident. This is why a correct understanding of the Millennium is so crucial to understanding God's purposes for Israel. In recent years there have been many conversions from Judaism to Christianity, and we praise God for this. But this is not and cannot be the national repentance spoken of by Zechariah.

In the section entitled 'Interpreting the Book of Revelation', Hoekema says:

"To see the background of the Amillennial view of the millennium, we should first of all concern ourselves with the question of the book of Revelation. Let us assume for example that the book of Revelation is to be interpreted in an exclusively futuristic sense, referring only to events that are to happen around or at the time of Christ's Second Coming. *Let us further assume that what is presented in Revelation 20 must necessarily follow, in chronological order, what was described in chapter 19. We are then virtually compelled to believe that the thousand-year reign depicted in 20:4 must come after the return of Christ described in 19:11.*"[7]

Emphasis is ours. Now that *is* an admission! We respect him for it. Virtually any Pre-Millennialist would accept that Revelation from chapter 4 to the end is futurist, although we would agree that there have been very important, but nevertheless secondary, messages for believers, particularly persecuted ones, down through the ages, and especially for 2nd century and for Reformation and Counter-Reformation ones. Hoekema continues:

"The system of interpretation which seems most satisfactory to me (though it is not without its difficulties) is that known as progressive parallelism, ably defended by William Hendrikson... According to this view, Revelation consists of seven sections which run parallel to each other, each of which depicts the church and the world from the time of Christ's first coming to the time of His second."[8]

He then lists these supposedly parallel passages, commenting upon each:

1–3   4–7   8–11   12–14   15–16   17–19   20–22

He makes some sort of case for each, and says that, although parallel, there is a certain amount of 'eschatological progress' within the series. Ingenious though this is, one feels that the Bible itself would have given some indication of this and not left it to clever men to dig out the essential facts. What Hendriksen and Hoekema believe the divisions to be within this Historicist format are quite different from what others believe. Variations are numerous.

The whole system encourages speculation and the avoidance of literal interpretation. The phenomena described in the Trumpets and Bowls which seem to conform closely to nuclear, ecological and other latter day happening are pushed back into Church history, where they lose their most obvious relevance. The Mark of the Beast, so very comprehensible now in the age of computer technology, loses its main significance.

What in Revelation perhaps seemed to be poetic licence or exaggeration even a century ago actually describes phenomena, not only known theoretically to modern science, but actually feasible and even dreaded. But most Amillennialists simply do not want to know. God-given portents are seen as too sensational. Christians, like Jews of two thousand years ago, become blind to the signs of the times (Matt 16:3). Those immensely important texts, which demonstrate that such catastrophic events as the December 2004 tsunami are signs of the times, lose their usefulness to the evangelist. The Bible is seen to be of no more relevance than Nostradamus. Whence came the main attacks on Hal Lindsay's "Late Great Planet Earth" in the early nineteen seventies?[9] Not from liberals as one might expect, but from conservative, reformed Christians who like to believe the Bible; but only provided they can be selective.

We return to Hoekema. What particularly concerns us is that, under this system of Progressive Parallelism, we lose any realistic Hebrew identity of the twelve tribes in Revelation 7; the twelve starred woman of chapter 12 is seen to comply with the Catholic teaching of Mary. Indeed, Revelation 7 supposedly becomes part of what is summed up by Hoekema as: "In this vision we see the church avenged, protected and victorious"[10]—a Church preposterously described by twelve tribal names of Israel! I have actually heard, albeit on video, Dr John Stott, one of Britain's best known preachers, who concurs with this approach, identify the 144,000 as being the same as the multitude of the same chapter, whom no man could number. A precise number and innumerable are supposedly synonymous; the mind boggles! But this is the crazy situation in which one finds oneself with this subjective scheme and its endless permutations. Revelation becomes the Replacement Theologian's playground. Of course no room remains for identifiable Jews, because the whole of Church history is supposedly in these seven 'parallels'.

One well-known Amillennialist at least is unblinkered enough to realise that the 144,000 can only be Jews. Jay Adams perceptively writes in contrast to so many others:

> "The 144,000 are Jewish Christians. The extreme care with which their ancestry is set forth removes all doubt concerning their Jewish character. Their Hebrew nature is further accentuated by the intended contrast between them and the great Gentile multitude. The former is a *small* easily counted group of one certain racial extraction, who escape the persecution. The latter is an innumerable host of heterogeneous people from the entire civilised world of that day, who have been slain." [11]

Splendid; we could re-echo his words; so much for Amillennial solidarity! However while it is commendable indeed that the Jewish identity of the 144,000 is recognised, it is somewhat astonishing to learn from the context of the above quote, that Adams sees this account in Revelation 7 as referring to events surrounding the AD 70 fall of Jerusalem, with the sealing referring to those preserved in Pella during the Roman siege. We say 'astonishing', because the ten Northern tribes were poorly represented within the Land at that time, and twelve thousand from, for instance, Simeon, is utterly improbable *at that time*. In the future God will call His 144,000 from wherever they have been scattered; the numbers no doubt are now available. The temple genealogical records were destroyed. God's have not been; He has remained as ever in control even of family trees. Moreover, dreadful though the persecution of Jews during and following Nero's rule was, the number of martyrs in those days in no way matches the Revelation description. The worst and final holocaust lies ahead. Amillennialism and its ambivalent or dismissive attitudes to latter day Jewish involvement have a soporific influence on enquiring Jews.

The fact is that Adams is a Preterist, quite different from the Progressive Parallel Amillennialists. He believes that the Olivet Discourse and most of Revelation were fulfilled in the AD 70 sack of Jerusalem; any further messages are simply principles. Nothing is quite so demotivating to the study of the signs of the times. However as Preterism is a central feature of most Post-Millennialism, we will devote special sections to it in the next two chapters.

But what does Hoekema say about the 144,000? Precisely nothing, or at least nothing about his own views! They are no doubt an enigma within this 'progressive parallelism'. He tells us what Dispensationalists believe them to be, however. Having explained very fairly about our assertion that they fall within Daniel's seventieth week or heptad, he writes:

> "Dispensationalists hold... that at this time a remnant of Jews will return to Jesus as Messiah—the 144,000 sealed Israelites of Revelation 7:3–8... This remnant will now begin to preach 'the Gospel of the Kingdom'—a gospel having as its central content the establishment of the coming of the Davidic kingdom, but including the message of the Cross and the need for faith and repentance; through the witness of this Jewish remnant an innumerable multitude of Gentiles will also be brought to salvation. The kings of the earth will now gather together to attack the people of God in the Battle of Armageddon." [12]

Now that would be an fair summary of what virtually every Dispensationalist or Pre-Tribulationist believes, but for two fatal flaws:

1. He has completely reversed the priorities of our understanding of the Gospel of the Kingdom. The Cross and the need for faith and repentance take precedence.

2. The kings of the earth gather primarily to make war not with the Jews, but with the Lord Jesus Christ Himself.

   "And I saw the beast, the kings of the earth, and their armies, gathered together to make war against Him who sat on the horse and against His army" (Rev 19:19).

   His army is a heavenly one—resurrected saints and angels. From Rev 16:14–16 we learn that it is God who has chosen the Israel battle ground of Armageddon.

These are immensely serious distortions; it is difficult to believe that Hoekema was not aware of these matters. But such tactics must be useful in defending a weak case; they seem rather out of character with the writer.

Denied Intervals

One of the most frequently found and understandable objections, of Amillennialists to the 1000 year interval between the Lord's coming in power and the end of this earth is the fact that such an accurately defined interval is nowhere indicated before Revelation.

We must concede this point, but believe that the explanation is perfectly simple. The Apocalypse is a very, very special source of prophetic detail, which God chose to disclose after all but one of the apostles had gone. It was not needed during Apostolic days; it was left until last. Certainly we can admit that, without Revelation 20, Pre-Millennialists would have to speculate how and when God would fulfil these ancient prophecies. But now they do not have to. All becomes abundantly clear. Revelation 20 should clear up rather than cause problems.

This book is Christ's own personal revelation, carrying its own unique blessings and warnings. If theologians cannot cope with the fact that such passages as Revelation 20 to 22 contain much new information, they should stay clear of the field of eschatology. But it is there for our enlightenment, and we believe it arrogant to ignore it or to make it subject to adjustment and amplification by earlier prophecies. It should be the other way round. Even should the earlier date for Revelation, which some claim, prove to be correct, it would not alter the futurist nature of this wonderful book.

The constant Amillennial complaint that there is no clear-cut statement that unfulfilled Old Testament prophecies to Israel fit in to this interval may deserve some attention. But consider this; we believe in the Holy Trinity, and, whether we are A-, Pre- or Post-Millennialists, vigorously defend this against JWs, who love to tell us that there is not single statement of this doctrine. There was no single clear-cut statement of First Coming eschatology in the Old Testament; yet Jesus, as we know from the Emmaus road incident, indicated that His disciples should have been aware of these matters. Must we have every detail written down like a train timetable before we will accept it? Where would be the blessing? (Rev 1:3; 22:7). The following are only a few of the quotes available on these matters.

Berkhof, in his *Systematic Theology*, indicates two precedents, one of which he accepts and applies; one of which, incongruously, he denies:

> "While the prophets do not clearly distinguish a twofold coming of Christ, the Lord Himself and the apostles make it abundantly clear that the first coming will be followed by a second... Present day dispensationalists distinguish between a twofold future coming of Christ, though they sometimes seek to preserve the unity of the idea of the second coming by speaking of these as two aspects of that great event."[13]

We would not quarrel with either statement. But, if we take Berkhof as representative of Amillennial thinking on this matter, we see indicators of a great anomaly. It is simply this. It is readily acknowledged that within the range of Old Testament Messianic prophecies there was, unknown to the writers, a long and most significant interval which we now know to be the Church Age. Why is it therefore that Amillennialists deny *on this basis* both the future intervals between the Rapture and the Coming in Power and between the Coming in Power and the end of the world? It is much their most frequently found argument. And yet it is flawed, inasmuch as there is the precedent, which Berkhof has eloquently described, in the previously unannounced interval between the First and Second Comings. Post-Tribulationists on the same basis deny the Rapture to Second Coming interval, but accept the Millennial interval. Where is the consistency?

If we go back to the opening verses of Isaiah 61, which we looked at much earlier, we are able to pinpoint two intervals not perceived by the prophet himself as he echoed miraculously beforehand the words of the Messiah Himself:

"The Spirit of the Lord God is upon Me...

1. *To proclaim the acceptable year of the Lord,*

2. *And the day of Vengeance of our God.*

> 3. *To comfort all who mourn, to console those who mourn in Zion... and they shall rebuild the old ruins, they shall raise up the former desolations... "* (Is 61:1–4).

Were we to read on we would see more of what is clearly an earthly, rather than a heavenly, restoration. The Amillennialist has no difficulty in recognising the interval between the first two missions, but is blind both to the interval between the second and third, and what is to happen within it. What does Cox say about this latter interval?

> "Amillenarians find no scriptural basis for an interregnum between the second advent and the eternal state." [14]

He then proceeds with some of the old arguments with which we have already dealt, including the seven 'parallel visions'. But let us turn to another Amillennialist, Bruce Milne, to refute Cox's statement. Milne is a very thorough researcher and is much better versed in the standard beliefs of those with whom he disagrees than others we have quoted. One feels that Amillennialism sits rather uncomfortably with him. Would that all Amillennialists presented Pre-Millennialism so fairly!

> "For pre-millennialists the thousand-year reign or its equivalent will take place after the second coming. The Parousia is before the millennium. The biblical support for this view is drawn from passages which describe the messianic kingdom in terms of an ideal earthly order" (a short but helpful list follows). "It also appeals to references which appear to present the coming age in material forms (Matt 19:28; Acts 1:6–7; Mk 10:35–40: Jn 5:25–29; Rev 5:9–10) or which is claimed to allow the idea of a passage of time between Christ's return and the eternal age (1 Cor 15:23–25; I Thess 4:13ff.; Eph 2:7). The major support however is clearly Rev 20:2–5. It is certainly doubtful whether this view would ever have been held on the basis of the other biblical passages cited had the passage in Revelation 20 not been present." [15]

Apart from reservations about the last sentence, we would not argue with this. It more or less describes where we stand. But we would re-emphasise what we said whilst reviewing some of Berkhof's comments. We should take time to look at the opening verses of Revelation:

> *"The revelation of Jesus Christ, which God gave Him to show His servants—things which must shortly (or in quick succession) take place."*

Revelation provides completely new information. It is exceedingly important to appreciate this. The fact that the whole picture cannot be seen until the closing chapters of the Bible, far from casting doubts about the place for Israel's glorious national future, shows how remarkable is the planning of this wonderful old book. Remove the first four chapters of Genesis and the last four of Revelation and we are left wondering how the rest of the Bible fits into time and eternity. Far too many remove or allegorise both sets of chapters and make shipwreck of their theology. Fundamentalist Amillennialists are inconsistent. They interpret the opening chapters of Genesis literally and the closing ones of Revelation symbolically. At least liberals are consistent, taking both allegorically. Had Revelation 20 not existed, we would have certainly been puzzled to know how and when God would keep some of His promises. But it would not have been grounds to doubt them. Milne, having come so near to the truth, continues:

> "Another problem with Revelation 20 being referred to as an earthly reign of Christ with his saints is that there is no indication that this reign is on earth at all. The whole book of Revelation spends much of its time with realities 'behind the scenes' in the heavenly order. John refers to the throne no less than 47 times in his visions… every other reference is to a location in heaven. Why then should chapter 20 be a single exception?" [16]

This is a good question, though we would point out that about half of Revelation concerns events on earth, albeit authorised by heaven. What Milne and other writers seem not to notice is that Revelation 19 describes Jesus' return to earth, conforming perfectly to Zechariah 14:11 and Acts 1:11. It does not conform to the Rapture descriptions of 1 Thess 4:17 or Jn 14:3, which give no indication of His coming down to earth, but rather His return with the resurrected saints to heaven. In Revelation 19

Jesus arrives spectacularly on earth, with much business to which to attend, including the Judgment of the Nations.

> *"When the Son of Man comes in His glory, and all the angels with Him, then He will sit on the throne of His glory"* (Matt 25:31).

Then, Jesus told us, He will judge the gathered nations, dividing them into two groups. Jesus tells us that this is on earth at His coming.

Would Amillennialists have us believe that the unsaved are going to be transported to *heaven* to hear their fate? As we saw in an earlier chapter, this is when *"The Lord shall be King over all the earth"* (Zech 14:9). This is the Revelation 19 scenario with a different emphasis, but with the clearest indication that there will be a restored nation of Israel (Zech 14:10–21). Allegorising a chapter like Zechariah 14 makes no sense at all. Reading it word by word does.

Neither Revelation 19 nor Zechariah 14 gives any indication whatsoever of the Lord's early return with His saints from earth back to heaven. His thousand-year rule on earth is just commencing. We do not get that from Zechariah, but we do from Revelation if we read through into the start of chapter 20. We accept Milne's point that there are no other references to Christ's earthly throne in Revelation; because no other earthly scene demands it. The Beast's kingdom has first to be overthrown. The aforementioned Judgement of the Nations is not about 'behind the scenes' happenings in heaven. Matthew 25 makes it absolutely clear that it will take place when Jesus returns here.

After all, Zechariah 14 describes the earth where Jehovah will reign, as *following* His return to the Mount of Olives, and that conforms perfectly to Rev 19:16 to 20:4. The break placed by Amillennialists at the end of Revelation 19 is one of the most unnatural anywhere; yet in desperation it has to be inserted in order to avoid the most obvious sense of the passage. Adams is a rare Amillennial exception, seeing no break of continuity between chapters 19 and 20. [17] Unfulfilled prophecies concerning the Jews and Jerusalem and other nations fit naturally there. Denial of the literal sense of these prophecies is escapism.

John Stott at least recognises the prophetic significance of new revelation of previously unknown truths. He makes a good case for this in relation to the Church, writing about Ephesians 3:1–6; but then proceeds to blunder over Israel.

> "These statements have puzzled Bible readers because the Old Testament did reveal that God had a purpose for the Gentiles. It promised, for example, that (1) all the families of the earth would be blessed through Abraham's posterity; (2) that the Messiah would receive the nations as his inheritance; (3) that Israel would be given as a light to the nations; and (4) that one day the nations would make a pilgrimage to Jerusalem and even 'flow to it' like a mighty river… But what neither the Old Testament nor Jesus revealed was the radical nature of God's plan, which was that the theocracy (the Jewish nation under God's rule) would be terminated, and replaced by a new international community, the church; that this church would be the body of Christ, organically united to him; and that Jews and Gentiles would be incorporated into Christ and his church on equal terms without any distinction. It was this complete union of Jews, Gentiles and Christ which was radically new, and which God revealed to Paul, overcoming his entrenched Jewish prejudice." [18]

It is perhaps appropriate that it is an Anglican who has produced this curate's egg—good in parts! But of course the point of the polite curate's egg story is that an egg bad in even one part is quite unacceptable. We have a good picture here of the Church Age, but of none other. We also agree with him that neither the Old Testament nor Jesus revealed the termination of the theocracy; *but neither did Paul nor any other Bible writer*. That was left to John Stott, and other Amillennialists who share his views! The theocracy, as we saw in an earlier chapter, is discontinued only *"until He comes whose right it (the crown) is, and will give it to Him"* (Ezek 21:27), or *"until Shiloh comes; and to Him shall be the obedience of the people"* (Gen 49:10). When He first came they were disobedient. This is about the earth to which He is coming again.

What is so inconsistent here is that Stott has listed (and the bracketed numbers are our addition) four major promises of God concerning the Gentiles, and then has immediately effectively annulled numerous other promises of God concerning the Jews. One could hardly blame an Orthodox Jew for questioning God's New Testament promises if His Old Testament ones are so unreliable. This sort of reasoning puts up barriers to enquiring Jews. What Stott is ignoring are all those 'until' conditions listed in our chapters three and four. He has no need for a future Millennium, because he has, with a single sweep of his pen, removed its *raison d'etre*.

Adams widens the topic under consideration. He brings Israel into the picture, so we must take note. We have already noted that Adams believed that the Jews *had* a future when Jesus gave His Olivet Discourse, but that the prophecies were fulfilled in AD 70. Adams, like Augustine, admits to having formerly been a Pre-Millennialist.[19] If Augustine's understanding of Pre-Millennialism was as erratic as Adams', it is hardly surprising he abandoned it.

> "Having rejected the unbiblical principle of an exclusively literal interpretation of Old Testament prophecy, many no longer look upon the so-called 'National Israel' as God's chosen people. They cannot agree to a 'Jewish' millennium, fully equipped with rebuilt temple and restored sacrificial system. They find no indication of a utopian-type millennium anywhere upon the pages of the New Testament. In fact apart from the twentieth chapter of Revelation, they wonder how anyone could come to the premillennial viewpoint at all. They freely admit that this one chapter is the sole purpose for their belief."[20]

Doctrinal Misrepresentations

Now Adams is a much more confused Amillennialist than the others whom we have quoted. In his foreword he writes "I simply do not know the source of many of my ideas".[21] We can well believe this. He is following a policy which is difficult to respect, of discrediting another school of prophecy by citing its weakest and least knowledgeable adherents rather than its strongest. His theology seems to include regarding Scripture at face value as 'unbiblical'; he makes no proviso for the difference between understanding heavenly and earthly scenes. His use of inverted commas has anti-Semitic undertones; his statement about the exclusiveness of Revelation 20 as a basis for Pre-Millennialism goes far beyond anything claimed by our other representative Amillennialists. Who 'they' are who make this 'free admission' I cannot imagine; he seems to have met them. Presumably they are accidental Pre-Millennialists who do not understand the basis of their belief. Every school of prophecy has such adherents; it is totally unethical to quote them as authorities.

Cox is equally guilty of misrepresenting others to bolster his own weak position. Consider the following:

> "Here then is the gist of much millennial thinking today: Christ offered to Israel a kingdom. This proffered kingdom was to have been an earthly messianic reign, patterned after David's kingdom of the Old Testament. The throne of David was to have been set up in the temple of Jerusalem, where Jesus was to rule with a rod of iron—forcing saved and unsaved alike to worship him and to perform the rituals and sacrifices performed in the Old Testament temple…". [22]

He has the unspeakable effrontery of crediting Lewis Sperry Chafer with this teaching. He does not of course give a reference. What he has apparently done is to latch onto certain things which Chafer very probably did write and then made a dog's breakfast of them. This is not the 'gist of millennial teaching today'. It is Cox's shocking distortion of what he would like his believers to believe about Millennialists in order to further his own arguments. It suggests that we believe that God is not sovereign and was unable to take into account the Fall, the Flood, Babel and a hundred other happenings up to and including Jesus' rejection by His own people, so that He could go to the Cross and die for us.

This misrepresentation of Dispensational Pre-Millennialism in order to promote Amillennialism is all too common. It is quite common, for instance, to find American writers asserting that Darby acquired his Pre-Millennial stance from Irving. This they capitalise on because later Irving was accused of heresy. There was indeed some contact between the two, but dates and facts have become muddled and sequences altered in order to discredit Darbyites. Not all Americans have been thus duped. Stanton points out that there is no evidence that Irving was a Pre-Tribulationist; he simply proclaimed the imminence of the Lord's return. [23] This distortion was first recorded many decades ago, and modern writers assume that because their authorities are perhaps a hundred years old, they must needs be correct.

One is usually left wondering whether such misrepresentation is conscious and deliberate, but one sincerely hopes that it is not. Many of the writers one feels are beyond reproach in this respect and merely mistaken; but a few seem be manipulative, as we have noticed, in that they take the worst or most obscure rather the best or most representative quotes. Take two statements of Walter Chantry; all that we can be sure about is that for one reason or another he quotes them as factual:

> "Some pre-millennialists and some post-millennialists slip easily into referring to the millennium as the kingdom (without Bible warrant)... Almost unconsciously some Christians begin to identify their loftier desires and expectations for blessing with what will happen in this present world during the temporary period called the millennium. Whatever your views of eschatology (and of the millennium in particular), you are on dangerous ground when the most profound longings of your heart and most energetic labours of your life have for their object a transient millennium instead of the final and eternal state of affairs toward which our Lord Jesus pointed us."[24]

We would agree with the danger, and see the application to some *Post-*Millennialists. But why bring Pre-Millennialists into the picture? No Pre-Millennialist believes that he or she will enter the Millennium in their earthly body. We are awaiting the return of the Lord Jesus Christ. The majority of us expect to be in heaven before we return to earth, and our hearts are set (or should be) on heavenly things. The joyful millennium is primarily there for those in their earthly bodies, although we will be there with our Lord in our resurrection ones. His second statement is this:

> "The scheme outlined by our Lord's kingdom teaching excludes the possibility of certain popular viewpoints. There is little wonder that dispensational pre-millennialists have relegated all kingdom references to the millennium. For Christ's teaching alone would disprove their chartered eschatology."[25]

Now this is a gross distortion of the truth. We have emphatically *not* relegated all kingdom references to the Millennium. The vast majority of Dispensational Pre-Millennialists recognise, as we discussed at some length in our previous chapter, the present Kingdom in Mystery. We quoted various Pre-Millennial authorities in earlier chapters. Such, for a good number of Amillennialists, are the defective building bricks of their school of prophecy.

One important argument which we have previously referred to is the remarkable Jewishness of much of Revelation. While we could usefully use it here to re-enforce the presence of special Jewish activity during the Tribulation period, we feel that it would be more useful to return to it in Chapter Thirteen.

Single Resurrection And Single Judgement?

Here are two Amillennial doctrines to which we could profitably devote as much time and attention as we have done to the Millennium interval (or its absence). If one believes, as we do, in the future thousand year interval of Revelation 20, then we find that the First Resurrection takes place before this interval and the Second after it, and that any judgements before and any after must be quite separate events.

We could safely go as far as to say that, if the Bible teaches that there are separate 'before and after' resurrections and separate 'before and after' judgments, we have gone a long way to proving Pre-Millennialism right, but that if these are not separate, but rather single, events, we have gone a long way towards proving that either A- or Post-Millennialism is right. However we are going to spend only the briefest time looking at these questions for two reasons:

- They add very little to the way into which Israel fits into the prophetic picture.

- The arguments we have used to prove a future identifiable Millennium upon earth are more or less the same as we would use here. There is no need to repeat them in full.

All of the previously quoted Amillennial apologists and most of the other Amillennial writers rest their case on the fact that they find no verses in Scripture prior to Revelation indicating separate resurrections of the redeemed and the lost, and no separate judgements for these two groups. Cox writes:

> "It is difficult to understand how so many persons can ignore these plain verses while they take an obscure passage from Revelation (20:5,6) and build a doctrine of two or more bodily resurrections upon it."[26]

When one considers Who gave John this Apocalypse, one feels that Cox's words are not far short of blasphemy—'obscure passage' indeed! Any respect which we might otherwise have for Cox as a theologian evaporates as we read this comment on the closing chapters of Scripture.

Cox and others ignore the fact that, while there are indeed many passages which do not state categorically that the resurrections about which they speak will take place in more than one stage, there is none which says that this *will* be a single event. It is an assumption. It is *exactly* the same as the Old Testament perspective of which we have already spoken, where the interval between the Lord's first and second comings was simply not apparent from their first prediction alone. It is similar to Peter, who refused to adjust his notions of the future when Jesus told him something which he had not previously heard (Matt 16:22). Jesus' reaction was very severe indeed. This time we have graciously been given extra last minute information to correct our perspective. If we choose to call this obscure, we are treading on dangerous ground. It was always a popular ploy among liberals and atheists to poke fun at those who take the Bible seriously. Fortunately few Amillennialists would go quite as far as Cox, but they do use much the same arguments.

However if one accepts the future Millennium (and in God's unfulfilled promises to Israel we have seen the clearest indicators to this truth), one can look back to the resurrection verses of other books of the Bible and see, with augmented understanding, how many of these do fit quite clearly into one resurrection or the other, whilst the partakers referred to in other verses are going to be split into two distinct groups to face very different judgements.

Berkhof puts his case for a single resurrection and judgement quite simply, quoting such verses as Dan 12:2; Jn 5:28; Acts 24:15, Rom 2:5–10; II Cor 5:10; II Tim 4:1 etc.[27] Certainly these particular verses do not actually differentiate, but they do raise questions when one considers the contrasting status before God of the redeemed and the unsaved. Revelation 20 answers any such questions. Note that in Lk 14:14 Jesus speaks specifically about the *"resurrection of the just"*.

Cox produces a long convoluted argument[28] to prove that the first resurrection is a spiritual one which takes place at conversion and that only the second resurrection is physical. Now, whilst of course the texts which Cox quotes do talk of a spiritual rebirth or resurrection, this is not what Revelation is talking about. Just look at Revelation 20.

Verses 4 and 5 talk emphatically about the bodily resurrection of people who have been physically dead.

> *"I saw the souls of those who had been beheaded for their witness to Jesus and for the word of God, who had not worshiped the beast or his image, and had not received his mark on their foreheads or on their hands. And they lived and reigned with Christ a thousand years."*

Now this is devastating for Amillennialists, because if the thousand years is the Church Age, these have been resurrected already, so cannot be included in the same resurrection as that described in II Thess 4:

> *"But the rest of the dead did not live again until the thousand years were finished. This is the first resurrection."*

The obvious conclusion leaves Amillennialism in tatters. We will look soon a little further into the first resurrection and how many stages are involved. We know however that it is exclusively for the Redeemer (the Firstfruits—I Cor 15:20) and the redeemed:

> *"Blessed and holy is he who has a part in the first resurrection"* (v6).

This playing around with the idea that the first resurrection is not physical, when all the indications in Revelation 20 are that it is, is extremely dangerous. This is the sort of argument that liberals use to deny the bodily resurrection of the Lord.

> *"If Christ is not risen your faith is futile; you are still in your sins!"* (I Cor 15:17).

Thus it verges on apostasy. The first resurrection is physical; verse 4 clearly shows that it is a different state from that which existed when John saw only their souls. They are now in their resurrection bodies. And nobody except the Lord himself will be in such a body before the Rapture (I Thess 4:15–17). That great Greek scholar, Dean Alford, said that claiming that one resurrection in Revelation 20 was spiritual and the other physical made a mockery of language.

Once we realise from Revelation 20, that the Great White Throne, which *follows* the Millennium, is only for those brought back from the grave in the second resurrection, we realise that there must be other prior judgements. Resurrected Tribulation saints are hardly going to reign with Christ before their personal judgement, are they? Their levels of honour and responsibility are going to be awarded by the Lord in proportion to their faithfulness in this life (Matt 25:21 etc.), not according to whether or not their names are written in the Lamb's Book of Life. Absence from the Lamb's book of life will be evidence for damnation (Rev 20:12). They will therefore be judged by their evil works, there being no atonement.

In the New Testament the resurrection of the just is frequently described as being *ek nekron*—'from the dead'. The AV and NKJV are fairly consistent; the JN Darby version is probably best at emphasising the significance of the original. The sense is 'out from among', implying that others remain among the dead. The NIV is inconsistent. In Acts 4:2 it reads *"proclaiming in Jesus the resurrection **of** the dead"*, but in verse 10, *"Jesus Christ... whom God raised **from** the dead"*. The Greek is the same—*ek nekron*; the *'of the dead'* in verse 2 is inappropriate. The unwary might reach the following conclusion: when Jesus left the dead, others remained (that we all know to be true); but when believers rise, no one will be left behind among the dead. Intentionally or unwittingly, the NIV thus promotes the Amillennial doctrine of a general resurrection. Most of the paraphrased versions miss altogether the significance of the resurrection of the saved being out from among the dead.

At the second resurrection nobody is left.

> *"The sea gave up the dead who were in it, and Death and Hades delivered up the dead who were in them. And they were judged, each according to his works"* (Rev 20:13).

Were we more like our Saviour, and unafraid to preach the bad news as well as the good news, we might have sorted these matters out in our minds.

If we look at the verses about the great judgments in other books of the Bible in the light of the fresh information in Revelation 20, it become so easy to see that there are in fact a number of separate judgements for different groups, in different places and at different times. For instance the sins of the redeemed were judged in Christ at Calvary. Only those whose names are not written in the Lamb's Book of Life will be judged for their sins, the Book bearing testimony to the fact that they rejected the salvation which had been on offer (Rev 20:12 et seq.).

We can see now that the Judgment of the Nations (Matt 25:31–46) is a separation, of the living saved from those who are about to die, and is not about the dead, which we are told is whom the Great White Throne deals with. Consider the contrasts in scenario, standards and processes between the Judgement of the Nations and the Great White Throne. Amillennialists would have us believe they are different pictures of the same thing. Neither is a 'picture'. Each is as clear a description of an actual event as we can presently understand. One is emphatically upon earth (Matt 25:32,33); the other is equally emphatically not on earth (Rev 20:11). How can we faithfully preach the Gospel and the consequence of rejecting it if we are dealing much of the time in allegories, rather than with simply explained facts?

We can see more clearly how the Judgement Seat of Christ (Rom 14:10; II Cor 5:10) is different from either of these two. The Greek *bema* is used there for judgement seat; as opposed to *thronos*, which is used for all other New Testament cases for God the Father or the Son being seated, including the Great White Throne. As we have emphasised, at the Bema believers cannot be judged for their sins, which were washed away by Christ's redeeming blood. Our *service* for our Lord will be judged in the refiner's fire. I Cor 3:10–13 tells us most about this—an under-preached topic. Ignorance of this leads to a belief in purgatory, a dangerous Catholic adaptation of an ancient pagan myth. Works may well be burned away, leaving nothing for reward. But it is entirely different from the judgement of the unbeliever.

The garments of the saints, witness of their righteous acts, as described in Rev 19:7–8, leaves us in no doubt that the judgement and reward of the Church will occur before the marriage of the Lamb, which in turn occurs before His Coming in Power. Indeed, the fact that the twenty-four elders, seen in Revelation 4, have crowns to cast before the throne indicates that the Bema will take place in heaven immediately after the Rapture and before the first Seal is opened.

Satan Bound Now Or Later?

One of the immense problems Amillennialists face when they claim that the Millennium equates to the Church Age is the fact that, according to Rev 20:2, the Devil, Satan, is bound throughout. They claim that He has been bound since Calvary. We do not dispute the fact that since Calvary and Jesus' resurrection Satan's sentence and ultimate destruction have been put beyond any shadow of doubt. But can we really agree that he has been bound in the terms of Rev 20:1–3? Let us read what God says through His servant John:

> *"Then I saw an angel coming down from heaven, having the key to the bottomless pit and a great chain in his hand. And he laid hold of the dragon, that serpent of old, who is the Devil and Satan, and bound him for a thousand years; and cast him into the bottomless pit, and shut him up, and set a seal on him, so that he should deceive the nations no more till the thousand years were finished."*

The Greek word translated here as 'bottomless pit' is *abussos,* whence we get the word 'abyss'. It is the place to which the legion of demons possessing the demoniac of Gadarenes (Lk 8:26–33) pleaded not to be sent by Jesus. Clearly the bodies of the swine—even dead swine—would have been a preferable fate to premature sentencing to the abyss. It is the prison from which a mighty hoard of demons will be temporarily released at the fifth Trumpet (Rev 9:1 et seq.). It seems likely from II Pet 2:4 that some of the most evil demons have been imprisoned there since the time of the Flood with their ruler, Apollyon. Do we get the impression from Revelation 20 that Satan is to be incarcerated in a place of total security, with the nations totally beyond his grasp for a thousand years? We certainly do. But Amillennialists argue otherwise. Why?

Because they have left themselves with no alternative if they are to maintain their stand.

Hoekema refers to a number of conflicting views of those who believe that Satan is currently bound[29]—this is hardly surprising as any such case is inevitably very weak in the light of Revelation 20; each case has to provide some means of evading the obvious implications. Many Amillennialists are quite unapologetic about this. However Milne is honest enough to recognise the difficulties:

> "This view has to cope with the problem that the devil does seem alive and pretty well in the period of the church and *not*, as would seem from the Revelation 20 language, shut up in a sealed pit and unable to deceive the nations any more. Certainly Christ has won a decisive victory over the devil and all the powers of darkness. The evil one is mortally wounded. The ultimate outcome of the conflict with the powers of darkness is not at all in doubt. Further they may, through the power of Christ working through faith and prayer, actually 'bind' the devil in human history so that the gospel can be preached and believed and the captives of the devil redeemed and set free. All that is true and gloriously so, but when all that is said, the description in 20:2–3 does not square very well with the realities of human history. Was the devil bound at Auschwitz? Was he 'bound' during Stalin's purges in Russia?"[30]

Thank you, Bruce Milne! Virtually all Amillennialists explain the binding as some form of limited restriction imposed by God on Satan during the Church Age, in contrast to total isolation and disarming of Rev 20:2,3. Of course there have been restrictions in the past—but the bottomless pit will be very different. Were we to trace the course of Jewish history, or indeed the history of the Christian Church, through the past almost twenty centuries, we would be reminded that, as Peter said:

> *"Your adversary the devil walks about like a roaring lion, seeking whom he may devour"* (I Pet 5:8).

Peter's words are tantamount to saying that the devil is most emphatically *not* yet bound in the way that the Bible says he will be in the future Millennium. Bound people do not wander; and we may assume that any binding ordered by God will be effective.

According to II Cor 11:14 Satan is at present masquerading as an angel of light, which seems to us more like deceiving the nations than languishing in the bottomless pit. According to Eph 2:2 he is the *"prince of the power of the air, the spirit who now works in the sons of disobedience"*. This is hardly an abysmal activity.

Amillennialists tend to describe the New Testament binding, as they see it, of Satan as something quite novel. Yet if one goes right back to that very early book of Job, we find that God even then restricted Satan's power, particularly over the righteous. In Job 1:12 and 2:6, he was given greater freedom than he had previously exercised. But God still imposed strict limitations. Elisha was well protected by an angelic army (II Kings 6:17). In addition to angelic powers, we Church saints currently have the extra protection of the Holy Spirit Himself. Israel's special champion is the archangel Michael (Dan 12:1), though God's wakeful eye is ever upon her (Ps 121:4). When Satan is eventually bound, no such special defences against him will be needed.

In Revelation 12:7–9 we encounter the great Dragon, Satan, the devil or malignant slanderer who accuses the brethren day and night, warring in the heavenlies before being cast to earth (v9)—not into the bottomless pit. The saints overcome him by the blood of the Lamb; such overcoming of Satan will not have to happen when he is bound. Then on earth we see the first Beast (13:1) and False Prophet (13:11). Thus we have the trinity of evil. In Rev 19:19–20:3 this evil trinity is dealt with by God immediately following the battle of Armageddon, when Jesus Christ returns in power. The chapter numbering is man's later insertion. The scenario is quite unambiguous. The Beast and False Prophet are cast alive into the lake of fire, and Satan, because he has still to be released briefly at the end of the Millennium, is bound in the Abyss. There will never be any return from the lake of fire. To disassociate the judgement of the other two from that of Satan seems passing strange; yet the great majority of Amillennialists would separate the start of the Millennium and the Lord's return. Even Satan apparently has to bow to their arbitrary sequence of events!

In contemplating Satan's ultimate defeat, we must never forget that right now we can and should be having victories over our tempter, as

Rom 16:20 confirms. But the ultimate victory is not for the Church, as some Post-Millennialists would teach, but for Jesus Christ, the Seed of the Woman (Gen 3:15). He delegates his binding to an angel. Until that day not even the Archangel is presumptuous with Satan (Jude 1:9). God has the final say (Rev 20:10).

Conclusion To Validity Of Amillennialism

In these two chapters on Amillennialism it may seem that we have frequently returned to the same points. This is because the case for Amillennialism is a circular argument. We have had neither the time nor the space to look at all the issues, but believe that we have given a very fair representation, with greater emphasis on typical views than on extreme ones. Taking the main tenets of Amillennialism, we have reasoning which goes something like this:

- There is no future Millennium.

- Therefore it must be either past or present.

- It cannot be past because events following it have yet to occur.

- Therefore it must be present.

- Because events described in Revelation immediately before it have yet to occur, there must be a break of vision between chapter 19 and 20, thus isolating the opening verses of 20 and the Millennium from the Lord's return.

- Because there is no future Millennium interval and because neither the events at the end of chapters 19 and the end of chapter 20 have not yet been fulfilled, they must all occur at the same time.

- Therefore the judgements described in chapters 19 and 20 are identical—a single judgement, whether or not the descriptions are similar.

- Because those appearing at this single judgement are raised in the second resurrection, they cannot be raised physically in the first; that must be spiritual.

- Because the Millennium is present, Satan must currently be bound, whether the facts confirm this or not.

- Because these things differ from the simpler implications of Revelation 20, they cannot be literal, but rather are symbolic or allegorical.

- This includes the Millennium itself, which need not be taken as the exact period of a thousand years as described six times in this chapter, but rather something different, such as the Church Age.

- Therefore there is no future Millennium.

Thus we have gone full circle. There are of course variations and different starting points. But, having dismissed so much of what we believe is primarily end-time prophecy and having relegated so much to subjective and inconclusive hypotheses, Amillennialists have very little left to study profitably. Only the very barest bones of prophecy remain relatively undisputed. And these do not require much depth of knowledge.

While we accept that all prophetic schools have their internal differences of opinion, these have struck us as being particularly wide with Amillennialism. They range from liberalism to extreme conservatism. We recognise that some fine evangelical theologians are Amillennialists. We accept that the title is unfortunate in that it implies a complete denial of any Millennium. Most see it as equating to the Church Age and leave it at that.

We have noted within the evangelical wing of Amillennialism much Historicism or Progressive Parallelism in the interpretation of Revelation and other end-time prophecies, but have also noted Preterism, which teaches that most end-time prophecy was fulfilled in AD 70 or thereabouts. The two views are of course mutually exclusive.

We have found remarkable inconsistency among those who claim to be Bible-believing, in their interpretation of Scripture. They read all Scripture other than that which is exclusively visionary at face value; generally they interpret as literally as possible the Old Testament prophecies concerning Jesus' First Coming, but they allegorise extensively those prophecies both Old and New, which refer to His Second Coming. Most of them claim in an allegorised form for the Church the future blessings promised to Israel, but tend to ignore the future curses promised.

Like us, they see Jew and Gentile entering the Church on precisely the same basis and with the same status during the present age. But most see the unconditional Old Testament prophecies for the nation Israel as being merely conditional, and therefore as having being annulled by their rejection of their Messiah two thousand years ago. They accept a 'seventy times seven' principle of God's forbearance and forgiveness for the Church, but set a double standard by denying this for the nation Israel. It is a pagan approach which gives greater priority to man's promises to God than God's towards mankind.

Attitudes to Israel vary very greatly, from the hard inflexibility of Metcalfe and the like to a complete assurance in others that God will somehow lead the nation to repentance. Some Amillennialists castigate Israel, some are indifferent and yet others love her. But unanimously they deny any future *opportunity* for a literal kingdom on earth, with a restored Israel and a re-established Eden-like environment. They assume Satan to be bound at present. They produce elaborate arguments which are totally unconvincing in the light of the present appalling depravity of the world. They believe in a single general resurrection and a single day of judgement for saint and sinner alike and living and resurrected alike. They find some Scriptural support, but fail to take into account the fact that the opening verses of Revelation indicate that much new information is about to be imparted; they refuse to adjust their prophetic timetables to allow any interval between judgements.

So, while only a fringe of conservative Amillennialists show any indications of Anti-Semitic prejudice, we find that all deny any future for Israel in which God's faithfulness to His promises can be demonstrated and where the Saviour can be glorified in the world which crucified Him. We believe Amillennialism thus to be invalidated.

> "Lo,! He comes, with clouds descending,
> Once for favoured sinners slain;
> Thousand thousand saints attending
> Swell the triumph of His train;
> Alleluia! Alleluia! Alleluia!
> **God appears on earth to reign.**"

While Charles Wesley, who wrote these familiar words, is not detailed in this eschatology, a prior Rapture is implied to allow resurrected saints to accompany Him. He returns not only to judge but to reign on earth. Precious few of the great revivalists were Amillennial.

So Why Bother?

We have seen many disconcerting things about Amillennialism, although we must admit that, regarding Israel, some forms are much more dangerous than others. We noted in our last chapter that it is currently a very dominant and widespread school of prophecy. That, we noted, may or may not be because it is less demanding of credulity. That would be unfair to some adherents; not to others. It allows people a wide degree of laxity in interpreting what it believes to be allegorical writing. This in turn leads to lack of precision in its teaching and even wooliness in the application of Scripture to the signs of the times. We believe that some of the most sincere Christians are falling into the same trap before Christ's Second Coming as devout disciples did at His First Coming.

Those believers who wish to be considered politically correct need look no further than Amillennialism. Within it there is room for discarding any future national place for Israel in God's plans for the remaining life of this planet. Therefore the 'Palestinian' claim to the Promised Land, and in particular Jerusalem, may be viewed sympathetically, and Jewish claims may be condemned. 'PC' Christians will escape the inconvenient moral dilemma of deciding whether three and a half thousand years ago God was right in saying to the Children of Israel:

> *"You shall dispossess the inhabitants of the land and dwell in it, for I have given you the land to possess"* (Num 33:53).

Of course the current situation is not an exact parallel, but there are similarities, including the avowed intention among many Palestinians totally to destroy Israel.

Yet, just as it was recorded:

> *"The Lord your God Himself crosses over before you; He will destroy these nations"* (Deut 31:3),

so, Pre-Millennialists believe, when He returns in power, as Captain or Commander of the Lord's army (compare Josh 5:14 with Rev 19:11–14),

He will destroy all who oppose Him. In Joshua's time the Lord led invisibly, except in the form of the pillar of cloud or fire. Next time *"every eye shall see Him"*.

Basilea Schlink, who did so much to bring home to Germans their guilt for the Holocaust, writes:

> "In the beginning anti-Judaism was mainly confined to the clergy, whose theological dissertations were conducted not only without love, but very often in open malice. To justify their stance, they argued that the Jews had killed Jesus and had persistently refused to accept salvation... In this way the devil succeeded in making Christians prepare the ground for him. The stone that had started to roll became an avalanche because no one checked its descent... The hatred manifested by the forerunners of the Antichrist such as Hitler will reach its final climax in the antichristian era proper." [31]

The parallelism interpretation of Revelation has deflected Amillennialists from being aware of the coming final holocaust. So even those Amillennialists who do not believe that God has finished with the Jews *as a nation* are lulled into a position which our Enemy welcomes—a position which, when the Church is caught up to heaven and the *"restrainer is taken out of the way"* (II Thess 2:7), will lead to the *"Time of Jacob's trouble"* (Jer 30:7). God said to Israel, *"I have loved you with an everlasting love"* (Jer 31:3). That was said to the nation, rather than to every individual. Most Amillennialists say it applies only to individual Jews, and we agree that individual repentance and response is also essential. But God has not cast away the nation. The great appeal of Hosea 14 will one day be answered. The appeal starts with the words, *"O Israel, return to the Lord your God"* (v1), is followed by lovely reassurances of forgiveness, and concludes with *"Who is wise? Let him understand these things"* (v9). Does it not grieve God that so many of His promises regarding others of His own are either allegorised, trivialised or ignored?

Chapter Eleven

Traditional Post-Millennialism And Israel's Future

Dealing With Post-Millennialism

We propose to tackle this in a rather different way from Amillennialism, because:

- Traditional Post-Millennialism has long been on the decline—we will explain later.

- Post-Millennialism is more recent than Pre- or Amillennialism; therefore its teachings are rather less complex.

- Some of the arguments which we used against Amillennialism apply here too, so we can refer back to the previous two chapters.

- Post-Millennialism, unlike Amillennialism, is a positive rather than a negative term. It describes what people believe rather than what they do not believe. Therefore it is easier to apply the Bible's tests for true or false prophecy in order to achieve an authoritative evaluation.

- While there is one distinct category of Post-Millennialism which we would describe as liberal, most adherents are comparatively conservative in their theology. There is a smaller 'grey area' between liberal and conservative than we encountered with Amillennialism.

- Whilst this school of prophecy is now in decline, much of its thinking has been transferred to the more aggressive and now widespread Neo-Post-Millennialism; the 'parent' is worth studying for the sake of understanding the 'child'.

- This 'child' is growing apace, so requires a dedicated Chapter Twelve.

We concede that the above are generalisations with which some Post-Millennialists might disagree in detail. However we believe them to be fair—in general terms!

Before we proceed any further, let us confirm that the Bible specifically teaches us a means of identifying which prophecies are true and which are false. It is a test which can be applied much more effectively to Post-than to A-millennialism, as the latter shares with Pre-Millennialism the teaching that the world is going downhill morally and socially. It is much easier to demonstrate that the world is plummeting downwards than otherwise. We refer to four texts which deal directly with the test.

1. In Deut 18:22 we read:

    "When a prophet speaks in the name of the Lord, if the thing does not happen or come to pass, that is the thing which the Lord has not spoken; the prophet has spoken it presumptuously; you shall not be afraid of him."

    This was a general warning for the people before they crossed into the Promised Land; God knew that they would need such a guideline. It is simple but practical. Anticipated is the fear which can be generated by a false prophet. Presumptuous false prophecy can be highly manipulative and dangerous, even when the individual responsible believes it to be a way to achieve a noble purpose.

2. In Jeremiah 23 we find a situation where false prophets claiming to speak in the Lord's name were rife.

    "'Behold, I am against the prophets' says the Lord, 'who use their tongues and say, "He says."'" (v32).

    These were within the religious hierarchy. The greatest caution must be exercised in evaluating any 'thus saith the Lord' statement which cannot be corroborated by Scripture. It can be mere attention seeking.

3. In Jeremiah 28 we encounter a false prophet within the Jerusalem establishment, who preached convincingly and dramatically a popular but totally false message regarding an

258

imminent peace. Jeremiah, whose message from the Lord was an unpopular one, proclaimed:

"As for the prophet who prophesies of peace, when the word of the prophet comes to pass, the prophet will be known as the one whom the Lord has truly sent." (v9)

God slew the false prophet the same year, just as Jeremiah had foretold. The impending fall of Jerusalem, which Hananiah had denied, took place soon afterwards. Prophesying short term good news can be a ploy for gaining popularity and spiritual 'kudos'.

4. Ezekiel, in chapter 13, has an equally stern message for those claiming to speak for God. What is particularly interesting here is that, evidently these false prophets actually hoped that God would co-operate with them and confirm their message;

    "They have envisioned futility and false divination, saying: 'Thus says the Lord!' But the Lord has not sent them; yet they hope that the word may be confirmed." (v6)

    Perhaps they were optimistic and well intentioned, trying to encourage the people. But in v10 God says that they have seduced His people. In v16 they are said to have had visions of a false peace; in v17 they are said to have prophesied from their own hearts.

We have in I Kings 22 a salutary case study, which cost Ahab his life, when the encouraging prediction of the presumptuous false prophet Zedekiah was heeded, rather than that of God's genuine prophet, Micaiah, whose warning was ominous. The important test which we have just summarised will be particularly relevant when we consider Neo-Post-Millennialism.

Categories And Definitions

There are or have been many variations, sub-groups and splinter groups within Traditional Post-Millennialism. However for the purpose of this study we will divide them into three broad categories:

- • Liberal Post-Millennialists. We will have very little to say about them, because they would not accept the authority of Scripture, were we to reason with them. Their optimism is based largely on the beneficial effects of anticipated human progress, science, knowledge, and moral and social evolution, God and Christianity being at best supplementary factors. They can be discredited by the above rules of prophetic validation. These rules may make some impact if expounded, as they have little strongly held doctrine to defend. Recent world events have reduced their numbers.

- Traditional Post-Millennialists, who have been around for about three hundred and fifty years. Most were, certainly until recently, generally sympathetic to Israel, with only low-key Replacement Theology. Like Amillennialists they deny any glorious national future. At least one scathing 'Neo-' scholar has dubbed them 'Archaic'!

- Neo-Post-Millennialists, who achieved sudden prominence in the nineteen seventies and seem to encompass a wide range of often confused attitudes towards the Jews. We will devote a separate chapter to them, although much of what we say in this chapter will apply to them also. Their denominational base is very wide indeed.

We must point out that there is no sharp divide between Traditional and Neo-Post-Millennialism, although there are very definite changes of emphasis, particularly regarding time scales. There are probably hundreds of thousands, if not millions, of Post-Millennialists who are quite unaware that they fit either description. Too many evangelical churches have too few members who take theology seriously.

These titles are not carved in stone. Some adherents would use different titles. We will in due course give brief histories of the second and third groups. We will start with the broadest possible definition of Post-Millennialism, which is that it is an optimistic belief that the world is getting progressively better, despite the odd set-back, and is heading for a golden age. However if we omit the liberal element, we can give a more precise definition which covers both the traditional and modern positions.

Boettner commences his 1957 Statement of the Doctrine thus:

> "We have defined Postmillennialism as that view of the last things which holds that the Kingdom of God is now being extended in the world through the preaching of the Gospel and the saving work of the Holy Spirit in the hearts of individuals, that the world eventually is to be Christianised, and that the return of Christ is to occur at the close of a long period of righteousness and peace commonly called the 'Millennium'. It should be added that on postmillennial principles the second coming of Christ will be followed immediately by the general resurrection, the general judgement, and the introduction of heaven and hell in their fullness."[1]

Now that statement comes from the pen of the person often considered to be the leading modern spokesman for Traditional Post-Millennialism, widely quoted by his fellows. Neo-Post-Millennialists would agree in principle with the statement, but they see all this happening much more dramatically and suddenly; or at least they did recently until it did not happen on schedule!

Two or three decades ago they claimed to be about to bring this all to fruition. Admittedly it was to be done through them by the agency of the Holy Spirit, rather than in their own power. But they were trying to fit God the Holy Spirit into their own timetable. While there was much genuine enthusiasm; there was also a great deal of arrogance and presumption around at the time.

Traditional Post-Millennialism—Background

The closing sentence of Boettner's statement demonstrates that some Post-Millennial beliefs, such as the general resurrection and judgement, are shared with Amillennialists. We need not add to what we wrote about these in our last chapter, except to say that their correlation of other events to the Millennium has obliged both groups to adopt this stance. Post-Millennialists do not look forward to the possibility of the Rapture within their lifetime; indeed, to most it is regarded as far distant. They have set far too many prerequisites. The eager expectation of the early Church is anathema to them.

The rest of his statement ties in very closely with what Blackstone wrote nearly a hundred years ago:

> "About the year 1700 a new error called postmillennialism crept into the church. It was instituted by Daniel Whitby, an English divine. He proclaimed a new hypothesis that the church would prosper and extend until the world would be converted, and this triumph of the church would constitute the Millennium; and that Jesus Christ would not come until after the Millennium."[2]

It has since been demonstrated that in fact the doctrine had been developing steadily within Puritanism for several decades previous to this. But it is still very much a Post-Reformation doctrine, and Whitby was its best known early exponent. The only claim to true antiquity might be that Constantine, towards the end of his life, tried to 'Christianise' the Roman Empire—and *that*, as any Protestant Church historian will confirm, led to widespread apostasy and the Dark Ages. To be fair to Whitby, he made no claims to such antiquity. We can find no call in the Bible for us to 'Christianise' the world, although the Crusaders, Conquistadores and others tried, only to achieve instant compromises with paganism, which have lingered on down through the centuries. One may 'Islam-ise' by conquest, but not Christianise.

There was at least in Whitby's day at a human level some apparent justification for this new optimistic view. Education, enlightenment and easier accessibility to the Bible, were all having an impact upon society. Major revivals occurred in Britain and America during the 18th century, and soon missionaries were being sent to hitherto unknown or unreachable lands, where colonial administrations and trading companies could give at least a degree of protection. These administrations benefited of course from the transformation of society which the Gospel brought. The so-called Pax Britannica, now much maligned, of the Victoria era was in fact pretty effective. Souls in their thousands were being saved in previously unevangelised lands, slavery was abolished and many benefits felt. Hymns of the period reflect the general optimism. Reginald Heber (1783–1826) had expressed these sentiments thus:

"Can we, whose souls are lighted
With wisdom from on high,
Can we to men benighted
The lamp of life deny?
Salvation! O salvation!
The joyful sound proclaim,
Till each remotest nation
Has learnt Messiah's Name.

Waft, waft ye winds, His story,
And you, ye waters roll,
Till, like a sea of glory,
It spreads from pole to pole;
Till o'er our ransomed nature
The Lamb for sinners slain,
Redeemer, King, Creator,
In bliss returns to reign."

Now this, as far as timing is concerned, is pure Post-Millennialism, though it lacks the arrogance and self-assurance which we will later encounter. Some of the sentiments are, of course, impeccable, and in no way would we wish to demean his evangelistic fervour. One can understand how a century or two ago it could have enjoyed credibility and fired the imagination of the saved and unsaved alike. It is probably fair to say that this eschatology did not carry so much 'excess baggage' with it as its modern counterparts. It did not pervade church life in quite the same manner as the modern variety. We must emphasis that Pre-Millennialism is *at least* as motivating towards missions, both at home and abroad, as Post-Millennialism; it has the added incentive of a foreshortened time in which to work.

In the face of this new optimism, Amillennialism, with predictions of a gloomy future but little else to capture the imagination, fell into decline. Only Pre-Millennialism in the 19th century arose from comparative obscurity to challenge it. It was the horrors of the Great War which vindicated the Pre-Millennialists and shattered the dreams of most Post-Millennialists. It gave the long disconsidered Amillennialists a major boost towards the dominance which they have now long enjoyed.

Some Post-Millennialists, however, stuck doggedly to their beliefs, sincerely seeing the Great War as 'the war to end all wars'. It was to be a brief respite; traditional Post-Millennialism has never recovered its dominant position. Boettner recognises the over-optimism of his own party at that time:

> "In his book *The Coming of the Lord*, Dr Snowden assumed that the First World War, then in progress, would come to a successful conclusion in the near future, would put an end to militarism forever and would be followed by a rapid development toward the millennial era." [3]

However we Pre-Millennialists have sometimes been equally guilty of anticipating times too precisely. We will decide for ourselves whether Dr Boettner's continuing optimism is well founded, both in the light of world events and in the teaching of the Bible.

We promised to explain our statement that Traditional Post-Millennianism is on the decline again. Some committed Post-Millennialists, despite the discouragement of two world wars, remained true to their beliefs; most notable of these was probably Charles Hodge, a reformed theologian of considerable stature, at a time when 'reformed' was not assumed to imply Amillennialist, as it generally is today.

Rousas Rushdoony, writing in 1971, expresses his indignation at a statement by Hal Lindsey, in a book published the previous year, which reads:

> "There used to be a group called 'postmillennialists'... World War I greatly disheartened this group and World War II virtually wiped out this viewpoint. No self-respecting scholar who looks at world conditions and the accelerating decline of Christian influence today is a 'postmillennialist'." [4]

Now, while I have much respect for Hal Lindsey and agree with him on every major point and most minor points of eschatology, I have to concede that on this occasion he has rather over-stated his case. However it is not far from the truth regarding the demise of *Traditional* Post-Millennianism. I have contacted several much-travelled British eschatologists, all of whom agree that, in the United Kingdom, whilst Amillennialism is on the increase and Neo-Post-Millennialism still flourishes in some quarters,

Traditional Post-Millennialism is almost a thing of the past. I have searched in vain for its literature in Christian bookshops and my library tells me that sought after volumes are obtainable only in the USA, and therefore unavailable for borrowing! With 'Neo-Post-Millennianism it is different. However as it is rarely styled thus by its own adherents, who have a host of other names, one can see why Hal Lindsey could make the above statement.

Rushdoony, in his critique of Lindsey, writes:

> "Postmillennial thought will flourish because it is Biblical and is therefore the eschatology of victory, or of salvation in its full sense." [5]

It may very well flourish, for a false eschatology will help 'left behind' religious leaders to cope with the theological crisis which is bound to arise following the Rapture of the Church. But it is foolish to speculate too wildly at present about the details of this future crisis. Perhaps, in summary, it would be more accurate to say that Traditional Post-Millennialism has been superseded rather than virtually wiped out. But, whilst the new variety is a development of the old, there are great contrasts, as we shall see in our next chapter.

One need only look at the caution exercised by Boettner, as quoted above, over Snowden's anticipation of an early Millennium. Neo-Post-Millennialism, which was about to explode on this side of the Atlantic, and was fairly new on the other side when Lindsey and Rushdoony were writing these quotes, is characterised by 'Kingdom Now' or 'Instant Millennium'. Predictably it has not arrived on schedule, in a world where the human birth rate is five times the church growth rate, and where Islam competes neck-and-neck with Christianity. Hal Lindsey was not far wrong in his comments about the Traditional variety, even if he was a little unfair over the scholarship.

Doctrine Of Christianisation

We have noted that Post-Millennialists believe in a coming golden age, when the world has eventually been 'Christianised'. Traditionalists are careful to claim no specific timescale for the achievement of this condition; some believe it may be in the yet very distant future. Neither do they make any claims for true perfection this side of eternity. We will stick for a while with Boettner as their spokesman; he is widely recognised within Traditional circles. He writes:

> "The changed character of individuals will be reflected in an uplifted social, economic, political and cultural life of mankind… This does not mean that there will be a time on earth when every person will be a Christian or that all sin will be abolished. But it does mean that evil in all its many forms will be reduced to negligible proportions, that Christian principles will be the rule, not the exception, and that Christ will return to a truly Christianised world."[6]

Readers may already be scratching their heads to remember which of the passages in Scripture describing the Lord's return depicts such a welcoming scenario, and recalling others which describe a very different one! We noted in Chapter Four that Jerusalem's welcome to her Messiah would be abrupt and dramatic, rather than as the result of steady progress. Boettner spends some time in both of his books from which we are quoting, trying to demonstrate how much better the world is becoming than it has hitherto been. We are in no way denying the enormous impact that the Gospel has often had down through the ages, but are disputing his 'Christianisation' of the world to date. He writes, for instance:

> "Today the world at large is on a far higher plane. Christian principles are the accepted standards in many nations even though they are not consistently practised. Slavery and polygamy have practically disappeared. The status of women and children have been improved immeasurably. Social and economic conditions in almost all nations have reached a new level. A spirit of cooperation is much more manifest among the nations than it has ever been before. International incidents which only a few years ago would have resulted in wars are now usually settled by arbitration."[7]

Who supplied the rose-tinted spectacles? We could challenge each one of those statements. Admittedly this was written, or revised, back in 1977. In almost every one of the above areas deterioration has taken place, sometimes markedly, over the intervening years. The Scriptural tests of prophecy are not indicating positive results for Boettner's proposition, rather the reverse. Commenting on his writing, Amillennialist Anthony Hoekema in the same year wrote:

> "Boettner's second argument is that the world is growing better. Many readers will be inclined to take issue with the author on this point. To begin with, his sketch of world conditions is seriously out of date. Little or nothing is said, for example, about the war in Vietnam, the tension in the Middle East, the ecological crisis, the world food shortage or the energy crisis... Besides, the author seems to pick out only the favourable aspects of world conditions while ignoring unfavourable aspects... Is it not more realistic to say that as the kingdom of God advances in the world there is a corresponding advance of the kingdom of evil?" [8]

If the answer to that last question is affirmative, much of the case for Post-Millennialism vanishes in one fell swoop. One needs to be neither a politician, soldier nor economist to realise that, were it to be up-dated now, Hoekema's statement would be even more devastating for Post-Millennialism. What is particularly serious is that we make Christianity look foolish in a world where fear is rapidly growing. Few people are so gullible as to see this approaching Utopia. Only those who are bent upon overthrowing our Christian-based laws are making progress. The 'man-in-the-street' is not to know that Post-Millennialism is not a universally held Christian belief; some churches and broadcasting stations proclaim it as if it were.

Boettner, admits to Lk 18:18 being a problem verse for Post-Millennialists *("Neverthelesss, when the Son of Man cometh. Shall He find faith on the earth?"),* and tries to find a way round it. [9] But he seems to ignore in this context even more awkward parallel passages predicting a latter day falling away, such as I Tim 4:1–3 and II Tim 4:3–4. He touches on them unconvincingly when avoiding the implication of 'the latter days'; [10] we say unconvincingly, because, whilst some *earlier* references to latter days do sometimes refer to the Church Age, the whole sense in I and II Timothy is very much a future one. He writes:

> "The golden age of righteousness is, of course, not to be thought of as beginning suddenly... it comes as the result of a long slow process, 'The kingdom of heaven cometh not

with observation' (Lk 17:20). It is 'first the blade, then the ear, then the full grain in the ear' (Mk 4:28)... To try to point the date on which the Millennium begins is like trying to distinguish the day or year when Mediaeval history ended and Modern history began." [11]

The Luke 17 and Mark 4:20 references apply to the Church Age, when the Kingdom is already here, but in mystery. He should forget about periods of history and look to the future and to what God has revealed to us in Revelation 20, where the precise opening and closing details of the Millennium are carefully given, as we noted in our last chapter; these are abrupt rather than 'almost imperceptible'. But then Revelation 20 presents him with major problems. We will see soon that Neo-Post-Millennialism expects a rather more sudden arrival than does Traditional.

Allegorisation Again

Pre-, Post- and Amillennialists all agree that the understanding of Revelation 20 lies at the core of the differences between each other's views. *At face value* it presents those taking Boettner's line with insuperable problems. It would hardly be unfair to talk about Pre-Millennialists' *understanding* of the chapter, but Post- and Amillennialists' *interpretation*. Boettner writes:

> "This passage contains much figurative language and admittedly is difficult to interpret." [12]

Of course it is difficult for him to interpret, because he is determined to wriggle out of the obvious implications! The sudden and dramatic Millennial changes indicated by other passages which we have quoted in earlier chapters are here too; most of our 'until' verses indicate sharp cut-off points. There is none of Boettner's creeping spiritual and environmental evolution. Christ will return suddenly, and the greatest geographical, geological, zoological, meteorological and environmental changes, at least since the Flood, will occur almost as suddenly.

> *"The Lord, whom you seek, will suddenly come to His temple"* (Mal 3:1).

The verses following make it quite clear that this is primarily a Second Coming prophecy and are devastating to Post- and Amillennialism.

At other times unwarranted changes suit him. Referring to Nebuchadnezzar's vision of Daniel 2,[13] he is happy for the gold, silver, bronze, iron and iron-plus-clay kingdoms to be earthly and visible kingdoms, but the stone kingdom which will destroy them and fill the earth must needs be invisible and spiritual! And yet were he to follow the vision through consistently, he would see that the invisible spiritual Kingdom in mystery has not as yet replaced the physical empires of this world, which are to remain in succession until Christ returns and sets up His visible one. Psalm 72 is instructive as to future visibility. Why are so many of the Old Testament prophecies, which he allegorised, furnished with so many geographical details if they are not to be literally fulfilled? Was it to fool the Jews, who had every right to take them literally? Surely not!

Marcellus Kik, another well known Post-Millennialist, uses complex arguments to avoid the plain language of Revelation 20. He has got himself into dreadful difficulties by denying the separate first resurrection for believers and second for the unsaved. Then he comes to v4:

> *"And I saw thrones, and they that sat upon them, and judgement was committed to them."*

In case you are naïve enough to believe that the Bible actually means thrones when it says thrones, be enlightened by Kik:

> "Surely they are not material, literal thrones. Surely we do not expect to see a million or more earthly kingdoms with a saint seated upon a throne ruling a number of subjects. Christ says: 'But so shall it not be among you, but whosoever will be great among you shall be your minister, and whosoever will be the chiefest, shall be the servant of all.' In the light of this teaching it is rather strange how a material, earthly and carnal conception of these thrones continues to hold sway over some minds. *Throne* is a figure of speech indicating the reign of the saint."[14]

This would it be funny, were it not so desperately serious. This is what happens when people try to separate Revelation 20 from 19. It is what happens when people get their dispensations, if they believe in them, confused. Indeed, it illustrates the confusion which arises when people reject dispensations. The problematical figure of a million plus and the separate kingdoms is entirely in Kik's own mind. He is forced, not only into believing, but into teaching, that the Bible's language is untrustworthy when there is no warrant whatsoever to doubt the literal meaning. He simply does not understand the Premillennialism which he opposes. He is throwing needless missiles at his own Aunt Sally.

Would he dare say that Jesus' promise to the Apostles was a 'material, earthly and carnal' conception when He said that they were going *"to sit on twelve thrones judging the twelve tribes of Israel"* (Matt 19:28)? That would be the logical conclusion of his remarks. The disciples have all died, and until they are raised physically in the First Resurrection, they cannot sit on thrones to judge Israel—they certainly did not do so whilst on earth in their physical bodies. Jesus said that this will happen when He sits on His throne in the regeneration. Perhaps Kik does not believe in Jesus' throne either; is it a carnal concept? The fact that we serve here humbly does not preclude Christ from bestowing honour, responsibility and authority upon us *after* the resurrection, does it? Such recognition and reward is actually taught in several passages. All this serves to emphasise that the Millennium is not on this side of the Lord's return and that all Old Testament and Church Age saints then will be in their resurrection bodies. Kik makes a remarkable statement:

> "The time of sitting on the thrones and reigning with Christ
> is the same as that of not worshipping the beast" [15]

This is all based on a complex juggling of the sequence of events and a quite inconclusive argument based on Greek tenses. The actual simple sequence as presented in Scripture is:

1. Christ descends from heaven (19:11–15).

2. The Beast and earth's armies gather to make war with Him (19:19).

3. The Beast and False Prophet are consigned to the Lake of Fire, and the armies are destroyed (19:20–21).

4. Satan is bound for a thousand years (the Millennium) (20:1–2).

5. The souls of the Tribulation martyrs, opponents and victims of the Beast, are seen (20:4).

6. The same are seen living (or having life) and reigning for the thousand years in which the Devil is bound and during which the rest of the dead will not live (20:4–6).

There is much more that we could add. But this is sufficient to show how extraordinary is Kik's statement, and how far allegorisation compels people to depart from the obvious.

Referring to Isaiah chapter 35—*'the desert shall rejoice and blossom as a rose'*, which surprisingly he decides not to spiritualise, Boettner refers to scientific work by Luther Burbank and others which are apparently bringing species of plant and animal life back to their original condition.[16] This being so, how does he cope with Isaiah 11, where God said that the wolf will dwell with the lamb, the leopard with the goat, the calf with the young lion and so on? Is Luther Burbank going to train them to behave thus? One cannot, unless one is an extraordinarily stubborn Post-Millennialist, conceive how these changes, which are dramatic and comprehensive, can take place without Divine intervention.

God did not require scientists to engineer the changes at the Fall of man (Gen 3:17,18); neither will He when Christ returns, however much He may at times bless human effort in the meantime. It is not part of, or even the result of, the Church fulfilling the Great Commission which will achieve this. This is one of the many places where Boettner gives the Church, in this case by 'man's proper management of the earth'[17] the credit which is due to God alone. If the Church is eventually to be involved in these tasks, it will be resurrected saints in their celestial bodies; some of us yet *might* be involved in actual mountain moving.

It will be becoming clear that Post-Millennianism, like Amillennialism, depends very largely on the assumption that any prophecy which does not conform to their time-table must be symbolic or allegorical. Indeed, neither 'ism' could exist rationally without it. Defending this policy and attacking Pre-Millennialism, Boettner writes:

> "This general principle of interpretation has been expressed as 'literal wherever possible' (H Bonar) or 'literal unless absurd' (Govett)."[18]

To deny the rule expressed by Dr Horatius Bonar, my neighbour separated by only a few miles but many years, a man of much greater scholarship than Boettner, is to put all theology at risk of abuse and private hermeneutics. He presents his case at some length. We dealt with this practice of superfluous allegorisation in Chapter 9; however it is worth quoting two more leading authorities. Dr Walvoord writes:

> "Early in the history of the church, especially in the third century, a school of prophetic interpretation arose in Alexandria which attempted to interpret all the Bible in an allegorical or a non-literal sense... Though the Alexandrian school of theology is labelled by all theologians as heretical, the effect of non-literal interpretation on prophecy was rendered acceptable by the theological writings of Augustine who applied allegorical interpretation only to prophecy... This influence continued through the Protestant Reformation to the present day." [19]

Thus a foundational tenet of A- and Post-Millennialism is derived from a heretical source. Dean Alford preached and taught at a time when Post-Millennial allegorisation was rife and was being applied to the great Rapture passage of I Thess 4:13–16. He wrote:

> "It will be manifest to the plain as well as to the scholar-like reader that attempts to interpret such a passage as this by the rules of mere figurative language, are entirely beside the purpose. The Apostle's declarations here are made in the practical tone of strict matter of fact and are given as literal details to console men's minds under an existing difficulty... Either these details must be received by us as matters of practical expectation or we must set aside the Apostle as one divinely empowered to teach the church." [20]

We have another example of Boettner's inconsistent 'spiritualising' with Heb 12:22, where he tries to convince us that Isa 2:2–3, where the nations shall *"flow to Jerusalem"*, means something entirely different:

> "In the book of Hebrews 'Mount Zion', God's holy mountain, is spiritualised to mean the Church. Hence in this prophecy it must mean that the Church, having attained a position so that it stands out like a mountain on a plain, will be prominent and regulative in all world affairs." [21]

This is precisely the kind of logic I occasionally have presented to me on my doorstep—by 'Jehovah's Witnesses', only they do it marginally better! The false equation of Zion with the Church in Heb 12:22 collapses when we find there that we believers come to (a) Mount Zion, (b) the city of the living God, (c) the heavenly Jerusalem, (d) to an innumerable company of angels, (e) to the general assembly and church of the firstborn, (f) to God the Judge of all, (g) to Jesus the Mediator of the new covenant. Why make (a) and (e) equate to each other when the others do not equate? There has been a heavenly Zion since Moses met God on Sinai, and doubtless before. See also Heb 8:2; 8:5; 11:10; Rev 16:1 etc. The heavenly Zion has not in the past precluded the existence of an earthly one, recognised and blessed by God. Why should it be as long as this old earth remains? Does its very history not testify? When we read that Jesus' *"feet will stand on the Mount of Olives, which faces Jerusalem on the east, and the Mount of Olives shall split in two, making a very large valley..."* (Zech 14:4), are we supposed to spiritualise this? Is the split Mount of Olives for instance the schism between Byzantium and Rome, the split between the Primitive and Wesleyan Methodists or something else equally bizarre? There is no end to the possibilities of such follies!

The problem is that, once licence is given to interpret figuratively passages which make perfectly straightforward sense to some believers, we are opening up the flood gates to liberalism. We have said that before, but it deserves repeating.

The Great Commission

The Great Commission is central to the doctrine of Pre-, Post- and Amillennialist alike. However the Post-Millennialist views it as something which must eventually be completed by the Church to the point of an overwhelming majority of converts. Boettner, reflecting this pivotal Post-Millennial teaching, writes:

"We believe that the Great Commission includes not merely the formal and external announcement of the gospel preached as a 'witness' to the nations, as the Premillennialists and amillennialists hold, but the true and effectual evangelisation of all the nations so that the hearts and lives of the people are transformed by it… Christ commanded the evangelisation of the world. That is our task. Surely he will not, and in fact cannot, come back until that task has been accomplished"[22]

Can't He? Who says He can't? Post-Millennialists say He cannot. It is seen by Post-Millennialists to be an inconceivable failure and a slight against the Holy Spirit and Christ's authority if this Great Commission of Matt 28:18–20 is not completed to the point of this alleged Christianisation. But this is based entirely upon the supposition that we are commanded to succeed. We are not. We are commanded to be faithful. Jesus said:

"The Spirit of the Lord is upon Me, because He has anointed Me to preach the gospel to the poor" (Lk 4:18).

Did Jesus 'succeed' in converting the vast majority of the poor? Was the fact that He did not due to His failure to exert His authority or fulfil that mission? God forbid! However sincere in their beliefs they may be, it is sheer arrogance that makes Post-Millennialists, believe that they will do what Jesus did not.

Ideally, of course, all would repent and be saved; but the epistles and Revelation chapters 2 and 3 indicate that spiritual decline had already set in over 1900 years ago. Post-Millennialists are triumphalist and do not see it thus. Boettner writes:

"Postmillennialism places a strong emphasis on the universality of Christ's work of redemption. Hope is held out for the salvation of an incredibly large number of the race of mankind… This does not mean that every individual will be saved but that the race, as a race, will be saved… God has chosen to redeem untold millions of the human race. Just what proportion has been included in his purposes of mercy, we have not been informed; but in view of the future days of prosperity which are promised to the church, it may be inferred that the great majority will eventually be found in that number."[23]

Probably all of us, applying human logic, would like to agree, although in the word 'eventually' one could almost hear echoes of purgatory, which admittedly Boettner does not teach. But dare we, in the face of what a loving but holy God has revealed? We hear Jesus say:

> *"Wide is the gate and broad is the way that leads to destruction, and there are many who go in by it. Because narrow is the gate and difficult the way which leads to life, and there are few who find it. Beware of false prophets..."*
> (Matt 7:13–15).

We can find no direct revision or reversal of this teaching later in Scripture. The nearest we can get is the passage of the innumerable number of the redeemed in Revelation 7, to which Boettner appeals. But do we really have the authority to say that this represents the majority of mankind? This teaching can only undermine the preaching of the Gospel by inducing widespread complacency among the unsaved and perhaps among evangelists.

Preview Of Preterism

Preterism is quite common among Post-Millennialists, and, as we saw with Adams in Chapter Ten, is also found in Amillennialism. It serves two main functions.

- It provides the only reasonable means of explaining how the world can be seen to be improving morally and in other respects, whist recognising that the Bible contains inspired prophecies of coming disaster. Its importance to Post-Millennialism will thus be self-evident.

- It provides extreme Replacement Theologians with some sort of basis for believing that God forever finished with the nation Israel over nineteen hundred years ago. We emphasise that some Post-Millennialists do not subscribe to this. Others adopt an intermediate position.

But it does an enormous disservice to our young people who may be desperately worried about environmental issues. By relegating to history all the prophecies which vividly and realistically describe coming catastrophes, and which confirm that God has fore-ordained them and will one day restore all, they are being horrendously misled by Christian

275

leaders whom they should be able to trust. Moreover their priorities are being diverted from the spiritual to the environmental.

If we can debunk Preterism, we will have gone a long way towards discrediting Post-Millennialism, especially in its more extreme forms. In Chapter Twelve we shall be looking at it in some detail. It seems more appropriate to examine it there, because we will be using some of the more outspoken and most recent Post-Millennialist authorities in order to alert ourselves to the real nature of the current threat to prophetic interpretation, especially regarding Israel. However we must take a brief look at Preterism whilst considering Traditional Post-Millennialism, because it is an underpinning factor there too, even if somewhat more subdued. Boettner oddly enough does not incorporate it into his exposition of Post-Millennialism, but rather into his critique of Pre-Millennialism.

Eschatological Preterism teaches that all the prophecies of judgement prior to the Lord's return have long since been fulfilled; most Preterists would see the fall of Jerusalem in AD 70 as constituting their completion. Thus, for the more extreme Preterists, the Olivet Discourse and Revelation chapters 6 to 19, plus lengthy Old Testament prophetic passages, are declared virtually obsolete in their prophetic application, and are deemed to contain only general principles and guidelines for subsequent generations. Others follow the common Amillennial Historicist pattern of seeing the various Tribulation passages applying to the history of the Church; such is Rushdoony, whom we will later quote and Guinness, whom we will meet in Chapter Thirteen.

One may very well ask why, given that the Synoptic Gospels were all written within twenty years of the fall of Jerusalem, the Church has for the past nineteen and a half centuries had these lengthy and detailed 'spent' or obsolete short term prophecies within the canon of Holy Scripture, and why God's last written word to the Church down through the ages was almost immediately, if not already obsolescent. One may also wonder why Revelation should have been addressed initially to seven congregations within the province of Asia, rather than to Jews in Jerusalem should it refer to AD 70. A date for the writing of Revelation sufficiently long before AD 70 for all believers in Judaea to become aware of its contexts is almost crucial for Preterism; and that most certainly cannot be confirmed. Insufficient evidence is available for a precise date, but most scholars other than Preterists, including those who have no axe to grind, opt for a later date. John was exiled to Patmos from Ephesus, where he probably went because of the sack of Jerusalem. If this is the case, Revelation must have been written no earlier than AD 73, and perhaps much later.

One may also ask, and this is an exceptionally important question, if we apply Preterism, why there were so many prophecies—give or take 330—in the Old Testament referring to the Lord's first coming, and so few, to His second coming. His first coming fulfilled a number of prophecies which had had previous minor fulfilments, such as Isa 7:14, *"Therefore the Lord Himself will give you a sign: 'Behold, the virgin shall conceive and bear a Son...'"*. The verses following confirm the first and more immediate partial fulfilment. Yet Preterists are scathing when Pre-Millennialists dare to apply the same principle to New Testament prophecies, where the first fulfilment was not on the grand scale of the original prediction, and simply do not satisfy its terms. We will see DeMar's paltry excuse in our next chapter.

Post-Millennialism And Israel

Post-Millennialism is almost as ambivalent as Amillennialism towards Israel. We see here both moderate and extreme Replacement Theology. The Post-Millennialist teaching which we have encountered up to this point leaves no room for a distinct and glorious place for Israel in the Millennium. The Church has grabbed the limelight, because it is seen to be on earth in mortal bodies throughout.

However some Post-Millennialists still see some sort of future for an identifiable Jewish people. Such is Marcellus Kik. He writes:

> "Romans 11 surely speaks of the conversion of Israel after the flesh. If the fall of the Jews brought richness to the Gentiles, how much will it add to the riches of the Gentiles when the Jews are restored?"

We would say 'Amen!' to this. But he then goes on to add:

> "When the Gentile world is converted then will come about the conversion of the Jews as a nation."[24]

Now this is very much more positive than some modern Post-Millennialists. It is only the sequence of events with which we would disagree. We need not repeat here our exposition of Israel's future vis-à-vis that of the Gentiles. We simply re-state our conviction that all surviving Israel will be saved:

- well after the Rapture of the Church;

- following the Great Tribulation with its final holocaust;

- after two third of Israel has been sifted out;

- immediately after the Messiah's return in power.

But for Post-Millennialists any future history for Israel would have to happen before the Lord's return, since for them the Lord's return heralds the start of the Eternal State. And they see the interim period dominated by the Church. Let us give a few brief quotes from Kik:

> "It was this Holy City, the Lamb's bride, the church of Christ for which Abraham looked as a fulfilment of the covenant promise. Christ stated in John 8: 'Your father Abraham rejoiced to see my day: and he saw it, and was glad.' And it is stated in Hebrews 11:13, 'These all died in faith, not having received the promises, but having seen them afar off.' This is not meant of the happiness of the heavenly state, for that they received at death. But this is meant of the happiness of the gospel economy. They had but the types and shadows; we have the reality. They looked for the coming of Christ and His church. We obtained the promises; they did not at any time they dwelt upon the earth." [25]

Now this is probably the most astonishing paragraph we have quoted in the entire thesis. We simply cannot do justice to every point raised, but will deal very briefly with a few of the most important ones:

- This side of glory we, the Church, are only the Lamb's espoused wife (II Cor 11:2), not yet perfected as the Bride (Eph 5:27), awaiting a consummation in heaven (Rev 19:7), before the Lord returns to earth with her. This conforms to the Biblical marriage pattern.

- Abraham has not yet been raised from the dead, so can never see the Church on earth in its present mortal state. One does not have to be a Pre-Tribulationist to see this from I Thess 4.

- Old Testament saints did not go to heaven at death, anyway; their souls went to Sheol, to the part described as Abraham's bosom (Lk 16:22, 23). In the Psalms it is referred to by David as 'down'; their souls had to remain there until Jesus' death, resurrection and ascension. Such comfort as they had was much less than the joy of the redeemed now in heaven awaiting the resurrection of the body.

- It is interesting to see a Post-Millennialist recognising different dispensations, because 'dispensation' and 'economy' have the same theological meaning.

- Whether the city Abraham sought is in heaven or on earth, it must be *after* his resurrection, and therefore it fits into a Pre-, rather than a Post-Millennialist programme.

- The New Jerusalem, which is to descend from heaven once this world has passed away, best fits the Heb 11:15 description, so cannot mean the Millennium. The gates bear the names of the twelve tribes of Israel and the foundations of the walls the twelve apostles of the Lamb (Rev 21:12–14). Redeemed Israel and the Church are thus both there. Abraham has his promised place; however he will be on earth in his resurrection body during the Millennium.

- The claim that the Church is the city which Abraham sought can be demonstrated only by assumptions; the timescales prove these to be faulty.

Some of the Messianic prophetic texts, which Kik and other Post-Millennialists claim for the Church, are very specifically addressed to Israel. Little wonder they cannot see Israel being restored until the Church has 'Christianised' all the Gentiles; they have purloined all her promises! Kik is generally careful to select certain Psalms or parts of Psalms which do not have direct reference to Israel, or to the geography of the Promised Land, but avoids those that do, or whose references are unmistakably Jewish. He argues at length that the whole world is going to be blessed in the Millennium, as if nobody else believed this. But of course Pre-Millennialists believe this—fervently. The difference is that we see the Lord ruling the world directly from Jerusalem, and we see Israel as *"the head and not the tail"* (Deut 28:13). This precedence is over the Gentile nations, not over the resurrected saints. This unconditional promise has yet to happen; God is faithful to His promises, even if they are inconvenient to Post-Millennial philosophy. As to Kik's assertion that Jewish national conversion will follow the conversion of the Gentile world, Zechariah 12 demonstrates the opposite sequence.

Consider very carefully this annexation by the Church (according to Kik) of a passage very specifically addressed to Israel. He starts in Isaiah 53:

> "It is upon Christ's atoning sacrifice that the victory of the church is built. It is after chapter 53, which gives such a clear picture of the vicarious atonement, that we read these exultant words in chapter 54: 'Sing, O barren, thou that didst not bear; break forth into singing, and cry aloud, thou that didst not travail with child: for more are the children of the desolate than the children of the married wife, saith the Lord. Enlarge the place of thy tent, and let them stretch forth the curtains of thy habitations: spare not, lengthen thy cords, and strengthen thy stakes; for thou shalt break forth on the right hand and on the left; and thy seed shall inherit the Gentiles, and make the desolate cities to be inhabited... No weapon that is formed against thee shall prosper.' From Isaiah 54 and 66 we have various pictures of the millennium. In these chapters we are informed of the destruction of Israel after the flesh for their refusal to behold and accept the Messiah. But that will not hinder the progress of the gospel church." [26]

In the Isaiah 54 quote it is *"thy seed"* who shall inherit the Gentiles; not the Gentiles who shall inherit *"thy seed"*. In the next verse, which Kik significantly omits, God refers to the widowhood of those whom He is addressing. Is that the Church, the espoused bride, or desolate Israel?

It is not the verses which He quotes, but those which he has left out, which speak volumes. The broken dots between 'inhabited' and 'No' are his, not mine. Now of course writers often have to jump sentences to save space. But look what fits into this space!

"'For your Maker is your husband, the Lord of Hosts is His name; and your Redeemer is the Holy One of Israel; He is called the God of the whole earth. For the Lord has called you like a woman forsaken and grieved in spirit, like a youthful wife when you were refused,' says your God. 'For a moment I have forsaken you, and with great mercies I will gather you.'" (Isa 54:5–7).

We could continue to the end of the chapter and beyond and see how explicitly the addressee is the nation Israel. The Church is at liberty to draw as many spiritual and moral lessons as she wishes from the passage. But the once abandoned wife is Israel. Read Hosea for confirmation:

"In the place where it was said to them, 'You are not my people,' There it shall be said to them, 'You are the sons of the living God'" (1:10);

"'And it shall be in that day,' says the Lord, 'That you will call Me "My Husband"'" (2:16);

"And they shall be wanderers among the nations" (9:17);

"O Israel, you are destroyed, but your help is from Me" (13:9);

"O Israel, return to the Lord your God" (14:1);

"I will heal their backsliding, I will love them freely" (14:4);

"Who is wise, let him understand these things" (14:9).

Indeed, where is the wisdom? We live in a generation of Christians where many doubt that the grace of God, which encompassed Israel after the Babylonian captivity, can still extend to the present nation. They forget that a substantial part of the Israel addressed by God through Hosea, was the Northern part, which did not include Judah, did not crucify the Messiah and has never to date returned to the Promised Land. They have been wanderers for twenty-seven centuries. But God has not forgotten them, though many Gentile Christians, who should love them, scorn them.

"No weapon formed against you shall prosper" (v17) refers of course to Israel, whose incredible and unparalleled four thousand year history bears eloquent testimony to God's everlasting care, even in dispersion

and extreme adversity. The Roman Catholic Church has been blind to this for fifteen hundred years and more. But why have Protestants not abandoned this folly? In whose interest is it that it should remain? Ponder this! But then, blindness was a characteristic of the Laodiceans, (Rev 3:18), and is rife in today's Church.

Kik is in no way actively Anti-Semitic. He is simply claiming too much for the Church and for the wrong dispensation. Loraine Boettner takes a harder line:

> "And because of their sin in rejecting and crucifying their Saviour, they were brought into a position in which, as Paul solemnly says, 'Wrath is come upon them to the uttermost' (I Thess 2:16). In accordance with this the entire Old Testament of Judaism has been abrogated and brought to an end. And in its place the New Covenant has become the authoritative and official instrument for God's dealings with His people, His Church."[27]

Now there are many points here that we have dealt with in earlier chapters, so we need only recap on one or two points and make a couple of further brief comments

- Paul says that it was the Jews specifically who crucified Jesus, not Israel. Even at that time far more Jews were scattered throughout the Roman Empire than were resident in the Promised Land. We do not want to make too much of this point.

- This epistle was written well before AD 70, so one may well dispute whether this was the reference to wrath.

- Even wrath to the uttermost does not compel God to break unconditional promises.

- The 'church' in the Old Testament was not the same body as that born at Pentecost.

- The future New Covenant for Israel is described in Jeremiah 31 in quite unmistakably Jewish terms, for the returning, deeply repentant remnant of Israel. Both Judah and Israel are identified. There have been partial fulfilments of certain statements there, but nothing on the grand scale of that passage. We have more to say of this elsewhere.

Boettner a page later adds:

> "In the Church there are no promises or privileges given to any one group or nationality which do not apply equally to all others... We should further point out that those who today popularly are called 'Jews' are in reality not Jews at all. Legitimate Judaism as it existed in the Old Testament era was of divine origin and had a very definite content of religious and civil laws, priesthood, ritual, sacrifices, temple, Sabbath etc. But with the destruction of Jerusalem and the dispersion of the people in AD 70, that system was effectively destroyed. It has not been practised anywhere in the world." [28]

While the first sentence may be true of conditions *within* the Church, he completely misses the point that, until the Lord returns in power and the 'until' conditions are met, the vast majority of Jews will remain outside the Church. Boettner's preoccupation with the true Church being a single entity in both Old and New Testaments is not common to all Post-Millennialists; but it is a popular view. It is worth quoting Unger to get a correct perspective:

> "In the NT the church fundamentally comprehends the whole number of regenerated persons specifically from Pentecost to the first resurrection united organically to one another and to Christ by the baptising work of the Holy Spirit... The word *ekklesia*, however is employed of any assembly, and the word in the Greek language implies no more; for example, the town meeting at Ephesus (Acts 19:38) and Israel called out of Egypt are spoken of as an assembly, *ekklesia*, in the wilderness (Acts 7:8), but in no sense was it an a NT church except as a type of that which was to come." [29]

Boettner is a Post-Millennialist sharing almost the same views as Amillennialist Metcalfe, whom we have already met. The system did indeed cease to be practised in AD 70. But it was actually obsolete from the moment when the veil in the temple was rent from top to bottom when Jesus died, rather than from AD 70. This is elementary theology which Boettner should know. The High Priest was recognised by God until Jesus' crucifixion, despite the decadence of the current Sadducee family, as we know from Jn 11:49–51, when Caiaphas spoke prophetically. Thereafter in the Acts he did not retain the same recognition except as religious head of state; consider Peter's attitude towards Caiaphas in Acts 4:19 or Paul's towards Ananias in Acts 23:2–5.

Any Orthodox Jew would be scandalised and further prejudiced against the Gospel by Boettner's above paragraph, and not without reason. Over the interim forty-eight years since it was printed, almost everything for the anticipated Jerusalem Temple has been prepared, even to the extent of employing DNA research for true Levitical priests and the finding of a genuine red heifer (Deut 21). Admittedly the one whom they will first accept will be turn out to be the Man of Sin. But the sheer preservation of so much for more than nineteen centuries is an outstanding testimony to God's conservation for future purposes. The fact that they have sought no alternative compromise site, and returned against all odds to their holy city, should speak volumes. Current affairs militate against Boettner and the like. On 9th February 2005, even as this chapter was being written, the Sanhedrin met in Jerusalem for the first time in over nineteen centuries. The intention was announced of rebuilding the Jerusalem Temple and re-instituting Levitical sacrifices in the foreseeable future. The scene is being set for Daniel 9:27, as interpreted by Dispensational Pre-Millennialists.

At the beginning of this chapter we said that the ultimate test for prophecy is the Biblical one, in which a prophet is validated or exposed by whether his prophecy comes true in the end. As the Lord has not yet returned, we cannot apply this test in full to the various schools of prophetic interpretation; but we can get very powerful indicators of levels of reliability. Traditional Post-Millennialists see little or no specific earthly future for Israel, or even for a current city of Jerusalem recognised by God as His future capital on earth—and this despite the extraordinary events of the past century. Contrast Boettner with JNDarby, much maligned by both A- and Post-Millennialists; his quarrelsome personality does not discredit his theology. Over a hundred and forty years ago, well before the birth of modern Zionism, and when the Holy Land was little more than a tract of wilderness with a few scattered towns, in a poverty stricken corner of the Ottoman Empire, he wrote regarding the two witnesses of Revelation 11:

> "'And their dead bodies [shall be] on the streets of the great city, which spiritually is called Sodom and Egypt, where also their Lord was crucified' (verse 8). It is perfectly plain that this is Jerusalem… God attaches the greatest possible interest to His people Israel, when His rights as to the earth are in question."[30]

We could have quoted many such passages from the work of Darby regarding Israel's future. Now we concede that some of Darby's surmising about how Israel and the Jews were to be re-established in the Land has been proved by history to be incorrect. Nobody could have been sure. But his basic facts about Israel's future, both before and after the Rapture are constantly being vindicated. Pre-Millennialism is scoring very, very much better than Post-Millennianism on these tests of prophecy!

Muted Replacement Theology

We have noted that some Post-Millennialists are much more sympathetic to Israel than others, holding only mild levels of Preterism or none at all. Drawing dividing lines between groups is well nigh impossible, because of the amount of overlapping and merging of views. However we will for convenience identify two writers for brief consideration. Both hold the view that God has indeed assured Israel of a bright future, but within the Church. Rushdoony is only slightly more Israel-friendly than some whom we have already met and does not raise many new issues. Murray is more so and produces quite different and very interesting data in his arguments.

Rousas J Rushdoony is typical of those Post-Millennialists who have a more Historicist approach to the Apocalyptic scriptures than the extreme Preterists. We will take his references to three passages from Revelation to illustrate this. Having referred to them already whilst reviewing Amillennialism and elsewhere, we can keep our comments very brief:

> "Revelation 7 gives us a picture of the sealed church in its ultimate victory. In Revelation 21 we are shown Jerusalem, symbolically portrayed as a perfect cube, the symbol of

perfection. Jerusalem has twelve gates, twelve foundations, the walls are 144 cubits in height and the population numbers 144,000. That this is a symbolic figure 7:9 makes clear. The twelve tribes of Israel give us a clear picture of the whole church."[31]

There is some very strange arithmetic here, not borne out by the figures in Revelation 21. No population is given at all in that chapter; he has imported it from chapter 7. It is all very ingenious, the best he can do to avoid the simple explanation that the twelve tribes are precisely who the Apostle says they are. The 144,000 are seen in Revelation 7, sealed for protection before the impending Trumpet judgments commenced:

"Do not harm the earth, the sea and the trees till we have sealed the servants of God on their foreheads" (7:3).

Revelation 21, as we have noted, is about the new creation after this present one has disappeared. His identification of the Church here, rather than Israel, is based upon the flimsiest of poor evidence. In Revelation 11, his evidence is even more flimsy, if that were possible.

"In 11:1, 2, 3 we see the security of the church in the midst of battle, and the security is the security of victory. We see the temple at Jerusalem, a type of the church..."[32]

We see no such thing. We see a piece of straightforward prophetic narrative centred around the city of Jerusalem, a city whose site God has preserved throughout history against incredible odds, the city to whose outskirts the Lord Jesus Christ will one day return in glory. Referring to the Woman of Revelation 12, he writes:

"We are given a picture of a woman clothed with the sun, clearly a cosmic figure. She is the true Church of God in every age."[33]

This teaching comes straight from the Vatican. Here we have the same misapprehension as that found earlier in Boettner, that the faithful of the Israel of the Old Testament are the same body as the New Testament Church. Rushdoony does refer to the Gen 37:9 imagery, but does not seem to see how powerful a confirmation this is of its being exclusively Jacob's (or Israel's) people; he conveniently ignores Isa 66:7–9, where the correlation is more striking. The Church did not give birth to the

Messiah. Tell a Messianic Jew that this is the Church, and wait for the reaction! He is in fact completely at odds here with those other Post-Millennialists who see this passage as applying to the Matt 24:16–20 warning to believers to flee from Jerusalem in AD 70. We must never assume Post-Millennialism to be a united front.

Iain Murray, writing in 1971, lists and quotes from various famous evangelists and teachers from Puritan times onwards. The trouble with this type of study is that one encounters great names which Pre-, Post- and Amillennialists all claim as their own on the basis of some utterance or written word. It was not until the birth of Zionism and the great events of the 20th century that the dividing lines between the three became sharply crystallised among those theologians who did not major in eschatology. However we do concede that there has been a great deal of both partial and total Post-Millennialism around in recent centuries, and that many adherents of the past have been outstanding Christians.

Israel in possession, or at least in occupation, of the Holy Land, was widely recognised by early and modern Pre-Millennialists as a prerequisite for certain end-time events. But when the Puritans were around, such a situation seemed so remote as to be either forgotten or irrelevant to believers, and in the meantime there was much to be done towards winning the world for Christ.

But long intervals in prophetic awareness have occurred before. One need only consider the approximately thousand and fifty years over which the canon of the Old Testament was being written. For several centuries there was comparatively little prophecy concerning either the Lord's first or second comings, except in David's time, compared with the latter four hundred years. Then there was a further four hundred year prophet-less period—"*The sun shall go down on the prophets, and the day shall be dark for them*" (Mic 3:6). We have referred in an earlier chapter to Daniel's sudden realisation from reading scrolls only two years before the event, that Jeremiah's prophesied ending of the Babylonian captivity was very near (Dan 9:2). Yet Daniel had been active for God for well over fifty years! Whatever mediaeval scholars and monks in their cells and cloisters may have discovered, throughout the Dark Ages, prophetic knowledge was very restricted indeed to the masses. Only now is the complete range of material readily available.

So the fact that 17th and 18th century theologians were preoccupied with the mission field and winning the world for Christ in no way disqualifies or discredits those who, in the 19th century, began to explore more deeply. Was God not over-ruling and allowing Christians to draw extra light from long misunderstood or neglected passages as the time drew near for activity in Israel?

Ian Murray in his Introduction, setting the scene for his book, makes the same mistake as other Post-Millennialists whom we have encountered. Regarding Acts 3:21 he writes:

> "He is to remain in heaven not until the commencement of a millennium, but until the times of the restoration of all things, elsewhere spoken of as 'the regeneration', which Jesus identifies with the last judgment (Matt 19:28)"[34]

This is totally misleading, because, were one to look at the Matthew 19 reference and assume it to be the last judgement, one would be compelled to accept that the twelve Apostles are to join *"Him from whose face the earth and heaven fled away"* (Rev 20:11) at the Great White Throne.

> *"The Father has committed all judgement to the Son"* (Jn 5:22);

> *"He will judge the world in righteousness by the Man whom He has ordained"* (Act 17:31).

The Apostles will judge administratively, like Moses (Ex 18:13–26), and that can only be on earth, but will have no active role in the last judgement. The regeneration and restitution can only be on earth; they imply setting to rights something which has gone wrong; it is quite different from the completely new beginning of Revelation 21:1 et seq.

We have with Murray the same old evasion of the significance of Revelation 20:

> "The truth is that Revelation 20 contains what has been called the 'darkest passage in all the Bible'; widely differing meanings have been given to it by those who share a common faith in the inerrancy of Scripture"[35]

The truth is that this great chapter is 'dark' only to those who refuse to take it at face value; and that is surely insulting to God the Holy Spirit. It is the very last chapter but two of the 1189 in the Bible, and the very last one about this old planet which had dominated Scripture since Genesis 1. Chapter 21 reveals a completely new, and therefore un-restored, cosmos. Did God really leave us with an indecipherable riddle? No. He left us with a challenging, but nevertheless clear, narrative of what is to follow immediately after the Lord's return in power. If some choose to obscure it, they are the losers; unfortunately so are their hearers and readers, just as 2000 years ago theologians seem determined to leave their charges in a prophetic limbo.

So his entire book starts off with false premises. This is sad, because there is much that one can respect elsewhere in his research, even if his claims as to who, down through the centuries, have been Post-Millennialists are sometimes questionable. Spurgeon's exposition on the Matthew version of the Olivet Discourse is clearly Pre-Millennial.[36] Yet Murray would like to claim him as a confused Post-Millennialist, devoting a lengthy appendix[37] to his "apparently contradictory thoughts on prophecy".[38] Alan Levett, writing about Murray's book, says, and I have to agree:

> "One of the chapters in Mr Murray's book is devoted to the so-called dichotomy in C H Spurgeon's views on prophecy, suggesting the great preacher was confused in his understanding of the subject. I suggest that this is a slight on one of the clearest minds in the history of Christendom. It is not Spurgeon who is confused, but those who do not understand that it is possible to interpret scripture in different ways as suggested above, to be enthusiastic about Jews being converted and brought into the body of Christ, but also understand that in a future day God will bring them into National blessing."[39]

Of course anybody who does not perceive that this restoration is to take place in a future dispensation, rather than in the Church Age, is bound to find that these harmonising truths seem to be contradictory to one another. If Murray can be so much in error over Spurgeon, one cannot help but wonder how strong his claims are for some of his earlier Post-Millennialists, for whom data is harder to obtain. Personally I raise my eyebrows over several of the names, such as John Bunyan, whom Murray claims to be Post-Millennial, whose flight of Christian from the City of Destruction strikes me as being in stark contrast to Post-Millennialism.

Murray makes another tactical error, common among Post- and Amillennialists, of treating Pre-Millennialism as if it implied only Pre-Tribulationism. If one is making a case for Post-Millennianism against the other two major schools, one must deal with those schools in general as well as looking at the groups within those schools. He makes the most of the 17th century antiquity of Post-Millennianism, whilst turning a blind eye to the 1st to 3rd century antiquity of Pre-Millennialism, preferring to attack the 19th century expansion of Pre-Tribulationism, which he does from the basis of his own shaky foundations. A variety of 17th to 19th century names cannot reasonably take precedence over Justin Martyr, Irenaeus, Hippolytus, Victorinus and so forth.

However Murray does draw our attention to positive attitudes toward the Jews in general, though not to some of *their* Covenant promises such as the Land. He quotes, for instance words of John Braidwood, a Scottish Free Church missionary in Madras, published in 1853 to stir up believers' hearts to faith and prayer for Israel:

1. "The national restoration of the Jews, and its blessed effects on the world. For what have they been preserved, but for some wondrous end?

2. The Jews are the whole world's benefactors. Through Jewish hands and eyes God has sent us his lively oracles of truth to us. They penned, and they preserved the Bible.

3. Our Redeemer—the God-man—who has all power in heaven and earth is their kinsman.

4. Viewed nationally, the Jews are the most miserable of all nations. The Messiah wept over Jerusalem, their capital, because the curse fell on it; ought we not to weep over the accumulated progressive woe springing from the curse, and drinking up the nation's spirit for eighteen centuries?

5. Their covenant prospects are bright beyond all conception. On the grand day of their realisation, will any of us all regret that we pitied Israel apostate and outcast?"[40]

Murray tells us of similar sentiments from many other well known theologians of the era, particularly in Scotland. One cannot help but wonder whether, in the light of 20th century events, they would not be Pre-Millennialists, were they alive on earth today! These faithful men of old knew full well that God keeps His promises. The only problem is one of timing—whether this restoration is to take place within or after the Church Age.

Summary Of Traditional Post-Millennialism

There seem to be nine main features which characterise Post-Millennial teaching, although we certainly cannot claim that all protagonists apply all of them, or that those who do apply them equally.

1. Symbolic, figurative and allegorical interpretation of texts which other eschatologists find easy to accept at face value.

2. Inference, assumption, oblique argument and wishful thinking, all made easier by the less literal interpretation of predictive prophecy.

3. Heavy reliance on Preterism to account for the otherwise incontrovertible evidence that the world is to become more evil before the Lord's return.

4. Appeal to popular sentiment, presenting an eternal scenario in which the vast majority will eventually be saved.

5. Compared with Pre-Millennialism, greater emphasis upon what the Church is to achieve in the world, compared to what God will achieve through direct action or Divine intervention.

6. An ambivalent attitude towards Israel's national future, with a transferring of specific Old Testament prophecies to the Millennial Church. However there is widespread recognition of some sort of national repentance or restoration for Israel, but within this dispensation.

7. No specific Millennial role for Israel, as they do not connect the restoration with the recovery of the Land.

8. No personal visible presence of the Lord on earth during the Millennium, inasmuch He is not expected to return until this is over.

9. Singling out Pre-Millennialism, which is regarded as the main 'opposition' for special attack, amounting in extreme cases to distortion, misrepresentation and ridicule.

We have dealt with the first eight as we have proceeded. Let us pause briefly to look at the final one, not out of pique, but because it helps to turn the spotlight on specific issues, particularly those which compel apologists to resort to desperate measures. Boettner is about to feature yet again!

> "There can be no doubt that Premillennialism lends itself more to an emotional type of preaching and teaching than does Postmillennialism and Amillennialism. It gives something definite to look forward to in the immediate future and charges the present with portentous possibilities."[41]

Some of the greatest evangelists have been emotional in their preaching because of their sheer burden for souls. In this writer's experience the most orchestrated emotive type of preaching, with short-term aspirations, has been among Neo-Post-Millennialists of the more extreme modern Charismatic churches. However Boettner should consider that the Lord's return is several times presented in the epistles as a message of hope and encouragement, and something to which believers should look forward. Traditional Post-Millennialism denies this. Does he subscribe to passionless preaching?

Writing about what he wrongly assumes to be the Pre-Millennial view of the Millennium, Boettner says:

> "During the millennium the saints in their glorified bodies mingle freely with men who are still in the flesh. This element in particular seems to present an inconsistency—a mongrel kingdom, the new earth and glorified sinless humanity mingling with the old earth and sinful humanity; Christ and the saints in immortal resurrection bodies living in a world that still contains much sin and scenes of death and decay. To bring Christ to live on the earth again in the

sinful environment of this world would seem to be the equivalent of introducing sin into heaven."[42]

Now where is the logic in that last statement, which is an odd mixture of truth and error? Jesus lived on earth for over thirty years and remained without sin. Can He and His risen and glorified saints not do so in that day, when we have been *"delivered from this body of death"* (Rom 7:24)? Would he dare say that in those weeks between Jesus' resurrection and ascension there was a 'mongrel situation', with Him in His resurrection body and the others in mortal bodies? That is his implication. But let us also consider Boettner's above statement in the light of a quite astonishing quote by him from Dr Snowden:

> "Premillenarians put their confidence in some 'rod of iron' with which Christ will 'smite down all opposition' when He comes."[43]

Now this is neither more nor less than ridiculing the words of the Bible. Are Boettner and Snowden referring to Ps 2:9, where God the Father addresses God the Son, or Rev 19:15?

> *"Now out of His mouth goes a sharp sword, that with it He should strike the nations. And He Himself will rule them with a rod of iron. He Himself treads the winepress of the fierceness and wrath of God."*

That verse follows immediately Jesus' return in power. They are quite right in this: Premillenarians put their confidence in the unadulterated word of God; not in some obscure allegorisation. Of course the rod of iron might not be appropriate for a Post-Millennial earth, with an unraptured but mature and perfect Church present; we would be inclined to agree, *supposing* such a Church is foretold; but it is not. The rod of iron will be for the rule of those born during the Millennium.

We quote Boettner for the last time:

> "Premillennialism thus despairs of the power of the Gospel to Christianise the world, and asserts rather that it is to be preached only as a witness."[44]

This is manipulative. How can one despair of what one does not believe? We do not believe that the world will be 'Christianised' before the

Lord's return. After all Post-Millennialism, as we have seen, means bringing the world up to a general level of Christian standards, with the vast majority but not everybody saved. We do not preach the Gospel to 'Christianise', but to lead men and women to a saving faith in the Lord Jesus Christ through personal acceptance of His redemptive work and shed blood. That always has a positive effect within society, but can also polarise it. But we maintain that God has given a free choice; thus while many will repent, many will not. If we despair, it is of the rebellious hearts of those who refuse the Gospel. And of course we are saddened by our own failures and by the widespread Laodicean attitudes and characteristics of the latter-day Church.

I noticed in one Post-Millennial book the old jibe that the Pre-Millennial attitude to the world is that 'one does not polish the brass on a sinking ship'. The accusation is too petty to waste time on trying to re-locate the reference. Possibly somebody did make such an injudicious remark, but one would have to know the full context before condemning it. Having been a Pre-Millennialist for over fifty-five years, I have to confess to never having heard it quoted except by sceptics. We do not deny that the Gospel can make a huge impact upon society, like the revivals under Asa around 950 BC, Hezekiah around 740 BC, and Josiah seventy years later (II Chron 15:12; 29:2 et seq.; 34:2 et seq.). These were immensely important, but did not stop the inevitable downfall of Judah. The Gospel has had an enormous impact upon the world; but it will not on its own bring about the Post-Millennial dream. The conquering Saviour will do that when He returns.

We have found that the vast majority of Post-Millennialism is not in any way Anti-Semitic. But we have noted that it denies, largely on the basis of Preterism, which considers AD 70 to have been God's final judgement on Israel for the rejection of her Messiah, any identifiable future fulfilment of those numerous Old Testament promises connected to Jerusalem and the Promised Land. A leading Messianic Jewish scholar sums up the distorted thinking thus:

> "The problem is not that God rejected Israel, but that Israel rejected the Messiahship of Jesus, which has led to the loss of blessing. The Covenant Post-Millennialists have placed the rejection in the wrong place."[45]

The consequences are serious indeed. False expectations of the Church are raised along with false expectations of the future. Tasks reserved for the returning Lord Jesus are claimed by the Church, as if robbing Him of His glory. As with Amillennialism, God's unconditional promises are seen to be breakable on the basis of Israel's failure. God's faithfulness is called into question; the implications are avoided only by an endless chain of subjective allegorisation. Moreover there is every indication that, despite the best of intentions, Post-Millennianism is based on presumptuous interpretation of prophecy, as we have seen it defined in Deut 18:22 and Jer 22:9.

We might seriously ask ourselves whether it is sufficient simply to be 'not Anti-Semitic'—at best a negative quality—if God still has a major place for Israel in His plans.

A comment in a newly published book, sympathetic to Post-Millennialism, speak volumes when compared to Peter's summing up of the reasoning of the latter scoffers:

> *"For since the fathers fell asleep, **all things continue as they were** from the beginning of creation"* (II Pet 2:3).

Jonathan Burnham, quoting W G Oliver, writes:

> "Accordingly, Premillennialists assumed a pessimistic attitude towards the world, viewing the end times **through a lens of discontinuity** and stressing a complete reversal of fortunes brought on by the bodily return of Christ. Postmillennialists, on the other hand, were optimistic in their hopes for political, social and spiritual reform, *emphasising continuity within the present order.*"[46]

We conclude Traditional Post-Millennialism to be discredited, especially by its stance on the nature of Israel's future in God's plans.

Chapter Twelve

Neo-Post-Millennialism And Israel's Future

Titles And Characteristics

Some people say that Post-Millennialism is dead, or virtually so. This is not true; it is very much alive and well on planet earth, but is usually referred to by one of a number of different tiles. We are more likely to encounter it under the titles of Kingdom Now, Restorationism, Reconstructionism or Dominion Theology. Associated ideas include Theonomy, Manifest Sons of God, Latter Rain and the Human Potential movement. Some are narrow terms, some broad; some overlap, others are self-contained. The majority who hold these views appear vague about their Post-Millennialism, which is a reflection of the lack depth of understanding which abounds. 'Theology' is once again becoming the province of the leaders, in churches where formerly most believers read the Bible in depth, even if they never read much else. All are more or less developments of the Traditional Post-Millennialism which we considered in the last chapter. The varying slants probably have as much to do with the original personalities involved as anything else.

- Restorationism is the belief that Acts 3:21 teaches that God had promised to restore the Church (as opposed to Israel) at some specific time in the future, and that supposed time, according to many proponents, was the final decades of the 20th century. We have already commented upon this and will have more to say.

- Kingdom Now means that the Old Testament Millennial promises are at last being fulfilled through the Church. This of course depends heavily on allegorisation. It simply brings the expectations of the Traditionalist into a present day, rather than a distant, fulfilment. Its roots are almost entirely Charismatic. Of course Kingdom Now also describes the wrong aspirations of many in Jesus' time on earth.

- Reconstructionism places upon the 'restored' Church the responsibility for imposing Christian laws, standards and

297

practices upon world governments. Political activism is claimed to be a legitimate means of achieving this. Its roots are largely Calvinist and Reformed. Indeed, Calvin tried it out in Geneva.

- Dominion Theology teaches that the dominion over creation, which man lost to Satan at the Fall, must now be reclaimed by a Church militant. This is widely reflected in Graham Kendrick's songs, some of which we will quote later. Old Testament Millennial passages are again invoked, but, intriguingly, expectations are not raised to the point of recognising the restitution of the physical and natural consequence of the Fall or Flood; they are confined to moral, cultural and social levels.

- Theonomy is a more extreme view, seeking to impose Levitical Law, including penalties for crime, upon all society. It is akin to extreme Islamic Law, as practised in the most militant states. Almost by definition it ignores the fact that *"If righteousness comes by the law, then Christ died in vain"* (Gal 2:21).

- Latter Rain, which pre-dates the other titles, claims that the late 20th century, extending possibly into the 21st, is the latter rain, as opposed to the former rain of Pentecost. If this is correct, Christians must currently be outshining all generations of believers since the 1st century morally, loving more sincerely and generally out-performing, in a way evident to the whole world. If it is true its influence should be glaringly obvious in our society. We should judge for ourselves and draw natural conclusions. Early expectations have not been met, and some Kingdom Now adherents will acknowledge that these 'latter rains' have been tardy.

- Manifest Sons of God, a development of the Latter Rains movement, is based upon the claim made by some in recent decades that Rom 8:19 is a prophecy referring to themselves. We are devoting a section to this.

- Human Potential Movement is a 'Christianised' version of 'inherent godhood' psychotherapy, mind-over-matter, holistic thinking, realisation of infinite potential and similar practices often associated with New Age and even occultism. This, supposedly, will be partly instrumental in achieving a sort of Utopia. Its appeal is mainly, but not exclusively, to liberals.

These are not intended to be comprehensive definitions. In practice, the distinction between the above are more blurred than our presentation of them suggests, and definitions may vary from country to country and locality to locality. It would be too massive a task to compare and dissect each of the above as we proceed to evaluate Neo-Post-Millennialism, and ultimately consider its relationship to God's future purposes for Israel. We trust that this is sufficient information for readers to be able to identify each as it occurs. Whatever differences may exist, the common theme can be summed up in DeMar's recent words:

> "Until whole nations come under the sway of the gospel and are truly discipled, we should not expect the coming of the Lord". [1]

How desperately depressing, when we look at the moral state of countries which have come under the sway of the gospel! Where is the blessed hope? Nowhere!

It must be emphasised that by no means all Neo-Post-Millennialists subscribe to all the above, or that they are evenly spread. Theonomy and the Human Potential Movement are more extreme views. Having been a leadership consultant, ever wary of the New Age thinking behind Maslow's Hierarchy of Needs and similar motivational theories, I am compelled to agree that distinct traces of HPM already exist in many churches.

Probably the most significant contrast between Traditional and Neo-Post-Millennialism is that, the one believes that the consummation of the Church's commission is still an indefinitely long way off, whereas the other believes that it has already started. Rather than applying our own personal, subjective judgements about whether the latter is true, we should be following the God-given guidelines for evaluating prophecy, mentioned early in our last chapter. They are very readily applied to the Post-Millennialism of recent decades, because this has been characterised by numerous bold claims and personal revelations about what God was doing or about to do in terms of prophetic fulfilment. If these claimed happenings have truly occurred in the place, manner and scale in which they were predicted by the prophets, they must be taken very seriously. If not, they must be suspect. I believe it fair to say that the 'Neo' variety of Post-Millennialism has been built upon and developed in ways which many of the Traditionalists of former years would have rejected. One thing that they have in common is that they are trying to bring about, in their own time and by their own efforts, the end of *"this present evil age"* (Gal 1:4), from which we are told that the Lord Jesus Christ will deliver us (v3).

The phenomenon is so unprecedented, so unique and so high in its profile that it cannot remain uninvestigated. It must either be totally genuine or utterly false. We quote Peter again:

> *"Be mindful of the words which were spoken of by the holy prophets, and the commandment by us, the apostles of the Lord and Saviour, knowing this first: that scoffers will come in the last days, walking according to their own lusts, and saying, 'where is the promise of His coming? For since the fathers fell asleep, all things continue as they were from the beginning of creation...'"* (II Pet 3:2–3).

Those Post-Millennialists who believe in the Rapture of the Church see this happening only at the *end* of their rule on earth. The ever-imminent Rapture is frequently described derogatorily as "helicopter escape" or in similar terms. Those who live in hope of this purifying hope are ridiculed. Their beliefs are said to be defeatist.

John Wimber and the Vineyard Fellowship are generally credited with the first of these new movements in Canada and the USA around 1948–49. But it was not until about 1970 that the ideas made any widespread impact in Britain. It was claimed to be a great new beginning, a work of the Holy Spirit. Most of the old Pentecostalists were profoundly unhappy.

Here I call on my own experience in the 'seventies, as a member of the national council of an evangelical mission threatened by destabilisation, and as a deacon in a Baptist church threatened by a split. Small groups— usually the same people—would go off for a few days or weeks to some centre, festival, camp or conference, and would return fired up, telling us what we were missing, but each time having some new idea, some different experience, some fresh revelation, some novel slogan. One perceived a contrast to the work of the Holy Spirit as recorded in Acts and reflected in the epistles. While sometimes new mysteries were revealed in the early Church, we are not told of new techniques, therapies or gimmicks. Some individuals assumed enormous authority, hardly in keeping with the New Testament pattern of local leadership, unless perhaps that of the self-styled 'apostles' of II Corinthians 11.

Everything new was transmitted to the congregation as something demanded by the Holy Spirit. Those who had put the new ideas into their heads may very well have argued from Scripture; but those tasked with spreading them back in their home churches were poorly equipped to present or to defend their cases from the Bible. Rather there was a sort of spiritual blackmail; weaker brethren and sisters were warned about 'resisting the Spirit'; this is a very solemn and dangerous threat to use against fellow believers.

Previously stable Christians became insecure; it was almost unfashionable not to have regular spiritual 'hang-ups' to declare for counselling, giving openings for influencing. 'Heavy shepherding' allowed stronger personalities to become 'control freaks' and weaker to become unstable; this was particularly true in house churches. Some of these trends will be reflected in excerpts of the songs of the period, which we will later quote.

My military duties at that time required me regularly to read the Soviet military press. I was intrigued to notice similarities to some of the techniques used by political officers to propagate Communism. One cannot deny that there was a great deal of trust, sincerity, enthusiasm and commitment among congregations. But this was capitalised upon by enterprising leaders, sometimes, though not always, manipulatively. Admittedly some congregations needed to be shaken out of their torpor, and this was sometimes achieved. But elsewhere in active evangelistic churches splits were common. I personally knew faithful pastors who were ousted from office. Huge generation gaps opened up. Ageism is not a Christian virtue, but it suddenly mushroomed, again usually justified by the accusation that those who wished to test everything by Scripture were 'resisting the Spirit'. This new spiritual bandwagon encouraged a fear of being left out.

From the beginning there were parties with conflicting priorities and approaches. According to Restorationist historian Dr Andrew Walker, in Britain in 1973–76 "the 'restored kingdom' (however fragile) had arrived", with the ministry and mutual recognition of 'The Fabulous Fourteen'!

> "Their vision at that time was for a worldwide church founded on the lines revealed to them in their deliberations together. However even during these years the 'kingdom' was in no sense a uniform structure. The evidence seems to suggest that it was the London Brothers and their associates who first developed a strong interest in discipleship... In the early 1970s, the 'fabulous fourteen' all thought that they were involved in the same work of restoring the kingdom."[2]

What was described as church discipline was all too often dictatorship. It is not profitable to pursue all the internal politics, rivalries, apostolic claims and counter-claims etc. of the so-called restoration of the kingdom. We noted in the last chapter that the promise of Acts 3:21 for restoration was not addressed to the Church anyway, but to Israel. We have hopefully thrown a little light on the cradle of Neo-Post-Millennialism in Britain. Dave Hunt's excellent books, *The Seduction of Christianity*, with T A McMahon as co-writer, and *Whatever Happened to Heaven?*[3] contain invaluable information on what was happening on the other side of the Atlantic. They have ominous points to make about the Human Potential Movement. Part of the appeal of the new style of church was that people who considered themselves as nonentities within their original denominations suddenly became influential leaders.

Neo-Post-Millennianism is more-or-less confined to Bible-believing churches, or at least to those who attend them, even if the definition of Bible-believing has to be diluted to permit generous levels of allegorisation and, in more extreme cases, the superior authority of claimed personal revelation. However there are some who are quite influential, but whose programme is largely humanist, though argued from Scripture but with a reduced supernatural content. It is very easy for humanists who accept Christian ethics to be caught up in the life of any church which believes in moral and social evolution. They can then exert their influence from within. The appeal to environmentalists is enormous. The world approves. The ability of the Creator to restore in His own good time the blighted environment is simply not considered.

Doctrine Or Indoctrination?

Much of the teaching has been absorbed through songs, rather than through conscious Bible study. One can hardly over-estimate the influence of songs and singers in the early days of Neo-Post-Millennialism in Britain. Some are written by people with a comprehensive knowledge of the Bible. Others are put together on the 'Judas went and hanged himself... Go thou and do likewise' principle. It's in the Bible, it must be okay; whether it fits together does not matter. The fact that they hold out some sort of popular cultural appeal is one of the secrets of their success. The appeal, if analysed, which it rarely is, is that they imply that the present generation of Christians is more spiritual, more heroic, more privileged, more dedicated and in every other sense more wonderful than any generation which has gone before. Some songs frankly flatter them. They will provide us with a convenient way to examine some of the main emphases of the movement.

Note that many of these songs talk about 'the Spirit', rather than God's Spirit or the Holy Spirit. This may be acceptable in songs where the context removes all doubt; otherwise it encourages abuse by false spirits. The repeated use of 'Jesus', avoiding saying 'Lord Jesus' or 'Jesus Christ', also becomes dangerous if not corrected. There is more than one Jesus and there are many spirits. Relaxed attitudes to theology can be lethal.

We referred very briefly in an earlier chapter to this song phenomenon. We appreciate that it is well nigh impossible to compile a hymnbook that covers every eschatological variation within a congregation or denomination, let alone an interdenominational community. For better or worse, one must expect different views to be catered for. But suddenly, at the time of the 1984 Mission England, a new book, *Mission Praise*[4], intended for inter-denominational use, was hi-jacked by Post-Millennial compilers. No new Pre-Millennial hymns were incorporated. It has since been enlarged and is in very widespread use. Some of the general traditional eschatological hymns were included, but there is practically no reference to an anticipated imminent Rapture. The verse with the lines, "If I shall walk the vale with Him, or meet Him in the air", a clear alternative to death, has been removed from "I know not why God's wondrous love"[5]. Hymns where escaping death is not an option were included. Hymns with a confused eschatology were accepted. The Blessed Hope has been blurred.

It was by no means the first, nor has it proved to be the last, of a number of new books containing vast numbers of Neo-Charismatic, Neo-Post-Millennial songs. But in this book the inclusion of a great many excellent traditional general hymns, and not a few very good new ones, puts people off their guard. They cheerfully sing doctrines which they would never acknowledge in any other form, such as the following two, which teach universal salvation, one even going as far as to say that eternal life is a reward, rather than a gift:

> "These are the facts as we have received them: Christ has fulfilled what the Scriptures foretold. Adam's whole family in death had been sleeping, Christ through His rising restores us to life."[6]

> "God has proclaimed the just reward, life for all men, alleluia!"[7]

The second quote is diametrically opposed to Rom 6:23. But who cares nowadays? The book was thrust upon many an unsuspecting congregation at a time of church splits; when challenging the new generation of leaders was seen as opposing the work of the Holy Spirit. Sometimes congregations of utterly diverse traditions and doctrines abandoned even the most precious and hardly won doctrines to get on the new bandwagon. Rigorous comparison with Scripture took second or third place to claimed private revelation and vision. Even within the Restorationist movement, some, like David Matthew, perceive the dangers:

> "Paradoxically, much of the unity-seeking has been against a backdrop of increasing liberalism."[8]

But a critical analysis was discouraged by such lines, often sung emotively, repetitively and manipulatively, as:

> "Bind us together, Lord, bind us together with cords that cannot be broken"[9]

"The Spirit won't be hindered by division, in the perfect work of Jesus that's begun."

The full context of the last line is below. Restorationism and allied forms were supposedly a new beginning in the Church, one which even seemed to put Pentecost in the shade, to judge by such triumphalism as:

"A body now prepared by God and ready for war,
The prompting of the Spirit is our word of command.
We rise a mighty army at the bidding of the Lord,
The devils see and fear, for their time is at hand.
And children of our Lord hear our commission,
That we should love and serve the Lord as one.
The Spirit won't be hindered by division,
In the perfect work of Jesus that's begun." [10]

Those who like to discredit Dispensational Pre-Millennialism by citing as founder, Irving, who, despite early connections, never was a Pre-Tribulationist, but was eventually classed as a heretic, should take note that he actually had Post-Millennial leanings, as Dr Walker records:

"Irving saw the Church revived again 'terrible and mighty like an army of banners'". [11]

However Post-Millennialist Walker is hopelessly inaccurate in his accompanying remarks about the history of Pre-Tribulationism. Irving's Catholic Apostolic Church had sown the seed a century or so before. For the sake of space we will use a prose, rather than poetic, print layout, for these quotes. The implication was that something totally unprecedented had just occurred in the Church, and that the current generation was to outshine the martyrs of the first three centuries and of the Reformation, the Counter-Reformation and the heroes of the pioneering missionary age. The same song writer elsewhere says:

"The Church that seems to slumber has now risen from its knees, and dry bones are responding with the fruits of new birth... the watchmen on the tower all exhort us to prepare, and the Church responds—a people who will answer the call etc..." [12]

These words accurately reflect the claims and predictions that were being made in the 'seventies. But whatever has happened to the sleeping virgins of Matthew 25? Had no previous generation produced fruits of new birth? We again challenge this 'unprecedented' awakening on the basis of the tests of true prophecy. If these claims for the Church's sudden dramatic new revived and restored state were genuine, surely we would see by now a huge impact upon the morals of society. A giant leap forward in the claimed 'Christianisation' of the world would have occurred. But where is this corroboration? Does not the failure of prophecies to materialise not indicate presumption, as defined in Deut 18:22? It is perfectly true that in some countries churches have multiplied numerically. Sometimes they have been very shallow based, with elements of former paganism never eradicated, such as a morbid fascination with demon possession. Others have shown healthy, vital growth. But in the countries where the claims were first made, morals have continued to plummet. Do we really see justification for the following?

> "This is the mystery, that Christ has chosen you and me to be the revelation of His glory... She's crowned in splendour and a royal diadem; the King is enthralled by her beauty. Adorned in righteousness, arrayed in glorious light, the bride in waiting for her King." [13]

Is this truly the state of the Church on earth today? No apostle ever made such a claim for the early Church. Look at the epistles of Paul, James and Peter, full of humility, awaiting a heavenly, not an earthly, consummation. Consider Paul's words in Rom 7:13–25. This song has been taken from thoughts from the Song of Solomon and Psalm 45, and has been muddled up as regards dispensations and locations. But people still sing it dutifully. The Church is never in Scripture pictured as crowned.

> *"So the King will greatly desire your beauty; because He is your Lord, worship Him"* (Ps 45:11).

The *"glorious church, not having spot or wrinkle"* (Eph 5:26) is seen thus in heaven (Rev 19:7,8), ready to accompany her Lord when He returns in power.

Many individual believers will be crowned, but only following their resurrection. Whatever has happened to the awareness of compilers who allow this type of travesty to enter our worship books? Contrast these words with the Christ-centred words of that old classic, based on the same scriptures, "Out of the Ivory Palaces"[14] Any true work of the Holy Spirit puts Him in the centre, not us. *"When He, the Spirit of truth, has come... He will glorify Me" (Jn 16:13, 14).*

"With a shout and trumpet sound He'll fetch His bride for the marriage feast"[15]

This is slightly more subdued in tone. But it raises an enormous problem for those who believe that the Church will be perfected whilst here on earth. Where and when is the Judgement Seat of Christ or *Bema* in such a programme? The word Bema is used only twice for Christ judging, both times for believers (Rom 14:10 and II Cor 5:10), never for the unsaved. We must all appear there to be judged for our service, not, of course for our sins. The questions raised by the quote are these:

- If the contemporary Church is to be perfected on earth, how can unresurrected believers appear before the same Bema as those who have gone before?

- Are half of the body of Christ to be judged in heaven and half on earth? Are latter day Church saints in a different class from their predecessors?

- Where will the Judgement Seat of Christ be if some believers are to remain on earth until the Marriage of the Lamb?

Further questions inevitably cross one's mind, but these will suffice here. One can appreciate why the Bema is so seldom preached about; certain schools of prophetic interpretation simply have no place for it. Dispensational Pre-Millennialism encounters no such problems, believing that I Thess 4:15–17 teaches that all Church saints will be resurrected at the same great event, which will precede the Bema, which will in turn precede the Marriage of the Lamb. It all fits together.

There is no doubting the sincerity, earnestness and conviction of some of these writers; however these are not the only qualities required for hymn writing. The following do not appear to lack earnestness:

"Right here in this place the Spirit is moving, as the prophet said it would be, right here in this place there's a mighty revelation of the glory of the Lord, as the waters cover the sea."[16]

Which prophet is he referring to that foretold what would happen in his congregation? Which prophet foretold a time such as our own, other than perhaps Paul talking of a latter day falling away or Peter predicting the scoffing generation? The Hab 2:14 part quote is quite out of place here. Now if this were merely a matter of differences of eschatological interpretation, it might not be so serious. But in fact it robs the Lord of *His* glory and also undermines the credibility of the Christian faith in the eyes of the world. All those Scriptural passages which refer to the Lord's return in power indicate that it will be quite unmistakeable, e.g. Mat 24:25–27. Here we have a song writer claiming a recent global phenomenon, which neither the world nor mature believers, would recognise as a revelation of the glory of the Lord *"as the waters cover the sea"*. Is that *really* all we expect of the Habakkuk prophecy? Some people may assume it to be because they are told it is. They are being brainwashed.

'Manifest Sons Of God'

The Manifest Sons of God movement was a development of the so-called Latter Rain movement and goes back to 1948–50. Associated with it sometimes is the idea of a special 'Joshua Generation'; which has not even the remotest prophetic authority. Some of the claims made were so extravagant that is quite outwith our terms of reference to examine them. But strange ideas based on Romans 8:19 persist.

Now here are some lines, rather better written than many others, because one of the authors, Graham Kendrick, is a very competent writer who has produced some highly commendable and indeed beautiful thoughts, sadly interspersed frequently with Post-Millennial lines. The individual parts are splendid, but the fitting of them together can be misleading. There is a recurrent Neo-Post-Millennial theme in this next one:

> "All heaven awaits with baited breath, for saints on earth to pray; majestic angels ready stand with swords of fiery blade. Astounding power awaits a word from heaven's resplendent throne; but God awaits our prayer of faith that cries 'Your will be done'." [17]

> "And the whole creation waits in expectation of the full revelation of the sons of God; as we march through history

to our blood-bought destiny, ever further and deeper into the heart of God." [18]

This is Church-centred rather than Christ-centred. It is immature and dangerous prioritising.

"When Christ, who is our life, appears, then you also will appear with Him in glory" (Col 3:4).

Such astounding heavenly power has been available to praying Christians throughout Church history; that is not new, though it has too rarely been invoked. Behind these thoughts is a novel interpretation of Rom 8:19:

"For the earnest expectation of the creation eagerly awaits the revealing of the sons of God."

The AV uses 'manifestation' where the NKJV uses 'revealing'. In the previous verse Paul writes:

"I consider the sufferings of this present time are not worthy to be compared with the glory which shall be revealed in us."

Paul is talking about events following the resurrection, or he would not have written 'us'. Matthew Henry and Bishop Ellicott, commenting on the verse, put it thus:

"The state of the church in this world always is an afflicted state. He tells them that they suffered with Christ, and should be glorified with Him." [19]

"The coming of Christ is always thus conceived as a visible manifestation of glory in those who take part in it." [20]

In other words, the glory of the Church does not precede the glory of the Lord, which is what this sinister interpretation implies. It tries to pre-empt for the Church of the glory that will be His when He appears; in that day the *lesser* glory that will be ours. Would we want it otherwise? Some do. It is the sort of philosophy which derides those who, like Paul, joyfully anticipate heaven.

"For our citizenship is in heaven, from which we also eagerly wait for the Saviour, the Lord Jesus Christ, who

will transform our lowly body that it may be conformed to His glorious body, according to the working by which He is able even to subdue all things to Himself" (Phil 3:21).

Neo-Post-Millennialists want this glory now.

Those who deride fellow believers who long for heaven would do well to consider the parable of the great feast (Lk 14:16–24), when invited guests are too busy getting on with legitimate earthly tasks to respond to the gracious invitation. Works may be evidence of faith, but they are *never* a substitute. Is there a greater disincentive to responding to the Gospel call than the denying of the possibility of the Lord's return, which, in the verses following the above quotation from Peter, is described as an incentive to *"holy conduct and godliness"* (v11)?

Creation has been groaning since the Fall of man. Its darkest hours are still ahead. According to the timetable suggested in the above song lines, nature should no longer be red in tooth and claw. Yet the curse is still evident wherever we look. Our planet is dying; only God can revitalise it for those promised thousand years.

A Post-Millennial Bible?

Neo-Post-Millennialism is powerfully supported by the pretentiously titled but popular *New Spirit-Filled Life Bible*, in which this school is represented by a variety of scholars, whose position may vary from very mild to quite extreme Post-Millennialism. The Scofield Bible used to be criticised for its unashamedly Pre-Millennialist slant; but this new study Bible is very much more overtly weighted in another specific direction. The Executive Editor, Jack W Hayford, in the Introduction writes:

> "One historian has referred to the Pentecostal-Charismatic revival as 'a movement without a man', thereby noting the phenomenon that its broadening tide of influence is dynamically global and impacting in every sector of the church. No one can proscribe the movement's boundaries, none can inscribe their name upon it, and who can describe it in any other way than by Peter's words at Pentecost, 'This is what was spoken by the prophet Joel'... And in the last days... I will pour out My Spirit on all flesh'" (Acts 2:16, 17).[21]

The 'old school' Pentecostalists are, or certainly were, largely Pre-Millennial and presumably would not want to be associated with this statement in its entirety. If Hayford subscribes to the formula that these things are to happen at the same time as the church fulfils its Great Commission, he should look around him. He should note the impact that Islam is having in nominally Christian countries He should note the overturning of Christian laws by the European parliament. He should consider the moral state of what was once known as Christendom, and think again. He should look at the growth of pagan and occult practice. Note the contrast here with Traditionalist Post-Millennialists, many of whom were scathingly dismissive of any who dared to claim that we were living in the last days.

Certainly he is right in claiming that this movement is impacting upon every sector of the church; whether this is positive is an entirely different matter. As for the claim that this is 'a movement without a man', has Jack Hayford never heard of John Wimber, Terry Virgo, Bryn Jones, Arthur Wallis, Earl Paulk and Michael Harper etc.? Dr Andrew Walker researched the Restoration movement of the nineteen seventies and 'eighties, *from the inside*, and lists an amazing array of personality cults, splinter groups and bizarre titles, such as 'the magnificent seven' and 'fabulous fourteen', claims and counter-claims of apostleship and much more. [22] A movement without a man, indeed!

Hayford implies that Joel's great prophecy, only partially fulfilled at Pentecost, is now receiving that more complete latter day fulfilment *before the great and notable day of the Lord* comes. We query whether God's Spirit has been poured out *upon all flesh*, because we fail to observe either the huge moral impact or the accompanying dramatic and visible cosmic signs. We know beyond any shadow of doubt that that Day of the Lord has yet to occur. It is sad that a potentially superb study Bible, using one of the very best translations available, should be devalued by its Executive Editor's distorted perception of where the earth is heading.

In a special section in this Bible about the Holy Spirit and Restoration, James Robison writes:

> "Restoration in every dimension of human experience is at
> the heart of the Christian gospel. It is woven through all the

Scripture and must be at the forefront of our ministry of the truth. Acts 3:19–21 makes the most pointed reference to restoration in the New Testament. Peter urges a return to God for cleansing of sins. He adds that this returning would pave the way for a period of refreshing renewal that would result from the presence of the Lord with His people. It would also prepare for the return of Christ, whom, Peter said, 'heaven must receive [or retain] until the times of restoration of all things, which God has spoken by the mouth of all His holy prophets since the world began' (Acts 3:21). Many feel it is now, in these last days, that all things prophesied will be fulfilled and restoration completed. The ultimate restoration is the return of the church, the bride of Christ, to the majesty and glory God intended for her. To accomplish this restoration God has begun to release His power and purity without measure through the church. The sifting has begun in order that the unshakeable kingdom may be revealed (Heb 12:27, 28)." [23]

We have commented in previous chapters about Acts 3:21. The terrifying aspect here is that, because this occurs within the pages of a study Bible, the unwary will assume that it carries the authority of the inspired word of God. One is staggered by the complacency and conceit reflected in the supposed spiritual progress of the latter day church. Has the Vatican ever sought or made greater claims for its status?

One's mind turns to that most self-satisfied and conceited congregation addressed by the Saviour, who is actually standing outside and knocking for admission—Laodicea (Rev 3:14–22). Jesus said:

> *"Because you say, I am rich and have become wealthy, and have need of nothing'—and do not know that you are wretched, miserable, poor, blind and naked—I counsel you..."* (vv. 17, 18).

It is not for us to criticise directly any church or congregation, but it is for us to evaluate, against Scripture and by what we see in the world around us, the 'signs of the times'. If the above claims are true, well and good. On the other hand, if the moral state of the world is static or deteriorating, we are fooling ourselves by believing them to be true.

As for Robison's claims of fresh purity, has there ever been a time when Scripture's injunctions for believers to keep themselves separate and unspotted from the world (Jude 1:23) been so disregarded? Worldly wisdom justifies our building bridges rather than blowing bridges in order to help achieve targets which we were never set.

Apart from anything else, the restoration of which Peter spoke is not of the Church, which had only just been born and did not need any restoration, but of Israel, which had just rejected and crucified her Messiah. It was of Israel's restoration that the prophets had spoken, although, as indicated by Peter, they were going to have to wait. The prophets had never promised any restoration of the Church. The disciples had asked Jesus about this on the ascension day:

> *"Lord, will You at this time restore the kingdom to **Israel"***
> (Acts 1:6).

Jesus' answer never denied their expectation, only their timescale. This is very significant. The whole fabric of Post-Millennialism has at its very foundation this failure to correlate the restoration, specifically of Israel, in Acts 1:6 and the restitution or restoration of Israel, the only candidate for restoration at the time Peter spoke, in Acts 3:21. Acts 1 and 3 use the verb and noun forms of the same Greek word. There are no semantic excuses here.

What strange logic is it that prompts Post-Millennialists to believe that Jesus is to remain in the heavens until the *end,* rather than the *beginning*, of the times of refreshing and restoration, when all parallel Old Testament prophecies indicate that it is the beginning, and that it is He who will accomplish the restoration personally?

Any further statement about the promised restoration of the Church is therefore irrelevant. However it is important to check what further misinformation Christians are being fed. A paragraph later Robison continues:

> "God multiplies when He restores. And so in His restoration work today, God is not only simply restoring the church to the glory it displayed in New Testament times. He is seeking to restore it to a state more powerful, majestic and glorious than anything the world has yet seen."

Since when have we to be perceived to be 'powerful, majestic and glorious' this side of the Lord's return? Is this not the image from which the Reformers rightly recoiled? Are we not rather to be meek, gentle and humble? With consistent Post-Millennialism they should be recognising that when the Lord returns, his surviving 'brethren' will be in anything but a 'powerful, majestic and glorious' state – just look at the Judgement of Sheep and Goats in Matt 25:31–46! Note carefully that the congregations most highly commended by the Lord were those of Smyrna and Philadelphia. To Smyrna Jesus says:

> *"I know your works, tribulation, and poverty (but you are rich)".*

Aspiration to be powerful, majestic and glorious seems to be more in keeping with Mystery Babylon (Rev 17:4), the final manifestation of apostate religion. Where are our leaders taking us? To the Philadelphian Church Jesus says:

> *"He who overcomes, I will make him a pillar in the temple of My God and the name of the city of My God, the New Jerusalem, which comes down out of heaven from My God"* (Rev 3:12).

Down here during this age we are to expect tribulation, not glory (Jn 16:33). Rev 21:1, 2 makes it abundantly clear that the New Jerusalem is to descend only after this earth has passed away completely. Paul says:

> *"Lest I should be exalted above measure by the abundance of the revelations, a thorn in the flesh was given to me, a messenger of Satan, lest I be exalted above measure"* (II Cor 12:7).

Neo-Post-Millennialists crave for glory prematurely in these mortal bodies; but they would no more be able to cope with such glory in *"these bodies of death"* than Paul could. The difference is that Paul was wise enough to acknowledge this. If people *think* that they are more spiritual than Paul, they are surely fooling themselves.

Paul writes:

> *"For I know that if our earthly house, this tent, is destroyed, we have a building from God, a house not made with hands,*

eternal in the heavens. For this we groan, earnestly desiring
to be clothed with our habitation from heaven... while we
are at home in the body, we are absent from the Lord
(II Cor 5:1, 2, 6).

So much for those Post-Millennialists who ridicule our 'pessimism' for
seeking our glorious future after this life. Our aspirations should be
heavenly.

"Here we have no continuing city, but we seek the one to
come" (Heb 13:14).

'Here' means here! While we expect one day to be with our Lord, in a
glorified situation ourselves, that is neither our present target nor our
priority for the future. In annexing Old Testament promises for earth, we
are effectively trying to elbow into the future blessing of restored Israel,
failing to realise that our promised blessing as the Bride of Christ is even
greater.

Robison's statement is completely out of line with the Lord's High
Priestly prayer of John 17:

"And now, O Father, glorify Me together with Yourself, with
the glory which I had with You before the world was" (v 4).

"I have given them Your word; and the world has hated
them because they are not of the world, just as I am not of
the world, I do not pray that You should take them out of the
world, but that You should keep them from the evil one.
They are not of the world, just as I am not of the world."
(vv. 14–16).

There is nothing there to suggest a 'Christianised' world before the
Lord's return. We are to be separated; not integrated, which is so often
the Post-Millennial policy. Any spiritual glory which we may or may not
possess, this side of death or the Rapture, is perceived by God rather than
by the world, which at present has diametrically opposed criteria for
measuring glory.

Now in no way are we suggesting that all Post-Millennialists suffer from
pride and that others are exempt. We are simply saying that a movement
which teaches that the earth is to be made ready by the Church for

Christ's return has more scope for pride, and that the Manifest Sons of God movement has perhaps the greatest scope. Too often pride takes the form of claimed greater spirituality or a perceived extent of being 'filled by the Spirit'. Only in the Cross may we glory. All believers are baptised by the same Spirit (I Cor 12:13). Our level of filling, if it can be perceived at all, will be evidenced by the *fruits* of the Spirit, not by *gifts*, which can be counterfeited.

There is a sinister and powerful type of spiritual blackmail afoot. It is the suggestion that one should never question anything which is said about or claimed to be in the name of the Holy Spirit. It is never a tool for bringing fellow believers into line. I remember my old Pastor, James Sidlow Baxter long ago saying that any one who feared sinning against the Holy Spirit was incapable of doing so; it was only those who were unafraid who might be guilty.

Preterism And Dismissal Of Israel's National Future

In our last chapter we found it useful to give a short preview of Preterism. Pre- and most Amillennialists believe that the world is foretold by the Bible to grow progressively more wicked before the Lord returns. It takes only a fairly elementary knowledge of Scripture to understand why, at face value, they believe this. Post-Millennialists believe, as we have noted, that the Lord will return when the world has reached its moral peak and has maintained a high level of morality, either for a thousand years or at least for a long time. How can this be, given all the Scriptures which Pre- and Amillennialists would quote to prove the opposite? Yet Post-Millennialists are not, by and large, foolish people; they must have some formula which the rest of us are missing. What is it? The answer, or at least the key answer, is Preterism. If Preterism can be proved to be correct, they have a case; if not, they have none.

To be fair to them, many Preterists are Bible-believing in a general sense. Liberal Post-Millennialists have no need to be, because they do not seek ways to reconcile their belief in evolving society, with detailed prophecies of end-time disasters and destruction in a Bible which they do not profess to believe anyway.

We encountered Preterism (sometimes spelt Praeterism) with some Amillennialists and promised to look at it under Post-Millennialism, where it is much more widespread. Marcellus Kik and Gary Demar, are leading Post-Millennialist spokesmen on this issue. The denial of Old Testament prophecies to the nation Israel is often closely interlinked with Preterism, something which has been around for fractionally longer than Post-Millennialism itself and which may even have encouraged it. Randall Price writes:

> "Preterist interpretation first appeared in a commentary on Revelation by the Spanish Jesuit Luis Alcazar (1554–1613). He interpreted symbols in Revelation as the victory of the Roman Catholic Church over paganism and especially over the Jewish people, whose divine rejection he believed was finalised in AD 70... The first Protestant preterist was Hugo Grotius (1538–1645), a Dutch Arminian who also originated the heretical governmental view of atonement, while Henry Hammond (1605–1660), who followed Grotius's approach, introduced it to British soil... post-Reformation groups, such as the Hugenots, denounced their views." [24]

One can see why the Jesuits were anxious to prove that events described in Revelation were 'spent' or 'realised' prophecies. The apostate Roman Catholic Church was well nigh universally identified by the reformers with Mystery Babylon and Babylon the Great of Revelation 17 and 18. Sir Robert Anderson, head of the CID (Criminal Investigation Department) a century or so ago, commented on the startling accuracy of this identification, though we know that the evil represented there has yet to reach its final form. Thus Preterism was born to satisfy the need to avoid the obvious.

This is hardly an ancestry to be proud of! DeMar of course would not agree, his argument being that the very early Christians believed that these prophecies would be fulfilled in their life time. [25] Many did; but that did not make them Preterists, which is a hindsight philosophy. We have noted elsewhere that the early Church was almost entirely Futurist and have quoted notable examples; it is most significant that Christians who lived in the two hundred years after the fall of Jerusalem were not Preterists, but rather studied with a futurist perspective what Preterists regard as obsolescent passages.

DeMar in 1999 wrote:

"Modern dispensational scholars like to argue that their prophetic teachings are as old as the hills, and that preterism is the wild new kid on the prophetic block. But a survey of Bible commentators will prove that the reverse is true. Dispensationalism is relatively new and has become popular only within the last hundred years."[26]

DeMar should not be comparing Preterism with Dispensationalism but with Futurism; they are different types of definition and therefore lead to unfair conclusions. Second century Justin Martyr and Iraeneus were Dispensationalists. Others, long pre-dating Darby, sometimes claimed to be the originator, can be quoted. His last statement is also quite wrong, as my own bookshelf testifies.

Second century Christian writers were not Preterists within the normal meaning of the word. This does not necessarily mean that they did not see an AD 70 application of the Olivet Discourse; but they believed that its *primary* application was to events surrounding the Lord's return in power. Radical Preterism teaches that the prophetic application was exhausted in AD 70, and yet history tell as that in the AD 135 Bar Kochbar rebellion, Jewish Christians heeded the warning of Matthew 24, Mark 13 and Luke 21 and fled Jerusalem; and that was certainly not within the life-time of those standing by when Jesus spoke. So we already have a precedent for a valid application to future generations. This destroys one of the main props of Preterism, that Jesus was addressing only those within His own generation.

DeMar describes Preterists and their view of the Olivet Discourse thus:

"Other Bible scholars, who take a more literal approach to the time texts, conclude that Jesus is addressing His contemporaries, that He is describing events that will happen to the first-century generation of Christians who first heard the prophecy. Advocates of this position are called *preterists*. A preterist is someone who believes that the fulfilment is in the past. The first-century *preterist* coming of Christ is a coming in judgement that led to the destruction of the temple and the judgement of the city in AD 70."[27]

That he of all people should claim a more literal approach staggers belief, when we note, for instance, that according to him Christ has already come! Yet in the same Olivet passage Jesus warns us not to believe in any claimed coming of His that is not universally visible and uniquely glorious (Matt 24:23–30). DeMar is recklessly including himself among those who proclaim a past coming of Jesus Christ which in no way matches these criteria. His theory stands only through massive and desperate allegorisation and figurative interpretation. We will return to this later.

But the heart of his case is based upon a highly manipulative distortion of what others believe and teach:

> "Of course, those who claim that Jesus did not teach His soon coming judgement upon Jerusalem can follow in the steps of the liberals and claim that Jesus and the writers of the New Testament were mistaken about the timing of prophetic events."[28]

He then proceeds to tell us about these liberals, with whom no Pre-Millennial theologian would wish to be associated. The implication, which remains throughout at least one of his books, and is found in other Preterist publications, is that only his party believe that Jesus predicted the AD 70 fall of Jerusalem. **This is simply not true.** Correct this misapprehension, and his readers may begin to view his rhetoric very differently. In his little volume, *Is Jesus Coming Soon?*, he constantly tacitly attributes to others this denial of an AD 70 application, for instance:

> "Notice that Jesus said, 'not one stone here shall be left upon another'. Jesus was not describing what would happen in some future rebuilt temple. He was speaking about the destruction of the very temple that stood before them at that time."[29]

Whoever is he trying to confound? Some imaginary Pre-Millennial monster? It would seem so. But it might impress the uninformed. Of course Jesus was talking about the contemporary temple, which they had only just left. We do not dispute that. The fact that, unlike him, we do happen to believe in a future temple does not invalidate the destruction in AD 70 of the old one! The whole point is that, while Pre-Millennialists see all except the early verses of the Olivet Discourse as pointing *primarily* to the future Tribulation period, and therefore spend more time on this future aspect, few if any deny the prediction of the then impending destruction of Herod's Temple and the first century city. People talking of the latter-day fulfilment may not find it necessary to comment on the AD 70 application at all, taking it as read, but that does not mean that they deny it. Back in 1843 Darby said, for instance, that Lk 21:9–19 referred to the sack of Jerusalem by Titus. The Schofield Reference Bible, F B Myer's Bible Commentary and Unger's Bible Dictionary, all well-known Pre-Millennialist and Futurist works, are quite clear about this.

It would be worth DeMar's time to ponder over the familiar setting, starting with Matt 23:39. Jesus said:

> *"'O Jerusalem, Jerusalem... you shall see Me no more till*
> *you say, 'Blessed is He who comes in the name of the Lord!'*
> *Then Jesus went out and departed from the temple."*

The Olivet Discourse ensued. Jesus had made it very clear indeed that the time will come when Jerusalem—the very same Jerusalem in the Judaean hill country—shall indeed repent and will welcome her visibly returning Messiah. What a sinister denial of God's faithful promises for Israel Preterism is, especially in its more extreme forms.

Dr Walvoord points out that Pre-, Post- and Amillennialists all have splits within their ranks over the precise timetable of the Olivet Discourse.[30] Most Pre-millennialists see the dual application, with either considerable overlap, or with a division at Matt 24:9, but opinions vary. This is not a crucial issue in this debate.

No Pre-Millennialist however sees such predictions as the Abomination of Desolation (v15), let alone the Lord's return, *"as the lightning comes from the east and flashes to the west"* (v27), as having had their main fulfilment already. There was a prior fulfilment of the Abomination very much in the pattern of Daniel 9 in the 2nd century BC; this sets a precedent for the fulfilment of the final such abomination, which will be greater, not lesser than the 2nd century BC one, which itself was much more elaborate than anything in AD 70, and led to the Maccabæan revolt and revival. There were of course minor abominations in AD 69 and 70, but no recorded event matched this desecration. The Roman soldiers, against their commander's wishes, had destroyed the temple to salvage the gold, before such an opportunity arose for anything like the fulfilment of Paul's amplification of Daniel 9:27 (see II Thess 2:4, quoted below). The AD 135 desecration was in turn on a greater scale than the AD 70 one. Antichrist's future abomination will be on a much more outrageous scale still, whatever Preterists claim.

As for the contention of some Preterists that the Lord's promised coming (Matt 24:27–30) took place in the form of the slow ponderous build up of the Roman invasion forces, we are appalled that any theologian who believes such an unlikely analogy can describe himself as Bible-believing. It makes a mockery of all interpretation.

Note that it is to a Gentile church in far off Macedonia, rather than to the church in Jerusalem, that Paul writes regarding this desecration. He refers firstly to our future gathering to Him (we being the Church) and then to the day of Christ:

> *"Let no man deceive you by any means; for that Day will not come unless the falling away comes first, and the man of sin is revealed, the son of perdition, who opposes and exalts himself above all that is called God or that is worshipped, so that he sits as God in the temple of God, showing himself that he is God... the coming of the lawless one is according to the working of Satan, with all power, signs, and lying wonders."* (II Thess 2:3, 4, 9).

That did not happen in AD 70. Revelation 13, written on a far off Aegean island, tells us more of this coming vile person, whose blasphemy will reach its peak in Jerusalem, which will be the epicentre of global, not merely local, events.

DeMar cannot even accept at face value Matt 24:30:

> *"And they will see the Son of Man coming on the clouds of heaven with power and great glory".*

He writes:

> "Clouds are symbols of God's presence. Why should Matthew 24:30 mean anything different?... Jesus was speaking of His ascension."[31]

Are we meant to re-interpret Acts 1:9 as, "And He was taken up, and a symbol of God's presence received Him out of their sight"? When one looks at the Matthew 24 context of the Son of Man's coming in the clouds, we ask why, *assuming* the Preterist interpretation, the associated national mourning, also described in Zechariah 12, did not take place in AD 70. The believers had already fled the city. Israel nineteen hundred years later has never repented nationally. Israel's repentance and the Lord's return are inseparable—except to Preterists. We ask why, again assuming this programme, the angelic (v31) gathering of the elect did not take place then and there. AD 70, for the survivors, was a time of further dispersal, not of gathering, as any historian will confirm. The crumbs of evidence scraped together by Preterists simply do not satisfy the demands of prophetic integrity.

DeMar's arguments, packed with Bible quotations and subjective interpretations, appear quite convincing to the unwary, until one tries to unravel their complexity. Unfortunately there are many unwary around. Regarding heaven and earth, he does not seem to know whether he is coming or going—seriously! Do we assume that almost two thousand years of believers have been wrong and that Gary DeMar is right? The editor of his books, which are influential in the USA as a negative reaction to Tim LaHaye's *Left Behind*[32] series, says the following:

> "Readers will no longer be bound by the idol of eschatological tradition which has paralysed the Church and minimised the impact of Christianity on the world. Don't be disturbed by what you read, because the truth is about to set you free!"[33]

This scoffing and arrogant diatribe goes on to ridicule those who expect the Lord's near return. This may not quite match all the prerequisites of a cult, but the approach is remarkably similar to that of well known cult founders. Of course Tim LaHaye and Jerry Jenkins have left themselves open to criticism by producing a series of novels based on the Rapture and Great Tribulation scenario. The overall picture is good, but some assumptions and guesswork are always necessary with novels, and not all Pre-Millennialists, including this one, will be happy with every detail, however much blessed the series as a whole may have been.

Many Preterist interpretations of the Olivet Discourse illustrate their dependency upon assumptions of exaggeration. We cannot take time to go through the Olivet Discourse word by word. We agree that we can find predicted there many of the things which happened in AD 70. But most of them were on a much smaller scale than is demanded by Jesus' prophecies. Was Jesus deliberately exaggerating? DeMar thinks so; naturally he prefers to talk about 'hyperbole',[34] but it amounts to the same thing. Did Jesus or did Jesus not really mean the following, for instance?

1. That there would be *"great tribulation, such as has not been seen since the beginning of the world until this time, no, nor ever shall be"* (v 21)?

2. That *"unless those days were shortened, no flesh would be saved"* (v 22)?

3. That the coming of the Son of Man will be *"as the lightning comes from the east and flashes to the west"* (v 27)?

4. That the *"sun will be darkened, and the moon will not give its light; the stars will fall and the powers of the heaven will be shaken"* (v 29)?

5. That *"all the tribes of earth will see the Son of Man coming on the clouds of heaven with power and great glory"* (v 31)?

According to DeMar, Jesus was deliberately exaggerating or using hyperbole; however he thoughtfully provides Him with an excuse!!!

> "All these passages describe calamitous events in terms of superlatives, stating that they were the worst that would ever happen. It is clear that the purpose of hyperbole in all these passages is to emphasise the disastrous nature of each event."[35]

Now where do we draw the line? Jesus was not talking in poetic language like the Psalm writers. He was talking factually and seriously two or three days before His crucifixion. What licence has DeMar for classing Jesus' words here as hyperbole and not others? Is this the only passage Jesus wanted to be taken desperately seriously? Are John 3:16 and a few dozen other key passages upon which we have built our theology merely hyperbole for the sake of emphasising the importance of certain facets? This is utterly unjustifiable inconsistency and leaves systematic theology in tatters. Taking just a very few points raised by the above five numbered and hitherto unfulfilled texts, let us consider:

1. This describes the same time as Daniel 12:1. Why does the Archangel stand up for Daniel's people if they are to be destroyed permanently by God? Tell this to Auschwitz survivors or Millennial Jews. Both groups have emphatically declared that AD 70 is not the worst thing that has happened to Israel.

2. This ties in with the culmination of the Seals, Trumpets and Vials of Revelation, which have every indication of becoming global.

3. Is this truly a different event from Zechariah 14, Acts 1, Revelation 1 and 19, all of which could be thus described and will be seen by Jew and Gentile alike and probably somehow be witnessed from Sheol?

4. The prophets and Revelation talk of global events. DeMar cites events which were either comparatively local or proved to be no more momentous in the course of world history than other sporadic bursts of cosmic activity. The Trumpet judgements of Revelation are described as being on a quite unprecedented scale. It is an appalling accusation to say that God's last written communication to the Church is full of exaggerations.

5. Our comments on (3) above apply.

We have referred to parallel passages of Revelation. However DeMar and other Preterists are compelled to place the book of Revelation before AD 70, as we saw in Chapter Eleven. The later dating is no good to Preterists, because it hijacks their theory. They have no option but to regard it as earlier in order to maintain their credibility. Neither date discredits A- or Pre-Millennianism. DeMar infers that the early date is unanimously accepted:

> "Keep in mind that all the New Testament books were written prior to AD 70" [36]

A quite astonishing statement comes from the pen of David Chilton, illustrating the extent of Anti-Semitic doctrine within some parts of Preterism:

> "The Book of Revelation is not about the coming of Christ.
> It is about the destruction of Israel and Christ's victory over
> His enemies... Revelation prophesies the judgement of God
> on the apostate Israel; and while it does briefly point to
> events beyond its immediate concerns, that is done merely
> as a 'wrapping' to show that the ungodly will never prevail
> against Christ's Kingdom"[37]

This is either unworthy of comment, or would require a whole book to
expose a view which must bring joy to the dragon of Revelation 12, the
ancient enemy of Israel; it reflects the level of apostasy which abounds
within Christian circles. It reduces the authority of Revelation to that of
non-canonical Jewish literature, written to portray various ideas. Chilton
should read the unique prologue and conclusion to this great book.

Of course many of the portents before AD 70 identified by Post-
Millennialists, and indeed by others, could very well have been God-
given signs of the impending sack of Jerusalem. God did indeed send
rumours of wars, famine, at least one comet and other portents to warn
believers to flee from Jerusalem at that time. But they were not on the
spectacular global scale that is to precede Christ's return. Why did the
Mount of Olives not split in two in AD 70? Why is there no resultant
great valley? Why has the Dead Sea not been healed? Why has the Gulf
of Aqaba not disappeared? All are prophesied. Why has most of the
world's marine life not yet perished? Why has the whole world not been
challenged and incensed by God's two witnesses in Jerusalem etc.?
Because all these things are yet *future*. That is why.

We must re-emphasise that the Old Covenant was annulled not in AD 70,
as some Preterists imply, when the temple was destroyed and Levitical
sacrifices ceased to be offered, but when Christ, the Pascal Lamb, offered
His own blood and the temple veil was rent asunder by God. The Old
Covenant had been anticipatory of Calvary, not of AD 70. In His mercy,
God gave Jerusalem clemency of around forty years, before their city
was sacked, but, as the writer to the Hebrews is at pains to point out, the
New Covenant was already in place before AD 70 for all believers, Jew or
Gentile. Jewish *national* repentance and their New Covenant are still
future. Jeremiah 31 still has preconditions for the nation, as their present
blind and deaf state confirms.

Key Preterist Texts

There are in fact only two groups of texts which give Preterism any
reasonable claim to validity, and DeMar and other Preterists make the
most of them; not that we would blame them for that. We have had a
great deal to say about others who do not accept what we believe are the
obvious meanings of Scripture, so it would be quite wrong to avoid
certain texts which at first sight appear to contradict us. The first occurs
in three Gospels in slightly different forms. These are:

- *"Assuredly, I say to you, there are some standing here who shall
  not taste death till they see the Son of Man coming in His
  kingdom"* (Matt 16:28). *"There are some standing here who will
  not taste death till they see the kingdom of God here with power"*
  (Mk 9:1). *"But I tell you truly, there are some standing here who
  shall not taste death till they see the kingdom of God"* (Lk 9:27).

- *"You will not have gone through the cities of Israel before the
  Son of Man comes"* (Matt 10:23).

- *"Assuredly, I say to you, this generation will by no means pass
  away till all these things are fulfilled"* (Matt 24:34).

Now the first three parallel verses in each Gospel clearly refer to the
Transfiguration which is the next event narrated in all three accounts. In
Matthew and Mark they have become separated from this event, but only
by chapter endings. Matthew tells us of a six day interval, but no other
intermediate happening is recorded; this juxtapositioning is highly
significant. As the chapter divisions were introduced by Roman
Catholics into the Vulgate in the 13th century, and into English by
Wycliffe's translation, which was from the Vulgate, we must not be
misled by them, even though they are generally useful. The 'but' in
Lk 9:27 indicates a contrast between what is predicted here and the
future coming in His Father's glory and angelic glory (v27); it also
indicates a contrast between what, for the apostles, will occur after death
and what before.

Any doubt about the Transfiguration reference is removed when we find
that Peter wrote:

> *"We were eyewitnesses of His majesty, for He received from God the Father honour and glory when such a voice came from the Excellent Glory: 'This is My beloved Son, in whom I am well pleased.' And we heard this voice which came from heaven, when we were with Him on the holy mountain."* (II Pet 1:19).

What the three privileged disciples saw on the mountain was real enough and glorious; but it in no way precluded a further future full-scale fulfilment.

Regarding the Matthew 24 quote, all these things were certainly to be experienced in some measure within that generation. Jesus knew the date. What the Father had withheld from the Son whilst He was yet on earth was the timing of the future Coming in Power (Mk 13:32). It is very much as when Jesus sent the message to the puzzled John the Baptist in prison, quoting Isaiah 35 and 61; the prophecies were being fulfilled in detail in Jesus' ministry, but not yet on the world-wide scale originally prophesied by Isaiah. It is like the Joel 2 prophecy which was fulfilled at Pentecost, but by no means in the full terms of the original.

It is understandable that Preterists should quote Jesus' words when He commissioned His disciples (Matt 10:23):

> *"You will not have gone through the cities of Israel before the Son of Man comes."*

The first point here is that in the context Jesus mentions a variety of things which were not necessarily about to happen during the immediate programme of the disciples, so at the very least some were to be beyond Pentecost. But even during the Acts period and beyond, right up to AD 70, there was no coming of Jesus which in any way conformed to that other reference to the 'coming of the Son of Man' (Matt 24:30). There Jesus, having in the previous verses specifically warned against believing in any coming to earth which was not spectacularly visible and glorious, describes a future event which has never been fulfilled to date. So Jesus was sending His disciples out on a task which, even when the Gospel of the Kingdom has reached *"the whole world as a witness to all the nations"* (Matt 24:14), will never be finished in the sense that all will repent. Thus what Jesus taught was quite distinct from Post-Millennialism.

We return to the *New Spirit-Filled Life Bible*, and find a section by Shira Sorko-Ram entitled 'Understanding Messianic Jewish Testimony'.[38] There is in fact much in these pages of which we would approve. However we are dismayed by one question, reproduced here in bold print, raised in the following paragraph and referring to Jer 31:31–37:

> "One popular view sees the Jews suddenly converting to Christianity and Israel ceasing to be identifiable as a 'Jewish' nation. But the text pointedly says the 'restored' 'Israel' will never cease to be a nation (vv. 35, 36). This declaration is made all the more dramatic by being an indivisible part of the New Covenant promises; a clear evidence that when 'all Israel shall be saved' (Rom 11:26), it is a direct result of massive numbers of Jews receiving Yeshua as Messiah. **One wonders what events could provoke such a readiness to respond spiritually through the land of Israel.** Certainly the promise is there and the prophecy is sure. Let those prompters alone motivate intercession for Israel, and as believers 'watch' (both in prayer and in observing the flow of international events). May faith for a spiritually cataclysmic outpouring of God's Spirit over the land and people fill believing interceding hearts."[39]

Reading this, we are reminded that Neo-Post-Millennianism is no undivided school of prophetic thought concerning Israel. Here is one of the better exponents, one who is neither a Preterist nor a Replacement Theologian. But, oh dear, what an amazing mixture of Bible-based conviction and of doubt! He actually wonders about the nature of the trigger which will spark off this restoration! It is the Lord's visible appearing, bearing the marks of Calvary.

> *"I will pour on the house of David and on the inhabitants of Jerusalem the Spirit of grace and supplication; then they will look on Me whom they pierced"* (Zech 12:10).

We quoted this in an earlier chapter, but it demands repetition here. This refers to all Israel who have rejected their Messiah. It was Romans who pierced Him, but Jews who condemned Him. We can only faintly grasp how God lays the charge of the crucifixion on all generations of rejecters. Perhaps it was to help us understand this truth when we consider that Jesus held the Pharisees responsible for all murders from Abel to Zechariah (Matt 23:35). But, because he is determined to be Post-Millennial, this writer cannot conceive the Lord's glorious appearance, with its penitential response from Israel, occurring before the Millennium.

We might close this section by reminding Preterists of two key verses already quoted. Both Dan 1:2 and Matt 24:21 speak of a time of great tribulation *"such as has not been seen since the beginning of the world until this time, no, nor ever shall be."* That simply is not true of AD 70. Even for the Jews things have been worse since. Supposing we just take Jesus at His word!

A Neo-Post-Millennial Programme

Books of the popular American writers, such as Earl Paulk and Gary North, are not easily obtainable in Britain, which is no great loss. So we will use one of those written by the English writer, Stephen Travis, to broaden our base of sources. His 'low key' style is probably more effective for use with thoughtful young Christians, and could appeal to would-be social activists. The book is entitled, *End of Story? What Jesus said about the Future of the World.* Jesus is not accorded an upper case 'J' on the cover, which is perhaps indicative of a work which has only a pseudo-Christocentricity, and where the true task of the Church, to which the book builds up, is a social gospel almost devoid of the Cross. It has a generous veneer of language which might make the unwary assume that it is orthodox and evangelical.

There is a dangerously misleading declaration under the heading "The Cross at the Centre", which might re-assure some readers. It is a subtle parody of the truth, but not the truth:

> "John's Revelation presents the crucified Jesus as the clue to God's purpose in history. Human experience does not depend on cold fate or meaningless chance. At the centre of history is Jesus, who, by his death, opened the way to life and showed that God is involved in the sufferings of the world. In chapter 5 Jesus is portrayed in language borrowed

from the Jewish practice of sacrificing a lamb in order to experience God's forgiveness."[40]

Firstly, it was Jesus Christ's Revelation, not John's (1:1). This alone should warn us not to fool around with this amazing book. Jesus' death was not a 'clue'. It was vicarious, substitutionary, effective and legally satisfying (Roman Catholics do not believe that). While it does show us an amazing amount about God's involvement in suffering (Roman Catholics believe that), that is secondary to the salvation wrought through the shedding of the blood of the Lamb of God. He *is* "the Lamb of God who takes away the sin of the world" (Jn 1:29); the Jewish sacrificial lambs were shadows of the Lamb of God, not the other way round. There is much around parading as evangelical which is nothing of the sort. This inversion of priorities is common within Post-Millennianism.

He starts his book by painting a depressing picture of the world, without making any reference to sin or our fallen nature, and concludes with a very humanist conclusion:

> "We need a new vision, a new way of looking at the world and at ourselves."[41]

He talks at length about God's reign. The rear cover, produced by IVF and presumably approved by the author, makes the startling statement:

> "In his lucid and lively style, Stephen sketches God's plan for the world. Through the coming of Jesus Christ, God has **begun** to reign on earth."[42]

The bold print has been added. Even Nebuchadnezzar knew better than to say that God's reign was going to begin only six hundred years later. In Daniel 4 both the angelic watchers (v17) and the Emperor himself (vv. 34, 37) witnessed to God's current and everlasting reign. Travis has a habit of presenting oblique or half truths, with little twists to provide secondary rather than primary meanings. For instance, talking of John's deputation from prison to enquire whether Jesus was the One for whom they were waiting (Matt 11:4, 5), Jesus is presented as the 'Liberator' rather than the Messiah, and we are told that Jesus' miracles were:

> "Signs that the power of God's reign was now at work in a new way."[43]

Now whilst this may have been true, the main point was that His works were testifying to who He was. Travis concentrates on the fact that he sees God's reign as progressive, and states, reasonably, that:

> "God's reign hasn't fully come... The coming of God's reign isn't a once-for all-event... But its complete coming remains an object of hope... God is moving forward in his plan to create a new world of justice and peace, of love and celebration, under his rule. Every time we see a Christian community truly living by the values of his reign we can say, 'I have seen the future and it works'."[44]

One is thus discouraged from anticipating the promised sudden intervention by God. Rather one detects here the spiritual evolution, so dear to the heart of Post-Millennialism and so contrary to the latter day scenario painted by Scripture. There are times when one is in doubt about whether he is talking about events in heaven or upon earth, or whether the earth he is talking about is the present one or the new one. He is apparently unaware that Revelation 21 makes it abundantly clear that the coming new one follows the complete destruction of the old one. Pre-Millennialists have no problem with the Millennial status of the patriarchs in Matt 8:11, but Travis's readers have to make their own assumptions about their role.

> "God intends to see that plan through to its completion. Jesus crammed a lot of his vision of the future into one brief picture: 'I say to you that many will come from the east and west, and will take their places at the feast with Abraham and Isaac and Jacob in the kingdom of heaven. Here we look forward to the time when God's reign would finally arrive in its completeness. He describes this reign as a feast, a party. That's always a good start! It's not about people being solemnly religious, but about celebration. It's the overflowing excitement of people caught up in God's plan for the world."[45]

Well, that explains a good deal about today's Church! The Christocentric nature of the Millennial prophecies have been forgotten. It's about Jesus' 'vision', rather than His authoritative foreknowledge. It's to be a party! Now we know. We are going to make the minimum comment about the following brief excerpts regarding the Lord's coming. However we are going to be kept wondering exactly what he actually means, because he makes statements with which we would be perfectly at ease, but he immediately follows them up with further remarks which seem to dilute or even emasculate them. Note Travis's use of inverted commas, suggestive of his less than factual understanding of certain texts:

> "Jesus' coming will bring the renewal of creation. Contrary to popular opinion, the Bible does not speak of the 'end of the world' so much as of a 'new heaven and a new earth'. It doesn't speak of people simply abandoning the earth and 'going to heaven', but of God transforming the whole created environment."[46]

> "It sounds simple. If Jesus left the earth from the Mount of Olives, he will return one day to the same place. His return will be like a film of his ascension played backwards. And that's exactly how many people understand it. If this were the only way in which New Testament writers described the coming of Christ, such an approach might be justified. But in fact a wide range of description is found, some of it much more symbolic and allusive."[47]

> "Christ's coming will be sudden and unexpected. At any time he may confront us with his demanding presence... The Son of Man will come with 'clouds and great power and glory'. This kind of imagery shows that he will come in triumph, with the full authority of God behind him."[48]

> "God is moving human history towards a goal. The Christian message isn't about God lifting a select group of people out of history into heaven, but about God moving with the ups and downs of history towards his grand finale."[49]

There are reminders here of the style of John Robinson, Bishop of Woolwich, in his notorious *Honest to God*, circa 1962. My copy was long ago consigned to the dustbin where it belonged, so I cannot give a reference. He then goes on to try to de-bunk his own representation of Pre-Millennialism, which is based on odd extravagant claims, rather than the basic doctrines and their Scriptural foundations. Examples of dangerous date-setting, subjective numbering of states in the EEC, and Hal Lindsey's rather rash statement that a US Marine friend identified the locusts of Revelation 9 with Cobra helicopters [50] are all fair game for him. Allegorisation and symbolism is applied in much the same manner as we have encountered with Amillennialists. Lindsey himself never thus identified them as helicopters, but Travis gives that impression. The Beast is a 'personification', not a person; Armageddon is 'not to be conceived of as an actual battle'. The substance of prophecy is generally degraded. [51] He concludes this section with the utterly unworthy jibe about Pre-Millennialism:

> "It doesn't stir Christians to compassionate care for the world, but paralyses them. What it offers isn't a hope but a kind of fatalism disguised as hope." [52]

What he ought to have said is that, rather than leading to his preferred programme of social reform, Pre-Millennialism induces people to preach a Gospel of Grace, to which he, Stephen Travis, to judge by his book, is a stranger. In his penultimate chapter, entitled, "Is there a Future for the World?", he quotes Ben Okri and Nelson Mandela, and reveals a 'Dream for the Universe':

> "First, God's reign will be universal. If we are to reflect the universal scope of God's love, we need to press for a more serious commitment to issues of world development... Secondly God's reign will create community. Therefore the nurturing of human community is our goal now. This means we will look for human solutions to the problems we face, rather than merely economic ones... The third point is that God's reign will bring peace. Therefore promoting and maintaining peace is our goal now... If Christ came into the world to make peace between humanity and God and to break down barriers of hostility between people, we are called to be peacemakers... Fourthly, God's reign will bring justice. Therefore justice is our goal... Fifthly, God's reign will involve bringing humanity and the natural world into harmony. Therefore we are to care for the environment now... Nelson Mandela said... 'I am more convinced than

ever before, it is not kings and generals that change history. It is the masses of the people.'"[53]

We do not condemn the details of this programme out of hand, even though some of Travis's personal politics shine through. I too have been a peacemaker, or at least a peacekeeper between warring communities, and put my life at risk in the process; but Travis might have disagreed with the policies involved. But then, we were applying pragmatism born of bitter experience in a fallen world; we did not rely upon theory. I and other Christian soldiers did not believe that we were bringing in the Millennium. And, no, we were not always successful and did sometimes, seen in retrospect, make errors of judgement. But there was a job to be done, and somebody had to do it.

What Travis is evidently trying to do is to put the world to rights by interpreting the Beatitudes as the heart of the Gospel. They are not. They were the ideals which Jesus set and communicated; they can and should be displayed in the lives of believers, where they will take the form of the fruits of the Spirit (Gal 5:22, 23). Paul adds:

"And those who are Christ's have crucified the flesh with its passions and desires" (v 24).

They are unique to those who are Christ's. Our task is to display the fruits, but preach the Cross, until the Lord returns for us. If we do not preach the Cross, we have little hope of having fruit to display. Most of us fall dismally short. Beatitudes will have complete fulfilments one day.

The evils identified by Travis were all noted and condemned long ago by God, through the prophets and by Jesus Himself in the Sermon on the Mount and elsewhere; and in no way should we condemn truly Christian efforts to right wrongs, provided that in doing so we recognise the limitations to success, as indicated by predictive prophecy, and do not try to improve upon God's declared agenda, which is what Travis does, by allegorising end-time prophecy. Above all, we must recognise that, without personal salvation and the removal of temptation, there can be no perfect world. He is deluding himself and his readers if he thinks that the above programme, however praiseworthy, will 'Christianise' the world.

Had there been a feasible political action plan to set the world aright, God would not have sent His Son into the world to die for sinners. Jesus before

His ascension would have bowed to Travis's superior knowledge and sent His disciples into all the world to preach a social gospel to all creatures.

We are not saying that all Post-Millennialists subscribe to Travis's views; his position is towards the liberal end of Post-Millennialism without being totally liberal. But these views are typical of the type of thinking, which becomes acceptable by and compatible with any programme which would postpone Divine intervention in the world's history until the Church has sorted everything out.

Stephen Travis is Vice-Principal of a theological college at Nottingham. Robin Hood would have been proud of this well-meaning but humanist ethical agenda with a thin Christian veneer. That is not intended to be sarcasm, but rather a neat way of putting it into perspective.

Post-Millennial Songs And Israel's Identity

We referred to the identity of Zion in our last chapter. The following song lines clearly identify Zion with the Church:

> "We are a chosen people... You have placed us into Zion,
> in the new Jerusalem." [54]

Where and what is the thinking behind these words? Whether or not we are citizens bound for the New Jerusalem, we are most certainly not there yet. (Rev 21:1 etc.).

> "Awake, awake O Zion, come clothe yourself with strength.
> Put on your garments of splendour, O Jerusalem; come sing
> your songs of triumph that your God reigns" [55]

The call to awaken comes from Isa 52:1, and applies to the Jerusalem which has *"drunk from the hand of the Lord the cup of His fury"*. The passage is so precisely the Jewish Jerusalem and not the Church that it makes a mockery of Preterism and Post-Millennianism old and new. It refers to the earthly city of Zion and her inhabitants in the future Millennium. Zion was originally a small, rocky, almost impregnable fortress within what became the city of Jerusalem. Unger's Dictionary gives a helpful summary of Zion:

> "**Theological use.** Zion has a threefold significance in the
> Bible apart from its original historical significance.

(1) **David's City**. In the OT Zion refers to Jerusalem, the city that David conquered and made capital of the United Kingdom of Israel. (2) **The Millennial City**. In a prophetic sense, Zion has reference to Jerusalem as the future capital of the nation Israel in the Kingdom Age. Amillennial theologians deny this equation and spiritualise, rather 'mysticalise', the term to mean the Christian Church of this age. (3) **The Heavenly City**. The NT also refers Zion to the New Jerusalem (Heb 12:22–24), the eternal city into which the Church will be received (cf. Rev chaps 21,22)." [56]

It is thus possible for a number of believers to sing the same hymn and yet have entirely different ideas of what the words mean! The song context may direct minds to one of these three legitimate significances, or to the incorrect mystical interpretation. We have covered this topic here because of the common Replacement Theology implications. The old Gospel hymn, with the words, "We're marching upwards to Zion, the beautiful city of God", reminds us that there is no Zion upon earth other than in Jerusalem, but that we and Abraham alike have a heavenly one in view. Unger might have added 'Post-Millennial theologians' had he not written the above at a time of their decline.

Perhaps the most outrageous compilation using the 'Judas went and hanged himself' technique, is the following:

"These are the days of Elijah, declaring the word of the Lord: and these are the days of your servant Moses, righteousness being restored... These are the days of Ezekiel. And dry bones becoming as flesh, and these are the days of your servant David, rebuilding a temple of praise." [57]

Had the writer said, 'These are the days of Noah', we might have found a prophetic connection, having checked with Genesis 6:5 & 13 to determine the state of the world at that time. Malachi's prophecy concerning the coming of Elijah (4:4) was potentially fulfilled in John the Baptist; the only other possible assumed reference is to the two Jerusalem witnesses of Revelation 11, a scenario which has yet to materialise. Were these the days of Elijah, a man who went to heaven without dying, he would be back on earth today. To date he has not appeared. Elijah's own age, with Ahab and Jezebel, was an evil one. Moses is not prophesied to reappear this side of the resurrection, unless he is to be the other witness of Revelation 11. David's rebuilt temple of praise within this age is not prophesied, and it is sheer arrogance to claim that modern praise is more spiritual than that of previous generations, unless perhaps amplification and spirituality are synonymous!

Ezekiel's dry bones prophecy at least is genuine, but it applies exclusively to Israel. Lest there should be any doubt about this, we find Judah and Ephraim, the leaders of the Northern and Southern kingdoms, being re-united for the first time in around three thousand years. It did not happen with the return from Babylon, which Post-Millennialists often cite as the final fulfilment of Jewish restoration prophecies. That has yet to happen and simply cannot be allegorised. Another song which is generally sung as if applying to the Church a promise made to Israel, and incorporating thoughts unconnected with the Isaiah quote, is:

> "No weapon formed or army or king, shall be able to stand against the Lord and His anointed." [58]

We have already noted the Isa 55:17 text partly quoted here. It is addressed unambiguously by God to the Israel whom He once forsook (v7). That is not the Church. If we must borrow or misapply God's promises, let us never forget the original recipients. A song which *might* have a Millennial application, but has no other justifiable one except in the writer's mind, goes:

> "O the valleys shall ring with the sound of praise, and the lion shall lie with the lamb. Of His government there shall be no end and His glory shall fill the earth, May your will be done, May Your kingdom come! Let it rule, let it reign in our lives. There's a shout in the camp as we answer the call, Hail the King! Hail the Lord of Lords!" [59]

The assumption is clearly for the future of the Church Age, unless there is going to be a change in animal as well as human nature. As this is not a standard part of the Post-Millennial agenda, we assume the lion and the lamb are understood by him to be allegorical, which is hardly the impression one gets from Isaiah 11 and 65. Jesus, incidentally, is the Church's Lord, not primarily her King. Post-Millennialist writers tend to ignore this and attribute the two titles to Jesus Christ in inverse proportion to their Biblical use. If in doubt, look at the epistles! He is Israel's King.

Neo-Post Millennial Conclusions On Israel

While there has been plenty of Replacement Theology, neither in song nor in teaching have we found any serious indication of conscious Anti-Semitism. There is some apathy, but, compared with Traditionalist Boettner, there is a more sympathetic, welcoming attitude, though sometimes tempered by equally sympathetic attitudes towards 'Palestinian'' territorial claims. But recognition of non-Messianic Jews is limited to the fact that they are God's special people, from whom the Messiah came, and to whom we therefore have a great debt. That debt can be repaid by making a special effort to evangelise and welcome them. That of course we should all do. But they recognise no place for Israel's national earthly future. Kirstie Kelly's remarks in a Restorationist magazine are typical:

> "The believer, surely, is interested in Judaism because God was preparing Israel in OT times for the coming of his Son. The development of Judaism after the coming of Jesus, however, is for the believer only of cultural interest. Believers in the arena of Arab-Israeli relations usually find themselves in sympathy with the Israeli side of the conflict, for various reasons, not all of them beautifully spiritual. One is the tendency to equate modern Israel with OT Israel." [60]

She then goes on to talk of the only solution as being reconciliation, but adds:

> "Many Spirit-filled Christians have got involved with Israel in a way that makes them not only blind to the needs of Palestinians but also blind to the fact that the West Bank is the only area in the Arab world where there is a complete legal freedom to preach the gospel... the urgent need is for fervent biblical evangelism." [61]

Well, we certainly agree with the last statement, and Jews and Palestinians are equally worthy of evangelisation. But how can a Spirit-filled Christian be blind? This suggests that there is a lot of spiritual pride around, some patronisingly claiming to be 'Spirit-filled' on some subjective and exclusive basis, such as the possession of the least of all the gifts. How, one wonders, should a Spirit-filled believer view God's declaration that when the Messiah returns, *"There shall no longer be a Canaanite in the house of the Lord of Hosts"* (Zech 14:21), other than at face value? The context is entirely unfulfilled and therefore future. Post-Millennialists have a greater chance of being politically correct, but not necessarily Spirit-filled, on such matters.

We return to Stephen Travis. He may be more liberal and less supernatural in some of his teaching than other modern Post-Millennialists, but his views on Israel are very typical. In fact it is a chapter with the encouraging title, "Good News for the Jews" to which we will be referring. He rejects Jesus' fig tree analogy for the nation, completely ignoring the significance of Jesus' cursing of the tree in relationship to its future recovery, which is the main reason for our identification of the tree with nation. [62]

He quotes from a Christian advertisement, evidently targeting Jews, about the fulfilling of prophecies regarding Israel, and adds:

> "I understand that a Bible-loving Jew might warm to this invitation. But how should I as a Christian respond?" [63]

He then goes on to use some of the arguments which we have seen before, claiming that the prophesied return took place at the end of the Babylonian captivity, typically ignoring most of the evidence for later applications. Then he moves to Acts 15:16–17, where James quoted Amos 9:11–12, and claims that this referred to Gentiles entering the Church during the Acts period. [64] But he fails to see that Amos goes on to prophesy about a return of Israel about which God says:

> *"I will plant them in their land, and no longer shall they be pulled up from the land I have given them"* (9:15).

There is no hint whatsoever of this being conditional. They were about to be 'pulled up' brutally twenty-one years after this Acts 15 statement, so a later re-planting within the Land of Promise is here guaranteed. This shatters Preterism. He writes:

> "Rabbi John Rayner argues that their millennia-old link with the land and their need for security from persecution give Jews a powerful claim on the land. But, he says, the

presence for centuries of Palestinian Arabs in the land gives them a claim also. So a way of sharing must be found."[65]

Now as Pre-Millennialists we believe, as we noted earlier, that:

> *"Jerusalem will be trampled by Gentiles until the times of the Gentiles are fulfilled"* (Lk 21:24).

And we do not believe that that 'until' has been met. We understand the current presence of 'Palestinians'. It is the Lord Jesus who will give the land back to repentant and redeemed Israel when He returns. In the meantime any pressure we might exert, if we feel led to, should be to ensure a just balance, counteracting the overwhelmingly greater bulk of Anti-Semitic propaganda. It is misguided to lead Jews to premature expectations via a human timetable. Above all, we should trust God. Time and again the prophets condemned Israel and Judah of old for seeking security from secular sources, e.g.:

> *"Woe to those who go down to Egypt for help, and rely on horses... But who do not look to the Holy One of Israel"* (Isa 31:1).

Let us end our brief exploration of Neo-Post-Millennianism with a final quote from Gary DeMar, who might have seen the light, had he not skipped one verse. As we have stressed earlier, we do not dispute the prediction of the AD 70 destruction of the temple.

> "The destruction of the temple took place when Titus and his Roman armies laid siege against the city in AD 70. This corresponds to what Jesus said to the Pharisees: 'Behold, your house is left to you desolate'!" (Matt 23:38).[66]

DeMar has failed to notice that Jesus had switched His attention from the Pharisees to the City, which He here addressed directly. Perhaps such details are not important to him. As we saw in an earlier chapter, Jesus did not leave Jerusalem with only the promise of desolation, as Preterists would have us believe. No. He immediately went on to declare:

> *"You shall see Me no more till you say, 'Blessed is He who comes in the name of the Lord.'"*

One glorious day they will welcome Him. We reject Neo-Post-Millennialism on many grounds; but chiefly on the grounds that it relies upon God breaking His promises to Israel.

Post-Millennialists love to describe others as pessimists, because they do not share their vision of an ever-brighter future of an evolving Church. But the Bible is not optimistic about end-time spirituality, and, although Jesus commands us to *"Occupy till I come"* (Lk 19:13), it urges us to set our sights on heaven and beyond:

> *"For we know that if our earthly house, this tent, is destroyed, we have a building from God, a house not made with hands, eternal in the heavens. For in this we groan, earnestly desiring to be clothed with our habitation which is from heaven... Now He who has prepared us for this very thing is God, who has given us His Spirit as a guarantee. Therefore we are always confident, knowing that while we are at home in the body, we are absent from the Lord"* (II Cor 5:1, 2, 5, 6).

Thus if we are truly Spirit-filled, we will share Paul's aspirations, not worldly ones.

Finally, much though we may respect many Post-Millennialists as fellow believers, we simply do not believe that Neo-Post-Millennial claims pass the tests of genuine prophecy as outlined at the beginning of the previous chapter.

Chapter Thirteen

Other Pre-Millennial Views

Why Only One Chapter?

We have just devoted two long chapters apiece to Amillennialism and Post-Millennialism in their many forms. We believe that they merited this level of coverage because these are the views which young believers are most likely to encounter and to assume to be orthodox and unassailably correct. In a Church apathetic towards doctrine, it does not seem to concern people that these two are in fact incompatible with one another. However they are the views which are most likely to undermine their understanding of God's future purposes for Israel.

This in turn can lead to a stumbling block to any witness to those Jews who have a good grasp of the whole of the *Tanakh* or Jewish Holy Scriptures, and can be deeply misleading to those other Jews, and there are a great many, who tend to concentrate on the *Torah* or Law, to the neglect of the prophets. We will include a short section towards the end of this passage to illustrate this. It seems that some Messianic Jews are much more susceptible to wrong teaching about their Tribulation role than they are about their Millennial one.

As we have seen, both A- and Post-Millennianism rely heavily on the allegorisation of numerous prophecies, especially those concerning Israel's future. And although some conservatives would hotly deny it, this in turn can lead to speculation over the reliability of God's other declarations and promises. We therefore considered them in considerable depth, though by no means using all the material available to us. Now it is time to move closer to home and to consider those schools whose teachings differ much less from our own, yet which, we believe, fail the 'Israel Test', at least in some respects. We will be re-visiting topics which we covered in Chapter Five.

The Other Pre-Millennialists

Whilst taking an unashamedly Pre-Tribulationist stand where appropriate, we have hitherto avoided as far as possible the debate between the two major divisions of Pre-Millennialism, namely Pre- and Post-Tribulationism, and the various minor divisions, such as Mid-Tribulationism, Pre-Wrath Rapture and Partial Rapture. We will use this terminology within this section, although, for the sake of clarity, we may as we proceed note alternative titles which readers are likely to encounter. The Historicist Pre-Millennialist view of Mede and Guinness is in so many respects different from the other views that we will ignore it for the time being, but devote a short section to it later.

As explained in our first chapter, we will, for the sake of clarity and convenience, continue to refer to the first half of the seven year false covenant period with Israel (Daniel 9:27), as the Tribulation, with a capital 'T' and the second half as the Great Tribulation. The entire seven years is also sometimes referred to simply as the Tribulation. The halves are also described as three and a half years, 42 months, 'times, time and half a time' and 1,260 days. Prophetic years last 360 days.

We have avoided the internal debates up to this point for the following reasons.

- Most Pre-Tribulationists take prophecies concerning Israel's future at face value, except where it is abundantly clear that language is allegorical or symbolic. A few Post-Tribulationists, such as Ladd, are ambivalent about Israel's role in the Millennium. We will explain this later.

- Pre-Millennialism is never Preterist and is almost always Futurist, with only the one Historicist exception referred to above.

- Pre-Millennialism invariably recognises a literal thousand year reign of Christ upon earth.

- Pre-Millennialism recognises the future repentance of survivors of national Israel and the fulfilment within Israel of numerous Old Testament prophecies; there may be slight variations in understanding of timing.

- A defence of Pre-Tribulationism, rather than of Pre-Millennialism, vis-à-vis A- and Post-Millennialism would have complicated the issue and denied us a level playing field by, to change the idiom, fighting on two fronts.

- The other Pre-Millennial schools, with whom we have much in common, are comparatively small and uninfluential, though Post-Tribulationism may be growing slightly.

All these reasons relate to our declared purpose of defending what we believe to be God's future purposes for Israel. Thus, as Pre-Tribulationists, we have fewer bones of contention with most fellow Pre-Millennialists than we had with the other two schools.

- We see a special key role for Israel during the seven-plus year absence of the Church. We expounded our views in some detail in Chapter Five. This role is greatly weakened and is almost anomalous if the Church is to be present during all or part of the Tribulation.

- All these other Pre-Millennial schools deny, in a way which we have not encountered even with some conservative A- and Post-Millennialists, the hope of an ever-imminent return of the Lord from heaven, so dear to Pre-Tribulationists.

Back in Victorian times the title 'Pre-Millennialist' was usually applied only to Pre-Tribulationists. For instance, back in 1876 we find T B Baines, in his book, *The Lord's Coming, Israel and the Church*, in a comparison of 'Pre- and Post-Millennialist systems of interpretation', writing of the former:

> "The Old Testament prophecies, except where manifestly figurative, are to receive a literal fulfilment. The promises made to Israel are to be made good to Israel, not to the Church... This coming, the date of which is purposely left undetermined, instead of being at the end of the world, is preliminary to the judgements awaiting the world, and to the reign of Christ with His saints. When it occurs, the living saints will be caught up to meet the Lord in the air, and at the same time will take place, in part at least, 'the first resurrection', when the dead in Christ will be raised."[1]

That was what was understood as Pre-Millennialism a hundred and thirty years ago. To us it is still by definition Pre-Millennianism, as it quite clearly states that the Lord's return is to be before the Millennium, which is the central criterion. That definition we will not surrender, although we may for clarity amplify it by describing it as Pre-Tribulationism.

Post-Tribulationists have tried to annex exclusively for themselves our Pre-Millennial title. They are entitled to share it, because it fits them too, but not to steal it! Ladd, probably the best known proponent, writing eighty years after Baines, says:

> "During the first half of the present century, occasional voices were raised within the circle of pre-millennial interpretation in defence of a modification of some of the details of this prophetic plan... Holding steadfastly to the premillennial coming of Christ to establish His kingdom, they felt they could no longer accept the teaching of a secret return of Christ to rapture the Church before the Tribulation."[2]

Ladd, who is a comparatively courteous writer, goes on to point out that there are totally committed Bible loving evangelical people on either side of this divide, and that Pre-Tribulationists remain very much the majority. We will attempt to maintain this courtesy. We re-emphasise that our primary aim must be to enquire whether God's future purposes for the Jews throw any light on who is right. We have chosen Pawson, Smith and Ladd as British, Canadian and American representative Post-Tribulationists respectively. Unlike some commonly quoted Post-Tribulationists, they are not paranoid about Pre-Tribulationism, and would take the same line as us with A- and Post-Millennialists. None of the three are gratuitously offensive, like Post-Tribulationists, Alexander Reese, George Fromow and sensational but inaccurate press reporter, Dave McPherson.

The implications of Ladd's statement are that, as the Church is not to be Raptured before the Tribulation, it must go through it. It will necessarily live through the great central part of Revelation (chapters 6 to 19), and be caught up to meet the Lord only as He returns in power. We will continue to refer to them as Post-Tribulationists. Their preferred modern title, particularly in the USA, seems to be 'Historic Pre-Millennialists' (not to be confused with Historicist); Fruchtenbaum refers to them as 'Covenant Pre-Millennialists'.[3]

One of the difficulties with some of these definitions—and we are criticising nobody, it is simply a fact of life—is that not all Pre-Tribulationists are Dispensationalists in the highly structured form associated with Darby, and Post-Tribulationists do not necessarily hold Covenant Theology. These are dominant or typical, rather than mandatory features. Saints down through the ages, who have never used this title, have been Dispensationalist to the extent that they have recognised that God, *"at various times and in different ways spoke in times past to the fathers by the prophets"* (Heb 1:1). It is probably also true that in the USA Dispensationalism tends to be more extreme than in Britain. There are several such minor differences in nomenclature which are rarely allowed for.

We referred briefly in an earlier chapter to this confusion over Pre-Millennialism and Dispensationalism, where there is natural overlap but by no means a total co-incidence. Dr Charles Ryrie, perhaps the best-known modern exponent, deals at length with the common false charges that Dispensationalism is an invention of J N Darby, popularised by Scofield. Under the heading "The Charge of Recency"[4], he shows that Justin Martyr, Irenaeus, Clement of Alexandria, John Edwards and Isaac Watts all taught Dispensationalism; indeed, Edwards in 1599 published a table of dispensations much more complex than Darby's, while Watts believed in six. There is nothing much wrong with Darby's exposition of Dispensationalism, apart from the fact that it is too often misapplied, misunderstood and misrepresented.

Occupying the middle ground between Pre- and Post-Tribulationists are two small groups. Firstly there is Mid-Tribulationists, held by people who believe that Post-Tribulationists had moved too far from the position of the earlier modern Pre-Millennialists. 'Mid-Tribs' believe that the Lord will come for His saints at the end of the first half of Daniel's week of years. Secondly there are Pre-Wrath-Rapturists, who believe that He will come for them before the Vials or Bowls of Wrath are poured out. As we have already mentioned, the groups have two features in common, which can be dealt with collectively rather than individually:

- Because they set certain prerequisites in place, such as the Seals, or both Seals and Trumpets of Revelation, they either do not teach that the Rapture should be regarded as ever imminent, or find it very difficult to make a case for imminency.

- Although most see Israel involved during the Tribulation period, they confuse the otherwise simple Pre-Millennial understanding of God having one programme for Israel and another for the Church. We will deal with this issue at the end of the chapter.

We do not propose to look into the pros and cons of each case in the same depth as we did with A- and Post-Millennialists. Obviously reasonable cases can be made for each view, and we are aware of these, but still believe that the Pre-Tribulationist view is much the strongest.

The Imminency Of The Rapture

Some people prefer to talk of 'imminence'; there is only the slightest difference in nuance. It is difficult to read the Church epistles without noticing the eager sense of expectancy which writers and readers held towards the Lord's return. This only slowly diminished as the years rolled by, but it was almost totally lost before the Dark Ages began. Modern believers are likely to occupy one of three positions regarding imminency:

- They may assume that after well nigh two thousand years, there is little point in expecting the Lord's long delay to end during their lifetime. We have seen something of this attitude within our Chapters Nine, Ten and Eleven. Signs of the times are rarely taken seriously; any occurrence which might be considered pertinent can usually be explained away. There are a hundred excuses for not believing He could be returning soon. The foolish virgins' excuse is seen by Jesus to be no excuse.

- They may adopt the 'not quite yet' position of the Mid- or Post-Tribulationist, which anticipates the start of the seven-year rundown to the Lord's return in power, expecting the signing of the Beast's covenant (Dan 9:27) and the earthly signs that the Lamb in heaven is opening the Seals and releasing the four Horsemen of the Apocalypse. In other words the Rapture must always be considered to be *at least* three and a half years, five and a quarter or seven years hence, depending on one's particular 'ism'! Post-Tribulationist George Ladd may call his standard work *The Blessed Hope*, but we believe Dennett's Pre-Tribulation 1876 work with the same title to be much more appropriately named!

- They may believe that the Lord could return for them literally at any moment. Admittedly very few maintain a constant sense of alertness. When one is at a spiritual 'high' one is more thrilled by the prospect, and, conversely, when one is in a spiritual trough, one feels more like a half-asleep virgin. Yet the signs of the times are important and ought to be truly uplifting and motivating towards the Lord's work without pin-pointing exactly the time of His Coming. This is, or should be, the position of the Pre-Tribulationist. It is truly a blessed hope.

Post-Tribulationists have the greatest problem with imminency in that, because they do not believe that the Lord will come firstly *for* His saints and secondly *with* them, they perceive a dichotomy between those passages which suggest suddenness and potential imminency and others which impose important prerequisites. Pre-Tribulationists have no problems whatsoever, because for them the coming *for* is to be sudden and the coming *with* is to be fully predictable at the end of the three-and-a-half year Great Tribulation, when the world's armies are gathered at Armageddon. Thus the specially detailed prerequisites are for the Coming in Power and the general prerequisites for the Rapture. This is simple and utterly comprehensible, we believe it to be validated by Scripture. But even Mid-Tribulationists and Pre-Wrath Rapturists, whilst recognising the separate *for* and *with* comings of the Lord, have problems in that they see at least half of the Tribulation preceding the Rapture. Dr Stanton writes:

> "By the very nature of the case, if the exact time of the rapture had been revealed, none but the final generation of Christians would have cause to look for the return of their Saviour, and for every other generation this vital hope and incentive would have been lost. Such is the mischief caused when any known event, such as the Tribulation, the coming of Antichrist, or the Millennium, is thrust between the Church and the coming of Christ for His own."[5]

Post-Tribulationist David Pawson, in a chapter entitled "The Doubtful Claim", writes:

> "While it is true that both Jesus and Paul said his coming would be as unexpected as a burglary ('as a thief in the night'; Matt 24:43; I Thess 5:2), at an 'hour' which is neither known nor expected, it does not follow that it will be without any warning or could be 'at any moment'. A clear distinction is drawn between unbelievers and believers in relation to this. To the former, it will come as a surprise, even a sudden shock... To the latter it will not come as a surprise, for believers live in the light and stay 'awake' and 'alert' to what is happening around them (I Thess 5:5–7)..."[6]

Sorry, David Pawson, but it was specifically to believers whom Jesus warned:

> *"Watch therefore, for you do not know what hour your Lord is coming"* (Matt 24:42).

Would that it were true that the prophesied scoffers were only outside the Church. How many believers today are in congregations where the signs of the times are carefully monitored in relationship to God's prophetic timetable? No doubt they were in David Pawson's church; but is that really typical? He then goes on to talk about some of the Tribulation signs, which will be immensely appropriate to those who will live through them. But we are warned to look up when these things *begin* to happen, rather than when they have almost finished happening (Lk 21:28).

> *"Watch therefore and pray always that you may be counted worthy to escape all these things that will come to pass, and to stand before the Son of Man"* (Lk 21:36).

It will not take much wakefulness to know when the Abomination is being set up or Armageddon is in progress! Jesus was surely talking of a much less precisely identifiable time than the Mid- or Post-Tribulational junctures when He spoke of sleeping and watching virgins (Matt 25:1–10).

While texts, such as the one just quoted for alertness, may occur in passages which culminate in Christ's return in power, this by no means indicates that the alertness points to the moment of this return. In fact His coming in power follows so many easily recognised precursors that any warning to be alert seems almost superfluous. Rather the point is that, the more we see a build up to these climactic events, the more alert and prepared we should be to be caught away to be with our Lord before they occur.

The Victorian writer, Edward Dennett, presents the alternatives of "A Present Hope" or a "Deferred Hope".[7] Deferred Hope might be a good description for all except Pre-Tribulationists. Elsewhere he writes:

> "For the Lord is at hand, and He desires that His people should be on the watch-tower, longing and eagerly waiting for His return. Surely therefore it is high time to awake out of sleep, knowing that our salvation is nearer than when we believed, 'For yet a little while and He that shall come will come, and will not tarry' (Heb x 37). And He Himself has said, 'Blessed are those servants, whom the Lord when He cometh shall find watching...'."[8]

Sadly, too many Pre-Millennialists are on the watchtower looking out not for the Saviour but for the Man of Sin, who, they believe, has to come first.

Post-Tribulationism

We have already observed that, despite the fact that the modern revival of Pre-Millennialism was almost entirely due to the teaching of Pre-Tribulationists, Post-Tribulationists now like to claim the Pre-Millennial title exclusively for themselves. They argue that the post-Apostolic early Church did not teach Pre-Tribulationism. The point that they miss is that, while they did investigate certain prophecies in great detail, the early Church did not, as far as we know, draw up a comprehensive plan of the Tribulation period which would conform precisely to *any* of the schools of prophetic interpretation within modern Pre-Millennialism. We could have a field day attacking each other on the grounds of what was *not* taught within the early Church. The prayerful study of Scripture is much our most important resource; Church history is instructive, but is very much secondary.

As we have seen, there was in the early Church a very deep sense of the potential imminency of the Lord's return. Few indeed had all the

Scriptures available, but prophecies concerning the Beast or Antichrist and Mystery Babylon were keenly studied. We have already noted the widespread acceptance of Chiliasm (Millennialism in general), though that is never a matter of contention among different Pre-Millennial groups. As we saw in the previous two chapters, the AD 70 destruction of Jerusalem in no way detracted from their interest in a coming Tribulation, as would have happened had they been Preterists. Living, as they did, in an age where wave after wave of Roman persecution swept over the Church, such study was natural, and God brought timely comfort and reassurance to His own, through prophecies that were still many centuries away from their main and final fulfilments. The present day lack of persecution in the privileged West is no doubt a major cause of the apathy towards the signs of the times and reluctance to believe in anything that smacks of sensation, even when this is foretold in Scripture. Soft option eschatology is more palatable and seemly.

Post-Tribulationists firmly believe that the Church will go through the entire Tribulation period, and are inclined to regard Pre-Tribulationists as being afraid to undergo this 'time of testing'; some Post-Tribulationist writers are quite scathing, mistaking faith for cowardice. Robert Cameron (no known relation of mine!), for instance writes:

> "This secret Rapture fly-away-from-tribulation theory is only
> a trick of the Devil to fool God's people so that they will not
> be on the firing line for God."[9]

That is a very dangerous comment indeed. To them the Rapture can therefore become a 'blessed hope' only when the Great Tribulation is drawing to a close. The Great Tribulation, which is to come first, will be anything but a blessed hope. To them the Rapture simply cannot be a going to the heavenly place He has gone to prepare (Jn 14:3), but a reuniting in the air of the souls and bodies of the dead in Christ, and a meeting with 'those who are alive and remain', and then a proceeding earthwards as the Lord intervenes in Armageddon and deals with the Devil, Beast, False Prophet and the demon-maddened armies. If you are a Post-Tribulational believer who hopes to survive until the Lord's return, don't expect to see heaven for at least a thousand and seven years. You will see a battlefield a thousand years before you see any mansion. **This is not only hope deferred, it is also hope diminished**.

For the Post-Tribulationist the Marriage of the Lamb takes place after the Lord's return in power; this is of course the natural conclusion to their timetable. Ladd writes:

> "Revelation 19:6–10 announces the marriage of the Lamb—
> the union of Christ with his bride, the church, which will
> occur at Christ's return." [10]

This brings us back to the problem already noted, namely, that Post-Tribulationism leaves no time interval for the Bema to take place before the Marriage. In fact, according to this programme, the Marriage of the Lamb is announced and the next event is Christ's judgemental intervention at the Battle of Armageddon! The programme creates far more problems than it solves. The marriage supper (Rev 19:9) is quite distinct from the marriage, and distinct again from the invitation (v17) to the birds of prey to the impending Armageddon slaughter.

Oswald Smith, the great Canadian evangelist, strikes one as being a reluctant Post-Tribulationist; we can concur with much of what he writes. But, writing of the Bema, he says:

> "The Time of Judgement. First of all, when will it take
> place? It will not take place at the end of the Millennium.
> That, as we have seen, is the Great White Throne Judgment.
> It will be at Christ's Second Coming." [11]

He also tells us, quite rightly, that the Judgement of the Nations will occur at this time. Having described it, he adds:

> "This judgement is still future and occurs when Christ returns
> to earth. It concerns the living nations, not the dead, and they
> are judged on the basis of their treatment of God's people." [12]

We have one Post-Tribulationist telling us that the Marriage of the Lamb occurs when the Lord returns and another that the Judgement of the Nations and Bema occur. Which is supposed to happen first? With any other Rapturist programme, the Bema comes first in heaven after the Rapture, and the Marriage also takes place in heaven, when the Bride has made herself ready, before Christ's return in power, after which the Judgement of the Nations will occur on earth. We will look at the implications for Israel's future in due course.

Ladd unwittingly highlights a further problem with Post-Tribulationism. He writes:

> "The Rapture means two things: 1). Union with the Lord... The emphasis in this meeting is not upon the place—in the air. Pretribulationists place the emphasis here and insist that Jesus does not come to the earth. This however is not asserted by the Scripture. Nothing is said about what happens immediately after the meeting... after this meeting Jesus continues His descent to the earth. 2). The second significance of the Rapture is the transformation of the bodies of the living believers." [13]

Now we do not dispute that the second statement describes something which happens at the Rapture, but this misses the point that what the word *Rapture* actually means is 'catching' or 'snatching away', not 'union'; the Greek verb is *harpazo* and quite unambiguous. Scripture *does* assert that this coming is not to earth, through Jesus' own words recorded in Jn 14:3:

> *"And if I go and prepare a place for you I will come again and receive you unto Myself, that where I am, there you may be also".*

We have quoted and commented already on this unambiguous promise, which *must* happen, but cannot be demonstrated to be fulfilled anywhere accept at a Rapture which has heaven as its destination—in stark contrast to Ladd's Post-Tribulational earthly destination.

For if the Rapture is to occur at Jesus' return to earth, we are left with the extraordinary anomaly of the Church being given resurrection bodies during their rapid ascent half way to heaven; and the 'sheep', at the Judgement of the Nations, which is definitely stated to be at the Lord's return to earth (Matt 25:21), being judged in their earthly bodies by different criteria and invited into the Millennial kingdom, where they will become the ancestors of all the other Millennial inhabitants. In the Post-Tribulation programme the 'sheep' are evidently not saved, else they would be raptured. Rather they are among a mixed group from the nations, who will be judged by their reception or rejection of Christ's 'brethren' (Matt 25:40), and be described by Him as being *"blessed of*

My Father" and welcomed into the kingdom (v34). Were they to be the same as those raptured, none would be left to populate the earth and raise children; and there is plenty of evidence that children will be born in the Millennium. This crazy anomaly is peculiar to Post-Tribulationists, and is greatly to their discredit.

Ladd seems to be hazy about the nature of the Millennium. His position lies between those of Amillennialists and most Pre-Millennialists. Fruchtenbaum, who has access to four of Ladd's books compared to my two, says that:

> "Ladd totally rejects the Jewish Nature of the Millennium."[14]

Ladd himself writes:

> "While the New Testament clearly affirms the salvation of literal Israel, it does not give any details about the day of salvation... The New Testament does not give any details of Israel's conversion and role in the millennium."[15]

We have dealt with all these points before. We simply wish at this juncture to emphasise that we cannot assume that Post-Tribulationists see a Millennial future for the Jews distinct from any other nation. It is pathetic to protest that he cannot find in the New Testament a prophecy which properly belongs to the Old. Surely he has read Zechariah! Much of this confusion could well be due to the implications of the numbers of extra happenings which they have attached to the Lord's return in power. Let him ponder the words of another Post-Millennialist, David Pawson:

> "Jesus... had announced that the kingdom of God will be taken away from you [i.e. Israel] and given to a people who will produce its fruit. This was not, as many have supposed, the cancellation of the national aspect. Too many scriptures point to a future place for Israel and Jerusalem in God's purposes to allow for this conclusion..."[16]

Some Post-Tribulationists believe in the literal fulfilment of Millennial promises concerning Israel; others don't. It is a school divided on an immensely important issue.

Mid-Tribulationism

This 'Mid-Tribulation' title tends to be used by others, rather than by those who hold it; some do not regard the first three and a half years as tribulation, therefore in their own way they are Pre-Tribulational. It is sometimes traced to a 1955 article by Dr Harold Ockenga, but in fact Norman B Harrison's 1941 and 1946 books set it forth, even if those who followed do not agree with some details. In fact Ironside, back in 1920, refers to such a belief. While we believe it to be wrong, we at least feel that it is more reasonable than Pre-Wrath, which we will be looking at next.[17]

Some features of Mid- and Pre-Wrath (what we might call 'Intra-Tribulationism'—my term) may conveniently be looked at together. The problem of imminence applies to both, inasmuch as the Rapture is believed in both cases to take place at a specific juncture within the seven years—what we might describe as the 50% and 75% points. The problems which we encountered with Post-Tribulationists regarding the sequence of events, such as the Marriage of the Lamb and the return in power do not arise here, because both see the Church absent from earth before Christ's return in power.

As both place the Rapture within the seven years, they are required to demonstrate a more precise understanding of the relationship between the three sets of judgements and other events than the other schools. The half-way point is straightforward enough in one respect; it is specifically the juncture at which the 'prince who is to come' will break his false covenant for the restoration of Jerusalem and its temple (Dan 9:26, 27), and set up the 'Abomination of Desolation'. This in turn ties in with Matt 24:15 and Mk 13:14 as probably the most accurately pin-pointed of all end time prophecies, and provides the start point for the Beast's public blasphemous identification (Dan 11:36; 12:11; II Thess 2:3–9 and Rev 13:1–8 etc.). Jesus has confirmed that it is still future, and so AD 70 in no way completed the terms of the prophecy. So none of us can reasonably question the mid-point of the seven Tribulation years. What Mid-Tribulationists have to demonstrate is that the Rapture takes place at this precise juncture; and this is another matter entirely. It requires them in fact to prove three things, namely:

- That the seventh trumpet of Revelation, the 'last trumpet' of I Cor 15:52 and the 'trumpet of God' of I Thess 4:16 are one and the same, thus signalling the Rapture.

- That the 'mystery of God' spoken of in Rev 10:7 is the Church.

- That this trumpet is sounded at the three-and-a-half year point when the Beast breaks his covenant and inaugurates his blasphemous tyranny.

Here is the case for the first two of these three propositions. It is well presented; we will hold the writer's name in reserve for a few paragraphs.

> "Then the same mighty angel lifts his hand to heaven and swears that the End-Time has come, declaring that during the days in which the seventh angel sounds his trumpet the mystery of God would be finished. It will be remembered that the rapture is to take place, according to I Cor xv 52, at the sounding of the seventh trumpet, and that the Church is spoken of as a mystery. Apparently the Church ascends as the seventh angel sounds his trumpet." [18]

This is a simple statement of fact, the logic of which is inescapable, *assuming* that the 'last trumpet', the 'trumpet of God' and 'seventh trumpet' are one and the same, and that the Church is indeed the mystery spoken of. But we simply cannot accept these assumptions, however reasonable they may at first appear to be. For a start, neither I Cor 15:22 nor I Thess 4:16 indicate that this will be the last of seven. Both Jewish and Roman readers knew a lot about last trumpets, usually the last of a series of three. The three trumpet blasts in Israelite journeyings were for assembly, advance and warfare (Num 10:1–10). In Roman times the last or third trumpet was the call to 'Quick march!', following the 'Stand to!' and 'Prepare to advance!' So the link between the Rapture and the seventh trumpet is tenuous indeed.

Revelation 10:7 reads:

> *"In the days of the sounding of the seventh angel, when he is about to sound, the mystery of God would be finished, as He declared to His servants the prophets."*

But the Church and its 'finishing' was *never* declared by the prophets. What was declared was the fact that God's astonishing patience with rebellious mankind would one day come to an end. The Day of Vengeance of our God (Is 61:2), symbolically postponed by Jesus (Lk 4:19), is to arrive at last (Is 63:4).

Regarding the third point that Mid-Tribulationists have to prove, the precise timing of the seventh angel's trumpet is highly debatable. If Seals, Trumpets and Vials or Bowls follow each other in 'end-to-end' succession, and if all the Trumpets are sounded before the three-and-a-half year point, then there is certainly a major Mid-Tribulationist happening of some kind. However we do not believe that this happening is the Rapture of the saints. As we argued in Chapter Five, the Seals, Trumpets and Bowls, whilst introduced and commenced in this sequence, do not necessarily end in the same sequence. They may indeed be coterminous; we are not adamant about this. The seventh Trumpet actually seems to take us right up to the Lord's return in power (see Rev 10:7 & 15), placing the Bowls within rather than following the 7th trumpet. If it does, Mid-Tribulation and Pre-Wrath are discredited on this ground alone.

It will be recalled that we withheld the identity of the writer of the last quote. It was in fact Dr Oswald Smith. And he is a Post-Millennialist! He uses exactly the same arguments as Mid-Tribulationists for the identification of the seventh trumpet, Rapture and the Church, but, because he sees the trumpets as being coterminous with the Seals and Bowls, rather than inserted neatly between them, he places the Rapture three and a half years later than the Mid-Tribulationists. Because we do not believe that the Church is the mystery or that the 7th trumpet heralds the Rapture, we cannot accept either case. The precise timing of the 7th trumpet, whilst significant, in no way impinges upon the credibility of Pre-Tribulationism.

The other perceived reference to a Mid-Tribulational Rapture is Rev 11:12,

> *"And they heard a loud voice from heaven saying to them,*
> *'Come up here.' And they ascended to heaven in a cloud,*
> *and their enemies saw them."*

Now, while the arguments for the timing of this event being Mid-Tribulational are good enough, there is no evidence whatsoever for its referring to the Church. It concerns two witnesses, who, on divine authority, have been preaching in Jerusalem declamatory judgement supported by retributive miracles. That is not the task of the Church. Jesus rebuked James and John when they asked for permission to emulate Elijah by bringing down fire from heaven (Lk 9:54). That is not the Church's task. If anything, this destroys Mid-Tribulationism rather than supports it. The Old Testament style prophetic activity in Jerusalem in Revelation 11 is highly suggestive of an absent Church and present Israel, supporting Pre-Tribulationism.

Pre-Wrath Rapturism

We now come to a form of Pre-Millennialism which has been around only since 1990, but which has caught on. Marvin Rosenthal can be credited or blamed, as the case may be, for the emergence of this new doctrine; the title was coined by him. On the front cover of his book we read:

> "Some believe that Jesus could rapture the Church at any moment; others say He won't until the middle of the Tribulation; still others place the Rapture at the end of the Tribulation. Are any of them right—or does the Bible teach something else? Find out in **'The Pre-Wrath Rapture of the Church'** a *new* understanding of the Rapture, The Tribulation, and the Second Coming." [19]

Such a claim sets warning bells ringing and sounds rather cultish. Well, it is not the latter, because Rosenthal is perfectly orthodox in his general theology. It is only his eschatology that is innovative; and even that has been only since he abandoned his Pre-Tribulationist stand. Rosenthal's former colleague, Dr Renald Showers, has written a thorough and devastating critique, apparently not yet published, of this new position, whilst Gerald Stanton has produced a first class exposure of its weaknesses. [20] This does not mean that his book is not well written; from the purely Pre-Millennial stand it has much of value. Rosenthal justifies his new stand by asserting that other Pre-Millennial schools are also recent:

> "Mid-tribulation rapturism is even more recent in origin, about fifty years old, it can make no appeal to age for support." [21]

We have shown it to be much older. In his prologue he tells of the two thousand people who wrote to encourage him as his book was in preparation. He does not provide us with statistics of the reactions following publication or how many disagreed. As in Athens (Acts 17:21) there are always those *"spending their time in nothing else but either to tell or hear some new thing"*. It is natural that we should want to know as much as possible about God's promises; but it is unhealthy and unwise to believe that we can extract every detail of God's programme from a Bible which, for many good reasons, does not disclose every detail.

Rosenthal's programme, in which the Rapture is supposed to take place half way through the second three and a half years, is dependent upon a highly elaborate and subjective timetable. He sees twenty-one months of Great Tribulation, followed by twenty-one months of the Day of the Lord. It is at what he says is the Day of the Lord point that he claims that the Wrath of God begins. All other Pre-Millennialists believe from Matt 24:21 that the Great Tribulation lasts until the Lord's return in power. He might be right in his timing of the Bowls; they must start to be poured out *somewhere* about this juncture; however we have no licence to be so precise in terms of months; it is pure conjecture. We cannot even claim that *only* the Bowls represent the Wrath of God. We know they contain the *"seven last plagues, for in them the wrath of God is complete"*. But in Rev 6:16, 17 in the sixth Seal, we read:

> *"'Fall on us and hide us from the face of Him who sits on the throne and from the Lamb! For the great day of His wrath is come, and who is able to stand?'"*

Mid-Tribulationist have at least as much justification for calling themselves Pre-Wrath Rapturists; but they choose not to.

Rosenthal's justification for the Church remaining on earth until the day of God's wrath, is based partly on when our Great Commission ends. He writes:

> "If the Great Commission of the Church is to evangelise the world up to the end, the church must enter the seventieth week of the book of Daniel in order to fulfil its holy calling, only then to be raptured before the Day of the Lord judgement. The phrase *end of the world* (Matt 24:3) is more

accurately translated end of the age and is speaking of the completion of this era in preparation for entrance into the next (the Millennium). The Day of the Lord will be the transition period from this age to the kingdom age." [22]

He is quite right about 'age' being the better rendering than 'world'. But Jesus was talking to the nucleus of His new Church and therefore surely of the end of the Church Age, rather than of some point within the seven years. There are important implications here for Israel, as we shall soon see. The Bible actually refers to a number of events, past and future, described as 'The Day of the Lord', as any good Bible dictionary will quickly confirm. Both he and we see the Church Age and our Commission ending at the Rapture, but he places the Rapture sixty-nine months later than we do. According to his theory the Church will know virtually to the day when the Rapture will occur. We know *neither the day nor the hour*. Gerald Stanton deals a final blow in the following unanswerable questions to Rosenthal:

> "Rosenthal does not explain the destiny of the Church at the Rapture. What happens to all the raptured saints, both dead and living, in the 630 day interval when Christ has a 'continuous presence' and is pouring out His wrath upon the wicked? The position of this book demands that the Church is not on earth during the time of outpoured wrath. But they are not raptured to heaven, for to Rosenthal that would imply 'two comings'. Will the Church triumphant which meets Christ 'in the clouds' continue to float about in those clouds for one-fourth of a seven year period while Christ has a 'continuous presence' and performs His work of judgement on earth below?..." [23]

Naturally this new 'ism' falls short on the question of imminency. However our main concern, as ever, is the question of Israel's role; we will return to this. It would be a very fair summary to say that, whilst the vast majority of 'other' Pre-Millennialists teach Replacement Theology neither in the Church Age nor in the Millennium, they effectively teach it for all or part of those future seven years which we refer to as Daniel's Seventieth Week.

Partial Rapturism

This has been around in a recognised form at least since 1945, when G H Lang wrote a book[24] representing the views of those who believe that the Rapture will take place before or during the Tribulation, but that only the spiritually mature will be caught up to heaven, while the remainder will be left to undergo the evil that will come upon the earth. There have probably been believers down through history who have been fearful of being left behind. Our comments must be extremely brief, as this belief does not impinge on the imminency of the Rapture, and affects Israel in precisely the same way as do non-Pre-Rapturist schools. Moreover it is not truly an eschatological problem. It is perhaps the believer's worst nightmare, assuming that they do have true saving faith, that they will be left behind at the Rapture. It is understandable, but wrong. It implies that our being taken to heaven is dependent upon our spirituality, or our fruit, or our good works. In fact it is dependent upon grace alone. None, when we meet our Saviour face to face, will be congratulated upon their being there. A Partial Rapture provides grounds for pride among those taken.

Again we have to point out the results of inadequate teaching about the Bema; we looked at this in our section on a single judgement in Chapter Ten. Paul writes:

> *"Each one's work will become manifest; for the Day will declare it, because it will be revealed by fire; and the fire will test each one's work, of what sort it is. If anyone's work which he has built on it endures, he will receive a reward. If anyone's work is burned up, he will suffer loss; but he himself will be saved, yet so as through fire."*
> *(I Cor 3:13–15)*

Our worst scenario should be finding ourselves empty handed and ashamed at the Bema. That is a real possibility. Works, not actual believers, go through the fire of testing. The idea of weaker believers remaining to go through the Great Tribulation whilst their stronger brethren and sisters are in heaven has been aptly described as a Protestant purgatory. A further problem with the teaching is that selected latter day believers are left to endure what previous generations of weak believers have not. L O Pritchard writes:

"In I Thess 4:16–17 there are only two kinds: (1) The dead in Christ, (2) The living in Christ. Now if the dead in Christ are safe, why not the living? If the partial rapture theory is correct we cannot be sure that any saint who has died has gone to heaven. For *all* the saints to come back with Christ, *all* must be translated. For all to appear before the judgement seat of Christ, all must be raptured (II Cor 5:10). You will not be raptured because of what you have done, you will be raptured because of what Christ has done."[25]

Partial Rapturists cannot by definition be Post-Tribulational. They are usually Pre- or occasionally Mid-Tribulationist. We are not aware of any who are Pre-Wrath. We will not be returning to them, when we consider their relationship to Israel's intermediate future, as this will be the same as that of others who share their view of the timing of the Rapture.

Historicist Premillennialism

Here is something entirely different, though rarely met nowadays. Grattan Guinness's book, *The Approaching End Of The Age*, first published in 1894 and widely circulated, was once quite influential and is still considered by some to be a classic. It is a massive and complex tome. It claims to be Pre-Millennial, but is strongly anti-futurist. Indeed, his 1897 edition contains a lengthy appendix[26] containing answers to the numerous Futurist objections raised against his previous editions. One is compelled to wonder whether he chose to deal with only the easier questions! Guinness was not original in this Historicist approach. He simply revived teaching which had been expounded by Joseph Mede in 1627 and had been elaborated by others until, by the early 19th century, important predicted dates and identifications had been proved false. Some of his teaching was valuable, but his big mistake was to assume that the 1260 days of Daniel and Revelation were years within the Church Age; Scripture guards against this error by describing them in several other ways. Even today some, mainly cult members, venture into this highly speculative type of deciphering of supposed encoded revelation. Regarding this Historicist approach to Revelation, Dr Ironside wrote:

"The historical schools believe that the momentous events of the last nineteen hundred years are the fulfilment of the seals, trumpets and vials, and other special visions of the book. According to this view, Revelation cannot be understood apart from a thorough knowledge of the history of the nations comprising Christendom—the sphere where Christ's authority is nominally owned."[27]

Guinness applies the principle to Daniel and other relevant prophets as well. Sidlow Baxter quotes Dr Joseph Angus's note on the multiplicity of solutions which can emerge from this subjective and almost random system of establishing some sort of relationship between prophecy and Church Age events. We believe this age to be a prophetic vacuum, with only general guidelines and admonitions to look out for the impending end-time.

> "It would be wrong to ridicule the mistakes and contradictions of interpreters whose solemn pursuit is that of truth, but… Where Elliot sees in the sixth seal a reference to Constantine, Faber sees allusion to the first French Revolution; where Bengel sees in the star fallen from heaven a good angel, Elliot discerns Mohammed; the scorpion locusts that have power for five months mean to Mede one hundred and fifty years of the dominion of the Saracen, but to Vitringa they mean Goths, and to Scherzer Jesuits. All this seems to be arbitrary and hazardous in the extreme."[28]

While there may indeed be wonders which we have missed in Scripture, which will one day enthral us, we simply do not believe that God has demanded such a detailed knowledge of history, obscure to all but a tiny learned minority, in order that believers might understand His word. Had our own school of prophecy not fitted together so well, we might have been compelled to turn to Guinness and his colleagues; but it does fit together. Were he alive today, Guinness would require to make massive modifications to adapt to events of the last hundred and ten years. That is not true of most other Pre-Tribulational writings of that era. His implications for Jews are strange indeed, as we shall see.

Résumé Of Pre-Tribulationist Position Regarding Jews

As we have already observed, virtually all Pre-Millennialists, irrespective of their views regarding the timing of the Rapture, believe that God has very specific plans and promises to fulfil for the nation of Israel during the coming Millennium. They do not doubt or try to explain away God's many unconditional Old Testament promises. All are fundamental, evangelical Bible-believing Christians with whom we have much in common, even regarding eschatology. Admittedly a few Post-Tribulationists are paranoid about our belief in the imminency of the Rapture and are aggressive or demeaning, but they are the exceptions. Before proceeding further, we will summarise very briefly what probably all Pre-Tribulationists believe about Israel in the intermediate future, or following the Rapture but before the Lord's return in power. This will help put in perspective our concerns about other schools. Our reasoning may be found in earlier chapters; we do not propose to repeat it here.

- God always has witnesses on earth to represent Him.

- God chose Abraham's descendents, but narrowed these down to the family of Jacob, whom He re-named Israel.

- In the Old Testament the Children of Israel were God's witnesses. Isa 43:10 and 44:8 contain perhaps the clearest of many statements to this effect.

- Israel failed miserably and has been side-lined from this central witnessing role by the largely, but not exclusively, Gentile Church, who are currently God's ambassadors.

- At the Rapture the Lord will resurrect His Church saints, whose bodies have been in the grave since death, but whose souls have been in heaven with the Him. The living saints will be caught up with them and will remain in heaven until the Lord returns in power.

- During this interval the Beast or Antichrist, posing as a benefactor, peace-maker or master-statesman will engineer or impose a seven year treaty which will 'solve the Jewish problem', allowing the Jerusalem temple to be rebuilt and sacrifices to be offered for the first time since AD 70. We do *not* know exactly how this will be achieved, though there is much that we can piece together, and which will become clearer to the truly repentant of that age.

- The relationship between Rome, capital of the Revived Roman Empire, Babylon and Jerusalem is a mysterious one; but there are many references to Jerusalem playing a key role within the seven years.

- God will seal 144,000 Jews from twelve tribes, whose ancestry is known to Him. It is most likely that they will be like Saul of Tarsus before his conversion, having a blind zeal for the Lord. There are many such Jews in the world today. The Holy Spirit will come upon them mightily. They will fill the witnessing vacuum left by the departed Church. They will preach to Jew and Gentile alike the Gospel of the Kingdom— *"Repent for the Kingdom of God is at hand!"*.

- An innumerable multitude from every nation, tribe, people and tongue will be redeemed. But the personal cost will be immense, particularly during the Great Tribulation, when there will be an unprecedented slaughter of believers—mass martyrdom.

- Satan, deprived of the access to heaven which he has always enjoyed, will be enraged. Jews once again will be his prime target. The sealed witnesses, though evidently preserved, like Job, from death, will be hungry, thirsty, naked and imprisoned. Those living in Judah who heed God's warning *in time* will be given divine refuge in some desert place for the duration of the Great Tribulation.

- God will send two supernaturally empowered witnesses to Jerusalem to preach repentance and coming judgement.

- Despite the massive numbers of converts, even greater numbers will remain unrepentant, and will openly blaspheme and defy God.

- Many, including some new believers, will be deceived and will be drawn into the mystic apostate harlot church and its political backing system. God will call His people out.

- Israel will be the focus of the world's armies, which will be drawn inexorably to it to meet their Creator, unbelievably in battle. The valley of Megiddo and the Judaean hills will be their two areas of concentration.

Other Pre-Millennialists And Israel's Intermediate Future

The Historicist Pre-Millennialist position, being unique, can be left until last. The others can be dealt with collectively, as they raise the same question: how can the Church and a partly awakened Israel co-exist as separately identified bodies representing God during the seven years? Answers vary considerably within these various schools; and these variations do not necessarily follow 'Mid-', 'Post-' or 'Pre-' lines. We will be particularly interested in the identity and assumed role of the 144,000 and of the Woman of Revelation 12, who is granted refuge in the wilderness for three and a half years. We have already made our own views plain.

All the other views except the Historicist recognise that the latter part of Daniel, most of the Olivet Discourse and the bulk of Revelation have much to do with Israel, yet few face up to the strange anomaly that, if the 144,000 are Jews and the Woman is Israel, then for the first time in history, Jews will occupy a specially sealed role on earth at the same time as a Church, whose latter day state is clearly prophesied as being apostate and lacking in faith. This is precisely the sort of assumed situation which encourages some Messianic Jews to believe that they are being groomed by God to take over the evangelisation of the world from the Gentile Church within this age. Of course we are asserting that only a tiny minority of Jews will be sealed, while the majority are either awaiting their own repentance or will be earning the awful penalty for those who will worship the false messiah. The 144,000 are only the firstfruits of repentant Israel (Rev 14:4).

Oswald Smith's and David Pawson's love for Israel is transparent. My copy of *When Jesus Returns* has been autographed "Shalom! J David Pawson". Smith has an excellent chapter, entitled "The Jew in Prophecy" in one of his books.[29] He is rightly very much aware of the presence of Jews during the Tribulation period. He writes:

"But the question that confronts us at this time is the relation of the Jews to the Antichrist. Will they receive him? Undoubtedly... a persecution of God's ancient people the like of which the world has never seen."[30]

He has much to say about the seven year covenant and suffering of the Jews in chapter 2 of the same book.[31] He recognises that it is in the rebuilt Jerusalem temple that the Antichrist will make his blasphemous claim to be God to be worshipped.[32] He recognises that it is to Jews that the warning is issued to flee when the Abomination of Desolation is set up.[33] However, he does not explain why God is suddenly communicating to the Jews through these Scriptures about these future events in detail which He has never used since the nation was sidelined. There were no such specific warnings to flee from Russia, Germany etc. for previous mass persecutions. If Israel is back on the mainline by then, as Pre-Tribulationists claim, it all fits together. But according to him, the Church will still occupy that mainline place.

Certainly in this volume, he says nothing about the identity and role of the 144,000, and says that Antichrist's reign will be characterised by hatred of God and persecution of the saints, quoting Dan 7:21,25; 8:24. The way he refers to these implies that these saints are the Church. While we in no way dispute the persecution of Tribulation converts of all races, we note that the three texts he cites point clearly to Jews—Daniel's people. He seems to have two lots of co-existing but distinct saints. He does not differentiate between the Gospel of the Kingdom and the Gospel of grace; neither does he say who will complete the world wide preaching of Matt 24:14.

Despite their inconsistent programme, we like David Pawson's approach to the Jews and their guaranteed future as much as we like Oswald Smith's. Here is a little gem of Pawson's with which to confront Replacement Theologians, based on the disciples' question of Acts 1:6,

"i.   Israel once had a 'kingdom'.

ii.   Israel has lost this 'kingdom'.

iii.   Israel will recover this 'kingdom'.

iv.   Jesus is the one to achieve this.

The only uncertainty they have is the timing: now or later?"[34]

Well, we agree with Pawson about the timing of (iv); it is to be during the Millennium. Our one disagreement with him is over the question of when the Church will be taken away from this scene and evangelisation handed over to God's original witnesses. Like Smith, he sees Jews and Gentiles co-existing, each having some unspecified place in God's plan during the seven years.

In Revelation he notes the three 'insertions' between the Seals, Trumpets and Bowls, namely chapters 7, 10, and 12–14 and says:

> "Whereas the three series of seals, trumpets and bowls are primarily concerned with what will happen to the *world,* the three insertions deal with what will happen to the *church...* On the one hand, a limited number of Jews are protected on earth (7:1–8). God has not rejected Israel (Rom 11:1,11). He made an unconditional promise that they would survive as long as the universe lasted (Jer 31:35–37). He will keep His word. They have a future." [35]

With much we can agree; but of course we would see the 'insertion' reference being to those redeemed during the Tribulation. They are converts, but not the Church. The Church is seen in heaven by then with some saints crowned; and they can be neither resurrected nor crowned until the Rapture and subsequent Bema have taken place. He has some interesting comments to make regarding the 144,000, but in no way disputes their national identity as presented in Scripture. But he has no suggestions to make as to their role, so again we are compelled to wonder why, if they have been sealed, they have not been absorbed into the Church, as they would be in the present dispensation. This is a crucial point.

Regarding the Woman of Revelation 12, he correctly rejects the Roman Catholic interpretation of Mary. But then he completely misses the option of identifying her with Israel, and perceives problems which do not arise if a comparison is made with Gen 37:9 and Isa 66:7–9.

> "Why bring Mary into the picture? After Acts 1 she disappears from the New Testament, her work completed... The interpretation which best fits all this data sees the woman as a personification representing the church in the end-time,

preserved outside urban areas during the worst of the troubles. Her man-child is also a personification, representing the martyred believers at this time, safe in heaven, out of Satan's reach. The 'rest of her offspring' are those who survive the holocaust yet 'obey God's commandments and hold to the testimony of Jesus'... There are still some tensions with the text in this view, but far fewer than with any other explanation."[36]

We cannot agree with the last statement. Nor can we agree that the Woman is the Church. This is a false identification imported from A- or Post-Millennialism. We have already justified our view that the Woman represents the faithful remnant of Israel, the nation who gave birth not to 'martyred believers' but to the Messiah. These heed Jesus' Olivet Discourse injunction to those in Judaea to flee to the wilderness. The link with Rev 12:14 is unmistakable:

> *"The woman was given two wings of a great eagle, that she might fly into the wilderness to her place where she is nourished for a time, times and half a time, from the presence of the serpent."*

This is the Dan 7:25 description of the three and a half years. Jesus' warning to flee must be heeded as soon as the mid-point Abomination is revealed. Refuge is apparently for three and a half years or not at all. Others will be saved later; they will miss this refuge and endure great suffering. When one correlates the Revelation 12 refuge and the Olivet discourse warning to flee, one wonders how Post-Tribulationists cannot perceive how the warning to flee from Judaea given to Jews alone is in itself an assurance that the Church will not be around at that time.

Ladd, whatever he may think of the Jewishness of the Millennium, is in no doubt about their suffering during the seven years; it is whether he sees any special role for Israel which is once again the problem; denial of a Pre-Tribulation Rapture almost makes any Jewish role redundant:

> "Another important element in these end times is God's treatment of the Jewish people. They are destined to be restored; the veil will be taken from their minds and they will turn at last as a people in faith to Jesus as their

Messiah. Refusing to worship Antichrist, they will become the object of his anger and will suffer fearful martyrdom."[37]

We agree in general, but have two reservations. Firstly, many Jews will in fact be deceived and will worship the Beast and will pay the consequences;

> *"If another comes in his own name, him you will receive"* (Jn 5:43).

Secondly, there is no reference to or explanation here for the 144,000 sealed Jews. But much later he comes to them and seems unable to decide whether they are Jews or not—he is thrown into this state of doubt, no doubt, by his assumption that the Church is still on earth:

> "Some insist that they are literal, racial Jews, for they are derived from the twelve tribes of Israel. Others insist that they cannot be literal Jews... Furthermore, we must note that the Apocalypse specifically distinguishes between true and false Jews, i.e. between those who are Jews literally but not spiritually (Rev 2:9; 3:9). It is possible therefore that by the 144,000 from the twelve tribes, the Spirit of God means to suggest that the true Israel, the true people of God will be preserved absolutely complete. Not one person who really belongs to the true Israel will be lost, even in the Great Tribulation."[38]

Ladd is having to scrape the bottom of the barrel to find arguments. Surely if God's Holy Spirit wished to indicate that these are not to be understood as literal, racial Jews, one thing He would not have done would be to name the tribes. We have not included his complex but weak argument about what he sees as an inconsistency in the tribal list; he is compelled to resort to this ploy due to his failure to understand dispensational differences. Several well known expositors have explained any apparent anomalies in the tribal list perfectly satisfactorily. Regarding his last sentence, we are left astonished, wondering where the Great Tribulation martyrs are going to come from, should this statement be true!

In fact the 144,000 are the straw which Ladd grasps to try to explain how the Church, which he assumes to be upon earth, will escape the outpouring of God's wrath. He makes a strong case for the Church not suffering this wrath:

> "The Church will certainly not experience these outpourings of the wrath of God. The seven bowls of the wrath of God are designed not for the world at large but for 'the men who bore the mark of the beast and worshipped its image'...." [39]

Mid-Tribulationists and Pre-Wrath Tribulationists would see the Rapture round about this juncture rescuing the Church; but Ladd, who would have the Church on earth throughout, has had to try to find a solution in the sealing of the 144,000!

However much other Pre-Millennialists dislike the Pre-Tribulationist view of the 144,000, a view which harmonises completely with a prior Rapture, they have either to ignore the significance of them, or to find an explanation which will conform to their co-existence with an unraptured Church. The sheer variety of explanations offered illustrates their difficulty. We will shortly look at the Messianic Jewish view of the 144,000 and the Woman.

Pre-Wrath Confusion Over Israel's Role

Rosenthal's views are in some respects quite different from anything we have yet encountered. He writes:

> "The 144,000 are also said to be 'the firstfruits unto God and to the Lamb' (Rev 14:4). They are the forerunner of a host of Jewish people who will survive the Day of the Lord and come to the Saviour at the end of the seventieth week... And whether they are regenerated (saved) at the time of their sealing (Rev 7:4) or sealed for physical protection and later regenerated (Rev 14:4) is a matter for speculation. What is abundantly clear and was obviously important to the angel is the fact that that 144,000 Jews must be sealed before the Day of Wrath begins." [40]

In fact Rev 7:3 suggests that they are sealed before the newly opened Seals begin to take effect and they are certainly sealed before the first Trumpet sounds:

> *"Do not harm the earth, the sea or the trees till we have
> sealed the servants of God on their foreheads".*

They are described as servants of God because they have a task to perform. That surely is why we meet them so early in the judgemental part of Revelation and why they are distinguished from the host of other Jews who will be saved during the seven years. Why, if Rosenthal's explanation is correct, are these not also sealed? All go through the Tribulation; some are sealed and some are not! We believe that they are sealed because at the start of the Tribulation they are God's *only* human witnesses upon earth. Like Rosenthal, we would hesitate in stipulating the exact moment of their sealing, but, if this sealing is with the Holy Spirit, it could very well be their equivalent of Saul's Damascus experience:

> *"That you may receive your sight and be filled with the
> Holy Spirit"* (Acts 9:17).

Again we ask why, in his programme, if they are sealed early in the seven years, as the description of 'firstfruits' suggests, they are not absorbed into the Church and in due course raptured. The answer is, of course, that there will be no Church on earth into which to be absorbed. They are saved after the Rapture, and constitute the firstfruits of the Israel who is about to be restored when the Lord returns.

Rosenthal makes no suggestion of how these 144,000 relate to the Woman of Revelation 12; the latter, on his own admission[41], represents Israel. Rev 12:6 and 14, say that she will be provided with refuge in the wilderness for the ensuing three and a half years or Great Tribulation. We have no reason to believe that those who flee are numerically limited.

Rosenthal's supports his timing with a strange interpretation of the opening verse of Daniel 12. The verse reads:

> *"At that time Michael shall stand up, the great prince who
> stands watch over the sons of your people; and there shall
> be a time of trouble, such as never was since there was a
> nation, even to that time. And at that time your people shall
> be delivered, everyone who is found written in the book."*

The AV (KJV) incidentally reads, *"At that time shall Michael stand up, the great prince which standeth for the children of thy people."* It is the first sentence which Rosenthal would retranslate, with a changed meaning for 'stand'.

The Hebrew word rendered 'stand up', 'stand watch', and 'stand for' is *amad*. It is an extremely common word which is frequently used for 'stand by', 'stand fast', 'stand firm', 'stand still' and 'stand up'. It is also used in the AV, in descending order of frequency, for 'stay' (x 15), 'endure' (x 8), 'remain' (x 8) and 'continue' (x 6).[42] Vine's *Expository Dictionary* says regarding *amad*:

> "The basic meaning of this verb is 'to stand upright'… It is what a soldier does while on watch (II Sam 18:30)…".[43]

Quoting 'certain Jewish scholars'—only Rashi is actually named—Rosenthal argues somewhat tortuously, from one of the more obscure renderings of *amad*, that Michael will be standing *aside* or be inactive during the Great Tribulation. The Archangel has a special role as Israel's protector. Is God going to withdraw him at the moment of Israel's greatest need? Was he withdrawn in the past, even during the Inquisition, Pogroms or Holocaust? Many and dreadful are the penalties listed as warnings to Israel in Deuteronomy chapters 28 to 30, but they are never told that, if they repent wherever they are, God will one day refuse to respond at all—rather the reverse.

His interpretation of Dan 12:1 is diametrically opposed to all nine commentaries which I have checked; not all of these have prophetic axes to grind. All speak of Daniel standing up for Israel, or words to that effect. After all, Michael and his angels have only just at this point cast the Dragon and his evil angels from the Heavenlies; are we really meant to understand that the Archangel, having cast Satan out, now gives him an open invitation to do his worst while he stands back and does nothing? It's preposterous! Of course the Dragon will do his worst, but only within permitted bounds. It is Michael's awesome task to see to that. But Rosenthal writes:

> "The archangel Michael will step aside, he will desist from helping Israel. That is why this period is called the 'time of Jacob's [Israel's] trouble'."[44]

He then proceeds at great length to tie this up with II Thess 2:2 et seq., which we agree is a Great Tribulation passage, and quotes v7,

"The mystery of lawlessness is already at work; only he (He) who now restrains will do so until he is taken out of the way, and then will the lawless one be revealed... and for this reason God will send them delusion that they should believe the lie, and that they all may be condemned who did not believe in righteousness."

He suggests that it is Michael who is to be 'taken out of the way' and Israel who will be deceived.

Now, however ingenious and original this identification of the restrainer as Michael may be, it simply does not make sense. For a start, it is indisputably at the *beginning* of the seven years that Israel is deceived into making the covenant with the Beast (Dan 9:27), not the *middle*; that is when his true identity will be revealed. The common, and very satisfactory, interpretation of the delusion of II Thess 2:11 is that it concerns those who had been presented with but refused the Gospel before the Rapture; they will not have a further option to repent. Toying with salvation and deliberately procrastinating are lethal practices. However, not believing a prior Rapture, Rosenthal does not have this interpretation available. Michael has constantly been standing watch— even through the AD 70 sack of Jerusalem and dispersal throughout the nations which were about to occur when Paul wrote. Why should he suddenly stand aside now? Rosenthal says it is for their rejection of their Messiah. But that is what the long AD 70 dispersion has been about. Had he been due to stand aside, it would have been then.

The Restrainer of II Thess 2:7 is usually taken to be God the Holy Spirit. This makes perfect sense, as His unique indwelling role in the Church will cease when we are raptured. Thereafter He will briefly cease from restraining evil in order to allow matters to be 'brought to a head'. He will not however depart totally from the earth. Both Tribulation witnesses and martyrs will desperately need His empowering. We know from many passages that the Holy Spirit was active in Old Testament times; so He will be then.

Again, how does this Michael identification tie in with the Woman of Revelation 12 and her refuge? If God is going to Rapture the Church twenty-one months after the mid-point, as Pre-Wrath people would claim, and all Jews are going to be *hors de combat*, who will be God's representatives during earth's darkest hour yet? Rosenthal would have an absent Church *and* a totally unprotected and unsupported Israel.

But perhaps the most significant point of all these deliberations is that Scripture tells us so much about the Jews during the Tribulation period. Pre-Wrath teaching is fully aware of this, yet fails to draw natural conclusions from the exceedingly significant absence of similar Scriptural coverage for those within the Church in the first three-quarters of the seven years.

Historicists And Israel's Intermediate Future

We are dealing here only with Historicist Pre-Millennialists such as Grattan Guiness. Because he sees the Apocalypse being unfolded in Church history, it is unreasonable to expect him to see Israel playing any part in events leading up to the Lord's return. At the time Guinness was writing, Pre-Tribulationists had for several decades been foretelling the return of Jews to their Land and describing their role, their suffering and, for many, their delusion during the Tribulation period. But Guinness did not see them involved in the Tribulation. In the Preface to his eighth edition, he admits that moves were at that time already afoot for Jews to return to Palestine.[45] But, as he sees the Tribulation period already nearing its fulfilment within the Church Age, he has no place for the Jews in prophecy until the Lord's return in power and their national repentance. Referring to one of the objections he has received, he writes:

> "The last, however, deserves a word of additional reply: 'Why are the Jews and Jerusalem excluded from Mr Guinness's theory?' The answer is simple. They are not excluded; on the contrary, they fill a very large place. The past history, and future restoration of the Jews, occupy most prominent positions on the pages of inspiration."

Then he explains their current spiritual condition and the physical consequences, quoting *"Blindness in part has happened to Israel, until the fullness of the Gentiles be come in, and then shall all Israel be saved."* What he has not foreseen, because his Historicist programme made it seem unreasonable, is that Jews were in fact to return in vast numbers and to occupy the Holy Land in blindness. Admittedly other

Victorians were similarly mistaken. He assumes the immediate repentance associated with the Lord's return in power. He continues:

> "The great anti-Christian power, symbolised as the 'little horn', and called the 'man of sin', and the eighth head of the beast, being the last form of Gentile power, and belonging to the 'times of the Gentiles', has little to do with the literal Israel, or the literal Jerusalem, or the literal Temple. He co-exists *not* with a recognised Jewish nation, but with the rejection and dispersion of the Jews, and with a recognised professing Christian Church. His sphere is not Palestine, but Christendom; his throne is not Jerusalem, but Rome; his victims are not Jews, but Christians; his end and doom are brought about by the events which mark the commencement of the restoration of Israel to God's favour—the second advent of Christ; when Israel shall look on Him whom they pierced, and mourn because of Him, and when the times of the Gentiles shall be ended." [46]

Here is a remarkable mix of truth and error. History has already demonstrated the error. The 'fig tree' began to bud during the 20th century. God, who preserved His ancient people, in a way quite without parallel in world history, allowed many Jews to return in blindness and to form and exist as a nation, albeit in the face of the fiercest opposition. God has already provided abundant evidence, for all who are alert to the signs of the times, that He has already allowed the stage to be partly but unmistakably set for the time when He *"will make Jerusalem a very heavy stone for all peoples; all who would heave it away will surely be cut to pieces, though all the nations of the earth are gathered against it"* (Zech 12:3). This chapter of Zechariah makes it clear that this will occur before—immediately before—her blindness is healed. Historicist Pre-Millennialism is therefore a major distraction from God's Pre-Millennial plans for Israel.

Guinness at least had the excuse, which no believer today can offer, that there were few signs of a Jewish nation state in his day. One might say that world events since his 1897 edition, from which the above quotes are taken, have proved one of the nails in the coffin of his theory. Like all Historicists, his views have constantly to be up-dated to keep pace with evolving history; his ideas have hit an insurmountable stumbling block. In his favour, it must be said that there is no trace of dismissal of Israel's *Millennial* future in his book, and from time to time one encounters most interesting and positive remarks, including those quoted in our introduction.

Messianic Jewish Views

We have from time to time pointed out the effects of Replacement Theology and incorrect eschatology upon both enquiring Jews and Messianic Jews. Fortunately Jews are much less susceptible than Gentile Christians to Replacement Theology and to the allegorisation of unconditional Old Testament prophecies to their nation. However they may nevertheless understandably be influenced by the eschatology of those who have evangelised them.

Post-Millennialists may have influenced them to believe that the Great Tribulation can and will be avoided. Post-Tribulationists can close their eyes to the future Tribulation Jewish roles and exhortations. Many Messianic Jews whom I know or whose work I have read are convinced Pre-Tribulationists. It is the school which best ties in with the Tanakh scriptures. But there are significant exceptions. In Chapter 12, in our section on Key Preterist Texts, we quoted Shira Sorko-Ram, who was unsure what will one day spark national repentance.

Orthodox and especially Cabalistic Jews fully expect, and have indeed prepared for, a rebuilt Jerusalem Temple, which we believe will comply with Daniel 9:27, Matt 24:15 and II Thess 2:4. The great mosque which dominates what is called the Temple Mount, lies within the Outer Court area, which has been temporarily given by God to the Gentiles (Rev 11:2). Contrary to public opinion, it does not stand on the true Temple site, which is slightly further North, and due West of the Mount of Olives. This prophesied temple is to be a dominant feature of and a witness to the blasphemies of the Tribulation period, although whether it will be built before or after the Rapture is more than any of us can at present say. It may well stand almost side by side with the mosque. But some Messianic Jews anticipate only one future Temple—that of Ezekiel 40 to 48. And that cannot be in the same place or fulfil the relevant Tribulation period prophecies, because the Mount of Olives will split East to West when the Saviour's feet touch the Mount of Olives (Zech 14:4), which is in direct line with the Temple site. A great valley is to be formed. However the Millennial Temple of Ezekiel and Micah 4:1 is to be elevated, and will most certainly not be neighbour to any pagan edifice. Thus we find some Messianic Jews who are blind to the horrendous events of their nation's intermediate future. This is a feature shared with them by many devoted and well-meaning Christians who are actively supportive of Israel, but whose eschatology is confused.

Dr David Stern is Messianic Jew. His eschatology is very muddled and he has several extraordinary views about Dispensationalism, which he says is 'manifestly anti-Semitic'. Having written an article about this[47], and being slightly worried at having been so critical of a Jewish believer, I was, whilst awaiting its publication, greatly cheered to acquire and read similar, and indeed much more detailed criticisms[48] by Dr Arnold Fruchtenbaum, a Hebrew Christian writer whom I greatly respect. His criticism was actually directed against Dr Dan Juster's book[49], which expresses many similar views to Stern's. Stern writes:

> "Unless the Church does everything in her power to restore that Jewishness, she lacks the key component of the Gospel. In consequence she cannot fulfil the Great Commission properly, and the Jewish people cannot be the 'right kind of light to the nations'."[50]

> "How will the Jewish people be blessed? By being able to realise its age-old goal of being a light to the nations, and also by receiving the deliverance for which she has waited so long... How will these blessings come to the Jewish people? From God, of course. But not directly! Rather, they will come through the Church, and specifically through Gentile Christians when they finally make Jews jealous!"[51]

> "The separation between the Church and the Jewish people, as it has developed over the last 2000 years, is completely out of God's will, a terrible mistake, the worst schism in the history of this planet."[52]

Now there is obviously scope for at least a whole chapter on the general theology and another on the eschatology of these quotes, particularly the last sentence; but that would be quite outside our terms of reference. Here we simply wish to illustrate the confusion which arises when one sees Jews and Gentiles separately tasked by God to preach the Gospel within the same age, be that the Church Age or the Tribulation. He sees Messianic Jews only half-integrated into the Church. Stern finds it crucial to 'restore their Jewishness', re-imposing the yoke on their necks *"which neither our fathers nor we were able to bear"* (Acts 15:10), implying among other things, the reliance on works and rituals, the roots of that ancient overweening pride which Stephen, Paul and Jesus Himself condemned. He wishes to take over from the Gentile Church without any Rapture. That does not fit into his programme. He wants to bring Jews again under the bondage of the Mosaic Law, having missed the truth of the epistle to the Hebrews.

But let us see what light Messianic Jews can throw on the 144,000 and the Woman of Revelation 12. We quote Stern's Jewish New Testament Commentary:

> "One objection sometimes made to interpreting these 144,000 as Jews is that there is supposedly no reason why Jews would be singled out for special protection... God, by his grace, has singled out the Jewish people for special protection for thousands of years. This protection is promised over and over again by the prophets, even when Israel becomes sinful and breaks the covenant; though it is not always promised to the entire people, but only to a remnant, such as the 144,000."[53]

> "The **woman** is not Miryam, Yeshua's mother, but Israel, in its normal sense, the Jewish people, because the imagery is from Isaiah 66:7–10 (compare also Isaiah 26:17, Micah 4:10)."[54]

While we cannot agree with all points of Stern's theology, we do acknowledge that it seems to take a Jew to recognise a Jew. Stern may not share our eschatology, but he is in no doubt about these two identities. If only more Christians would stop stubbornly denying the renewed central position of Jews in Revelation from Chapter 7 onwards, they might be more inclined to recognise that the Church will not be in the Tribulation! If only more Jewish believers would fully comprehend the fact that they will be Raptured as part of the Church before the

Tribulation, they would appreciate better their present role to win fellow Jews for the Messiah before the final holocaust, that their refuge might be in heaven, rather than in the wilderness! Of course many Messianic Jews do believe that they will partake in the prior Rapture; I have had the privilege of being able to join with some as a fellow contributor to the Pre-Tribulational press.

Conclusion To Other Pre-Tribulationist Positions

At the beginning of this chapter we expressed two concerns about these 'other' forms of Pre-Millennialism, namely those which see part or all of the Tribulation period occurring before the Rapture. Our first concern was for the undermining of what we believe to be the precious and sanctifying truth of imminency—an expectation which may be heightened by signs of the times, but which does not demand absolute observable prerequisites. Our second concern was that Israel's special role during the Tribulation period should neither be under-estimated nor ignored. We have delved into many obscure and unexpected corners in the process, as well as the obvious.

There are numerous references in the prophets to events of the seven years, and particularly to the second half; most of the Olivet Discourse and much of Revelation are given over to them. Notable in the prophets are passages in Isaiah 34 and 63, Joel 3 and Zechariah 12 and 14; but most Tribulation references are short, being interspersed with promises of the First Coming, Millennial blessing and sometimes even current matters. Israel, the Jews and Jerusalem dominate in Tribulation prophecies. Topographical details forbid allegorisation. Why has God arranged it thus? Why are the Church epistles not equally well provided with details of this critical time? There is only one viable reason; and it is an obvious one. It is certainly not that God loves Israel more than the Church; that is quite untrue. The reason is that the Church will already be in heaven with her Lord; she will be safe. The special attention given to Israel at this time proves beyond all shadow of doubt that the Church will be Raptured before the Tribulation begins. Israel, in the form of a faithful remnant, will be back on the main line after a long, long absence.

This is wonderful news for Church members, be they Jew or Gentile. But what about those who will be left behind? Some may seek out and scrutinise the material which Raptured saints have left on their bookshelves. We cannot be sure, but it seems eminently reasonable. We are doing them no favours if we leave to them books and articles which claim that the Jews will have no role. Neither do we want them to believe that some true Church believers will be left behind. Sealed witnesses will indeed preach the Gospel throughout the world. But *"false christs and false prophets will rise and show great signs and wonders, to deceive, if possible, even the elect"* (Matt 24:23). Elect there will soon be, an innumerable multitude, described in Revelation 7 immediately after their evangelists. We can rely upon the One who will seal the 144,000 to ensure that they at least are not deceived, but rather empowered. As we rejoice in our Blessed Hope, let us not add to the deception and confusion of those who will be left behind.

Chapter Fourteen

Conclusions

Surprises

When I commenced the thesis which led to this book, I was not so open-minded to believe that I might be compelled to abandon my Pre-Tribulation position. I had held it too long and defended it too often. I had considered some of the other options in my youth. But I was prepared to learn, and I have indeed learned much. My own stand has been further underpinned, although I confess there have been certain arguments from the 'opposition' which were challenging. These are dealt with mainly in Chapter Eight. Where I have not encountered any intellectual challenge has been over Israel's future. If anything, I am more confirmed than ever in my belief that many of God's promises to Israel as a nation are absolutely unconditional, and that the closely related Father's promises to the Son, such as in Psalms 2 and 110, cannot possibly be anything other than unconditional. The denial of unconditional promises to imperfect Israel involves denying equally unconditional promises to the perfect Son. More than ever I see most of the allegorisation of these promises as a stubborn form of escapism from inconvenient truths.

What has surprised me is the way in which theologians, whom I would in every other respect regard as fundamental and conservative, have used excuses, such as the fact that there is no mention in the New Testament of a Millennial kingdom for Israel. We have demonstrated that there are a few such prophecies there, but most are precisely where one would expect them to be—in the Old Testament. One cannot see how these theologians fail to see this, yet they persist in presenting the excuse to their readers. Just as many Orthodox Jews tend to regard the Torah as being twice as authoritative as the Prophets and Writings, so it would seem, from what I have read during this study, that many Christian writers treat the Old Testament as being less reliable and less literal than the New. One would expect this from liberals, but not from Conservatives. I have been mildly surprised by the number of times I have found occasion to quote the same texts to refute entirely different arguments. This suggests that there are a number of key prophetic passages which are consistently avoided or ignored by some schools.

From time to time in Chapters Nine to Thirteen we have referred to claims based on the comparative antiquity of various schools of prophetic interpretation. For some people, antiquity seems to be the sole criterion for establishing authenticity. But consider this. While we found that Pre-Millennialism was dominant for the first two Christian centuries, it was only in the second quarter of the 19th century that Dispensational Pre-Millennialism began to be widely recognised again. Should we not wonder whether such timing was because God perceived the imminent need for influential Christians, who would be supportive of Israel's forthcoming resettlement and ultimate nationhood? Can we not allow for the fact that God, in His good time, raised up men like John Nelson Darby and allowed a period of sometimes heated but ultimately profitable debate, until God's programme for Israel was better understood? Is it mere co-incidence that the greatest international evangelist of his time, Dwight L Moody, fearlessly preached Pre-Millennialism at the same time as Theodore Herzl was founding modern Zionism? Was it not God Himself who allowed a devout Christian, General Allenby, to take Jerusalem from the Turks in 1917, and to dismount from his horse as he entered the city, because he knew Whose right it was to enter mounted? Did not God Himself ensure that Lord Balfour's understanding of Scripture regarding Israel was untarnished by Replacement Theology?

God not only controls the words of the prophet; He also controls the comprehension of the devout hearer or reader. However, while God's timing is perfect, the Enemy's timing is pretty good too. He knows the implications for himself. By espousing the cause of the so-called Palestinians, many modern churches are unwittingly doing the Dragon's work (Rev 12:17). The 'Palestinian' appetite for Israel's Promised Land is like the leech's two insatiable daughters (Prov 30:15). It can never be satisfied. But God the Holy Spirit, speaking through His prophet Zechariah (14:21), specifically took the trouble to assure us that there will be no sharing of holy sites in the Millennium. God always has the last word.

Final Comment Upon 'isms'

I have also been surprised by the range of widely varying and contrary opinions which I have encountered *within* both Amillennialism and Post-Millennialism; and that was discounting the liberal wings. Obviously some variations were to be expected, owing to the nature of prophecy.

In Amillennialism I met no active Anti-Semitism, and from some writers there was true respect for the Jews. But there were teachings which could give comfort to those who wished to justify or practise Anti-Semitism. Most seemed to be so tied to their Anti-Dispensational position that they simply could not conceive that there could ever be any situation this side of eternity when saved Jews could not be welcomed and absorbed into the Church. They are preoccupied with the Church Age *status quo*. Admittedly this is consistent with their timing of Christ's Coming in Power. Much is based on their refusal to accept the obvious sequence of events as presented in Revelation 19 and 20. Amillennialists cannot cope with this, and they go to great pains to justify deviations from the plain narrative. The fact that we are not, within Revelation 20, furnished with details of what happens within the 1000 years does not seem to compel them to ask what other unfulfilled prophecy could fit into what is patently an earthly scenario. They assume it to belong to the Church Age, even though it plainly follows the Lord's Return in Power.

Amillennialism is totally reliant on infinitely subjective allegorisation of Old Testament prophecy. It effectively implies that God can be unfaithful to His promises. I am therefore compelled to reject it.

Post-Millennianism seems to have revived in recent decades more through song writing than through exposition. I have noted that it is quite incompatible with Amillennialism; yet the two seem to co-exist happily in many a congregation. This is not unity; it is ignorance. It is unhealthy, suggesting an apathy towards the serious study of Scripture. One could indeed argue whether it is driven by conviction or by triumphalist pride mixed with misguided enthusiasm. It is dangerous, because outsiders simply cannot recognise in the current world the extravagant claims which are frequently made for improvement and transformation through Christian action. In this respect it fails the Bible's own tests of prophecy. Most dismiss or circumvent the New Testament teaching that apostasy and lack of faith will be rife in the latter day Church.

Towards Israel it is generally more consistently sympathetic than Amillennialism. Few if any deny a future spiritual revival of Israel, but that is all. Seeing the Millennium as a Church responsibility, they have no place for any glorious future for Israel in a restored Promised Land, neither do they see Jesus Christ ruling from Jerusalem. To justify this stance, they too see much allegorisation of Old Testament prophecies, ignoring the cursings and annexing for themselves the blessings. Within Post-Millennialism is a significant minority of Preterists, who see the bulk of end-time prophecy having been fulfilled in events surrounding the sack of Jerusalem in AD 70. The fact that many of the horrors foretold for the Great Tribulation did not materialise at that time is explained by them in the prophecies having been deliberately exaggerated to emphasise their seriousness! Any teaching which leaves the door so wide open for the abuse of interpretation cannot, I believe, be taken seriously. I therefore am compelled to reject Post-Millennialism.

With the other forms of Pre-Millennialism we had potentially much more in common. What, however was sad, was the quite bitter antagonism of some Post-Millennialists to an imminent Rapture. As I based my research of this 'ism' on four less extreme books, I did not personally encounter this attitude, but have an abundance of reliable 'Post-' quotes from other Pre-Tribulationist writers. The problem over Israel was that, while most saw Israel featuring prominently within the Tribulation period, and all without exception recognised Daniel's seventieth 'week' of years, they saw the Church still on earth, occupying the 'mainline' for part or all of the seven years. Thus there was no logical or coherent role for either the 144,000 Jews or for the Woman of Revelation 12. I saw how misleading and perplexing to present day Jews this could be. I therefore believe these teachings to be discredited.

I am deeply conscious of the fact that many whose works I have quoted are fine fellow-believers, perhaps much better Christians than I am. However I do most sincerely believe that the truth concerning the Lord's Return and His ancient people, Israel, cannot be sacrificed upon the altar of respect and friendship. In Part One we found the case for Israel's national future within God's will to be proved. It is therefore non-negotiable. Any school of prophetic interpretation which denies this or makes no provision for it must necessarily be wrong. Healthy debate is the best solution for resolving differences; but here few are prepared to enter into serious debate. 'Christian unity' can give false respectability to evading serious doctrinal issues. I remain more convinced than ever that (1) the Lord Jesus Christ could come literally at any moment for His espoused Bride, that (2) earth's darkest hour ever will follow, but that (3) sealed Jews will almost immediately begin to fill the evangelistic vacuum left by the Church, that (4) the Lord will return visibly in great glory and power and that, (5) having put down His enemies and judged the nations, He will (6) reign from Jerusalem for a thousand years when Israel is at last the 'head and not the tail'.

More important, however, than the accuracy of the *details* of the Bible's predictive prophecy, is the wonder that God has chosen to reveal so much to us. If the only outcome of reading this book is to help confirm the sheer consistency of God's revelation, and if any reader is thus challenged to enquire after their own soul's eternal salvation, the little time and effort taken to write it will be infinitely repaid. Heaven is not some ethereal place of our fancy; Hell is a real alternative; both are eternal. God has decreed that there are no further options. Had there been other options, God might never, at such great cost, have sent His Son to die on a cross in our place. *"How shall we escape if we neglect so great a salvation?"* (Heb 2:3).

Readers will find in Appendix II what is hoped will prove a helpful, concise list of reasons for believing in a Pre-Tribulational Rapture.

Appendix I

Past, Present And Future Events Of Prophetic Significance With Special Reference To Israel

Most events listed are referred to in the text, but a few have been outside the scope of this book, yet may be of interest to readers. Only a few key references are given. The exact sequence and duration of events with the seven year Tribulation period is difficult. Some events are contemporaneous rather than consecutive. The same applies to the period immediately following Christ's Coming in Power. Many questions will be answered only as events transpire.

Past Event	Comments
Times of Gentiles (Dan 2), represented by Nebuchadnezzar's vision.	Successive world empires with sovereignty over Land of Israel. Gap for Church Age.
End of 70 years Babylonian Captivity (Dan 9:2).	Vast majority of ten Northern Tribes plus many of Judah, Benjamin and Levi remained in lands of exile.
Start of 70 'weeks' of years (Dan 9:24), adding up to 490 years.	Divided (Dan 9:25–27) into 7, 62 and 1 groups of seven years.
Jesus presented His credentials as Messiah (Ps 118:22–26, Zech 9:9, Matt 11:3–5); rejected and crucified.	End of all but final 'week' of years. Church Age intervenes before final seven years.
Pentecost and start of Church Age.	Time given for individual repentance (Acts 2:36–39) and establishment of Church.
Jerusalem sacked by Romans in AD 70, as foretold by Jesus (Matt 24:2).	Mass deportation of Jews.
Bar Kochbar rebellion, AD 135. Jerusalem sacked again.	Final dispersal (Diaspora) of Jews remaining in Land.

Present Event	Comments
Church Age. Kingdom in mystery (Matt 13:3–52).	From Pentecost to Rapture. Individual Jews may become part of Church (Gal 3:28, Eph 2:14).
Jews remain dispersed, persecuted by Romans and in Crusades, Inquisition, Pogroms, Holocaust etc. (Deut 28:65).	No detailed prophecies concerning Israel, but all dire warnings given in Deut 28:15 et seq. implemented.
Birth of modern Zionism in late 19th century.	Trickle of Jews settled in Land, having bought their property from Arab owners.
Balfour Declaration (Great Britain), of November 1917, recognised principle of Jewish homeland.	Britain given League of Nations mandate 1922 for governing 'Palestine'. Many more Jews return to settle.
Flood of refugees arrived following WWII.	Britain over-strict in controlling entry numbers, turned many away.
Israel declared independent statehood, May 1948.	Three militarily vastly superior neighbours immediately attacked and were convincingly defeated.
Frequent military and constant terrorist attacks upon Israel. International ostracism.	Remarkable preservation in face of enormous odds (Isa 54:17). Only most stubborn Christians can fail to see the hand of God. USA main ally, but even there far from unanimous. Support will cease after Rapture.

Future Event—In Heaven	Comments
Rapture of the Dead in Christ and all living believers (I Thess 4:14–17) and return to Heaven, the place He has 'gone to prepare' (Jn 14:2,3).	Souls and spirits of Dead in Christ are already with Him; bodies are in the grave until Rapture.
Bema or Judgement Seat of Christ (I Cor 3:13–15 & II Cor 5:10).	Our service or works will be tried and judged, not our sins. We may be rewarded or suffer loss, be commended or suffer shame, but our salvation will remain unaffected.
Opening of the seven Seals by the Lamb (Rev 6:1 et seq.).	Tribulation judgements begin on earth. Events on earth are carefully monitored by those in Heaven.
Sounding of the seven Trumpets (Rev 8:7 et seq.).	More severe judgements commence on earth.

Future Event—In Heaven	Comments
Souls and spirits of Tribulation martyrs arrive in Heaven as they are slain (Rev 6:9,10).	These will wait until Christ's return to earth to receive their raised bodies (Rev 20:4), along with Old Testament saints (Dan 12:2,3).
Two supernaturally empowered slain witnesses return bodily to Heaven (Rev 11:12).	Almost certainly Enoch and Elijah, who have never died, or Elijah and Moses, whose body God buried.
War in Heaven; Satan denied future access to Heaven. (Rev 12:7–11).	The 'Malignant Accuser' is cast out in great fury.
An angel sent to preach the Gospel (Rev 14:6).	Apparently unprecedented—God's final act of mercy before the Vials of Wrath.
Rejoicing in Heaven over destruction of Mystery Babylon, apostate church and religion (Rev 14:8).	
From Heaven Christ reaps the over-ripe harvest of the world (Rev 14:15).	The heavenly Temple is briefly closed (Rev 15:8), suggesting temporary suspension of access to Mercy Seat for salvation.
The seven Vials or Bowls of Wrath are poured out upon the earth (Rev 16:1 et seq.).	The time of trouble unequalled since the foundation of the world (Dan 12:1, Matt 24:21).
The Marriage of the Lamb (Rev 19:7).	The Bride (Church) has made herself ready (Rev 19:8).
Heaven opened, Jesus Christ gloriously revealed coming in power to judge and make war (Rev 19:11).	King of kings and Lord of lords, followed by armies of heaven—saints and angels (Rev 19:14,16).

Future Event—On Earth	Comments
Following Rapture, no true Church on earth. Unlimited scope for deception (Matt 24:5).	Those who have already consciously rejected Gospel deceived, unable to repent (II Thess 2:9–11).
Political realignment, notably emergence of final form of Beast's dominant ten nation kingdom, or feet of iron and clay (Dan 2:41–43).	Within area of old Roman Empire, therefore including much of EEC. Will probably happen much more quickly than seems possible. Daniel's incompatible iron and clay feet *could* indicate Christian-Muslim coalition.
Rapid rise to power of Beast or Antichrist (Dan 7:8, 8:23).	Also known as Son of Perdition, Little Horn, First Beast etc.

391

Future Event—On Earth	Comments
Beast 'solves' 'Middle East Crisis' by agreeing or imposing seven year peace treaty with Israel, Dan 9:27a. This, rather than Rapture, marks start of Daniel's final 'week' of years. The interval between the two events may be very brief indeed.	Terms of treaty will allow resumption of Levitical sacrifices in Jerusalem (Dan 9:27b). Virtually everything is now ready in Jerusalem including temple parts. Beast with super-charismatic personality likely to be seen as world benefactor; will be hailed as Messiah by many Jews (Jn 5:43). Multitudes of Jews likely to return to perceived safety of Israel.
Initial period of peace and prosperity quickly disrupted as four 'Horsemen of the Apocalypse' (first four Seals) (Rev 6:1–8) take effect.	The 'Beginning of Sorrows' (Matt 24:8). Some of these prophecies have been fore-shadowed in history, but await final fulfilment.
144,000 Jews from 12 tribes sealed (Rev 7:4–8) as witnesses, preaching the Gospel of the Kingdom worldwide (Matt 24:14).	Will be severely persecuted (Matt 25:35–40), but have their lives preserved.
A bloc of nations, usually thought of as being led by Russia, will invade Israel from the North (Ezek chaps 38 & 39) and be decisively and miraculously routed.	Some suggest this will occur before the Rapture or between the Rapture and the seven year treaty. But the undefended state of Israel (Ezek 38:8) suggests that it will happen sometime after the treaty is signed.
The earlier trumpet judgements will take effect and create enormous devastation, ecological disaster and terrifying cosmic activity (Rev 8:7–13).	The unrepentant will look to other sources of help than God. Demonic reinforcements will arrive from the Abyss (Rev 8:2–11).
Satan, having been cast out of Heaven, will descend to earth with great wrath (Rev 12:12).	"Woe to the inhabitants of the earth!" (Rev 12:12).
After three-and-a-half years the Beast will renege on his treaty with Israel, desecrating the Temple, setting up therein an image of himself and demanding worship from Jews (Dan 8:11, II Thess 2:4).	This coincides with Satan's exit from Heaven and marks the start of the Great Tribulation (Matt 24:21, Rev 7:14). The image is the Abomination of Desolation (Dan 9:27, 11:31, Matt 24:15).
Believing Jews, heeding Jesus' warning (Matt 24:15–17) will flee to a miraculously provided refuge in the desert (Rev 12:13–16).	Refuge for three-and-a-half years; may well be in Petra or elsewhere in Edom.
Remaining Jews will be the special object of Satan's fury; the final holocaust will begin. Two thirds of Jews will perish before the Lord returns in power (Zech 13:8).	This onslaught will last for three-and-a-half years (Dan 7:21, 25).

Appendix I: Past, Present And Future Events Of Prophetic Significance With Special Reference To Israel

Future Event—On Earth	Comments
The 'trinity of evil', Satan (the Dragon), Antichrist (the First Beast) and the False Prophet (the Second Beast) (Rev 13:1–15) will blasphemously take control of world religion, demanding universal homage and worship on pain of death.	The False Prophet will exercise stupendous miraculous powers in support of the First Beast (13:12–15).
The Mark of the Beast (666) on the right hand or forehead will be universally enforced for all commerce. It will be given only to those who swear allegiance to the Beast (Rev 13:16–18).	Life without the Mark will be desperately hazardous. Refusal will demand great courage. But, because of what it entails, there can be no salvation for those who accept it (Rev 14:11).
After Satan tightens his stranglehold on worship, the entire fabric of apostate and pagan religion will be destroyed by its chief sponsor and his bestial kingdom. Spiritual Babylon, which has dominated human religion virtually since the Flood (Gen 10:9–11) will also receive the wrath of God (Rev 14:7).	Nimrod, founder of Babylon, was the mighty hunter in the face of God or who faced up to (defied) God. (Gen 10:9). Most idolatry and apostasy can ultimately be traced back to him. After the sack of ancient Babylon it eventually passed to Pergamos, then to Rome, but could well return to its original site. God will appeal to some genuine believers, who are still entrapped within this false system, to leave (Rev 18:4).
The final wrath of God, in the form of seven Vials or Bowls will be poured out in quick succession (Rev 16:1), as Seals, Trumpets and Vials together reach their climax with destruction and suffering unprecedented since the Flood.	Countless millions will still refuse to repent (Rev 16:9), but will blaspheme God, whom they evidently recognise as having ordained the judgements.
From all over the devastated, denuded world demons will drive the surviving armies to a final confrontation with God and with His client state, Israel (Rev 16:12–14).	This may seem crazy, and in fact *is* crazy; but such will be the fear and desperation, combined with hatred and bitterness, that logic will not be a consideration.
The Battle of that Great Day of God Almighty, concentrating upon Armageddon, but also including a massive assault on Jerusalem (Zech 12:3, 12:2, Rev 16:14, 15).	Generally referred to as the Battle of Armageddon, a perennial battle site in the North of Israel.
Heaven open and Christ seen visibly coming to conquer in power and great glory as King of kings and Lord of lords, followed by saints and angels (Zech 14:2, Jude 1:14, Rev 19:11–16).	

Events At And Following Christ's Return In Power—The Millennium	Comments
The Beast and False Prophet cast alive into Hell (Rev 19:20).	The lake of fire and brimstone.
Satan securely incarcerated in the Abyss for 1000 years (Rev 20:2, 3).	The bottomless pit, where he can have no influence in the world, in utter contrast with the Church Age, where he prowls as a lion.
The armies destroyed personally by God the Son (Zech 12:9, 14:12, Rev 19:15, 21).	A great individual and national mourning will take place in Israel, as the Holy Spirit is poured out (Zech 12:10–14).
Jesus recognised as Messiah by surviving Jews (Zech 12:10).	
Jesus recovers His Jewish believers from their desert refuge (Isa 63:4)	We are not emphatic about this timing.
Old Testament saints will be resurrected (Job 19:25–27, Isa 26:19, Dan 12:2).	They will not have participated in the Rapture, which is for the Church only.
The Tribulation martyrs are raised (Rev 20:4–6).	Thus ends the First Resurrection, of which Jesus was the Firstfruits of them that slept (I Cor 15:20), the raptured Church being the main harvest, and Old Testament and Tribulation saints the gleanings.
The Judgement of the Nations or Gentiles (Matt 25:31–46). The 'sheep' will be welcomed into the Millennial Kingdom, the 'goats' assigned to Hell (vv. 34, 41).	Judged according to their treatment of God's Tribulation period witnesses and response to the Gospel of the Kingdom. (Matt 25:40, 45). Any other interpretation implies salvation by works.
The remaining scattered of Israel will be re-gathered, helped by angels (Deut 30:4, 5, Isa 5:26, 51:11, Jer 31:11, Zeph 3:20).	
A mighty earthquake, when Jesus' feet touch the Mount of Olives (Zech 14:4). Other major geomorphological changes (Isa 11:15).	May be world-wide changes of continental proportions, hiding devastated world and its infrastructures. Resurrected saints may literally move mountains. Process will have started towards the end of the Great Tribulation with a global earthquake destroying all Gentile cities and moving mountains and islands (Rev 16:18–20).
Ecology will be restored, climate altered, deserts made fertile, disease eliminated (Isa 35:5–7).	Formerly predatory beasts will live at peace with their prey (Isa 65:25).

Events At And Following Christ's Return In Power—The Millennium	Comments
Limitations of human lifespan (Gen 6:3, Ps 90:10) will be reversed (Isa 65:25). Sin and death will be the exception (Isa 65:20); some will live through the whole 1000 year Millennium.	To them will be born children who have never known a fallen world or external temptation (Isa 11,6,8, Zech 8:5).
Jesus Christ will be acclaimed King of the earth (Dan 7:14, Zech 14:9). His capital will be Jerusalem, He will judge the world in righteousness (Isa 11:4) and impose peace and disarmament (Mic 4:1–3).	Rev 19:15 says most specifically that Jesus will descend from Heaven to rule the nations with a rod of iron, rather than to end the world . Ps 2:2–9 summarises these events. The A- and Post-Millennialists are utterly confounded.
Resurrected David will be regent over Israel (Jer 30:9, Hos 3:5, Ezek 34:23). The 12 Apostles will rule over 12 tribes of Israel (Lk 22:30).	
Church saints will reign in the Gentile world with Christ.	Resurrected saints will be in immortal, incorruptible, sinless bodies (I Cor 15:40–44). Authority and honour will be proportionate to our faithfulness and service in this life (Matt 25:21, II Tim 2:12).
All nations will desire (Mic 4:2) or be required to come periodically to Jerusalem to worship (Zech 14:16, 17).	
At the end of the Millennium Satan will be released briefly to deceive, in order that the true attitudes of those born in the Millennium may be tested and revealed (Rev 20:7).	There will have been no opportunity to demonstrate inward rebellion during Christ's rod of iron reign.
An immense army from the Gentile nations will flock to join Satan and attempt to attack Jerusalem. Fire from God will destroy them. (Rev 20:8).	The age-old link between hatred of God and Anti-Semitism will re-appear for the last time.
Satan will be cast into the Lake of Fire, Hell or Gehenna (Rev 20:10).	He will join The Beast, False Prophet and such fallen angels as have preceded him. These are sufferers in Hell, not rulers. It is described as everlasting in the same way as Heaven.
The world and present universe will be destroyed by fire (II Pet 3:7, Rev 21:1).	

Events At And Following Christ's Return In Power—The Millennium	Comments
Jesus will take His seat on the Great White Throne as Judge (Jn 5:22, Acts 17:31, Rev 20:11).	
The Second Resurrection of all the unsaved of all ages (Rev 20:13) to be judged for their works.	No salvation is recorded of them in the Lamb's Book of Life (Rev 20:15). Hell is the only option.

The Eternal State	Comments
A new heaven and earth are created, quite unlike the old (Rev 21 & 22).	Here we end this sequence, but note two things: 1. The names of the twelve tribes of Israel are preserved for all eternity on the twelve gates of the New Jerusalem (Rev 21:12). 2. The Lord Jesus Christ is identified seven times in Rev 21 & 2 as the Lamb. Our eternal redemption is secure.

Appendix II

Fifty Reasons For A Pre-Tribulation Rapture

This is an adaptation of my article published in *Prophetic Witness* in February and March 2004 and was part of an earlier thesis. It assumes some knowledge of the prophetic Scriptures on the part of readers, and also assumes that they do not dispute the divine inspiration of the Bible. I have collected these points from many sources over many years; the chief source has been the pages of Scripture itself. Each is dealt with only briefly. There may be the odd point here, such as number 30, which some may consider debatable. Please however look at the overwhelming impression given by the majority, before discounting a Pre-Tribulation Rapture on the basis of one or two points of disagreement. This is a consolidated list for reference. Virtually all the data may be found elsewhere in the book.

1. Jesus promised that He would return *for* us and not *to* us. His words in Jn 14:1, 3 are unambiguous: *"I go to prepare a place for you, and if I go... I will come again, and receive you to Myself, that where I am, there you may be also."* He went, and, except in vision, has not been seen on earth since. We will go to the same place.

2. If the Lord has gone to prepare a place for us, we have every reason to believe that it is in heaven and not on earth. That leads us to believe that when He returns for us, it will be to take us to heaven, not back to earth, as some think. The linguistic argument, which says that 'meet' in I Thess 4:17 implies Christ's onward passage to earth, is fallacious.

3. *If* the Rapture is to take place after the Tribulation but before the Millennium, then the 'dead in Christ' would not see, in their resurrection bodies, the place the Lord has gone to prepare, for a further thousand years; *"those who are alive and remain"* would not see it at all until after the Millennium. Are we seriously meant to interpret Jn 14:1–3 like that?

4. These John 14 verses are conditional: *"If I go, I <u>will</u> come again and receive you to Myself."* The condition was fulfilled at His ascension. It follows that the blessed consequence will be fulfilled too.

5. When Enoch was taken to heaven (Gen 5:24), he could not be found (Heb ll:5). When Elijah was caught up to heaven, search parties spent three days looking for him (II Kings 2:17, 18). If the Rapture is to take place after the Millennium, what will immediately happen to those left, in other words the unsaved? The Bible says nothing; is that not because this timing is wrong?

6. There is a further problem with a Rapture at the end of the Millennium. Rev 20:7–10 expressly tells us of a brief final revolt at that point, and of the beloved city, Jerusalem, being surrounded by a vast army. Should the Rapture take place at the end of the Millennium, the implication would be that the encircled city would be empty. Does that make sense?

7. There is no hint of the Rapture in the 20th chapter, which six times states a thousand year period. Why? Because the Rapture has occurred between chapters 3 and 4! Neither do we find any hint of a collective Rapture among the Old Testament prophets. That is because it concerns the Church only and will occur at the end of the Church Age.

8. In the I Thessalonians 4 passage Jesus will bring those that sleep in Him only as far as the meeting point in the air. Their spirits and souls have been with the Lord since their death. But they have to meet up again with their resurrected and transformed bodies. The living saints will meet their Lord in the air. Loved ones will meet each other. Then we will proceed to His place; we will not return to ours until much later.

9. The promise to return for us made by the Lord on the night of His betrayal is in stark contrast with several texts which describe His Coming in Power. Others will be mentioned later, but Jude 1:14 & 15 says: *"Behold, the Lord comes with ten thousands of His saints to execute judgment..."* This cannot conceivably refer to the same event as John 14. The saints are going in opposite directions! Logically we must go before we can come back with Him.

10. While it is *"this same Jesus"* who will come for His Church and return in glory, He will return in different roles. For the Church He will come as Lord and Bridegroom coming to collect His Beloved. As Saviour He will come to claim His redeemed; it will be a glorious appearing which will fulfil a blessed hope (Titus 2:13). To the world He will return as a conquering King of kings, appearing in awful majesty on a white war horse, with a sword going forth from His mouth, to smite the nations and tread the winepress of the wrath of God. (Rev 19:13–17). These cannot surely be one and the same event. To quote Dr Alec Passmore, "One is Wedding, the other Warfare".

11. Contemporary Jewish marriage customs are often referred to in the New Testament. The bridegroom always took the bride to his father's house. Before heaven is opened and the King of kings and Lord of lords, who is the Bridegroom, descends to smite the nations, we see the Church in heaven, the Father's House, as the *wife* of the Lamb (Rev 19:7–9).

12. We are told to watch for Christ, not for tribulation (Matt 24:44, Lk 21:36 etc.). These passages have many tribulation preconditions to be met—specific signs before Christ returns in power. The Post-Tribulationist has nothing to watch for but the Antichrist.

13. *"Now when these things begin to happen, look up and lift up your heads, because your redemption draws near."* (Lk 21:28). While there is here an important general warning to the Church to anticipate the Rapture as these events loom on the horizon, the detailed information in this passage is primarily for the benefit of the Tribulation Jews who will need to know precisely when to flee Jerusalem. It is a very carefully identified faithful remnant of Israel, the woman crowned with twelve stars (see Gen 37:9 and Isa 54:6), for whom a refuge in the desert is to be prepared (Rev 12:1–6). The crowned image of Mary purloined via Rome by the European Community is an ancient Babylonian symbol and should not be confused. The things which Jesus has just been speaking of are terrors which have not yet taken place in human history. So it is still appropriate to look up.

14. The whole central part of Revelation, from chapter 6 to 18, demonstrates that the Coming in Power cannot be imminent. Unless we are to accuse God of gross exaggeration, we cannot claim that the events forecast under the Seals, Trumpets and Bowls in Revelation have taken place to date, so awesome are the Bible's descriptions. Yet some claim that Revelation is a picture of the present age. That's preposterous! The Lord's coming for His Church is prior to and distinct from His Coming in Power. Logically only one can be imminent.

15. *"Watch therefore, and pray always that you may be counted worthy to escape all these things that will come to pass, and to stand before the Son of Man."* (Lk 21:36). *"These things"* are the events of the Tribulation. Those who watch and are worthy are the redeemed, who will not undergo the Tribulation, but shall, in contrast, appear before Christ at the *Bema* or Judgement Seat of Christ, where service is evaluated and rewarded. (I Cor:3:13–15, II Cor 5:10). Standing before Christ when He comes in power is not something to be desired.

16. The Rapture or catching up is declared to the Church as a mystery. In I Thess 4:15 it is a revelation specially authorised *"by the word of the Lord"*, whilst in I Cor 15:51 it is stated to be a mystery that Paul is disclosing that we shall not all sleep, but that we shall all be changed. Contrast this mystery revealed in this early epistle to the church at Thessalonica, two decades after the birth of the Church, with the clear teaching of a dramatic, visible glorious return as found in Zech 14:2,3, Matt 24:30, 25:31 and 26:64, Jude 1:14 and Rev 1:7. That was far from being a mystery at this juncture. Old Testament prophets had foretold it; so had Jesus.

17. The Old Testament gives us precedents or 'types' of the Rapture. Provision was made by God for Noah and his family to escape the Flood and ride above the waters for a year, until judgement was passed and they were able to return to a transformed earth. Lot was called out from Sodom before the judgement fell. Jesus refers to both in Luke 17. The children of Israel in the land of Goshen were saved from the plagues that befell Egypt by being kept separate. (Ex 8:22 etc.).

18. What some call a rapture of the wicked at the end of the Great Tribulation is no rapture at all. *"(They) knew not until the flood came and took them all away... one will be taken and the other left."* (Matt 24:39,40). The 'taking' here is in judgement—being slain to await the resurrection of the unrighteous—*"but the rest of the dead did not live until the thousand years were finished."* (Rev 20:5). Contrast this with the *"twinkling of an eye"* resurrection of the redeemed and Rapture of the living saints (I Thess 4 and I Cor 15).

19. Enoch was caught up *before* the Flood. *"By faith Enoch was translated so that he did not see death".* (Heb 11:5) Remarkable? Yes. But God does remarkable things. *"And Elijah went up by a whirlwind into heaven"* (II Kings 2:11). What God has done in the past for individuals, He can do again in the future for the Church. He who created DNA can create distinctive, flawless new bodies as readily as He called the worlds into being.

20. So many of these splendid Old Testament precedents and miraculous happenings are singled out for significant mentions in the New Testament, by Jesus Himself, by Paul and by other writers. God through His Holy Spirit in the New Testament writers confirmed the reliability of these ancient witnesses. Yet the Rapture is not in the Old Testament; it cannot be; but it is foreshadowed. It lies within a prophetic gap or dead ground which was hidden from the view of the old prophets. Daniel picks up the prophetic sequence again at the very start of his seventieth week of years, so we can take it that the Rapture of the Church has preceded that, occurring, as it does, at the end of the hidden interval.

21. If the Rapture is to take place at the end of the Tribulation, rather than before it, what will happen to all those Jews who repent when they see the Lord returning and observe the wounds in His hand and feet (Zech 12:10–13:6)? Are they going to be a matter of minutes too late to be included in the Rapture? What about the Gentile 'sheep' of Matt 25? They are evidently considered as being saved, yet they too are going to miss the Rapture by hours or days, *if* it is to be Post-Tribulational. We expect more from the Rapture than merely going half-way to meet the Lord and then returning to earth with Him, which is what some would have us believe!

22. Peter warned that *"Scoffers will come in the last day, walking according to their own lusts, and saying, 'Where is the promise of His coming'?"* (II Pet 3:4). The Rapture is probably more targeted by scoffers than any other prophetic doctrine. Those who believe in its potential imminence or who talk about it are increasingly ridiculed. It is easier to acknowledge a Rapture which is so far into the future as to be scarcely relevant. Admittedly the fact that one is considered somewhat 'way out' is no guarantee that one's theology is sound. But when one adheres to all the fundamentals of evangelical faith, and is distinguished only by holding what was a common view among evangelicals a few decades ago, one ought at least to be seen to be standing out from the scoffers.

23. *"God did not appoint us to wrath, but to obtain salvation"* (I Thess 5:9). The context is the Lord's return. Some assume that this is a reference to the devil's wrath when he is cast down to earth from his position as Prince of the Power of the Air (Rev 12:12). However all twelve uses of 'wrath' in Revelation refer to God's wrath—the righteous wrath of a longsuffering and holy God, Who has promised to remove His Church from the earth before it begins.

24. When John had been given the messages for the seven churches, which (a) were actual contemporary churches of Asia Minor, (b) represented a broad band of typical congregations at any given time, and (c) marked the progress of the Church through the ages, John was commanded, *"Come up here, and I will show you the things which must take place after this"*, i.e. after the Church Age. What he then saw was the seven years of the Tribulation from the perspective of the Church, which will then be in heaven.

25. In the first three chapters of Revelation the word 'church' occurs nineteen times. After chapter 3 there is no mention of the word until the epilogue (22:16), when the Lord refers back to the beginning of the book. Believers are seen on the earth in the interim period, but they are either identified as Jews or as persecuted Gentile believers— the Tribulation saints. They are not members of *the* Church any more than anyone who died before Pentecost could have been. Of course, as the word translated 'church' also means assembly in general, one may occasionally find other applications.

26. In Revelation 4 the redeemed are seen in heaven with crowns, and must therefore be in heaven in their resurrection bodies following the Rapture. They must already have appeared at the Judgement Seat of Christ, where crowns are to be awarded. (II Cor 5:10, II Tim 4:8 etc.). This is early in the great vision which goes on to reveal the opening of the seven Seals which inaugurate the judgements of the Tribulation. Thus the Rapture can only be 'Pre-Tribulation'.

27. In Rev 19:6 et seq. we read of the Marriage Supper of the Lamb. We read that His wife, the Bride, which is the Church (Eph 5:25–27), has made herself ready. We are currently the *espoused* bride. Surely nobody can seriously suggest that members of the Church are to be judged for their works *after* the marriage supper! This event precedes the Lord's Coming in Power (19:11–16) in a passage which gives every indication of being continuous narrative.

28. We have noted that, in addition to Revelation 19, the Coming in Power is also described in Zech 14:5, Matt 24:30, Jude 1:14, etc. Taken together, the setting is the divine intervention whilst the battle with its epicentre at Armageddon is raging, at the climax of the Great Tribulation. It follows that resurrected saints must be in heaven in the first place to be able to follow their Lord.

29. Jude 1:14 and Rev 19:14 tell of the saints who will follow the Lord when He returns in power. This will fulfil the passage (Rom 8:18–23) which tells of the sons of God being gloriously manifested at the time when creation will cease to groan and our bodies, as well as our souls, will at last be redeemed. The rather silly and extravagant claims made in the 1970s by some to be the manifest sons of God completely ignored the context. Paul said: *"I consider that the sufferings of this present time are not worthy to be compared with the glory which shall be revealed in us."* The Church, ridiculed, disconsidered, sometimes persecuted and, in her future absence, vilified by the briefly triumphant Mystery Babylon (Rev 17), will be revealed glorified, when the once rejected Lord of Glory returns to earth as King of kings and Lord of lords. This demands a prior Rapture and later Pre-Millennial return with our Saviour. It is little short of blasphemy to expect the Church to be glorified on earth before her Lord.

30. *"The mystery of lawlessness is already at work, only He who now restrains will do so until He is taken out of the way"* (II Thess 2:7). The NKJV rightly gives a capital letter to 'He', for this is God the Holy Spirit, who was given to the Church at Pentecost in an unprecedented way. Throughout the Church age He has been restraining evil and preventing the arrival on the scene of the Beast (or Antichrist) and False Prophet (see Rev 13). When the Church is taken into Heaven, the special relationship which He had with believers on earth will end, although we cannot doubt that He, who is infinite and omnipresent, will have a vital relationship with Tribulation saints, just as He did with Old Testament ones.

31. Only a Pre-Tribulational stand allows God's faithfulness to be recognised in the literal and detailed fulfilment of His unconditional promises to Israel. Others are compelled to resort either to inconsistent programmes, or to embrace Replacement Theology, that device which underpins virtually all Anti-Semitism within 'Christendom'.

32. When the Church, the *ekklesia* or called-out body, is complete and the Lord takes us home, He has a future earthly task for the Jews to fulfil. This does not, of course, include Church Age Jews, who are an integral part of the Church (Eph 2:14) and who will have been raptured. *"God at first visited the Gentiles to take out of them a people for His name... After this I will return and will rebuild the tabernacle of David which is fallen down. And I will rebuild its ruins, and I will set it up, so that the rest of mankind may seek the Lord..."* (Acts 15:14–17). James was talking some fifteen years after Pentecost, long after the apparent end of the house of David. But God will honour those unconditional promises made to David (see II Sam 7:6 and Ps 89:36,37). Thus it is quite clear that, after the Church will be complete and taken home, God will still have business to do on earth, where there will still be people requiring to be saved.

33. We, the Church, are presently ambassadors for Christ (II Cor 5:20) and witnesses (Acts 1:8), responsible for teaching all nations (Matt 28:19) until the *end of this age*. In the Tribulation period, which is a detached portion of an earlier age, the Lord will still need representatives. These are described as witnesses—genuine Jewish Jehovah's witnesses as opposed to cult figures!!! (Isa 43:10,12).

They failed in the past. But 144,000 will be sealed to preach during the Tribulation—Revelation chapter 7 unambiguously emphasises their Jewishness. They would not be needed were the Church still on earth. Also two miraculously empowered Jerusalem-centred prophets will preach for three and a half years. (Rev 11). Jerusalem will again be the world's religious centre, even though it will be usurped for a further three and a half years by the Antichrist.

34. Matthew 24, Mark 13 and Luke 21, which are specifically Tribulation passages, give careful instructions for threatened Jews in their land at that time. There is nothing comparable for the Gentile Church. Does God not care equally for her? Of course He does. But the Church will be in heaven and will have no need of such advice. Everything points to the land of Israel being the correct place for Jews to be.

35. Not only the many Old Testament prophecies concerning the Tribulation period, but the entire central part of Revelation, are Jewish orientated, with appropriate geographical references. There is nothing comparable in the Church epistles.

36. Daniel was told (9:24): *"Seventy weeks (groups of seven or heptads) are determined for your people and for your holy city."* The sixty-ninth was to end with the death or cutting off of the Messiah, which duly happened (vv. 25, 26). The perfect timing has been historically demonstrated. The whole of this passage refers unambiguously to Daniel's earthly people, the Jews. The seventieth, which has never been fulfilled, also refers unmistakably to the Jews (v27).

37. The sixty-ninth 'seven' ended before the Church was born. If the Church was not in the first sixty-nine groups of seven years (483), whatever would she be doing in the final seven years? The Church occupies the long gap between the 69th and the 70th.

38. It was given to Paul to reassure the young Church that, despite severe persecution at the time, they were not going to undergo the Great Tribulation: *"concerning the coming of our Lord Jesus Christ and our gathering together to Him, we ask you not to be shaken in mind or troubled..."* (II Thess 2:1, 2). This was a message of comfort and reassurance. Paul then went on to write about that which would have been anything but comforting, were it to occur prior to the Rapture,

in other words the revelation of the 'man of sin', the Antichrist. That person will therefore be revealed only after the 'gathering' of the Church.

39. The Tribulation saints are seen before the throne (Rev 7:9–17). They are a quite distinct company from the Church, whose members are around the throne, and even in it (Rev 3:21). The Church is in its celestial bodies—*"conformed to His glorious body"* (Phil 3:21). The martyrs of the Great Tribulation are a separate group. They are seen in heaven *awaiting* their resurrection bodies (Rev 6:9): *"I saw the souls of those who had been beheaded for their witness to Jesus... who had not worshipped the beast..."* (Rev 20:4).

40. In I Tim 2:1 & 2 Paul tells us to pray for all in authority. This is valid for the Church Age only, although it has sometimes been difficult to observe. It is currently appropriate because we must believe that at present even the vilest political dictator is not beyond redemption. Those living in the Tribulation period cannot possibly pray for those in supreme political authority, or indeed for any who will wield power at that time. All these will have accepted the *"mark of the beast"*, and are consequently already condemned to eternal damnation (see Rev 14:9 and 19:20). Clearly that will be a different dispensation or time period in God's order of things.

41. Jesus, in His last recorded message to the whole Church (Rev 22:1), portrays Himself as the *"Bright and Morning Star"*—that which heralds but precedes the dawn. But to the Jews and the shattered world which shall emerge from the Great Tribulation, He is the *"Sun of Righteousness with healing in His wings."* (Mal 4:2). Earth's darkest hour will be immediately before the dawn of a new and glorious day for the earth. But the Church will not be here to undergo that dark hour.

42. Significant is the different sequence of the dead being raised and the translation of the saints at the Rapture and the resurrection sequence following the Lord's return in power. At the Rapture, *"the dead in Christ shall rise first; then we which are alive and remain shall be caught up..."* (I Thess 4:16,17). But at His Coming in Power the raising of the Tribulation saints appears last in a series of events which is to mark the beginning of the Millennium (Rev 20:4).

43. The Millennial Kingdom is not to be brought about by the actions of the Church. We read in Daniel 2:44 that, when the worldly kingdoms, which conclude with the Revived Roman Empire or feet of iron mixed with clay, described earlier in that chapter, are finished: *"the God of heaven will set up a kingdom which shall never be destroyed... it shall break in pieces and consume all those kingdoms, and it shall stand for ever."* In the vision of which this is the interpretation, this is described as *"a stone cut out without hands"* (without human agency) which will smash the final earthly kingdom. (2:34, 35). In Psalm 2, God the Father tells God the Son that it is He, not the Church, who will break the nations with a rod of iron and dash them in pieces like a potter's vessel. The already raptured Church will accompany her Lord when this happens. This kingdom will never cease, but will, at the end of the Millennium be handed over to the Father (I Cor 15:24).

44. Who would be left to repopulate the earth were the Rapture to follow the Tribulation? Peter spoke of Jesus, *"whom the heaven must receive until the time of restoration of all things, which God has spoken by the mouth of all His holy prophets"* (Acts 3:21). From this we understand that Jesus will remain in heaven until this promised restoration which is to be found throughout the prophetic books. Then He will return. He, Himself, told us of this return and of the Judgement of the Nations which will immediately follow, with some, described as 'sheep', invited to *"enter the kingdom prepared for you by My Father from the foundation of the world"* (Matt 25:34). This will be Eden restored. We read of the splendid conditions in Isaiah 11, 35 and 65 etc. *"The wolf also shall dwell with the lamb, and a little child shall lead them... The nursing child shall play by the hole of the cobra..."* (11:6, 8). Those who are raptured will be in their resurrection bodies, and as such will neither marry nor have children (Matt 22:30). Children will most certainly be born; but not to members of the Church!

General Comments

45. The following sequence is the only one which allows much of the vast store of unfulfilled Bible prophecies to be taken at face value, rather than being arbitrarily 'spiritualised' or allegorised:

    (a) The Resurrection of those who sleep in Christ and the Rapture of living saints.

    (b) The final 'week of years'—three and a half years of the 'Beginning of Sorrows' and three and a half years of Great Tribulation.

    (c) Christ's Coming in Power with the destruction of the Armageddon armies, the Judgement of the Nations and the resurrection of the Tribulation martyrs.

    (d) The Millennial Kingdom on earth.

    (e) The final brief rebellion.

    (f) The resurrection of the unsaved and Great White Throne judgement.

    (g) The eternal state—the new heaven and earth.

46. Revelation is a much more straightforward book from a Pre-Tribulationist stance, as shown in the above paragraph. It allows for a generally undistorted sequence of events from the Church Age (chapters 1–3) right through to the eternal state. Granted, there are parenthetical glimpses of significant personalities and phenomena, but these do not distract from the overall sequence.

47. Most other perspectives, particularly the Amillennial and Post-Millennial, imply that the prophetic Scriptures are full of highly exaggerated, gloomy, portentous prophecies which either will not actually be fulfilled or have already been fulfilled in an emasculated manner in history. Pre-Millennialism, of which Pre-Tribulationism is a significant element, is not sensationalism. It is simply a matter of accepting in the most obvious terms what God has graciously revealed. It is an acceptance of the way in which God has informed us that He will allow mankind in rebellion to bring the world to the brink of destruction before He decisively steps in. It is recognition

of God's holiness, and His need to deal finally and effectively with the sin of those who refuse to repent. It is recognition of the truth that His ways are infinitely higher and wiser than ours, even although at times we, with our present mortal perspective, may not always feel comfortable with them.

48. Pre-Tribulationism leaves less room within the Church for pride. Recent years have seen a great increase in the confidence that the Church, without her Lord's personal return, will accomplish the Kingdom programme. Neither the broad trend of Bible prophecy, nor the state of our world, justify such conclusions. Ours is increasingly a Church which revels in fads, opinions and novelties. Generally it seeks earnestly to study what the Bible has to tell us about the future. While the Church has many tasks to perform, making the world 'good enough' to bring Christ back is not one which we find listed in Scripture. Yet many of the songs which we now sing advertise such an agenda.

49. Pre-Tribulationism probably provides the greatest contrast with man-made religions. Many of these see a gradual and painful progression or evolution towards higher spiritual planes, towards a Utopia or even to simple oblivion. Some of this has rubbed off on Christians. Those pagan religions which recognise a future judgement see a single general tribunal where the criterion for salvation or damnation is the degree of goodness or wickedness. How different from the provisions and demands of God's plan of salvation in the Cross, where everybody must be born again or be damned! *"When we were still without strength, in due time Christ died for the ungodly."* (Rom 5:6). Much of the teaching of the 'ultimate triumph of good over evil' has pagan roots and shuns God's way. That too is pervading Christendom. We are ever in danger of leaning towards a compromise with pagan aspirations and means.

50. Failure to recognise the various injunctions in the New Testament to be watchful, expectant and prepared for the return of the Lord at any moment, has deadened the sensitivity of many congregations to the prophetic message. Christians are thus seen by the world to have neither the authority nor the ability to tell people about the future of the planet. People therefore turn to the false prophets, soothsayers,

fortune-tellers and horoscopes, who are only too willing to fill this void. If our interpretation of prophecy fails to enthuse us or inspire us to tell others of God's plan of the ages, it must surely be suspect. It gives opportunity to the occult. Only a Pre-Tribulationist perspective allows for the expectation of an imminent meeting with our Lord, in a way which bears any relationship to Scripture. *"Even so, come, Lord Jesus!"* (Rev 22:20).

Bibliography

For ease of reference, each chapter is self-contained. The full details of a source are recorded only for the first entry within a chapter. Thereafter only the author's name is given, except where there are two or more titles by the same writer.

Introduction

1. Fruchtenbaum, Arnold G, *Israelology: The Missing Link in Systematic Theology* (Ariel Ministries Press, Tustin, Ca, Revised 1994 edition).

Chapter One: Prophetic Principles And Definitions

1. *Prophetic Witness* is published monthly by Prophetic Witness Movement International, Leyland, Lancs. From 1983 until 1998 it appeared under the title *Your Tomorrow*, before reverting to its previous name.

2. Walvoord, John F, *The Revelation of Jesus Christ* (Moody Press, Chicago, 1989) p.20.

3. Unger, Merrill F, *Unger's Bible Dictionary* (Moody Press, 3rd edn. 1966) p.588.

4. Walvoord, John F, *Matthew – Thy Kingdom Come* (Kregel Publications, Grand Rapids, Mi, 1974), p.201).

5. Richards, Lawrence O, *Expository Dictionary of Bible Words* (Marshall Pickering, Basingstoke, 1988), p.303.

Chapter Two: A Future For Israel—The Big Issue

1. Walvoord John F, *Major Bible Prophecies* (Zondervan Publishing House, Grand Rapids, Mi, 1991), p.66.

2. Pollock, Algernon J, *The Amazing Jew* (The Central Bible Truth Depot, London, 3rd revised & enlarged edn., c.1939), p.97.

3. Pollock, Algernon J, *Things Which Must Shortly Come To Pass* (Bible Truth Publishers, Oak Park, Il, reprint of 2nd edn., 1936), p.61.

4. Ibid. p.12.

5. Prasch, James Jacob, *The Final Words of Jesus and Satan's Lies Today* (St Matthew Publishing Ltd, Cambridge, 1st British edn., 1999), p.14.

6. Meyer, F B, *Christ in Isaiah* (Marshall, Morgan & Scott, London & Edinburgh, 1950 edn.), p.39.

7. Ibid. p.41.

Chapter Two: A Future For Israel—The Big Issue

8.   Vine, W E, *Isaiah – Prophecies, Promises, Warnings* (Oliphants, London & Edinburgh, 1st edn., 1946), pp.7–8.

9.   Milne, Bruce, *The End Of The World – What The Bible Says* (Kingsway Publications, Eastbourne, 1997 reprint of 1983 edition), pp.68, 71).

Chapter Three: Some 'Untils' Concerning Israel

1.   Ryrie, Charles C, *Everyman's Bible Commentary: Revelation* (Moody Press, Chicago, 1996), pp.139–140.

2.   Newell, William R, *The Book of The Revelation* (Moody Press, Chicago, 1935), p.344.

3.   Girdlestone, E A, *The Unsealed Book* (Marshall, Morgan & Scott, London & Edinburgh, 1935), p.88.

4.   Baines, T B, *The Lord's Coming, Israel And The Church* (W H Broom, London, 2nd edn., 1876), p.103.

5.   Walvoord, John F, *Prophecy Knowledge Handbook* (Victor Books, Wheaton, II, 1990), p.372.

6.   Vine, W E, *Isaiah – Prophecies, Promises, Warnings* (Oliphants, London & Edinburgh, 1st Edition), 1946, p.32.

7.   Walvoord, John F, pp.453–4.

8.   Vine, W E, *The Epistle to the Romans* (Marshall, Morgan & Scott, London, 1948), pp.169–170.

9.   Savage, John Ashton, *The Scroll of Time* (Kingston Bible Trust, Lancing, Sussex, 1982 reprint), pp.27–28.

10.   Rice, John R, *The Son of Man* (Sword Of The Lord Publishers, Murfreesboro,Tn, 1971), pp.495–6.

11.   Kelly, William, *An Exposition of the Book of Isaiah,* 2nd edition, London 1896 (Bible Truth Publishers, Oak Park. II, 1975), p.259.

12.   Meyer, F B, *Bible Commentary* (Tyndale House Publishers, Wheaton, Illinois), p.32.

13.   Fruchtenbaum, Arnold G, *Israelology, The Missing Link In Systematic Theology* (Ariel Ministries Press, Tustin Ca), Revised 1994 edition, p.835.

14.   Skevington Wood, A, *Your Tomorrow* (Prophetic Witness Movement International, Leyland, Lancs), p.11 of May 1991 and p.10 of June 1991.

15.   King, Geoffrey R, *Daniel* (The Midnight Cry, Ilford, Essex, 3rd edition, *c.*1957), pp.243–245.

Chapter Four: 'Untils' Concerning Israel And Her Messiah

1. Baines, T B, *The Lord's Coming, Israel And The Church* (W H Broom, London, 2nd edn.. 1876), p.95.

2. Ibid. p.98.

3. Ibid. pp.99–100.

4. Ibid. pp.104–105.

5. Ibid. p.106.

6. Walvoord, John F, *Prophecy Knowledge Handbook* (Victor Books, Wheaton, Il, 1990), p.438.

7. Baron, David, *The Visions and Prophecies of Zechariah*, (2000 edition by The Messianic Testimony, Barking, Essex, of Morgan & Scott, London, 1918) p.435.

8. Ibid. p.498.

9. Meyer, F B, *The Prophet of Hope: Studies in Zechariah* (Ambassador, Belfast, 1995 reprint) p.114.

10. Jamieson, Fausset & Brown's *Commentary* as contained in Power Bible CD, Philip Lindner, Online Publishing Company Inc, 1999–2002.

11. Gardiner, A, of Middletown, Ct, as quoted in the *Bible Commentary for English Readers* (edited by Bishop John Ellicott, Cassell & Company, London etc., n.d.), Vol V, pp.634–64.

12. Walvoord, John F, *Matthew – Thy Kingdom Come* (Kregel Publications, Grand Rapids, 1974) p.214.

13. Richards, Lawrence O, *Expository Dictionary of Bible Words* (Marshall Pickering, Basingstoke, 1988) p.364.

14. *Tanakh – The Holy Scriptures* (The Jewish Publication Society, Philadelphia, Jerusalem 1985) p.1243.

15. Walvoord, John F, *Major Bible Prophecies* (Zondervan, Grand Rapids, Mi, 1991) p.365.

16. Tatford, Frederick A, *Prophecy's Last Word – an Exposition of the Revelation* (Pickering and Inglis, Basingstoke, 1947) p.254.

17. Newell, William R, *The Book of the Revelation* (Moody Press, Chicago, 1947) p.326.

18. Ibid. p.327.

Chapter Five: Israel's Nearer Future

1. Lahaye, Tim, *Revelation Unveiled* (Zondervan, Grand Rapids, 1999) p.132.

2. Ibid. p.157.

3. Ibid. pp.158–9.

Chapter Five: Israel's Nearer Future

4.   Stanton, Gerald B, *Kept From The Hour* (Schoettle Publishing Inc, Miami Springs, Fl, 4th edn., 1991), pp.35,36.

5.   Girdlestone, E A, *The Unsealed Book* (Marshall, Morgan and Scott, London & Edinburgh) p.34).

6.   Newell, William R, *The Book of the Revelation* (Moody Press, Chicago, 1947) p.111.

7.   Baines, T B, *The Revelation of Jesus Christ* (4th edition, London, 1905, 1991 reprint by Gute Botschaft Verlag, Germany) pp.102,104.

8.   Kelly, William, *The Collected Writing of J N Darby, Prophetic Vol II* (G Morrish, London), p.35.

9.   Scott, Walter, *Exposition of the Book of Revelation* (Pickering and Inglis, London, 4th edn., n.d.) p.162.

10. Ironside, H A, *Revelation – Ironside Commentaries* (Loizeaux Brothers, Neptune, N J, Revised edn., 1996) p.89.

11. Ibid. pp.91,92.

12. Tatford, Frederick A, *An Exposition of the Revelation,* Pickering & Inglis, London, 1947, p.96.

13. Miller, Ernest J, *The Final Battle* (New Wine Press, Chichester, 1987), p.115.

14. Ryrie, Charles C, *Revelation – New Edition* (Everyman's Bible Commentary, Moody, 1992) p.60.

15. Kelly, William, *Lectures on the Revelation,* new edn., (G Morrish, London, *c.*1871), pp.152, 153.

16. Lindsay, Hal, *There's a New World Coming* (Coverdale House, London & Eastbourne, 1974 edn. of 1973 Vision House, Santa Ana, Ca), p.120.

17. Walvoord, John F, *Matthew – Thy Kingdom Come* (Kregel Publications, Grand Rapids, Mi, 1974). pp.200, 201.

18. Ibid. p.202.

19. Barnhouse, Donald Grey, *An Expository Commentary on Revelation* (Zondervan, Grand Rapids, 1971) pp.261–262.

20. Baines, T B, p.134

21. Lahaye, Tim, *Revelation Unveiled* (Zondervan Publishing House, Grand Rapids, 1999) p.201.

22. Lindsay, Hal, p.21.

Chapter Six: Completing Our Case For Israel's Future

1.	Dennett, Edward, *The Blessed Hope* (W H Broom and Rouse, London, 1879), p.48.

2.	Pollock, A J, *Things Which Must Shortly Come To Pass* (2nd edn. London, 1936, Bible Truth Publishers, Oak Park, II, n.d.), pp.60, 61.

3.	Hislop, Alexander, *The Two Babylons* (B McCall Barbour, Edinburgh, 1998 reprint of 1929 4th edn.), p.167.

4.	Blackstone, William E, *Jesus is Coming* (Kregel Publications, Grand Rapids, 1989 reprint), p.161.

5.	Hunt, Dave, *A Cup of Trembling* (Harvest House Publishers, Eugene, Oregon, 1995) p.149.

6.	Ibid. p.158.

7.	Ibid. p.328.

8.	Schlink, Basilia, *Israel – My Chosen People* (Kanaan Publications, Darmstadt, Germany, 1995) p.28.

9.	Prasch, James Jacob, *The Final Words of Jesus and Satan's Lies Today* (St Matthew Publishing Ltd, Cambridge, 1st British edn. 1999), pp.64–66.

10.	Phillip, John & Vines, Jerry, *Exploring the Book of Daniel* (Loizeaux Brothers, Neptune, NJ, 1927) p.196.

11.	Kelly, W, *Jeremiah – The Tender-Hearted Prophet to the Nations* (CA Hammond, London, 1937) p.80.

12.	Walvoord, John F, *Major Bible Prophecies* (Zondervan Publishing House, Grand Rapids, 1991) p.176.

13.	Ibid. p.41.

14.	Pollock, A J, *The Amazing Jew* (Central Bible Truth Depot, London), c.1939, p.10.

15.	Fruchtenbaum, Arnold G, *Israelology, The Missing Link in Systematic Theology* (Ariel Ministries, Tustin, Ca, 1992 revised edn.) p.341.

16.	Pentecost, J Dwight, *Things to Come: A Study in Biblical Eschatology,* (Dunham Publishing, Grand Rapids, 1958), pp.72–73.

17.	Fruchtenbaum, Arnold, pp.570–571.

18.	Ibid. pp.588–589.

19.	Baines, T B, *The Lord's Coming, Israel and The Church* (W H Broom, London, 1876), pp.170–171.

20.	Lightner, Robert, *Last Days Handbook* (Thomas Nelson, Nashville, Tn, 1997), pp.153–159.

21.	Pollock, Algernon J, *Things Which Must Shortly Come to Pass,* pp.66–67.

Chapter Six: Completing Our Case For Israel's Future

22.   Cameron, Donald C B, *Your Tomorrow* , (Prophetic Witness Movement International. Leyland, Lancs), articles published from June to November 1998.

23.   Phelan, M W J, *The Israel of God* (European Theological Seminary monograph), pp.19, 20.

24.   Baxter, J Sidlow, *Explore The Book* (Marshall, Morgan & Scott, London & Edinburgh, 1952), Vol 4, p.254.

25.   Ibid. p.256.

Chapter Seven: Taking Stock

1.   Lahaye, Tim and Jenkins, Jerry B, *Left Behind* series of books (Tyndale House Publishers Inc, Wheaton, Il).

2.   Pawson, David, *When Jesus Returns* (Hodder and Stoughton, London, 1995), pp.xi, xii.

3.   Kelly, William, *Lectures on the Gospel of Matthew* (Loizeaux Brothers, New York, 1950 edn. of 1868), p.220.

4.   Ryrie, Charles C. *Biblical Theology of the New Testament* (Moody Press, Chicago, 1959), p.64.

5.   Walvoord, John, *Major Bible Prophecies* (Zondervan, Grand Rapids, Mi, 1991), pp.206–207.

6.   Vine, W E, *Complete Expository Dictionary* (Thomas Nelson Publishers, London & Nashville, Tn, 1984). p.344.

7.   Unger, Merrill F, *Unger's Bible Dictionary* (Moody Press Chicago, 1966) p.632.

8.   Pentecost, J Dwight, *Thy Kingdom Come* (Victor Books, Wheaton, Il, 1990), pp.18, 19.

Chapter Eight: Some Proof Texts Of Replacement Theology

1.   Young, Robert, *Analytical Concordance to the Holy Bible* (Lutterworth Press, London, 8th ed, n.d.), p.67 of Lexicon.

2.   Hamilton, James, *The Gospel of St John in Greek, Interlineal & Analytical Translation*, (Francis Hodgson, London, 1893), p.148.

3.   Chantry, Walter J, *God's Righteous Kingdom* (Banner of Truth Trust, Edinburgh and Carlisle, Pa, 1980), p.36.

4.   Ibid. p.28.

5.   Cox, William E, *Amillennialism Today* (Presbyterian & Reformed Publishing Co, Philadelphia, Pa, 1966), p.23.

6.   Cameron, Donald C B, *Your Tomorrow* (Prophetic Witness Movement International, Leyland, Lancs), November 1988, p.10.

Chapter Eight: Some Proof Texts Of Replacement Theology

7. Blackstone, William E, *Jesus is Coming* (Kregel Publications, Grand Rapids, 1989 updated edn. of 1908) pp.121–2.

8. Scofield, C I, *Reference Bible* (Oxford University Press) n.d.,

9. Rice, John R, *The Son of Man, Verse-by-Verse Commentary on Luke* (Sword of the Lord Publishers, Murfreesboro, Tenn, 1971), p.414–5.

10. Blackstone, William E, pp.123–4.

11. Vine, W E, *Complete Expository Dictionary – Old and New Testament Words* (Thomas Nelson Publishers, London, Nashville Tn, 1984), p.125.

12. Berkhof, Louis, *A Summary of Christian Doctrine* (Billing & Sons, London, 1960 edn. of USA, 1938), p.181.

13. Adams, Jay, *The Time is at Hand* (Presbyterian & Reformed Publishing Co, Philadelphia, Pa, 1966), pp.12, 13.

14. Pawson, David, *When Jesus Returns* (Hodder & Stoughton, London, 1995), p.231.

15. Kelly, William, *Notes on The First Epistle of Paul The Apostle to the Corinthians* (G Morrish, London, 1878) pp.281, 282.

16. Cameron, Donald C B, October 1998, p.10.

17. Blackstone, William E, pp.125, 126.

18. Glasson, T Francis, *His Appearing & His Kingdom* (Epworth Press, London, 1953) p.124.

19. Augustine of Hippo, *The City of God*, xx.7

20. Hislop, Alexander, *The Two Babylons* (B McCall Barbour, Edinburgh, 1998 reprint of 1929 4th edn.) pp.176 et seq.

21. Kelly, J N D, *Early Christian Doctrines* (Adam & Charles Black, London, 1958) p.466.

22. Campbell Morgan, G, *The Analysed New Testament – Epistle to the Romans* (Hodder and Stoughton, London, 1919) pp.140, 159.

23. Vine, W E, *The Epistle to the Romans* (Marshall, Morgan and Scott, London, revised edn., 1948), p.136.

24. Baxter, J Sidlow, *Explore the Book* (Marshall, Morgan & Scott, London & Edinburgh 1955), vol 6 p.75.

25. Pawson, David, pp.230–231.

26. Phelan, M W J, *The Israel of God* (European Theological Seminary monograph) p.32–33.

27. Vine, W E, *The Epistle to the Romans*, pp.67–68.

28. Kelly, William, *Lectures on the Epistle to the Ephesians* (Bible Truth Publishers, Oak Park, Il, 1972 reprint of London, n.d., pp.100–101.

Chapter Eight: Some Proof Texts Of Replacement Theology

29.   Fruchtenbaum, Arnold, *Israelology: The Missing Link in Systematic Theology* (Ariel Ministries, Tustin, Ca, 1992) pp.706–707.

30.   Fruchtenbaum, Arnold, p.711.

31.   Glasson, T Francis, p.8.

32.   Ibid. p.32.

Chapter Nine: Amillennialism And Israel's Future—Background

1.   Walvoord, John F, *The Millennial Kingdom* (Dunham Publishing Co, Findlay, Oh, 1959) p.71.

2.   Cox, William E, *Amillennialism Today* (Presbyterian and Reformed Publishing Co, Philadelphia, Pa, 1966) p.3.

3.   Ibid. p.1.

4.   Ibid. p.1.

5.   Adams, Jay E, *The Time is at Hand* (Presbyterian & Reformed Publishing Co, Nutley, NJ, 1966) p.41,

6.   Cox, William E, p136.

7.   Glasson, T Francis, *His Appearing and His Kingdom* (Epworth Press, London, 1953) p.126.

8.   *Hutchinson's Encylopaedia* (Century Hutchinson Ltd, London, 7th edn.), 1986.

9.   Glasson, T Francis, pp.127–9.

10.   Augustine of Hippo, *The City of God*, xx. 7.

11.   Needham, Nick, *Augustine – Vessel and Champion of Grace* (Evangelical Times) November 2004, p.21.

12.   Renwick, A M, *The Story of The Church* (Inter-Varsity Fellowship, London, 1958) p.58.

13.   *Watchtower* (Brooklyn, N J, 15 September 2003) p.29.

14.   Ferguson, Sinclair B, *The Westminster Confession in the Church Today* (edited by Alasdair I C Hutton, Saint Andrew Press, Edinburgh, 1982) p.34.

15.   Blackstone, William E, *Jesus is Coming* (Kregel Publications, Grand Rapids, 1989 reprint of 1908) p.5.

16.   Ibid. p.42.

17.   Cox, William E, p.136.

18.   Ibid. p.4.

19.   Milne, Bruce, *The End of the World* (Kingsway Publications. Eastbourne, 1983), p.84.

Chapter Nine: Amillennialism And Israel's Future—Background

20. Metcalfe, John, *The Son of God and Seed of David* (John Metcalfe Publishing Trust, Penn, Bucks, 1979) p.89.

21. Ibid. p.88.

22. Ibid. pp.152–3

23. Chantry, Walter J, *God's Righteous Kingdom* (Banner of Truth Trust, Edinburgh, 1980) pp.44–45.

24. Ibid. pp.50–51.

25. Ibid. pp.122–3.

Chapter Ten: Amillennialism And Israel's Future—Doctrinal

1. Berkhof, Louis, *A Summary of Christian Doctrine* (Billing & Sons, London, 1960 edn. of USA, 1938) p.173.

2. Ibid. p.176.

3. Berkhof, Louis, *Systematic Theology*, (Banner of Truth Trust, Edinburgh, 1958).

4. Hoekema, Anthony A, *The Bible and the Future* (William B Eerdmans, Grand Rapids, Mi, 1994 edn. of 1979), p.142.

5. Ibid. p.144.

6. Ibid. p.145.

7. Hoekema, Anthony A, *The Meaning of the Millennium* (edited by Robert C Clouse, Inter-Varsity Press, Downers Grove, Il, 1977), p.156.

8. Ibid. pp.156–7.

9. Lindsey, Hal, *The Late Great Planet Earth* (Marshall, Pickering, London, 1971).

10. Hoekema, Anthony A, *The Meaning of the Millennium* , p.24.

11. Adams, Jay, *The Time is at Hand* (Presbyterian & Reformed Publishing Co, Nutley NJ, 1966), p.65.

12. Hoekema, Anthony J, *The Bible and the Future*, p.190.

13. Berkof, Louis, *Systematic Theology*, p.695.

14. Cox, William E, *Amillennianism Today* (Presbyterian & Reformed Publishing Co, Philadelphia, Pa, 1966) p.4.

15. Milne, Bruce, *The End of the World,* (Kingsway Publications, Eastbourne, 1983), pp.82–83.

16. Ibid. p.83.

17. Adams, Jay, p.83.

18. Stott, John W, *God's New Society,* (Inter-Varsity Press, Leicester, 1979), pp.117–118.

Chapter Ten: Amillennialism And Israel's Future—Doctrinal

19.   Adams, Jay, p.ix.

20.   Ibid. p.3.

21.   Ibid. p.viii.

22.   Cox, William, p.57.

23.   Stanton, Gerald B, *Kept From the Hour*, (Schoettle Publishing House, Miami Springs, Fl, 1991), p.309.

24.   Chantry, Walter J, *God's Righteous Kingdom,* (The Banner of Truth Trust, Edinburgh, 1980), pp.18–19.

25.   Ibid. p.58.

26.   Cox, William E, p.103.

27.   Berkhof, Louis, *A Summary of Christian Doctrine,* p.180.

28.   Cox, William, pp.99–102.

29.   Hoekema, Anthony, *The Bible and the Future*, pp.176–8.

30.   Milne, Bruce, p.94.

31.   Schlink, M Basilea, *Israel – My Chosen People*, (Kanaan Publications, Darmstadt, New English Translation, 1987), pp.35–36.

Chapter Eleven: Traditional Post-Millennialism And Israel's Future

1.   Boettner, Loraine, *The Millennium*, (Presbyterian & Reformed Publishing, Phillipsburg NJ, 1957), p.14.

2.   Blackstone, William E, *Jesus is Coming* (Kregel Publications, Grand Rapids, 1989, updated edn. of 1908), p.43.

3.   Snowden, J H, quoted by L Boettner in *The Meaning of the Millennium,* (Edited by Robert G Clouse, Inter-Varsity Press, Downers Grove, Il, 1977), p.130.

4.   Lindsey, Hal, *The Late Great Planet Earth* (Marshall Pickering, London 1971), p.176.

5.   Rushdoony, Rousas J, Introduction to *An Eschatology of Victory* (Presbyterian & Reformed Publishing, Phillipsburg NJ, 1971), p.viii.

6.   Boettner, Loraine, *The Meaning of the Millennium* (as at Snowden above), pp.117–118.

7.   Ibid. p.126.

8.   Hoekema, A, *The Meaning of the Millennium* (as above), p.150.

9.   Boettner, Loraine, *The Millennium*, p.382.

10.   Ibid. p.342.

11.   Ibid. p.58.

Chapter Eleven: Traditional Post-Millennialism And Israel's Future

12. Ibid. p.68.

13. Ibid. p.25.

14. Kik, J Marcellus, *An Eschatology of Victory* (Presbyterian & Reformed Publishing Co, Phillipsburg, N J, 1971) p.44.

15. Ibid. p.45.

16. Boettner, Loraine, *The Meaning of the Millennium*, p.131.

17. Ibid. p.131.

18. Ibid. 134.

19. Walvoord, John F, *Prophecy Knowledge Handbook* (Victor Books, Wheaton, II, 1990), p.15.

20. Alford, Henry, quoted by James McWhirter, *Is Christ Coming?* (Methuen & Co, London, 1940), p.vi.

21. Boettner, Loraine, *The Millennium*, p.24.

22. Boettner, Loraine, *The Meaning of the Millennium*, pp.118–119.

23. Ibid. pp.123–124.

24. Kik, J Marcellus, *An Eschatology of Victory*, p.28.

25. Ibid. p.22.

26. Ibid. p.27.

27. Boettner, Lorraine, *The Millennium*, p.380.

28. Ibid. p.381.

29. *Unger's Bible Dictionary* (Moody Press, 1966), p.204.

30. Darby, J Nelson, *Lectures on the Book of the Revelation* (G Morrish, London, 1866), p.266.

31. Rushdoony, Rousas J, *Thy Kingdom Come* (Presbyterian & Reformed Publishing Co, 1970, USA), p.148.

32. Ibid. p.163.

33. Ibid. p.168.

34. Murray, Iain, *The Puritan Hope* (The Banner of Truth Trust, London, 1971), p.xvi.

35. Ibid. p.xviii.

36. Spurgeon, C H, *A Popular Exposition of Matthew* (Marshall, Morgan & Scott, London & Edinburgh), 1962 reprint of 1893), pp.210–219.

37. Murray, Iain, pp.255–266.

38. Ibid. p.260.

Chapter Eleven: Traditional Post-Millennialism And Israel's Future

39. Levett, Alan, *The Puritan Hope* (*Your Tomorrow*, Prophetic Witness Movement International, Leyland, Lancs), June 1992 issue, p.10.

40. Braidwood, John, 1853, quoted by Iain Murray in *The Puritan Hope* (q.v.), p.176.

41. Boettner, Loraine, *The Millennium*, p.7.

42. Boettner, Loraine, *The Meaning of the Millennium*, p.122.

43. Snowden, J H quoted by Boettner in *The Millennium*, p.28.

44. Boettner, Loraine, *The Millennium*, p.16.

45. Fruchtenbaum, Arnold G, *Israelology, The Missing Link in Systematic Theology*, (Ariel Ministries, Tustin Ca, 1992), p.121.

46. Burnham, Jonathan D, *The Story of Conflict* (Paternoster Press, Carlisle, Cumbria, 2004), p.102).

Chapter Twelve: Neo-Post-Millennialism And Israel's Future

1. DeMar, Gary, *End Times Fiction* (Thomas Nelson Publishers, Nashville, Tn, 2001), p.212.

2. Walker, Andrew, *Restoring the Kingdom,* (Hodder & Stoughton, London, 1989), p.73.

3. Hunt, Dave, *The Seduction of Christianity* and *Whatever Happened to Heaven?* (Harvest House Publishers, Eugene, Or, 1985 & 1988).

4. *Mission Praise*, numbers taken from Complete edition, hereafter referred to as *CMP* (Marshall Pickering, London, 1999).

5. Whittle, D H, *CMP*, No. 279.

6. Saward, Michael, *CMP*, No. 687.

7. Fishel, Donald, *CMP*, No. 30.

8. Matthew, David, *Restoration Magazine* (Bradford, Yorks, Nov/Dec 1983), p.37.

9. Gillman, Bob, *CMP*, No. 54.

10. Wilson, Ronnie, *CMP*, No. 274.

11. Walker, Andrew, p.228.

12. Wilson, Ronnie, *CMP,* No. 274.

13. Lawson, Phil & Bowater, Chris, *CMP*, No. 947.

14. Barraclough, Henry, *Alexander's Hymns No. 3* (Marshall, Morgan & Scott, London, n.d.), No. 380.

15. Levers, Greg & Burt, Phil, *CMP*, No. 692.

16. Turner, Roy, *CMP*, No. 18.

Chapter Twelve: Neo-Post-Millennialism And Israel's Future

17. Kendrick, Graham & Rolinson, Chris, *CMP*, No. 15.

18. Kendrick, Graham, *CMP*, No. 718.

19. Henry, Matthew, *Commentary* (Marshall, Morgan & Scott, London & Edinburgh, 1960 edn.), NT p.570.

20. Ellicott, *A Bible Commentary for English Readers* (Cassell & Co, London) vol vii, p.18.

21. Hayford, Jack, *The New Spirit-Filled Life Bible* (Thomas Nelson, Nashville. Tn, 2002), Introduction, p.vi.

22. Walker, Andrew, p.22 et seq.

23. Robison, James, *The Holy Spirit and Restoration, The New Spirit-Filled Life Bible* (as above), p.1859.

24. Price, Randall, *Israel My Glory* (Friends of Israel Gospel Ministry, Westville NJ), Jan/Feb 2005, p.23.

25. DeMar, Gary, *Is Jesus Coming Soon?* (American Vision, Powder Springs, Ga, 1999), p.17.

26. Ibid. p.18.

27. Ibid. Introduction.

28. Ibid. p.8.

29. Ibid. p.21.

30. Walvoord, John F, *Prophecy Knowledge Handbook* (Victor Books, Wheaton, Il, 1990), p.381

31. DeMar, Gary, *Is Jesus Coming Soon?* p.42.

32. LaHaye, Tim, & Jenkins, Jerry B, *Left Behind* and sequels, (Tyndale House Publishers, Wheaton, Il, 1995 and later).

33. DeMar, Gary, *Is Jesus Coming Soon?,* rear cover.

34. Ibid. p.33.

35. Ibid. p.33.

36. Ibid. p.9.

37. Chilton, David, *Paradise Restored – An Eschatology of Dominion* (Reconstruction Press, Tyler, Texas, 1985), p.43.

38. Sorko-Ram, Shira, *Understanding Messianic Jewish Ministry, The New Spirit Filled Bible* (as at Ref 21 above), pp.1874–1882.

39. Ibid. p.1881.

40. Travis, Stephen, *End of Story?* (Inter-varsity Press, Leicester, 1997), p.85.

41. Ibid. p.17.

Chapter Twelve: Neo-Post-Millennialism And Israel's Future

42. Ibid. rear cover.

43. Ibid. p.35.

44. Ibid. p.42.

45. Ibid. p.44.

46. Ibid. p.48.

47. Ibid. p.49.

48. Ibid. p.51.

49. Ibid. p.53.

50. Lindsey, Hal, *There's a New World Coming* (Coverdale House, London, 1974), p.141.

51. Travis, Stephen, p.64.

52. Ibid. p.68.

53. Ibid. pp.140–145.

54. Kendrick, Graham, *CMP*, No. 716.

55. Hadden, David, *CMP*, No. 46.

56. Unger, Merrill F, *Bible Dictionary* (Moody Press, Chicago, 1966), p.1190.

57. Mark, Robin, *CMP*, No. 1012

58. Dowall, Tom, *CMP*, No. 483.

59. Bilbrough, Dave, *CMP*, No. 525.

60. Kelly, Kirstie, *Restoration Magazine* (Bradford, Yorks) Nov/Dec 1983, p.23.

61. Ibid.p.24.

62. Travis, Stephen, p.70.

63. Ibid. p.71.

64. Ibid. pp.73–74.

65. Ibid. p.76.

66. DeMar, Gary, *End Times Fiction,* p.51.

Chapter Thirteen: Other Pre-Millennial Views

1. Baines, T B, *The Lord's Coming, Israel & The Church* (W H Broom, London, 1876), pp.v & 2.

2. Ladd, George E, *The Blessed Hope* (Wm B Eerdmans Publishing, Grand Rapids, Mi, 1956), p.9.

Chapter Thirteen: Other Pre-Millennial Views

3.   Fruchtenbaum, Arnold G, *Israelology: The Missing Link in Systematic Theology* (Ariel Ministries, Tustin, Ca, revised 1994 edn.), p.245.

4.   Ryrie, Charles C, *Dispensationalism Today* (Moody Press, Chicago, 1965), pp.66–78.

5.   Stanton, Gerald B, *Kept From The Hour* (Schoettle Publishing Co, Miami Springs, Fl, 1991), p109.

6.   Pawson, J David, *When Jesus Returns* (Hodder & Stoughton, London, 1995), p.185.

7.   Dennet, Edward, *The Blessed Hope* (W H Broom, London, 1879), p.9.

8.   Ibid. pp.2–3.

9.   Cameron, Robert, *Scripture Truth About The Lord's Return* (Revell Co, New York, 1922).

10. Ladd, George E, *The Meaning of the Millennium* (Edited by Robert G Clouse, Inter-Varsity Press, Downers Grove, Il, 1977), p.34.

11. Smith, Oswald J, *The Voice of Prophecy* (Marshall, Morgan and Scott, London & Toronto, 1948), p.81.

12. Ibid. p.82.

13. Ladd, George E, *The Blessed Hope* (as above), p.78.

14. Fruchtenbaum, Arnold G, p.314.

15. Ladd, George E, p.228.

16. Pawson, J David, p.204.

17. Harrison, Norman B, *His Coming* and *The End: Rethinking the Revelation* (The Harrison Service, Minneapolis, 1941 and 1946).

18. Smith, Oswald J, *The Voice of Prophecy*, p.70.

19. Rosenthal, Marvin J, *The Pre-Wrath Rapture Of The Church* (Thomas Nelson, Nashville, Tn, 1990).

20. Stanton, Gerald B, pp.374–400.

21. Rosenthal, Marvin J, p.266.

22. Ibid. pp.229–230.

23. Stanton, Gerald B, p.395.

24. Lang, G H, *The Revelation of Jesus Christ* (Oliphants, London, 1945).

25. Pritchard, L O, *Partial Rapture* (End Times Journal, New Zealand, c.2004).

26. Guinness, H Grattan, *The Approaching End of the Age* (Hodder & Stoughton, London, 13th edn., 1897), p.699.

27. Ironside, Henry A, *Revelation* (Loiseaux, Neptune, NJ, 1996 revised edn.), p.20.

Chapter Thirteen: Other Pre-Millennial Views

28. Angus, Joseph, cited by J Sidlow Baxter, *Explore The Book*, (Marshall, Morgan & Scott, London & Edinburgh, 1955) vol 6, p.338.

29. Smith, Oswald J, *Prophecy – What Lies Ahead?* (Marshall, Morgan & Scott, London & Toronto, 1948), pp.82–89.

30. Ibid. p.88.

31. Ibid. pp.21–31.

32. Ibid. p.77.

33. Ibid. pp.78–79.

34. Pawson, J David, p.233.

35. Ibid. pp.134–135.

36. Ibid. p.140.

37. Ladd, George E, p.7.

38. Ibid. p.126.

39. Ibid. p.125.

40. Rosenthal, Marvin J, p.182.

41. Ibid. p.259.

42. Young, Robert, *Analytical Concordance to the Holy Bible* (Lutterworth Press, London, 8th ed, n.d.).

43. Vine, W E, *Vine's Complete Expository Dictionary* (Thomas Nelson, Nashville, Tn, 1984), p.243.

44. Rosenthal, Marvin J, p.260.

45. Guinness, H Grattan, pp.iv–vii.

46. Ibid. p.717.

47. Cameron, Donald C B, *Another Prophetic View* (Prophetic Witness Movement International, Leyland, Lancs), July/August 2004.

48. Fruchtenbaum, Arnold, pp.857–895.

49. Juster, Daniel C, *Jewish Roots* (Destiny Image Publishers, Shippensburg, Pa, 1995).

50. Stern, David H, *Restoring the Jewishness of Gospel* (Jewish New Testament Publications, Clarksville, Md, 1988), p.1.

51. Ibid. p.74.

52. Ibid. p.11.

53. Stern, David S, *Jewish New Testament Commentary* (Jewish New Testament Publications, Clarksville, Md, 1992). p.811.

54. Ibid. p.833.

The European Theological Seminary and College Of The Bible

The European Theological Seminary and College Of The Bible is an international and non-denominational accredited Seminary that stands unequivocally for the literal truth of the Scriptures of the Old and New Testaments, and is firmly opposed to both Modernism and Liberalism.

The seminary offers a very wide range of courses, from Certificates and Diplomas to Doctorates. Evidence Of Prior Learning is warmly welcomed, and the seminary is able to offer its students the benefits and convenience of Distance Learning and Continuous Assessment.

The Honorary President would welcome applications for enrolment with the seminary by readers of this book, and will do all he can to accept them as suitable candidates for *European Theological Seminary and College Of The Bible* scholarships.

Please write for a free Prospectus to;

Professor G. S. Beck, (Dept. TES/AFF)
170 Shore Road,
Greenisland,
Carrickfergus,
County Antrim, BT38-8TT.

Other books published by Twoedged Sword Publications

Try the spirits: volume 1

Cecil Andrews

ISBN 0-9547205-2-0

- Was C S Lewis truly 'Our greatest Christian writer'?

- Philip Yancey—'turning the grace of God into lasciviousness'?

- Alpha—Attend or Avoid?

When the writer first formed 'Take Heed' Ministries some fourteen years ago most of the warnings issued on spiritual deception would have referred to matters outside of professing Christendom. Today the spiritual make-up of that professing Christendom is both very different and very dangerous. There has been a biblically-predicted (1 Timothy 4:1 and 2 Timothy 4:3) marked decline in discernment amongst professing Christians and the result is that the questionable views of certain apologists, authors and advocates, who are viewed by many as Christian, have increased dramatically both in popularity and influence. This book is an attempt to bring biblical truth to bear on three such current dangers that are deceiving many.

Try the spirits: volume 2

Cecil Andrews

ISBN 0-9547205-5-5

- Catholic Catechism—some non-Christian teachings

- 'Father' McCafferty—Catholic but not Christian

- Alister McGrath—misrepresenting the Catholic Catechism?

- ECT Ireland—the myth of Evangelicals and Catholics Together in Ireland

- Evangelising Roman Catholics

Almost five hundred years ago the Roman Catholic domination of professing Christendom was broken as God, by His Spirit, moved in the hearts, minds and understanding of many who had found no peace with God through their adherence to, and reliance upon, priestly Roman Catholic ritual. The rediscovery of the great biblical truth of 'justification through faith alone in Christ alone' became central to what is known as The Reformation. Today, many appear to have forgotten the spiritual lessons of that crucial period and for a number of decades now Romanism has once more been rising to a position of dominance like the proverbial Phoenix from the ashes. This bodes ill for the eternal well-being of countless souls. May the One who alone has saved His people from their sins be pleased to use this little volume to counter the claims of a false anti-Christian system that is so loved by the world today.

Condemned, Condoned or Confused?
The Contemporary World in the Light of God's Word

Timothy Cross, BA (Hons), BD (Hons), Th.D.

ISBN 0-9547205-3-9

- Bad language

- The cult of the celebrity

- The family

- The status and role of women

- Homosexuality

- Gambling

- Alcohol

This book considers these, and many other prominent aspects of our modern world, in the light of God's Word—which is the correct standard by which to *prove all things* (1 Thessalonians 5:21). Sadly, when our contemporary society is tested in the light of God's unchanging Word it is often *weighed in the balances, and... found wanting* (Daniel 5:27). But the situation is not hopeless, for the Bible shows us where we have strayed from God's way and how we can return to God's way, the only way to true happiness, peace and eternal life. Only the Bible can make us truly wise, as only the Bible can impart the wisdom of God.

Some Postcards from John:
2 and 3 John for today

Timothy Cross, BA (Hons), BD (Hons), Th.D.

ISBN 0-9547205-7-1

The 'postcards' that John wrote to the churches of 2 and 3 John are packed full of useful instruction and exhortation. John sent these 'postcards' on ahead of hoped for, and longed for face to face visits: in 2 John to *the elect lady and her children* and in 3 John to *the beloved Gaius.*

Both churches had their problems. The problem in the church of 2 John concerned deceiving deviants from outside the church — *men who will not acknowledge the coming of Jesus Christ in the flesh,* whilst the problem addressed in 3 John was concerned mainly with a dreadful dictator from within the church — *Diotrephes, who likes to put himself first, does not acknowledge my authority.* These problem personalities from the first century will ring many present-day bells with us in the twenty-first century.

In John's 'postcards', we encounter doctrine, duty, affirmation of truth, and warning against error. We meet love and discipline along with affection and sternness. Overriding everything, as everywhere in the Bible, we glimpse something of the supernatural glory of God in contrast with the sinful humanity He sent His Own Son to save.

At the end of each chapter there is a set of thought-provoking and stimulating questions, each of which could be the subject of a Bible study group.

An Exposition of I Peter Chapter I

Robert A. Penney B.D., D.Min.

ISBN 0-9547205-4-7

The lessons that Peter brings to us might have been written with our current times in mind, such is the relevance and agelessness of Scripture. In expounding these great truths, the author considers the following subjects:

- Apostleship

- Election

- Worship, Mercy and Lively Hope

- The Preservation of the believer

- Heaviness

- The Trial of Faith

- Unseen but Loved

- The Desire of Prophets

- The Desire of Angels

- Holiness

- Redeemed by Blood

- The Christian's Hope and Faith in God's Power

- The Transient Nature of our Existence and the Eternal Nature of the Word of God

- Vain Glory: The Enduring Word

An Exposition of II Peter chapter 3

Robert A. Penney B.D., D.Min.

ISBN 0-9547205-9-8

The old adage says: "Your bible is more up-to-date than your morning's newspaper." Such a statement was never more true than when applied to this third chapter of Peter's second epistle. It has to do with the present state of affairs and gives us a brief insight into the end time and also a glimpse of the nature of the future kingdom. To live amid this present godless world with such Scriptures saturating our minds and our souls is richness indeed and fills the believer with hope, confidence and faith in these modern times of unbelief and apostasy.

These addresses are sent forth trusting that the result will be the strengthening of all who read them, that hope may be instilled within those who may be discouraged in these wicked times and that even thrill and excitement may be aroused as one contemplates the believer's lot in this present evil world and the glories which will follow. Nothing is more needful today than for the Christian to be encouraged in the things he has most surely believed.

The author has written this small book to encourage Christians to rejoice in the hope of their high calling and to consider the eventual triumph of Christ and His Church over Satan and his forces and over the ungodliness of men which is so characteristic of these last days. But the chapter under consideration is also full of warnings for the believer—the appearance of evil on an unprecedented scale, the ultimate wrath of God in judgment upon it all and how we must get back to spiritual basics by heeding the teaching of the apostles and prophets.

Angels Everwatching

One family's testimony of God's protection and mercy

Robert Baghurst, Rosemarie Baghurst, Timothy Baghurst, Amy Baghurst

ISBN 1-905447-00-0

"Liberia's motto has always intrigued me... 'For the Love of Liberty brought us here.' It has always been their boast to be the first African nation that was free, all the others having first been colonised. Actually this has been to their disadvantage since they had no strong Western influence to educate, support, and give them a good basis from which to work and grow. To the contrary, they have always been a poor nation, proud to be free, but wholly enslaved to the animistic traditions which they tenaciously hold."

The Liberian civil war erupted in December 1989, when the National Patriotic Front of Liberia (NPFL), a military force led by Charles Ghankay Taylor, a former official of the Liberian government, invaded Liberia from the Ivory Coast. He received the assistance of mercenaries from other nations, with many recruits from the Mano and Gio ethnic groups. The Baghurst family found themselves in the path of this force and for a time found themselves captives. During their experience they learned that the "angel of the LORD encampeth round about them that fear him, and delivereth them" (Psalm 34:7). This is that story.

The Army and I

An account of life in the Army as a non-combatant Christian during the Second World War

Robert B. Carter

ISBN 1-905447-01-9

This is an account of one individual's impressions and experiences in the Second World War. It is based on the author's memory and on a notebook in which, throughout the war, he entered names and addresses, locations, train journeys, leave dates, rates of pay, and so on. Many have recorded their experiences during those terrible years, but few have written of service with non-combatant status within the Army.

He whose words can never pass away said:

> "Render to Caesar the things that are Caesar's and to God the things that are God's" (Mark 12:17).

In times of national danger, Caesar inevitably tends to enlarge his claims upon us and it is good if there are statutory safeguards. Throughout the history of the church, there has been difficulty for many in discovering where, in practice, the boundary between these two responsibilities lies. The conscience of the believer is enlightened by, and subject to, the Word of God, but as one Christian said when called to answer before the Great Council in Zurich in the early part of the 16th century:

> "Do not oppress my conscience, for faith is a free gift of God's mercy and is not to be interfered with by anyone."

May any who read this record be encouraged to commit their lives to Him who "worketh all things after the counsel of His own will" (Ephesians 1:11).

A Faith for the Times

Robert A. Penney B.D., D.Min.

ISBN 0-9547205-8-X

Only One Message • Liberty in the Spirit • The Power of the Spirit • The Demonstration of the Spirit • The Power of God • Impossibilities • Divine Revelation • Divine Commission • Departed Glory • The Flickering Lamp • Leadership • The Function of the Local Church • Treasures of Darkness • Fire! • Scotland's Finest Hour • Righteousness

Dr Robert A. Penney addresses the problems of a people that has turned its back on God: materialism, moral depravity, humanism, philosophy, sin in high places. He reflects on the ways in which God dealt with the people of Israel and its leaders, the early New Testament Church as well as some of the problems in the modern Church.

'When you read the Bible and get to know it thoroughly, you will find that it is a book that speaks to every age and generation, because mankind remains the same in all its essential qualities, and God remains the same.'—Dr. Martyn Lloyd-Jones

Dr Penney spent over twenty years as a Probation Officer in the Birmingham courts. On early retirement he studied at the Scottish Congregational College and New College, Edinburgh, whilst serving as an assistant to the late Dr Nelson Gray at Portobello Congregational Church. He pastored Beith Congregational Church, Ayrshire, for a short period before resigning to devote himself to writing and itinerant ministry. He now lives in Kirkintilloch, his home town, near Glasgow.

The Christology of Philippians 2:6–11
An examination of the Person and Work of Christ

M. W. J. Phelan, B.Th., M.Th., Th.D.

ISBN 0-9547205-1-2

By accepting that all the Scriptures centre on Christ; that all the believer's hopes centre upon Him; and that we are acceptable to God only through Him and His Work, all true believers practice Christology. This book exposes the so-called Kenotic Theology as a falsehood. This doctrine teaches that the Deity of Christ was compromised when He took our flesh. The danger of this doctrine is made worse by the fact that it may seem to be correct, but, as this book reveals, it is based upon a fundamental misunderstanding. Many believers will find this book to be of real interest and benefit, especially as it could easily be used as the basis for a small study group, in which believers may explore together the exhilarating truths dealt with by the writer.

The Inspiration of the Pentateuch
or
The Graf-Wellhausen Fallacy

An examination of the origins of the Torah, the inadequacies and contradictions of cynical Source Criticism, and the merits of Faithful Source, and Form Criticism.

M. W. J. Phelan, B.Th., M.Th., Th.D., Ph.D.

ISBN 0-9547205-6-3

Christianity claims the Bible is a comprehensive collection of truths concerning the nature and purposes of God, and the nature and destiny of mankind. It claims that this Divinely Inspired, and therefore, utterly inerrant revelation was transmitted to us through the New Testament. However, this collection of documents rests upon the Hebrew Canon, or Old Testament, and the very foundation of the Hebrew Canon, is the Torah, or Pentateuch, or Five-Books-Of-Moses; namely, Genesis, Exodus, Leviticus, Numbers, and Deuteronomy. It is the Pentateuch that has been the target of the most unremitting assaults of sceptics and critics down the years, and the Book of Genesis has suffered the most brutal of these attacks. It is these assaults upon the Pentateuch that form the subject of this book.

The Genesis 'Gap Theory'

Its Credibility and Consequences

M. W. J. Phelan, B.Th., M.Th., Th.D., Ph.D.

ISBN 1-905447-02-7

The interpretation of Genesis 1:1–2 has taxed the minds of exegetes for many years. The controversy has centred upon whether or not there is a chronological gap of unspecified duration within the compass of what, at first glance, seems to be continuous narrative. This proposed gap is the basis of what might be termed theories-of-accommodation. By some the proposed gap is used to accommodate the alleged vast ages of cosmic, geological, and biological evolution, and has certain similarities with the theory that views the days of Genesis 1, not as literal days representing but one complete rotation of the earth upon its axis, but as entire epochs, during which the earth was subject to profound, but extremely slow evolutionary change. This is a view frequently advocated by so-called Theistic-Evolutionists, who seek to harmonise Scripture with human wisdom in the form of evolutionary dogma.

The facts are that;

1) the six days of Genesis 1 are each defined as comprising but one 'evening and morning' (verses 5, 8, 13, 19, 23, and 31),

2) Exodus 20:11 and 31:17 state that the basis of the seven-day week which regulates our calendar still, is the hexameron, or six days of creation followed by the Sabbath rest,

3) death did not exist before Adam, and came through Adam (Romans 5:12), ruling out the possibility of millions of years of plant and animal deaths before man, and,

4) the concept of the history of the events of Genesis 1, being greater in duration than all the rest of Scripture history taken together, and of it outlasting it by a truly prodigious amount which the adoption of an evolutionary time-scale would demand, is absolutely contrary to the conceptual basis of the Word-of-God.

The desire to accommodate entire epochs such as are suggested by evolutionists within a chronological gap to be located within

Genesis 1:1–2 then should not be a serious consideration for sincere students of the Word.

But the proposed gap is used also to accommodate the Luciferic Rebellion and Fall. It is taught by believers in this view that the original creation was marred, if not ruined altogether by this rebellion, or by a Divine Judgement which fell upon the earth as a consequence of it, and that the hexameron details the actions of God in restoring the, by then, ruined earth.

Finally, there are those who see such a gap accommodating *both* evolutionary epochs, and the Luciferic Rebellion.

What the sincere student of God's Word needs to know is; whether or not there is any real basis in the Scriptures themselves for the existence of such a gap, or whether the proposal is based only upon human speculation. It is the authors' aim to address this question.

The Integrity of Isaiah: New evidence of single authorship

A practical demonstration of the literary unity of the book of Isaiah

M. W. J. Phelan, B.Th., M.Th., Th.D., Ph.D.

ISBN 1-905447-03-5

For over two thousand years the book of Isaiah was accepted as the exclusive work of the son of Amoz, the friend of Hezekiah. The translators of the Septuagint regarded the book as a single work. The well-known discovery at Qumran in 1947 of two different copies of Isaiah also testifies to its unity. One of these scrolls is virtually complete and is normally dated to the late second century B.C.E.

The New Testament adds its very considerable, and for the believer, decisive weight to the traditional viewpoint, as may be seen from the eighty-seven occasions where it cites the prophet's words. In no less than twenty-one of these instances, the quotation from the book is accompanied by a reference to the prophet Isaiah by name.

In addition to this, the Masoretic Text, the standard Hebrew text of the Hebrew Canon, and the unanimous testimony of all the ancient texts, versions, Jewish traditions, and the early Christian Church, report the book to be a single work.

At the end of the eighteenth century however, this view that had held sway for millennia began to be challenged. Isaiah, it was asserted was a compilation by different authors, and various so-called proofs of this were brought forth by the critics. Since then, this view-point has gained a massive momentum so that it is now considered to be the orthodox scholarly position. We are assured that critical scholarship has demonstrated the separate existence of the work of no less than three authors, usually referred to as Proto-Isaiah, Deutero-Isaiah, and Trito-Isaiah.

The issues raised by this challenge to the traditional belief, are firstly and obviously, that the Hebrew Canon is charged with containing pseudonymous works, but secondly, and more importantly, the authority of the New Testament is gravely undermined, as the twenty-one occasions where Isaiah is referred to by name, relate to every section of the book, and, therefore, to all three of the modernist's authors.

Either the evangelists and Paul were unaware of what has supposedly been unearthed by the critics, and thereby face the charge of gross ignorance; or they were not ignorant at all, but accommodated themselves to the prejudices of those they wrote for, and, thereby, knowingly and deliberately maintained a falsehood. For believers then, the matter is not merely of academic interest, but affects his or her faith in the Inspiration of the New Testament. A New Testament that through ignorance or deliberate policy propagates and maintains a falsehood cannot be Divinely Inspired, or relied upon as our guide in the most vital issues which confront us all, the issues of life and death in their eternal dimensions. Clearly then the matter must be resolved, and either the New Testament, or the views of the critics must be abandoned; the matter is as stark as that.

Things which must shortly come to pass: a study of Revelation

Paul Rose

ISBN 0-9547205-0-4

The things John wrote in the book of Revelation were revealed to him by the Lord Jesus Christ Himself. They are *things which must shortly come to pass* (Revelation 1:1). Many Revelation prophesies have already been fulfilled and those who keep an eye on the political arena can see the way being prepared for the fulfilment of more Revelation prophecies. In the writer's opinion we should study Revelation with renewed enthusiasm because *these things must shortly come to pass.*

Recapturing the Wonder of Christmas

Timothy Cross

ISBN 1-905447-05-1

The trend in our current society is to celebrate and remove all reference to any religious, let alone Biblical basis to Christmas. 'Goodness, they are bringing religion into Christmas. What next?' is a common feeling of a busy shopper on seeing a nativity scene in a shopping centre. This precious and warm celebration has become increasingly secular over the years. Few would deny that materialism has taken over almost completely. This book seeks to counter the current trend. It explains and informs the reader as to the true meaning of Christmas, and explores the different aspects we have come to believe and know about Christmas as committed Christians.

Whilst this book is definitely seasonal, its message is also eternal, for the purpose of the incarnation is eternal.

> *'You shall call His name Jesus,*
> *for He shall save His people from their sins.'*

The Good News underlying Christmas is that when the Christmas experience actually happens in us, and the living Lord Jesus is known in our hearts, then the Christmas joy is not just seasonal but everlasting.

Printed in the United Kingdom
by Lightning Source UK Ltd.
110247UKS00001B/82-99